Wakashan
Salishan
Chimakuan

Yuki

Keresan

Beothuk

Aztec-Tanoan

Hokan

Macro-Algonkian

Macro-Siouan

Na-Dene

Paleo-Siberian

Penutian

MAJOR LANGUAGE GROUPS

NATIVE AMERICAN HERITAGE

NATIVE AMERICAN

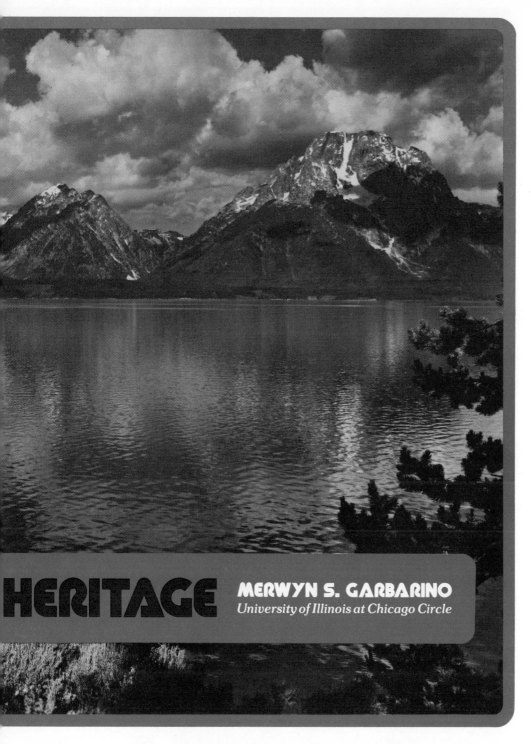

HERITAGE

MERWYN S. GARBARINO
University of Illinois at Chicago Circle

LITTLE, BROWN AND COMPANY BOSTON TORONTO

Library of Congress Catalog Card No. 75–33520

First Printing

Published simultaneously in Canada by Little, Brown & Company (Canada) Limited

Printed in the United States of America

Cover and book design: Clint Anglin

Maps: David Lindroth

Photo research: Designworks

Manuscript editing: David W. Lynch

Editorial-production supervision: Diane E. Shluger and Freda Alexander

Frontispiece: Union Pacific Railroad Photo

Cover photo: Charles Moore/Black Star

The author gratefully acknowledges permission to adapt portions of the following pages
from Time-Life Books: *The First Americans* (1973), pp. 17, 35,
36, 67, 68, 70, 91, 92, 94, 96, 99, 100, 109, 111–117, 134–138, 140, 145; *The Indians* (1973),
pp. 60, 61, 92. © 1973 Time, Inc.

Credits for text photos appear on p. 532.

PREFACE

There comes a time when one must explain why he or she wrote a book—especially if many ably written works are already available on the same subject. My defense is that none is organized the way I think makes best sense. As a result of my years of teaching North American ethnology, I have concluded that the best way of presenting the material is the scheme I have used in this book, a four-part division of prehistory, culture areas, general aspects of Indian cultures, and the contemporary scene. Fine scholars have produced a myriad of works on the native people of this continent—works I could not improve upon except, in a sense, by combining them, and that is what I have tried to do. I have tried to include what I believe students (and people in general) should know about the subject, as well as those things students (and people in general) always ask me about.

Part I is a résumé of the origins and antiquity of the native peoples of North America. Part II uses the culture area concept to cover the variety of native life. Coverage is not the same for all culture areas because I have tried to characterize each to indicate its distinctiveness. Therefore I may have emphasized technological adaptation in one while stressing values or ideology in another in order to point out particular qualities that contribute to the individuality of the cultures. Part III generalizes about topics of Indian life before European contact; Part IV presents a history of the contact between Indians and explorers, traders, soldiers, and settlers from overseas, and it ends with an account of Indian life today.

Charts within each of the culture area chapters should help students review the differences and similarities of Indian groups across the continent. The glossary at the end of the book includes definitions of important terms that may be new to readers. At the end of parts I, III, and IV, a few books are suggested for further study. In Part II, I have included suggestions at the end of each chapter. The books recommended for further study should be available in college libraries and even in public libraries of most cities. A bibliography with full citation appears at the end of the text. I hope that the numerous photographs, charts, and drawings throughout the book will make the peoples and customs more vivid than they are in many introductory books.

This book has been a tremendous undertaking, and I would be foolish to expect to please all people. There will be those who disagree with my emphases. Specialists will find details missing or perhaps feel that I have slighted their areas of expertise. I apologize on the grounds that time and space force me to neglect many controversies and special interests. I have tried to indicate where major disagreements exist. However, the point of view is my own, as are any interpretations not specifically attributed to others. There may well be those, too, who disagree with my data or their interpretation. Because I had to limit the field somehow, I have chosen to use the present international boundary between Mexico and the United States as the southern border of the study. It is an academic choice. Indians recognized no such border, and many scholars will correctly point out that the Southwestern culture area extended well into Mexico.

I have tried to write this book so that it will be interesting and understandable to students who will never be professional anthropologists or even majors in the subject. It is directed toward an audience interested in learning more about the native Americans, but it does not assume that readers will have had any previous course in anthropology. Where professional or technical terms were necessary, I have explained them in the text as well as in a glossary at the end of the text; where they were not necessary, I did not use them. Thus I hope this book will be enjoyable and instructive to the general public as well as to students. I especially hope that if descendants of the first Americans read it, it will help them understand their cultural heritage as well as deal to some degree with the questions, Why am I what I am? What forces have shaped me? What difference does my cultural heritage make in terms of my existence in today's world?

In a broader sense, perhaps some readers will wonder not only why I wrote this book, but also why anyone spends so much space and time on ways of life that no longer exist. There are numerous answers to this question. Perhaps the most persuasive is that knowledge of other human ways can help us in solving problems we must face today. We need to be more aware of the full range of human possibility. Industrial societies often think that they control nature and their own destinies; many people of the world, including the American Indians, are under no such illusions. They stand as people who recognized their small part in the natural scheme of things. No American Indian conceived of an egocentric universe. No one of them thought that the sun revolved around the human inhabitants of the earth. They offer us a new perspective. Indian people, past and present, can give us information about the diversity of human adaptation and flexibility. They can tell us of options and alternatives to the ways of life many of us blindly pursue.

I find myself under obligation not only to those who have assisted in the labor and bringing forth of this creation, but also to all the many people who encouraged and challenged me for years before I ever thought of such a work. They must know who they are: in anthropological jargon, my family of orientation and my family of procreation, living and deceased, and my greatly esteemed professors and colleagues at Northwestern University and the University of Illinois at Chicago Circle. I am grateful to them all.

In addition, my special appreciation for help with this book goes to my graduate research assistants, Janice Ableman, Robert Mucci, and Janis Johnson, and to Carol Verburg, developmental editor at Little, Brown and Company. Frank Lee Earley of Arapahoe Community College, Munro S. Edmonson of Tulane University, Catherine S. Fowler of the University of Nevada, Don Lenkeit of Modesto Junior College, David S. Phelps of East Carolina University, Allan Richardson of Whatcom Community College, and Peter Z. Snyder of the University of California at Los Angeles provided valuable criticism. In addition I would like to thank Dr. Robert L. Hall of the University of Illinois at Chicago Circle and Dr. Elizabeth Brandt of Arizona State University for taking time to read parts of the manuscript and for making helpful and insightful suggestions, and Dr. Nancy Lurie of the Milwaukee Public Museum for her invaluable help with the illustrations.

CONTENTS

2   CULTIVATION AND AMERICAN CULTURES   39

▼▲▼▲▼▲▼▲▼▲▼▲▼▲▼▲▼▲ II

CULTURE AREAS OF NORTH AMERICA   69

Contents

x

6 THE GREAT BASIN AND THE SOUTHWEST 199

▼△▼△▼△▼△▼△▼△▼△▼△▼ III

NATIVE AMERICAN CULTURE   335

9   TECHNOLOGY, ART, AND RELIGION   339

10   SOCIAL AND POLITICAL SYSTEMS   387

IV VAVAVAVAVAVAVAVAVAVAVA
CONFLICT BETWEEN CULTURES   423

11 INDIAN-WHITE RELATIONS   429

12   CONTEMPORARY INDIANS   467

MAPS

CHARTS

NATIVE AMERICAN HERITAGE

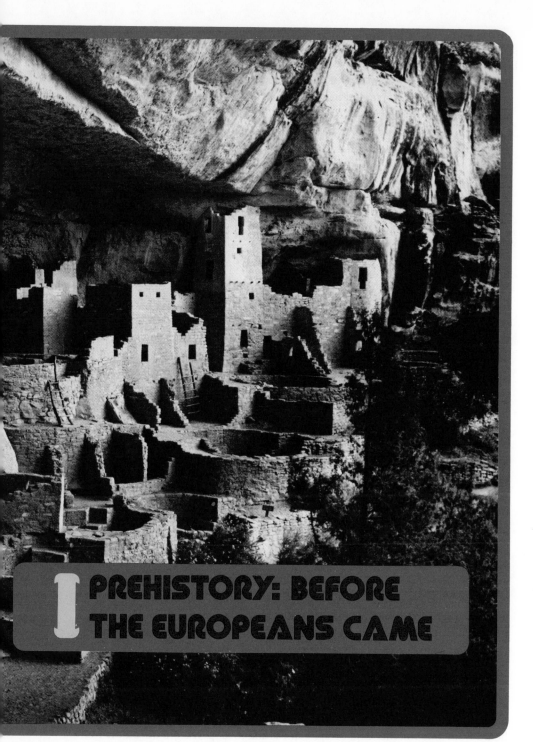

PREHISTORY: BEFORE THE EUROPEANS CAME

In 1492, Christopher Columbus sailed westward across the Atlantic Ocean from Spain in search of a passage to the Orient. He never found it. Instead, he landed on islands off the coast of a continent unknown to Europeans of that time, though Norsemen had landed on the northeast coast sometime during the eleventh century. Thinking he was in the Indies off the coast of Asia, Columbus called the inhabitants he met "Indians."

The so-called Indians had been living in the New World for many thousands of years before any Europeans knew of their existence. By the time Columbus "discovered" them, they occupied all the land from the far reaches of North America to the tip of South America. They spoke many different languages, and had no single word for themselves as a racial or cultural group that would be the equivalent of our word "Indian." Each group had its own term for itself, usually meaning something like "we, the people," and other words for those who did not belong to the group. Navajo, for example, called themselves Dine, meaning "the people" or "people of the surface of the earth."

We continue to use the name Columbus gave the native people, although some scholars have suggested that "Amerind" is more accurate, and many people today prefer "Native American." In Europe, especially in Britain, the American Indians are often called Red Indians to distinguish them from the natives of India, and the slang terms "redskin" and "red man" were once popular in stories and films. Since Indian skin is not red, but shades of brown, these terms may have arisen from the Indians' use of red body paint for their religious and battle dress.

Indian societies varied, ranging from simple hunting and gathering bands to populous urban centers. Some groups spent their lives in one place, cultivating the soil; others lived part of the time in villages, leaving them only for seasonal activities; still others, the nomads, moved around all year long, hunting and gathering wild plants. It was many years before Europeans realized the variety of Indian cultures and how different each group was from all the others. The Indians Columbus met in the West Indies, those the Pilgrims lived among on the northeast Atlantic seaboard, and those the Spaniards found in Mexico and Peru were as unlike each other as the Pilgrims and the Spanish themselves. They had countless languages—linguists believe that over three hundred were spoken north of the Rio Grande, though only some Mexican Indians had written languages. Some Indians were tall, like the Mojave and Yuma; others were short and stocky. Some looked like the Indian on the old buffalo nickel, with hawklike noses and high cheekbones; others had flat noses, round and generally oriental faces. There never was a typical American Indian, culturally or physically.

The Europeans who were curious about where these unknown people had come from suggested many theories, of which a few have survived and are still heard from time to time. One of the earliest and most persistent traced the Indians to the ten lost tribes of Israel, who had somehow made their way to the New

Preceding pages: Mesa Verde cliff dwellings in Colorado.

Columbus presenting Indians to Spanish royalty at the court of Barcelona in 1493.

World. Others linked Indians with a variety of peoples, both real and mythical. One tale tells how the soldiers of Alexander the Great sailed east from India after their leader's death and eventually populated the Americas. The Indians' origin also has been attributed to Trojans, Phoenicians, Romans, Egyptians, Welsh, and the people of the mythical lost continents of Atlantis and Mu.

A few of the imaginative histories came very close to the one the scientific community now accepts. Early explorers and settlers speculated that Indians had come to the continent from the northwest and that animals from the Old World had come in at the same place. They pointed out physical likenesses between Indians and people of eastern Asia. How this migration must have happened is the story that opens Chapter 1.

Bibliography

Jennings, Jesse D.
1968   *Prehistory of North America.*
      An introductory college text in North American archaeology. This is a highly regarded book which deals with methodology and definitions as well as prehistoric developments. It contains an excellent bibliography for beginning students, as well as a glossary.

Suggestions
for Further Study

Jennings, Jesse D., and Edward Norbeck, eds.
1964 *Prehistoric Man in the New World.*

Prehistory: Before
the Europeans Came

4

A more advanced book, compiled by leading authorities in New World archaeology, both North and South American. It tells of the findings of specialists and
discusses some of the controversies. The papers were originally given at a sym-
posium on New World archaeology at Rice University.

Willey, Gordon R.
1966 *An Introduction to American Archaeology,* vol. 1, *North and Middle America.*
A college textbook that includes Mexico as well as regions to the north. Pro-
fusely illustrated with excellent charts, it covers origins and cultural developments by culture area, and has a good bibliography and glossary.

Other
Pertinent Works

Caldwell, Joseph
1958 *Trend and Tradition in the Prehistory of the Eastern United States.*

Griffin, James B., ed.
1952 *Archaeology of the Eastern United States.*

Martin, Paul S., George Quimby, and D. Collier
1947 *Indians before Columbus.*

McGregor, John C.
1965 *Southwestern Archaeology.*

Meggers, Betty J.
1972 *Prehistoric America.*

Sanders, William, and Joseph Marino
1970 *New World Prehistory.*

Wedel, Waldo R.
1961 *Prehistoric Man on the Great Plains.*

Wormington, Hilda Marie
1957 *Ancient Man in North America.*

1 FIRST SETTLERS IN THE NEW WORLD

The last major geologic epoch was the Pleistocene, which began more than 2 million years ago and ended about 10,000 years ago. During its last 100,000 years, great quantities of snow fell in the northern hemisphere, and huge glaciers spread over much of North America. A few stretches of land were free of ice from time to time; one of these was central and coastal Alaska. Vegetation grew in these areas, allowing browsing and grazing animals to feed almost up to the glaciers' edges.

With so much water locked up in the glaciers, the oceans were lower. A strip of dry land as much as a thousand miles wide emerged between Asia and Alaska, connecting the continents where now the Bering Strait—fifty-six miles of open ocean—separates them. This land too eventually grew vegetation, attracting large game animals from both northeast Asia and Alaska. People from Asia, taking advantage of the good hunting, began to follow them into the New World. Like Columbus thousands of years later, they were not looking for a new world, nor did they realize they had found one. They probably wandered eastward for many years, and may even have meandered back to Siberia occasionally.

Now and then over the ages the ice sheet melted in places, opening corridors southward. People, still hunting, must have passed from Alaska south to the land we know as the United States. They probably followed one of the temporary, ice-free corridors around the Alaska coast north of the Brooks range or up the Yukon River valley into the Mackenzie River valley and then southward, along the east slope of the Rocky Mountains to the Dakotas.

Direct evidence telling just when and how people first came to North America has not been found. It may be lost beneath cold ocean waters, destroyed under advancing and retreating glaciers, or lying undiscovered in Siberia or Alaska. But we know they came, probably by these routes, and most archaeologists believe they came between 20,000 and 28,000 years ago.

To reconstruct a picture of these early American settlers, we can draw much indirect evidence from geology, archaeology, anthropology, and other disciplines. Another useful tool is *ethnographic analogy,* comparing the facts we have about prehistoric peoples with what we know about tribal people who live today or who lived in the recent past. Such comparisons can be very helpful if they are used with careful control. The people compared must have some historical connection with one another, living in about the same environment and being not too different technologically. To reconstruct ancient Indian groups, we have used knowledge about more recent American Indian societies with low population density and simple tools, making their living in difficult environments. From this information we can arrive at informed guesses about how the Indians' very early ancestors lived.

Most archaeologists now think that the ancestral Indian population, or part of it, had come into this continent by 20,000 B.C. Others would set the date much earlier. We will side with the majority, recognizing that new evidence might turn

Preceding page:
Ceremonial pipe
(height, 8 inches),
fashioned 2,000
years ago by the
Adena, the early
mound builders.
Found in Ohio, the
dwarflike figure has
spools in its ears
and a thick neck.

up at any time to push that date much further back. Beyond any doubt, people had reached Tierra del Fuego, the southern tip of South America, before 6000 B.C. How long would a hunting and gathering group, following its food, take to travel from Alaska to the end of the South American continent? Uncounted generations must have lived and died as the people drifted southward. Some must have stopped, settling and adapting to local conditions—one reason that Indian societies are so numerous and so different. In two hundred centuries or more, even people with the same ancestry can develop marked cultural and physical

The Bering Strait land bridge during the last glacial period and the ice-free corridor that provided access from Siberia to Alaska and then to the North and South American continents.

differences. The Indians may be descended from many successive waves of immigrants, but they could just as well have sprung from a few groups arriving from Asia centuries apart.

The First Americans

We have only a general idea of what these very early Americans were like and what kind of life they led. Physically, all we know of them comes from a few skeletal remains, and the dates of those are in doubt. Even these fragmentary traces, though, show clearly that they were of the *Homo sapiens* species, our own. They show that man did not evolve in the New World, but entered in modern physical form. We have found no fossil remains of earlier species of man or his nearest relative, the great apes, in the Americas.

Reconstructing a human being's physical appearance from bone material is moderately chancy. Judging from skeletal remains and descriptions of Indians by early European arrivals as well as the appearance of contemporary Indian people, physical anthropologists believe that early Americans were of a Mongoloid type, less oriental in appearance than today's East Asians, but with dark hair and eyes, light to medium brown skin, and relatively little facial and body hair. Generation after generation of adapting to new environments would have left them with the variations in height and body build that the European visitors found in North America at the time of contact. Nothing in the New World, though, compared with the physical differences to be found in Africa, where stature ranges from the tallest to the shortest people on earth, living just a short distance apart.

A physical trait or distinguishing characteristic that sets Asian and North American Indian populations apart from other peoples is the *shovel tooth*. This is a kind of hollowing out of the inner side of the upper central incisor teeth, giving them a scoop or shovel shape. The fact that this trait is common in both populations is very strong evidence that they had common ancestry.

The Eskimo population, which is not considered Indian but a separate group physically and culturally, arrived later, and probably crossed the strait by boat. Anthropologists agree that the ancestral Eskimo were established in the New World Arctic around 2000 B.C. Physically they are a more specialized Mongoloid type than the Indians, with *epicanthic eye folds*—the so-called slanted eyes— as well as yellower skin and flattened noses. The Eskimo are the only society on earth whose geographical range coincides with a climate zone, the Arctic, and who have a common language and common culture with only minor local variations.

Many questions still remain about how the New World was populated. When did the earliest migrants come? How many migrations were there? Where did

Shovel-shaped incisors (top), characteristic of American Indians, Eskimo, and East Asians, are compared with the incisors with no shoveling.

they come from in Asia? Some weak similarities have been suggested between material remains such as tools in the New World and some found near Lake Baikal in Siberia.

How They Lived

The early people had simple tools. They needed protection from the cold, so we can assume that they knew techniques for working hides into clothing and probably into simple shelters—though their shelters may well have been no more than windbreaks, not leather tents. Remains of ashes are good evidence that those people knew how to make and control fire, which would have been important, considering the climate. The scarce stone remains tell us that their tools were very simple: scrapers, bearing out the idea that the people knew how to work hides, and flakes of stone that must have been useful for many jobs, among them cutting, punching, and chopping. We doubt that those stone pieces were meant to be attached to lances or arrows; that is, the people probably did not use them as part of a projectile to be thrown or shot.

That these people lived by hunting seems certain. In the Arctic and Subarctic they would have little choice but to hunt for most of the year, even today. The short summers brought greater variety: vegetable foods, edible roots, seeds; eggs from the migrating birds that nest at that time of year by the millions; and clams and mussels gathered along the beaches and tidal flats. And fish and sea

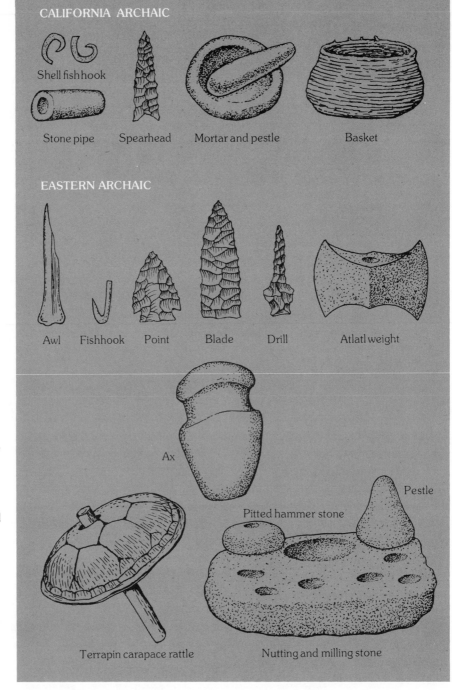

CALIFORNIA ARCHAIC

Shell fish hook

Stone pipe   Spearhead   Mortar and pestle   Basket

EASTERN ARCHAIC

Awl   Fishhook   Point   Blade   Drill   Atlatl weight

Ax

Pestle

Pitted hammer stone

Terrapin carapace rattle   Nutting and milling stone

Archaic artifacts. Artifacts of the California Archaic made of shell, fiber, and stone (top; variable scale). Eastern Archaic artifacts (bottom; all one-fourth actual size except the weight, the ax, and the milling stone). All these items are of stone except for the awl and the fishhook, which are made of bone, and the carapace, or turtle shell, which is a restored rattle.

STONE TOOL MANUFACTURE

DRILLING

Tool technology. Stone tools were manufactured by various steps. First, a suitably
hard stone was selected and flakes were chipped off it by means of a hammer stone
(A). Next, the edges of a flake were chipped by applying pressure with a bone tool,
thus making a sharp-edged tool (B). Finally, by pecking (C), grinding, and polishing, such tools as axes and chisels were manufactured; a hammer stone was
used to peck tiny bits from the tool's surface to make it smoother.

Drilling. Holes in stone and bone tools could be drilled by different methods.
The simplest tool was a hand drill (D), made of a wooden shaft with a point of
stone, bone, or copper; the shaft was rotated in opposite directions by rolling it
back and forth between the hands. The Eskimo and some other northern tribes
used variations of the bow drill (E). The Eskimo steadied the drill by holding the
bone mouthpiece in his teeth and revolved the drill by moving the bow back and
forth; a bow drill can also be worked by holding the top of the drill with one hand
and working the bow with the other. A simpler version of this drill has a mouthpiece but no bow—only a cord that is pulled to turn the drill.

mammals could be added to the land animals. But for most of the year, then as now, that northern land was frozen, snow-covered tundra. The plants were buried or dormant, and the birds were nesting in the south. Shellfish beds were locked under ice, and streams were frozen over. It was hunt or starve, and the remains of stone tools mean that the hunt was vital.

Hunting must have been difficult and tiring, and the hunters often would have to return to camp empty-handed. Then, dried plantstuffs or fresh plants gathered during the growing season would be their diet. We lack fossil evidence of these foods because they decay quickly, but we know that primitive hunting tribes today commonly depend on wild plants as a stable food supply. It is likely, then, that the men hunted, and the women and children gathered wild plants. When the hunt was successful, everyone feasted on meat; but plant foods must have been a more reliable daily food, depending, of course, on what grew in the region during that season.

A Society of Bands

Once again we use ethnographic analogy and assume that as groups became more populous—and they must have done so sometimes in spite of the rigorous climate—some couples probably moved off to fresh hunting and gathering grounds. The amount of food the environment could produce would have strictly limited population size; even later people with more complex technology such as more effective hunting tools could not escape that limitation. Also, the population limits set by the technology and the food supply would have kept political structures simple. We describe their social organization as *band level,* groups of fifty to one hundred people in families or other kin groups that lived and found food together. Bands probably were composed of brothers with their wives and younger children, the oldest brother or the best hunter usually acting as leader, making suggestions and offering guidance. No one would have held the leadership except by community agreement, and no one would have had coercive power to enforce his decisions. Group decisions would have been made after thorough discussion and by unanimous agreement. Brothers would have been a good core for a band of hunters because, having grown up together, they would know how to hunt together and would know their environment. Cooperation and intimate knowledge of animals, surroundings, and weather conditions are essential for efficient hunting. Strangers brought together as husbands of a group of sisters would exploit the environment for hunting far less effectively, but women who started as strangers would not suffer as much disadvantage in gathering wild plant foods for their families.

Although the land was vast and the populations were small, bands must have met from time to time, perhaps by arrangement to organize marriages or en-

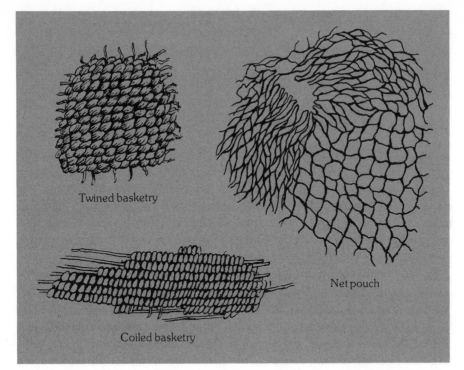

Twined basketry

Net pouch

Coiled basketry

Examples of basketry fragments from the Desert Archaic. The net pouch was probably used like a shopping bag.

gage in communal hunts. Such hunts would have required more hunters than any one band usually could muster. Some of the animals they hunted—as we know from bone remains—were large; the best way to hunt them would be to stampede them over cliffs or into bogs where they would be mired down, killed, or disabled. The bands probably planned such activities together, and, if the hunt was successful, followed it with communal celebrations and feasting. When the supply of meat dwindled, the bands would break up, perhaps planning to meet during a good hunting season when they could find enough food for the larger population. We can also guess that bands sometimes met each other unexpectedly; the results of such contact may have been less than peaceful.

As the earliest Americans wandered, following the game they hunted, they moved southward and eventually entered new environmental zones. The southward movement was slow, bringing no abrupt changes in climate, vegetation, or animal life. The people had plenty of time to adapt their traditional ways to new environmental requirements. The food quest would have changed as the need arose, modified by past customs. People would have responded to new circumstances, but their responses must have varied widely, depending not only on new geographic conditions and old accustomed ways, but also on the frequency of contact between bands. Various groups would doubtless have exchanged information and techniques, a process called *diffusion* or *cultural borrowing*. Those who lived where people often passed through would show more variety than those who became isolated from contact with others. The people who moved into environments rich in natural resources would begin to show a richer material life. As the years passed, cultures would have diversified.

The Big Game Hunters

The country stretching from the Rocky Mountains to the Mississippi and south to Mexico had a chilly and moist climate in late Pleistocene times. Winds blowing off the continental glaciers to the north cooled the plains and brought enough rainfall to sustain lush vegetation even in regions that later turned arid or semiarid.

On the northern plains, the lower and wetter areas were forested with pine, spruce, and tamarack; the higher land, except for wooded lake margins and river valleys, was open and carpeted with grass. Farther south along the Mississippi the plains extended hundreds of miles in a broad belt of prairie grasslands scattered with lakes and ponds, and with woodlands of birch, alder, and other deciduous trees as well as many conifers. Toward the Rockies the long-grass area was mostly treeless. West of the Rockies, parts of today's Nevada and Utah were covered by Lake Bonneville, and even Death Valley was well vegetated.

The plains area was an enormous open zoo, filled with some of the most remarkable animals the continent has known: giant moose, beavers as large as modern bears, ground sloths, bison, caribou, musk-oxen, gigantic mammoths, and in the wooded areas, mastodons. Peccaries, rabbits, and smaller animals were everywhere, along with a species of camel that later became extinct. In season, waterfowl formed a living blanket on the prairie ponds. A fearsome array of carnivores—meat eaters—preyed on the plant eaters. The dire wolf, nearly half again as large as the later timber wolf, was armed with powerful, bone-crushing jaws. There were also bobtailed sabertoothed cats, and a panther larger than the biggest lion.

People on the Great Plains

Human beings, lured by game, wandered southward, and were drawn toward the great plains by the promise of even better hunting. Why did they go south? They could not have known what awaited them there, but consider the sights that met their eyes yearly. As daylight decreased in the northern latitudes, watchers saw swans, geese, ducks, curlews, plovers, and other birds fly southward from arctic breeding grounds. The birds were followed by the great browsers and grazers. The snow drifted deeper and deeper, and less and less game appeared. People would have needed no great imagination to deduce that by following the vanishing sun as the birds and the beasts did, they might find more game. And so the people came to the great plains.

Few traces of these first pioneers of the American West have been found, but enough to tell us that as they entered the plains their hunting and living practices began to change from the ways of their northern forefathers. The food resources of the plains were radically different from those in the northland; plants in particular were far more plentiful. The new resources could not help affecting people's ways of life. As the glaciers passed their peak and began to retreat, people moved into the grassland areas—not only the places that are the plains today, but the grasslands and woodlands that extended to the east beyond the Mississippi and into the territory that later became the desert of the Southwest.

In this vast area, the people began to specialize in big game hunting. The period of the Big Game Hunters ran from about 15,000 to 8000 B.C. in general, but it lasted much longer in the true plains than elsewhere—long after the desert area had grown so arid that it could no longer sustain the herd animals.

Folsom People. Archaeological research in the plains area has helped us understand the Big Game Hunters, and has also established the antiquity of man in the New World. Scholars long believed that the first migrations from Asia had come as recently as 2000 B.C. During the first quarter of this century, in fact, no one even bothered to search for evidence of an earlier arrival, so convinced were scientists that man's entry was recent.

Then one day in 1925, riding in search of lost cattle near the town of Folsom, New Mexico, a man named George McJunkin noticed a layer of bleached bones twenty feet down in a deep gully. He was familiar with cattle bones, and recognized immediately that the bones, though resembling modern cattle bones, were not quite like any he had ever seen. Among them McJunkin found several bits of worked flint, somewhat like arrowheads he had seen, but of a different shape— parallel instead of tapered edges, with the base chipped into a concave curve. Both sides of the points had been grooved or fluted.

News of McJunkin's discovery spread eventually to archaeologists and paleontologists (scientists specializing in fossils), who identified the bones as those of a bison that had become extinct about 8000 B.C. The bison's antiquity was not startling, but its clear association with man-made flint points was most exciting. The official theory at that time was that man had not been in the New World when that bison variety lived. Either the bones and the flints had become mixed long after the bison died or else the date of man's arrival in the New World had to be changed.

Unanimously the scientific world agreed that the conjunction of bones and artifacts was no mere accident: the points had actually been used in hunting the bison. That bison pursued by Folsom man, as we call those ancient hunters, was *Bison antiquus,* a long-horned beast that stood six feet high at the shoulder and weighed a ton. At the original Folsom site, the arrangement of the bones shows that twenty-three animals had been trapped and killed as a group in a blind gully. Here, and at some other Folsom kills, the hunters' main object seems to have been hides rather than meat; the bones are not scattered as they would have been if the bison had been butchered, and the tail bones, which would have come away with the hide when it was removed, are nearly all missing.

Clovis People.   In 1932, another New Mexico site, near Clovis, yielded the bones of extinct animals accompanied by stone points different from those found at Folsom. But these Clovis points were discovered beneath layers of earth containing flints of the Folsom type, indicating that Clovis was older, and pushing the time of man's arrival in North America still further back. Clovis-like spear points have turned up from coast to coast, as far north as Alaska and as far south as Mexico. Folsom points, on the other hand, are known only from the

Points used by the plains Big Game Hunters, with the names of the sites where the points were found.

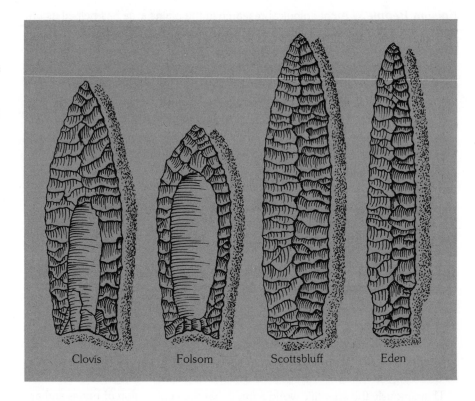

Clovis   Folsom   Scottsbluff   Eden

high plains. The Clovis point is larger than the Folsom, and the fluting on the Clovis does not extend as far along the blade. We have some evidence that the Clovis type is associated with mammoth hunting and the Folsom with bison hunting.

How They Hunted

The people of the Big Game tradition were probably not physically different from the earlier immigrants. We have few human skeletal remains from either period, and those we have are fragmentary. But the difference in their skill at manufacturing stone tools is noticeable. The Folsom and Clovis points are far finer than the choppers and scrapers of earlier times, and the fluted points, though delicate looking, were lethal to giant animals.

The fluted points were probably set into spear or lance handles and hurled from an implement called an *atlatl* (an Aztec word) or spear thrower. The atlatl may have been brought over from Asia or it may have been invented in the New World. It was a truly revolutionary tool which allowed the hunter to attack a dangerous animal from a relatively safe distance. (The bow and arrow did not appear in the New World until much later.) The atlatl could hurl a spear with such force that it would penetrate the tough hides of the large game animals; that force came from the length the atlatl added to a man's arm and the extra joint that created more leverage.

Even with spear throwers, it was hard to kill the large animals, and as in earlier times, the hunters often drove them into sites where they were disabled and could not escape. Grass fires started at the right places sent game in a panic over cliffs or into swamps. At one site the bones uncovered are all from young animals, suggesting that the hunters had managed to separate the less dangerous and tenderer individuals from the herd. They had other ways of minimizing the risks. The Clovis people who hunted mammoths seem to have made a practice of lying in wait at water holes where the animals drank, and attacking them there. In one Clovis kill site, the leg bones of a mammoth were found intact, standing upright just as they had been when the beast was mired down. The rest of the skeleton was scattered about as if the hunters had butchered their kill from the top down, ignoring the hard-to-reach legs.

The sign that the Big Game Hunters worked hides from the animals they hunted is the number of scrapers in the sites. The hunters used stone knives to cut the hides and butcher the animals. Because these people wandered, like the earlier people, we would not expect to find remains of permanent shelters, and their housing appears to have been nothing more than rude windbreaks of brush and grass or perhaps hides. In fact, except for the Lindenmeier site in

The atlatl, or spear-thrower, has a wooden handle and a hooked tip into which the haft of the spear was fitted (length, about 2 feet). The use of the atlatl enabled the hunter to add range to his spear—he could stay at a distance from his prey—and to increase the speed of his weapon by the flipping action with which it was thrown. The round weights around the atlatl were probably adjusted to the individual hunter.

Atlatl

Atlatl in use

Spear in position

northeastern Colorado, camp sites from the time of the Big Game Hunters are all but unknown; most of our knowledge comes from kill and butcher sites.

Although all the remains that would tell us how these people used plants have long since decayed, we can guess from the amount and variety of vegetation that grew around them that plants were important in their food supply. Their social organization would have continued to be bands that came together during good hunting seasons to hunt game communally. Mass bison drives suggest that at least several dozen individuals cooperated in these. One archaeologist estimated that something like 60,000 pounds of meat must have been butchered at one site; at least one hundred fifty people would have been required to carry away even a third of it.

A New Diet

Around 8000 B.C., though the people continued to depend upon game, they seem to have turned more and more to plant foods. Sites of the late Big Game period show more equipment, such as grinding stones, for processing plants. Why the shift in eating habits? The answer is tied up with a hotly debated puzzle: why did many of the big game animals disappear? The phenomenon is often referred to as the Pleistocene extinctions. Between about 10,000 and 5000 B.C., more than a hundred species of mammals became extinct in North America, among them the mammoth, the mastodon, the horse, the camel, and all but the modern variety of bison often called buffalo. Were the animals wiped out by man, by climate, by both, or by causes yet to be determined?

We cannot hope to answer these questions. In any case, the extinctions made people change their subsistence patterns and caused important changes in their ways of life. In some places hunters began to seek small game; in others fish became a major food; in still others the food was mostly wild plants. Those new subsistence patterns led to other new patterns. Instead of wandering over broad areas searching for large game, hunters began to use more of the food resources they could find in limited areas. In one way this restricted the food search: people no longer ranged over great distances; in another way, it expanded their diet: they began to use more kinds of foods. The new local conditions varied from place to place, so there was no longer just one major way of life.

The shift from Big Game Hunting to an economy varied by plants and animals introduced the period we call the Archaic, to which we add a word describing the region: Desert Archaic, Eastern Archaic, and others. Although the Big Game Hunting tradition had seen regional modification, it was recognizable as one coherent tradition from the tools the people used.

The Archaic Period

The stage called Archaic spans generally the years from 8000 to 2000 B.C., though its length varied from region to region. From the kinds of tools that were most common in that period, we can see the changes the people went through in finding subsistence. Along with the hunter's projectile points, people made new kinds of tools. Special devices for spearing, hooking, netting, and trapping fish showed how sophisticated technology was becoming. Stone itself came into broad use in a new form—tools were ground into shape instead of being chipped or flaked. This change in manufacturing was much more than a refinement. It enormously expanded the supplies of raw materials from which tools could be made. Almost any tough stone, such as basalt, could now be ground into a serviceable ax, and an easily split material like slate, which cannot be chipped as well as flint because it splits too easily, could be ground into a very good spearhead, and soft stone could be hollowed out to make containers.

In this period we see the first evidence of many significant inventions: boats, baskets, and cloth woven of plant fibers, and in the late Archaic in the Lake Superior region, even some tools and adornments made of copper. The size and complexity of the tool kit and the changes it made in people's ways of life varied according to environment. In the western deserts, resources were sparse, and the possibilities were somewhat limited. In the eastern woodlands, countless new possibilities opened up to the inhabitants, who worked out a highly efficient technology for exploiting them.

About 8000 B.C., the North American climate began to change. The weather became drier and the grasslands started to shrink. The continental ice sheets had withdrawn and the land that had been under ice was exposed. The meltwater from the ice sheets ran into river beds, filling the Great Lakes and others, and the ocean began to submerge the Bering Strait. The Southwest and parts of Mexico became so hot and dry that they turned into deserts. The shorelines of the continents began to change as the oceans grew deeper. All these new climatic and geographic conditions altered the animal life and also forced the people into different ways of life. Big Game Hunting gave way to more intensive plant collecting and small game hunting.

Desert Archaic People

The first evidence that Big Game Hunting was declining comes from the Southwest and Basin areas, which were turning into arid zones by 8000 B.C. This vast region lies between the Rockies and the Sierra Nevada and Cascade ranges, covering all of Nevada, Utah, and Arizona, and parts of Oregon, Idaho, California, New Mexico, and northern Mexico. As the Pleistocene closed, it was becoming desert land, one of the most rigorous habitats in North America, imposing severe limitations on human existence.

Life in the Desert. People in this area had to shift from hunting to foraging—some would even call it scavenging. They changed their dietary habits to include rats, snakes, lizards, gophers, and other small desert species, though unquestionably most of their diet was desert seeds, tubers, and other vegetable foods. Deer and elk must have been rare delicacies in the desert, though Big Game Hunting continued on the grasslands to the east. For the new diet the Indians developed grinding stones, which they used to reduce the vegetable foods, indigestible when raw, to a condition suitable for cooking. Baskets for harvesting and storing wild plants became common household utensils. The women gathered all kinds of seeds including those of pickleweed, sunflower, and yucca, from good-sized acorns to tiny Indian millet seeds. Placed on the surface of a grinding stone and ground with a small stone held in the hand, the seeds were reduced to a coarse meal. This milling equipment was the prototype of the stone slab *(metate)* and hand-held stone *(mano),* still widely used in rural Mexico to grind corn. The cooks then either formed the meal into cakes to be baked or boiled it into a mush in watertight baskets by dropping hot stones into them—a method known as stone boiling.

These people had a domesticated animal, the dog, by mid-Archaic times, around 4000 B.C. Dogs helped in hunting, as scavengers about the camp, as a warning if animal predators or human enemies came near—and occasionally as a source of food.

The once large lakes of the region were drying up and turning brackish by Archaic times, but migrating fowl stopped by, attracted by realistic decoys made of reeds sewn together with fiber threads and covered with duck feathers. The people searched the reedy shallows for eggs in the nests of grebes or mud hens and caught fish in fiber nets weighted on the bottom edge with stones: six or seven boys or men waded out waist-deep to bring the net around in a loop to scoop up the fish.

By early summer, the heat was intense, and the waterways and lakes began to dry up. No longer did people have to wear fur blankets and robes; breechcloths for the men and short hide aprons for the women were all the summer clothes they needed. Brush shelters that had given protection against winter cold gave shade during summer midday heat. Women harvested the seeds and plants as they ripened, carrying the foodstuffs in tall, conical collecting baskets and roasting them by shaking them with live coals on wickerwork trays. The heat split the inedible husks and freed the seeds inside for grinding.

This life-style spread to nearly all the arid and semiarid regions of the West. In some places it persisted until historic times (documented after European contact), as in the cultures of the Shoshoni, Ute, and Paiute tribes, from whom we get our descriptions of the rabbit hunt.

The Rabbit Hunt. An important cooperative activity, hunting for rabbits added meat to the mostly vegetable diet. Rabbits were caught in nets more than two hundred feet long but only about two feet wide, woven of milkweed fiber. Only the very old and mothers with babies did not take part in the hunt. Some of the people tied nets together and set them up, and others served as beaters, thrashing the underbrush with sticks. Rabbits ran from their hiding places into the nets, where they were met with throwing sticks and clubs. As the animals approached, the hunters killed as many as they could short of the net, because if too many rabbits hit it they could tear the delicate net fibers. A second line of hunters disposed of animals entangled in the mesh and caught many of those that managed to get through the net.

The hunt was followed by a rabbit feast, and then the women dressed the skins. Beginning at the outer edge of a pelt and cutting around and around in a spiral, they converted the skins into long strips and stretched them between trees until they dried. Thirty or so six-foot lengths of fur rope woven side by side with bits of skin made a winter robe or blanket.

People of the Coastal Archaic

Along the borders of the western desert and in the lands stretching to the Pacific coast, life was much less harsh, but the people's adaptations were much the same. The main difference was the amount and variety of food available: the supply of animals and plants was more bountiful beyond the desert, and fish and seafoods abounded along waterways and coasts. In central California, where oak trees were plentiful, the main crop was acorns, which women gathered and ground into meal for cakes or mush. The foraging groups along the seacoast exploited the rich food resources there: abalones, clams, mussels, many kinds of fish, and even marine mammals like seals and sea otters. In the California area, communities were larger than in the desert, and life went on around more or less permanent base camps.

The northwest coast, then as now, was mountain terrain with deep valleys whose rivers rushed to the sea. The archaeological record, still very incomplete, shows Archaic adaptations to the plentiful fish and shell foods of the rivers and coast. Bone remains tell us that people also took sea mammals such as otters and seals as well as land mammals like elk and deer. The hunting and fishing adaptations of the northwest coastal people appear to have begun 7,000 or more years ago.

Living in the Arctic and Subarctic Archaic

Scholars agree that North America's native populations entered the continent from the extreme northwest, but the archaeological material they have to work with from the far north is much scantier than from almost any other region. The reason is obvious: the excavators face formidable obstacles in a land of permanently frozen soil. Some ancient sites are accessible—one is conveniently on the campus of the University of Alaska—but others lie in remote and almost un-mapped regions, reachable only recently by helicopter. Digging still can be done only during the summer, and even then it poses unique difficulties. After remov-ing one shallow level, the excavator must wait for the sun to thaw a few more inches of soil before digging deeper. This natural deep-freeze has the advantage, of course, of preserving otherwise perishable materials. Ancient refuse does smell as it begins to thaw, but it is full of information about prehistoric diet.

Tiny tools known as *microblades,* dating from about 4000 to 2000 B.C., have turned up in the Arctic. This development is known as the Small Tool tradition. The blades probably were set in antler and bone to make composite tools, one of which was a kind of toothed saw, useful for working hides. Other types may well have been serrated points used for spears or harpoons. People of the Small Tool tradition probably were not Eskimo, but they seem to have handed down many of their tool designs to subsequent people who undoubtedly were Eskimo. The Small Tool makers spread across the northern part of the continent in the Arctic and Subarctic from Alaska to Hudson's Bay and eventually to Greenland. Archaeologists think that their tools resemble certain Asiatic types. Some of those people seem to have hunted sea mammals in summer and passed the winters farther inland hunting caribou, elk, and small game. They also fished, for net sinkers have been found among the stone equipment, especially in sites in the subarctic forests.

We know from a few tool remains that other people also lived in the frigid zone across northern Canada. These tools include spear points that are stubby and notched on either side for lashing to a shaft, and cruder tools that point to an even earlier culture, still undated. The record of those traditions is still so in-complete that little can be said about them.

Forest People of the Eastern Archaic

From the plains eastward to the Atlantic, forests were prominent in the environ-ment after about 8000 B.C. Those eastern forests were not scattered patches of woodland as they are today, but endless tracts of trees covering mountains, roll-ing hills, and valleys. The forests sheltered countless woodland animals; deer were most common, but squirrel, opossum, bear, raccoon, and wildcat also in-habited the forests. The region was well watered by rainfall and by rivers and streams. Those watercourses and the many lakes and large and small ponds held many species of fish and turtles and attracted many waterfowl. The Indians of the East were forest people. Trees provided the materials for their houses and equipment, and the game lived in the forests.

The women gathered many forms of wild plants, seeds, nuts, fruits, tubers, and roots. Around Lake Superior, people often ate a grass seed that we now call wild rice. The forest residents constructed rather elaborate dwellings, as we can tell from the postholes found at some Eastern Archaic sites. They must have been more settled than the desert or arctic people of the same period. The enormous heaps of fresh-water shells near inland rivers and seashells on the coasts imply a population that was not only more settled, but more numerous. In addition to supplying food, shellfish also provided raw material for utensils and shell ornaments.

The tools the easterners used included many implements for exploiting the wood that was so plentiful: axes, drills, gouges, and other woodworking tools of ground and chipped stone. They made specialized items, too: many styles of fishhooks, harpoons, and nets for game and fowl as well as for fish, and mortars and pestles for crushing and grinding plant foods. Out of bone and shell they carved beads, pendants, and awls. Around the Great Lakes, they hammered tools as well as ornaments out of the copper nuggets they found—the first instance of metalwork in the New World. The copper was hammered as if it were another form of stone; the people had no knowledge of smelting, and the cop-

**Copper tools of the
Archaic period
(about one-half
actual size).**

per workers never learned to cast metal. Consequently, metal craft was restricted to a small area around Lake Superior where lumps of pure copper could be found ready for use. Archaeologists have given the name "Old Copper Culture" to the Archaic development of copper technology in the Great Lakes region.

It was probably during the late Archaic that the birchbark canoe was invented in the densely forested north woods that stretched from Wisconsin and Minnesota into Canada and to the eastern seaboard. Such a boat would have been particularly useful here, where thousands of lakes are connected by a network of streams and rivers, but with gaps in the connections. Only a lightweight vessel could negotiate shallows and be carried across land between waterways. Once available, the bark canoe opened up the formerly impenetrable north woods and converted the region's web of lakes and streams into routes for trade and communication.

In the East, fishermen not only hooked and netted fish, they also trapped them. One huge fish trap, or weir as it is called, was built about 2000 B.C. in what is now Boston. It was an enclosure extending over two acres of a shallow lagoon, allowing water to pass through but keeping fish back. Building the weir would have required an estimated 65,000 stakes, sharpened with stone axes and set in double rows interlaced with brush. The labor it took shows that it was not intended for short-term use, but to bring in a sure food supply for many years—enough for the fairly large population that would have been needed to build such an extensive installation. The large number of workers required meant that there must also have been some central authority to mobilize people and materials for such a large public work.

Like the Desert Archaic, the Eastern Archaic tradition left a record telling of a remarkably stable way of life over a long period. Unlike the Desert, though, the Eastern shows a big difference in population growth, because resources there could support many more people. Although the wooded eastern region as a whole may be characterized as we have done here, this one general tradition included an infinite variety of local environments and thus considerable diversification.

The Woodland Tradition

In the East, two major new developments set off the period from about 1000 B.C. to A.D. 800 from the Archaic: large earth mounds and pottery. Eastern people also began to focus their attention on certain species of the wild plants they harvested. Whether it is necessary or even appropriate to classify these 1,800 years separately has been debated, because in much of the eastern

area the simple Archaic tradition continued; in fact, many Archaic traits continued until European contact. Some areas, however, showed such intensified development and so much new sophistication that most prehistorians feel it is reasonable to separate this period from the Archaic. It has become known as the
Woodland tradition.

Within the Woodland tradition, different groups constructed spectacular earthworks as burial and effigy mounds, and apparently traded luxury items like
pearls, shells, and mica. Thus the period is not only of great interest but also of
great importance. Those local changes showed how bountiful natural resources,
complex and sophisticated technology and social organization, and opportunity
for new ideas to enter (probably by the connecting river routes) all came together to create a new social and economic level. This led, though indirectly, to
even more complex societies. Important stimulation may have come from as far
as Mexico, although archaeologists by no means agree about Mexican influence
in this early period.

The two most outstanding Woodland cultures are known as Adena and Hopewell. As you read these descriptions, keep in mind that Adena and Hopewell are
a biased sample of Woodland. Most groups were not so technologically or socially sophisticated, but merely added pottery and occasional rather insignificant
mounds to the Archaic adaptations. Indeed, for some societies, Woodland has
been described as "Archaic with pottery."

Adena People

No one knows just why, around 1000 B.C., some people began a new type of
construction, variously shaped earth mounds, most of which covered burials.
Mounds were not all built at the same time, nor were they built by the same people. The first of the major mound-building peoples were the Adena, named after
an estate near Chillicothe, Ohio, where earthworks were excavated in 1901. The
Adena modes of subsistence followed the Archaic pattern. The people lived by
harvesting wild foods in a systematic way, taking advantage of nearly all the
available plants, and hunting woodland animals. We say harvesting rather than
cultivating because, though no sign of domesticated plants has been found, the
Adena people had gone beyond the simple gathering practiced by earlier
groups. The Adena folk may even have sown the seeds of such plants as sunflower. This kind of work with wild plants may well have predisposed these and
other peoples to horticulture, the cultivation of plants. Evidence that squashes,
gourds, and pumpkins were used has shown up in some archaeological sites.
Other wild foods included those of the Archaic period, both plant and animal.
We do not have much excavated evidence of habitations, but the remains that

Serpent Mound, longest of all effigy mounds (a quarter mile), contained no burials as far as can be determined; it is located in southern Ohio. Woodland mound building took the form of effigy mounds in Wisconsin, Illinois, and Iowa, usually with burials. The effigies may have been connected with religious beliefs, but no one really knows.

have been found show that Adena houses were round, built of posts leaning outward, with mats hung from them to form walls. The roofs were thatched.

The finest remains of the Adena people are their burial mounds and the structures that went with them. People began erecting these mounds sometime around 600 B.C., surrounding many of them with ridges of piled-up earth through which long avenues, similarly bordered, approached the mounds. The mound structures seem to have been connected with Adena ceremonial life.

Because so much excavating has been done in the Adena people's ceremonial complexes and so little in their villages, we know much more about their ornamental objects than about their ordinary tools and equipment. These tools differed little from those of the Archaic people except that they had been developed further. The Adena people made pottery, pendants of ground stone, and pipes. Perhaps the latter indicate tobacco smoking, but we have no direct evidence. They also wove cloth from plant fibers and made items of copper: body ornaments like bracelets, pendants, and rings, as well as some tools.

The burial mounds were large, and much care was lavished on them. The people built them by piling up small basketloads of earth. The dead interred in these mounds were probably high-ranking people, because not all bodies got

A reconstructed Adena house and a floor plan (diameter, 26 feet) on which the reconstruction was made.

this treatment. Some were laid on the ground and merely covered over; others were placed in pits lined with logs and roofed with more logs, over which a mound was built. Some bodies were cremated and some were merely buried.

Grave goods placed with the dead included designs cut from sheets of mica, and ground and polished stone tablets elaborately carved with an image of a bird associated with the Adena people. This was probably a bird of prey like a hawk or an eagle, along with an *eye* motif, and is found in this culture and later southern cultures. Although Adena certainly influenced other cultures in the East, it appears to have been confined mainly to parts of Kentucky, West Virginia, and southern Ohio.

Hopewell People

Early Hopewell existed around the same time as Adena and was certainly influenced by that culture. Adena probably was earlier and Hopewell lasted longer, though they had generations of overlap; the dating is still not clear. Hopewell appears to have started in central Illinois, but it reached its peak in Ohio, where it got its name from a mound-studded Ohio farm owned by a man named Hopewell. The Hopewellians, like the Adena folk, were mound builders, but their mounds were even more sophisticated and complex, and their burials were much more richly furnished with personal adornments.

Hopewell Trading.   The Hopewellians also are distinguished by their far-flung trading system. Trade had been going on throughout the Midwest and East for some time, especially trade in copper nuggets, but it was informal, not systematic. The Hopewellian trade appears to have involved at least semiprofessional traders. The Ohio Hopewell sites were well suited to such commerce. To the north, rivers gave access to the Great Lakes and the copper areas of Lake Superior. To the east, through Lake Ontario, were routes to the St. Lawrence, Mohawk, and Hudson valleys. The Ohio River led south into the Appalachians, where mica was found. From the Gulf of Mexico, trade in shells moved north via the Mississippi. Up the Missouri River, to the west, traders could get grizzly bear teeth and obsidian (volcanic glass).

What did the Hopewell people trade for these items? The complexity of their society implies much specialization of labor, at least part-time, so they probably had craftsmen turning imported raw materials into finished goods for trade. The Ohio Hopewellians had a valuable raw material of their own, a flint of distinctive

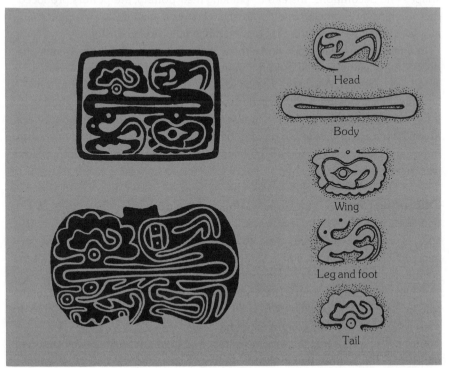

Head

Body

Wing

Leg and foot

Tail

Elements of the Adena bird design and two engraved tablets which show the elements.

and fine quality dug from a deposit known today as Flint Ridge. Another local product was a fine-grained stone used for making pipes, much desired throughout the East and Midwest.

Traders did not have to travel as far as Lake Superior, the Gulf, or the Rockies. Articles from those areas were almost unquestionably passed from tribe to tribe along a network of commercial routes. But Hopewell traders probably sought business as far as several hundred miles away.

Crafts from the Tomb. Proof of the wealth that trade funneled into Hopewell communities is plentiful in the mounds where they buried their important dead in log-lined tombs. Accompanying the burials are not only spear points and tools, but also embossed breastplates and ornaments of hammered copper, delicately chipped obsidian knives, fragile silhouettes cut out of sheet mica, and conch shells engraved with designs representing men and beasts. Some skeletons have been found covered with thousands of fresh-water pearls, which had apparently decorated a cloak or blanket.

These rich goods do not always reflect the results of trade, however. Some show how culturally sophisticated the Hopewellians were themselves. Pipes of local stone were beautifully carved into naturalistic animal or human forms by artisans. Pottery shows imagination and remarkably skilled workmanship in its shapes and decorations. Instead of painting their pottery, the potters produced their designs by engraving and by varying its texture. One design element many Hopewellians used is a bird of prey, resembling the Adena design.

In addition to carved pipes and almost sculptural pots, the Hopewellians produced true sculptures: little pottery figurines that show how the people sat, stood, and dressed. A woman, seated with her feet to one side, wearing a mid-length skirt, suckles her baby; another stands beneath an elaborate headdress, long hair hanging down her back in a sort of tassel, a crescent-shaped necklace around her neck and wide bands of either beads or tattooing around her wrists, upper arms, and ankles. And a little kneeling man, clad in a breechcloth, holds a war club or a hoe.

Cultivating Crops. The Hopewell folk definitely cultivated their crops. We find some indication of maize (the grain called corn in the United States) and species we think of as weeds were sown and harvested: pigweed, lambsquarter, and sunflower. The large, stable settlements, the broad geographic range of the culture, the wealth, and the elaboration of burials all indicate that the Hopewellians had some sort of central authority and a large, organized work force, and also an assured food supply they could have gotten only by combining some domestication with the wild plant and animal foods.

Around A.D. 500–800 the prosperity that had marked the Hopewell culture diminished. The great earthworks were no longer built, and the funeral offerings

Mica silhouette.
The brittle, trans-
parent mineral from
which silhouettes
were cut was traded
by the Hopewell
Indians. Found in
Ohio some 400
miles from the
nearest source of
mica, this silhouette
had been buried
with an Indian
about 1,500 years
ago.

A Hopewell ceramic
figurine of a mother
carrying a child
was found at the
Turner site.

became crude and sparse. What caused the decline is unknown, though some scattered evidence of invaders and warfare has been found. Booming population growth may have caused competition for resources. The people generally abandoned the ceremonial centers, and simple local forms developed in place of the once grand and widespread Hopewell tradition.

Contacts across the Pacific

It would not do to conclude our discussion of the early prehistory of the New World without a brief look at the question of trans-Pacific contacts other than those which may have come across the Bering Strait. There is no serious doubt that the New World was populated from Asia over land that emerged during the Pleistocene. The early immigrants had a very simple technology: they could control and make fire, work stone by chipping, work hides, and apparently make very little else. In much later periods, however—from 3000 B.C. to perhaps A.D. 1000—some traits show up in the New World that are strikingly like traits in the Pacific Islands and Southeast Asia. To explain this similarity, some archaeologists have suggested contacts between peoples across the Pacific Ocean.

The items that may be signs of contact with Asia are cultural and botanical, and most are not more than similarities between remains from South America and trans-Pacific cultures. Some botanists and archaeologists believe the similarities are too striking to have been independently invented, and that they must have been carried by voyagers across the ocean. Certainly some resemblances came about as adaptations to similar conditions. Or the forms may look alike where function and meaning are quite different—in other words, they are sheer coincidence. Some similarities, though, cannot be so casually dismissed, and at least one is cultural.

Botanical Evidence

Before any Europeans had arrived in North America, certain domesticated plants appear to have been known both in the New World and in Southeast Asia and some of the Pacific Islands. The most important of these—those for which we have the best evidence—are cotton and the bottle gourd. Some people have taken the existence of these two cultivated plants in both hemispheres as evidence that people brought them from the Old to the New World. Since domesticated plants must be carefully tended to survive, whenever they appear outside the area where they were originally domesticated it usually means that they were moved by people.

Those who oppose the theory of trans-Pacific contact point out that the seeds of the gourd can still grow even after long soaking in ocean water, and therefore could have come to the New World simply by floating across the ocean. Cotton is a botanically complicated puzzle, but recently scientific opinion seems to have swung to the point of view that modern forms could have arisen independently by natural crosses between two wild New World species. Cotton, then, is no longer considered very good evidence for the trans-Pacific theory. The presence of other cultivated plants in both Old and New Worlds, such as the sweet potato and the yam, might have explanations other than transmission by prehistoric cultivators, and all in all, domesticated plants do not seem very convincing evidence for contact. It is particularly weak when we consider that voyagers would have had to cross the Pacific *before 2000 B.C.* to bring these domesticates to the New World, because archaeological remains show that they were already here by that date.

Cultural Evidence

A number of investigators have been interested in stylistic similarities between the Old and New Worlds, such as decorative designs using crosses, serpent deities, and intertwined ribbons or laces. The question is: are those designs so complex that they would not have been thought up more than once in the vast history of mankind? Another objection to proving contact by anything so tenuous as art styles is that the spread of style would have required more interaction than just a few people landing from a boat. On the other hand, if a flood of people came across the Pacific, so many that they would make an impression on the native population, how can it be that they left anything so nebulous as an art style, but not one object of material culture, not one tool or pot from their homes? We may also ask if those sailors or fishermen would have been so artistic that they could reproduce the art styles of their homelands. It seems more likely that some design components turn up almost everywhere in art, like spirals and scrolls; finding such items in two widely separated areas does little to prove human contact between the two places.

Sounder evidence of contact is the appearance of more complex items in both the Old and New Worlds: pan pipes, blowguns, and a way of casting metal that was known in South America. These items are elaborate enough that it seems unlikely they would have been invented independently. Nevertheless, no one has determined how complex or complicated an item must be before it definitely could not have been independently invented in several areas. What about the principle of evolution, for instance, simultaneously but independently formulated by Darwin and by Wallace?

Some evidence cannot be so easily discounted, though, and it comes from pottery remains. Scientifically established dates for pottery found in the Valdivia complex on the coast of Ecuador fall around 3000 to 2500 B.C., and these dates are believed to be sound. That makes the Valdivia pottery the oldest known in the New World. Although it is sophisticated pottery, no simpler forms have been found to indicate how it might have developed. We could say that because it is so well made and of such advanced design, it must have come in full-blown from somewhere else. The dates of the Valdivia find are consistent with dates of pottery made in Jomon, Japan, and the shapes and surface designs are consistent with the Jomon forms and decoration. The Valdivia find is too concrete and plentiful to be disregarded. Yet those who know the subject still disagree about what it proves, and we must await further information or new finds before using it as a basis for any definite statements about trans-Pacific contacts.

Even if contact is proven eventually, it is still clear that most aspects of the high civilizations in America were truly indigenous. The important *cultigens* (that is, cultivated plants), especially corn, are native to the New World, and we know that the early Americans manipulated them over many years to bring them from the wild state to domestication. The same is true of urbanization and complex political and economic structures, as well as native art styles.

Summary: People in the Arctic, Plains, Desert, and Woods

At some time before 20,000 B.C., small groups of people moved into the New World over the open land that at that time connected eastern Asia and northwestern North America. They were not deliberately migrating to a new land, but simply following the animals they hunted. Those early people had only the simplest technology: stone equipment to butcher the game they killed and to work the hides. They appear not to have hafted their stone points to a shaft but used them as hand-held chopping, scraping, and hammering tools. Over the millennia, moving through the ice-free corridor between the eastern and western ice sheets, succeeding generations came to the great plains area to the east of the Rocky Mountains.

The great plains were home for a number of species of large herd animals, and as time passed, the hunters began to concentrate on these large browsers and grazers. Thus the period from around 15,000 to perhaps 8000 B.C. is

NEW WORLD CULTURES, TRADITIONS, AND EVENTS COVERED IN PART I.

Date	Arctic and Subarctic	Northwest Coast and Plateau	California	Great Basin and Southwest
Modern times A.D. 1600			California tradition (seed gathering)	Great Basin and Southwest traditions
A.D. 1500	Eskimo tradition			Pueblo life abandoned in many places
A.D. 1000		Plateau and Northwest Coast traditions		Pueblos built Anasazi culture Hohokam culture Mogollon culture
A.D. 1				
1000 B.C.	Old whaling culture			
2000 B.C.	Eskimo population established			
3000 B.C.	Small Tool tradition	Coastal Archaic tradition (fishing and gathering)	Coastal Archaic tradition (hunting, fishing, and gathering)	Desert Archaic tradition
4000 B.C.				
5000 B.C.				
6000 B.C.				
7000 B.C.				
8000 B.C.	Pre-Eskimo population (hunting and fishing)			
9000 B.C.		Salmon fishing		Big Game Hunting tradition
10,000 B.C.				
20,000 B.C.				
40,000 B.C.	Entry of Asiatic population into New World			

European contact

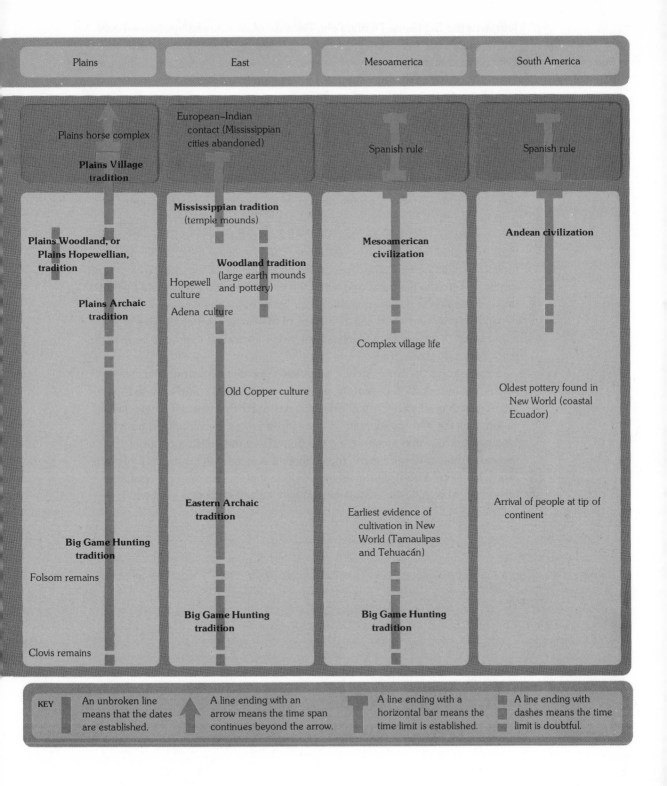

Plains	East	Mesoamerica	South America

Plains

Plains horse complex

Plains Village tradition

Plains Woodland, or Plains Hopewellian, tradition

Plains Archaic tradition

Big Game Hunting tradition

Folsom remains

Clovis remains

East

European–Indian contact (Mississippian cities abandoned)

Mississippian tradition (temple mounds)

Woodland tradition (large earth mounds and pottery)

Hopewell culture

Adena culture

Old Copper culture

Eastern Archaic tradition

Big Game Hunting tradition

Mesoamerica

Spanish rule

Mesoamerican civilization

Complex village life

Earliest evidence of cultivation in New World (Tamaulipas and Tehuacán)

Big Game Hunting tradition

South America

Spanish rule

Andean civilization

Oldest pottery found in New World (coastal Ecuador)

Arrival of people at tip of continent

KEY

An unbroken line means that the dates are established.

A line ending with an arrow means the time span continues beyond the arrow.

A line ending with a horizontal bar means the time limit is established.

A line ending with dashes means the time limit is doubtful.

known as the Big Game Hunting era. Because of climate change, human over-kill, or causes yet undetermined, the animals began to die out, and slowly the Big Game tradition gave way to less specialized ways of life that varied region-ally. That period of diversification and adaptation to many local environments we call the Archaic.

In the Southwest, the climate became hotter and drier. The desert dwellers began to use more plant food, for the desert animals were small and scarce. Many archaeological remains of implements for collecting and grinding seeds have turned up in desert regions. The desert people also gathered berries, bulbs, and roots, and ate nuts in season. Sometimes they added meat to their diet in the form of rabbits, prairie dogs, snakes, rats, and occasional deer.

In the North and East, where ice and snow once covered the land, great forests grew up. The animals that lived in those forests were smaller and swifter than the earlier types, such as mastodons. The Woodland Indians changed their tools to exploit the new environment and its animal life. They invented axes and adzes, and around the lakes and along the rivers the people increased their fish-ing and trapping of ducks and other water birds. Along the new coastlines they began to gather and eat shellfish. Indians of the Archaic left great piles of shells along some of the coasts and inland waterways, indicating that quite large popu-lations lived on those foods.

In some areas the basic Archaic adaptation lasted until historic times. In others, the introduction of pottery, an increase in cultural complexity, and popu-lation growth produced more advanced styles of life that warrant a new classifi-cation; thus the eastern adaptations are referred to as the Woodland tradition. One new practice that arose during this period was the building of burial mounds. Another development, the deliberate selection and cultivation of plant foods, led to corn horticulture, an introduction that made possible social and technological complexity unattainable in hunting and gathering societies.

2 CULTIVATION AND AMERICAN CULTURES

In the highlands of central Mexico the Archaic period followed much
the same course as the Desert Archaic north of the Rio Grande. The climates were not very different as the continental ice melted, and in each region
the people adapted to differences in altitude, water, and supplies of plants and
animals. The changing climate, in Mexico as in the north, brought to an end the
hunting tradition specializing in big game such as bison and mammoth. Less archaeological work has been done on early sites south of the Rio Grande than to
the north, but evidence has been unearthed that people shifted from big game
hunting to dependence on plant foods in both areas. Fluted points found in the
northernmost part of Mexico indicate that early people north and south of the
Rio Grande had made contact, probably often. After all, the border between
Mexico and the United States is the result of political history, and did not keep
prehistoric southwestern peoples from carrying their way of life into what is now
northern Mexico.

Corn, Beans, and Squash

The archaeological record of the mid-Archaic in some Mexican sites
clearly tells us that people were living more and more on plants. One new
food, corn, was not native to the more northerly regions. It became the heart of
the diet for Indians in Mexico as well as in the outlying regions where cultivation
spread. Corn, beans, and squash are the major cultigens of the Americas, the
trinity of American agriculture. Most important was corn, and by the time Europeans came, it was being grown wherever conditions allowed. Varieties ranged
from the bushy form suited to desert conditions to the tall corn of the eastern
area, and came in more than six colors.

Corn has been studied for many years by the archaeologists and botanists trying to trace its origins. Botanical information pointed to a wild ancestor that was
probably a popcorn with its kernels in pods. Drilling for the subway in old lake
beds under Mexico City brought up pollen grains of ancestral wild corn dating
back to 80,000 B.C. The area around the Valley of Mexico was therefore certainly one logical place for archaeologists and botanists to hunt for the earliest
domesticated corn. After years of research, the earliest domesticated corn was
found in the Tehuacán Valley, somewhat south of Mexico City. The archaeological record there shows a sequence from early Archaic wild plants and animals to
domesticated corn. Domesticates show up alongside increasingly abundant
equipment for grinding and processing plant food, indicating that people were
depending more on vegetable foods. We can see in the record too that the
human population was slowly growing over several thousand years. The increase

Preceding page:
**An Anasazi earth-
enware vessel in the
form of a man,
found in Chaco
Canyon, New
Mexico (height, 7¼
inches). The gray
pottery is marked
with black and
white.**

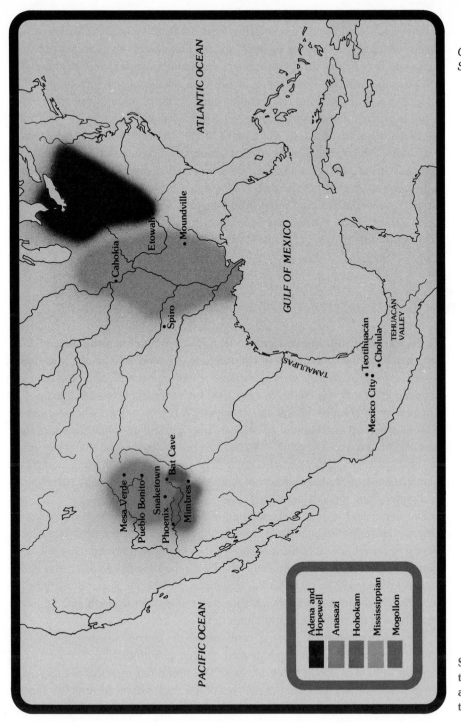

ATLANTIC OCEAN

GULF OF MEXICO

PACIFIC OCEAN

Cahokia
Etowah
Moundville
Spiro

Mexico City
Teotihuacán
Cholula
TEHUACAN VALLEY
TAMAULIPAS

Mesa Verde
Pueblo Bonito
Snaketown
Phoenix
Bat Cave
Mimbres

Adena and Hopewell
Anasazi
Hohokam
Mississippian
Mogollon

Sites and cultures in the United States and Mexico mentioned in Chapter 2.

came not from a change in climate, but from something new in the culture, the cultigens, which allowed a more secure food supply. People of that time ate plants we recognize today as edibles and also other plants we now think of as mere weeds. Some of today's weeds were truly domesticated, and though these are no longer cultivated, we cannot ignore their significance in early times.

Squash was domesticated earlier than corn. As far as we know, people first raised squash in Tamaulipas to the north, where scientists have dated the earliest forms at about 7000 B.C. The people of the Tehuacán Valley had domesticated squash by 5000 B.C. The earliest variety of corn found in Tehuacán was not much more productive than its wild ancestor, and until a hybrid appeared, corn was not a big part of the diet. We think that between 5000 and 4000 B.C., only 10 percent of the food came from domesticated plants. By about 3400 B.C., agricultural plant food may have been up to 30 percent of the diet. People were cultivating some plants, but they still depended heavily on foraging and hunting.

Changing Culture

In the early period, domestication was just one of the many adaptations we have described as typical of the Archaic. Around 2300 B.C., however, when the Mexican Indians were growing several corn hybrids, cultural change speeded up among the cultivators. By 1500 B.C. the people were making pottery and had a complex village life, depending on cultivated crops for their staples. Pottery, first used on the coasts, was an important invention for agriculturalists because it made a rodent- and insect-proof container and a superior vessel for boiling foods. It is probably no coincidence that the spurt in social complexity that led to village life began when superior strains of corn had been hybridized and pottery had begun to spread.

The shift from the wild food gathering of the Archaic to a settled village life relying on domesticated plants was slow. As the shift went on, the flow of culture change reversed and went from Mexico to the north. No longer did peoples and ideas drift from north to south as they had from the time the Asians came into the New World until about 4000 B.C. Even pottery, whether it was brought in from Asia or a native development, appeared earliest to the south and diffused from there to the more northerly cultures.

The only domesticated mammal north of the Rio Grande was the dog. We do not know much about how domesticated dogs originated on this continent: were they tamed here or brought in from Asia? The only other mammal put to service was in South America, where the peoples of the Andes domesticated the llama, using it as a pack animal and a source of wool. Because the Indians outside the Andes had no suitable domestic animal, they did not have dairy foods or animals to ride or to haul large loads. The dog was sometimes eaten but was never an important food animal; it was helpful in hunting, as a scavenger, and for protection. Without farm animals, the New World never developed the mixed farming complexes that arose in the Old World. Until the Europeans brought sheep, cattle, and swine, wild animals remained the main source of meat protein.

Many plants that began in America have become very important to the rest of the world. Today corn and potatoes (also an American cultigen) are second only to wheat and rice as commercial food crops everywhere. Other plants domesticated by Indians of North and South America and now used by many peoples include beans, manioc (the source of tapioca), squash, pumpkin, peanuts, cashew, pineapple, tomato, chocolate, vanilla, and tobacco. Among the medicinal herbs used by pre-Columbian Indians are quinine, curare, and cocaine.

The paths by which corn, beans, and squash diffused to the north are not known. Seeds and the idea of cultivation may have passed from group to group, or migrating groups may have transmitted them, but we have no archaeological evidence. The earliest domesticated corn to show up north of the Rio Grande came from a site in southwestern New Mexico, Bat Cave, where a very primitive but domesticated variety has been dated between 3500 and 3000 B.C. Corn cultivation in the East came much later. The exact date has not been determined, but probably some corn was grown in the East as early as 1000 B.C. However, at that early date it was not an important foodstuff.

The Southwest

The environment in the Southwest after 2000 B.C. was much as it is today. There were no lush green fields or fertile bottom lands as in the East, but stony, dry desert, hot in summer, cold in winter, swept by winds, dotted with straggly mesquite and spiny cactus. It may very well have been this poverty of the land that influenced its inhabitants to try farming where water supplies allowed it. Vegetation was too slight to attract large animals, and only enough small animals could be found to support a relatively small population. So the idea of helping food plants to grow must have had great appeal for the southwestern Indians when at last it reached them.

The Beginnings of Agriculture

These people were well acquainted with the life cycles of plants, having for many generations followed the ripening vegetation of the area on foot. Like all Archaic folk, they had learned to use all the food resources of their environment because they had to, and in the desert that meant focusing on plant foods. The tools they had developed for wild plant gathering and preparation were usable on domesticated plants without modification. Thus, if not ready and waiting to turn to cultivation, they were at least well disposed toward it. They were also close to Mexico, so it is not surprising that the idea of farming, as well as the important cultigens, showed up first in the desert Southwest.

It was a long time, just as in regions farther south, before agriculture could provide even half the food supply of the southwestern peoples. For centuries they continued to get much of their subsistence by foraging. The climate held back agricultural advances, and so did the plants themselves. The earliest corn grown in the Southwest was only a step or two removed from its wild ancestor. Its cobs were little more than an inch long, holding only a few dozen kernels. These miniature ears, unlike those of modern corn, were not enclosed and protected in a tight husk, so the grains were exposed to competitive foraging by birds and rodents, and they shattered easily when ripe, not waiting for people to harvest them. The types of corn that followed were only a little more productive, but gradually over the centuries the people acquired improved plant strains. Some unquestionably were imported from Mexico, but some came from natural crossing, probably helped along by human selection. Besides the problem of im-

The development of corn: (A) an ear of today's corn; (B) the probable look of extinct wild corn; (C–G) domesticated corn's evolution.

proved hybrids, the people also had to face and overcome the shortage of water, especially the limited rainfall, which to this day makes simple dry-land farming, without irrigation, painfully uncertain in much of the region.

Precipitation in most parts of the Southwest comes mainly in summer, usually as brief thundershowers so intense that water runs off downhill before much seeps into the ground. To make the most of the limited moisture, the early farmers learned to build dams of loose stones across the small gullies that channeled the runoff. These dams slowed the rushing water to help the ground absorb more of it, and also trapped sediment, forming little terraces of better than average fertility. Where a spring seeped out along the base of a cliff, a group of farmers might wall off a small area, filling it with dirt and trash to make a garden. On lower ground, along the larger streams and rivers, a community would arrange its fields to take advantage of flooding from showers or from melting snow in the mountains upstream. Some people probably employed "pot irrigation" like that still used in parts of Mexico and the Southwest, carrying water to the fields in clay-caulked baskets, skin bags, or pottery containers. And in a few places southwestern Indians ultimately built irrigation systems, storing water in reservoirs and distributing it through canals.

Farming techniques also improved, though tools seem not to have developed much beyond the simple digging stick of pointed hardwood, useful for unearthing wild roots, punching holes in the soil to plant seeds, or gouging out a new irrigation canal. Crops were sown in early spring when the lower levels of soil were still moist from winter seepage. The people planted corn in deep holes, in clumps widely scattered over the plot, to make best use of the limited water, each clump containing enough seeds to produce ten or a dozen stalks. As the stalks grew—seldom more than three or four feet high—the outer plants shielded the inner ones from the hot, dry winds of summer, so that they could live long enough to yield a few ears at harvest.

Three Cultures

Between 100 B.C. and A.D. 400, three local cultures began to develop in the southwestern area, the Mogollon, the Hohokam, and the Anasazi. All were farming societies, but their environments demanded different techniques. They did have traits in common—pottery, cultivated plants, and permanent settlements— and probably had some interaction in the form of trade. In all three, wild plant collecting was still of some importance, and wild game was their major source of meat. At some time during the generations that these three regional cultures took to develop, the people began to raise turkeys, the only domesticated creature native to North America except for the dog.

The Anasazi of prehistory became the Pueblo Indians of historic times. The sequence for the Mogollon and Hohokam is less clear. Although both cultures faded after about A.D. 1400, the Hohokam were probably ancestral to the Pima and Papago Indians, and the Mogollon may have merged with the Anasazi, or perhaps joined with some Hohokam groups. It is possible, but not proven, that the Zuni Indians are in part descended from the Mogollon.

Mogollon: The Earliest Farmers

Around 300 B.C. some cultivators began to settle in villages in the valleys of the Mogollon mountain range in New Mexico. Because they found little land suitable even for modest farming in the steep mountains and narrow valleys of their Mogollon heartland, they still counted heavily on hunting and gathering to supplement their sparse crops. In this early period, their villages rarely amounted to more than about a dozen pit houses.

These dwellings were built over roughly circular or rectangular excavations no more than two or three feet deep, above which rose a framework of stout posts supporting a roof of saplings laid across poles. The whole was probably covered with woven reeds and a mud plaster that would keep out all but the worst of the infrequent rainstorms, and the earth into which the house was dug was effective insulation against the desert heat. In the Southwest, temperatures often go over

Two Mogollon house styles, showing floor plans and reconstructions of cross-sections, from the Harris Village site.

Pueblo III period artifacts (A.D. 1100–1300): (A–C) polished stone hoes or celts; (D) carved wooden bird; (E) basket; (F) black-on-red pottery jar; (G) black-on-white pottery ladle (Mesa Verde); (H) black-on-white pottery jar; (I) manos; (J) metate.

100 degrees Fahrenheit in the summer, but a few inches below ground level they are far less extreme. The kangaroo rat and half a dozen other species of desert animals long ago learned to take advantage of this difference by spending the hottest hours of the day in their holes or burrows. The pit houses would have insulated equally well against cold, which is not as rare in the desert as one might think. Thanks to the clear, dry air, 100 degrees at noon can drop close to freezing at dawn, and winter cold snaps, particularly at high altitudes, can be even more biting. In later times, perhaps around A.D. 900, the Mogollones began to put together dwellings in the pueblo style, clusters of rooms with walls in common, making one large structure containing many families.

A Mimbres pottery bowl (diameter, 9 inches). The Mimbres potters excelled in their craft and decorated their typically black-on-white pottery with whimsical animals, insects, and people. Bowls with damaged bottoms ("killed" on purpose) have been found in graves with their owners' bodies.

Mogollon equipment shows how much of the diet was plants: digging sticks, several styles of metates and manos, and baskets for gathering and storage. Their hunting implements were snares, bows and arrows, nets, and many styles of flint points for spears.

To the Mogollones, perhaps the earliest potters in the Southwest, pottery became increasingly important. One settlement, Mimbres, became known for its fine ceramics with whimsical painted designs of insects, animals, and people. Many consider Mimbres pottery the artistic climax of the prehistoric Southwest.

Mogollon seems to have been the earliest farming life in the Southwest, a style of life that spread to the other subareas. It may have been the first, but Mogollon life-style was not the most durable, perhaps because it developed in a part of the land so difficult to live in that it quickly reached its climax and could go no further in cultural elaboration; its cultural energy seems to have gone to the Hohokam and Anasazi.

Hohokam: The Irrigators

To the west of the mountainous Mogollon territory, much more elaborate farming communities arose in the valleys of the Salt and Gila rivers in southern Arizona. Here conditions might seem even less promising for agriculture, since the two watercourses flow through some of the bleakest desert in North America. Though the region appears forbidding, its soil is made surprisingly rich by deposits of silt laid down each spring as the rivers, swollen with rain and melted snow from the mountains to the east, overflow their banks. A people whom archaeologists call the Hohokam developed a system to take advantage of this rich soil.

Flood Irrigation.   Around 100 B.C., the Hohokam practiced a crude form of flood irrigation, building dikes and little dams and diverting water from the Salt and Gila to cultivated plots near the riverbank terraces. Soon, with more advanced irrigation methods, probably learned from people in Mexico where irrigation had been practiced and developed for more than a thousand years, they were constructing ditches to carry the life-giving water farther from the rivers. The Hohokam's first simple efforts are hard to trace today, most having been obliterated by modern irrigation, agriculture, and urban development (several

An example of a Hohokam irrigation system.

Hohokam settlements lie beneath the city of Phoenix). However, it has been estimated that the early irrigation ditches were as much as fifteen feet wide, although no more than one or two feet deep. Later, presumably to cut down evaporation of precious water by reducing the surface area exposed to the air, canals were built only eight feet or so wide, but six or more feet deep. Many were lined with clay to reduce loss by seepage.

In a few places the Hohokam built large earth dams to divert the water from the riverbeds into their canal system. Some of their major canals carried water thirty miles, with branch canals leading into fields along the way. The flow of water was controlled, as in many modern irrigation systems, by a series of head gates, movable devices for blocking and unblocking a branch channel. The Hohokam are thought to have made them of tightly woven grass mats, backed by stakes, which could be raised or lowered as needed.

These complex irrigation systems clearly required imaginative engineering, enormous amounts of labor, and organized management. The ditches apparently were gouged out entirely with digging sticks, the marks of which have been found on the walls of canals uncovered by archaeologists, and the loosened earth was carried off in baskets. Once built, moreover, the canals had to be maintained. Silt deposited by the muddy spring floodwaters had to be removed periodically, and a flash flood from a summer thunderstorm could break through the sides of a canal and cut gullies across fields at a lower level. In exchange for

This Hohokam ball court shows features similar to the courts in Mexico.

their exertions, the Hohokam canal system could carry water to the rich valley soil far from the rivers, making possible a denser population and larger communities than those of the Mogollon.

Mexican Contacts. The basic Hohokam dwelling was like the simple Mogollon pit house, but their other structures, ball courts and pyramid-like mounds, were much more elaborate. The ball courts, similar to ball courts in Mexico, had oval clay playing floors as small as a basketball court or as large as a football field. At either end of the court was a goal of stone markers or a basin, into which a rubbery ball, probably made from the coagulated juice of a desert plant called *guayale,* could be struck.

When one looks at a Hohokam ball court it seems strikingly likely that its builders were strongly influenced by more advanced societies in Mexico. This possibility is even more apparent in the pyramid mounds that the Hohokam built. Made of hard-packed clay and comparatively small, they are clearly simplified versions of the enormous stone-faced platforms of Mexico and, like the Mexican counterparts, may have been topped by temples.

More evidence of contacts with Mexico appears in the Hohokam artifacts and art motifs. The serpent being attacked by a bird painted on some Hohokam pottery resembles an ancient Mexican design (the serpent and bird motif, which is displayed today on the Mexican flag). And polished slate mirrors and little copper bells unearthed at some Hohokam sites are almost certainly Mexican imports, the bells especially, because no evidence has come out that the Hohokam worked metal.

Anasazi: The Pueblo Farmers

Hohokam agricultural practices were sophisticated, but their way of life was confined to river valleys that were broad enough and had water enough to make large-scale irrigation possible. The Anasazi flourished to the north of the Hohokam and Mogollon, spreading at their climax over more territory by far than any other prehistoric southwestern farmers. Their name was given to them by archaeologists; it means "the old ones" in Navajo.

The Anasazi were not only successful farmers, they were just as clever at building. They were the first to raise the remarkable structures that come to mind when we hear southwestern Indians mentioned, the apartment-like dwellings of clay, mud, and stone that the Spanish explorers called *pueblos,* meaning "towns." The most unusual pueblos are built into natural clefts high in the walls of steep canyons. The best known of these, in Mesa Verde National Park in southwestern Colorado, are still almost livable 650 years after their last inhabitants left.

Hohokam pottery bowl from Snaketown. This red-and-buff earthenware bowl, made about A.D. 800, has the typical Hohokam design of human figures (diameter, 10¾ inches).

The Anasazi originally occupied a fairly limited area known today as the Four Corners, where Arizona, New Mexico, Utah, and Colorado meet. At their peak, around A.D. 1200, their villages were scattered across much of those four states. Wide, barren tracts there make any sort of agriculture impossible, but much of the region over which the Anasazi eventually spread is better suited to farming than the rugged Mogollon country and needs less irrigation than the desert river valleys cultivated by the Hohokam. Its high mesas and plateaus guarantee relatively copious rainfall; some of this water could be stored in man-made reservoirs, so that in most years the people could farm without building extensive irrigation systems. In this region too are some of the Southwest's highest mountains, the Rockies in Colorado, the Sangre de Cristo in New Mexico, and the Wasatch range in Utah, with many vigorous rain-nourished streams that the Anasazi farmers used for flood irrigation in the foothills and valleys.

The earliest Anasazi settlements, dating from around the beginning of the Christian era, gave little hint of accomplishments to come. They were dome-shaped structures which, unlike the Mogollon and Hohokam pit houses, were built over shallow saucerlike depressions in the ground. Built up of concentric layers of logs laid in a sort of rail fence arrangement and cemented with mud mortar, they seem to have lacked one feature that most prehistoric people considered essential, an interior fireplace. Probably the homes were heated by stones warmed in outdoor fires and then laid in a pit in the house floor. Such heating pits have been found during excavation. A possible reason for this arrangement is that the log houses were covered with flammable brush or grass, making an interior fire dangerous. A few centuries later, though, the Anasazi were building more conventional pit houses with more usual heating, a central fireplace, the smoke from which escaped through a hole in the roof. Perhaps to prevent sudden flareups caused by gusts of wind through the doorway, the fireplaces were protected by deflectors, low screens made of stone slabs. These must also have helped block off uncomfortable drafts in winter.

The Pueblos.   It was not until about A.D. 900 that the Anasazi began to build pueblos. These singular structures are unlike anything elsewhere in North America. The early Spaniards correctly named them towns, for an entire village could be housed in a compound structure that was, in effect, a single building. Pueblo Bonito (p. 55), whose ruins lie in the valley of the Chaco River, was four to five stories high and had more than eight hundred rooms arranged in an immense "D" around twin plazas. Many smaller pueblos were no more than a helter-skelter collection of roughly cubical units added at different times.

Curiously, the pit house, or something very like it, survived amid the new style of architecture, though its earthen walls were now lined with stone. These circular, semiunderground chambers, entered by ladder through an opening in the mud-covered roof, were prototypes of the *kivas* that some southwestern tribes still use for ceremonial purposes. Probably they served the same function among the Anasazi peoples.

We can only guess what inspired the Anasazi to devise their pueblos in the first place. One possibility is a growing shortage of timber as their increasing population, nourished by agriculture, was compelled to build more and more dwellings. Substituting stone and clay for timber would almost necessarily have given the pueblos their vertical walls, limiting the shape a building could take, but at the same time would have made it easy to add a room by simply attaching three more walls to one in the original structure.

An even more pressing influence than lack of timber may have been a need for physical security. The expanding population of the pueblo dwellers could have caused friction between groups, leading to conflicts. Certainly many pueblos have the look of walled fortresses. On the first story, at least, doors and

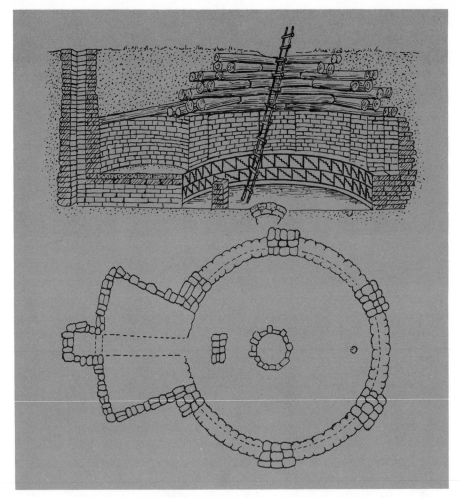

A kiva of the Mesa
Verde type, showing
the cross-section
(above) and the
floor plan (diameter,
14 feet).

windows open only to the enclosed interior courtyard. The only way of getting in
from the outside is by ladder, and ladders can, of course, be drawn up to leave
only the blank exterior walls to confront hostile strangers.

   Security seems to be the best explanation for the development of the cliff
dwellings. They are among the most inaccessible homes ever inhabited. Built
among high mesas deeply scarred with narrow canyons, they occupy lofty ledges
in the faces of sheer cliffs. Most were too high to be reached from the canyon
floors, and from the mesas above could be gotten to only by steep paths down
the cliffs, some pathways no more than a series of shallow toeholds hacked out
of the rocks. A few of the dwellings can be reached today only by experienced
mountain climbers, who must lower themselves down the cliff face on a rope.
Yet the Anasazi, men and women carrying babies and bundles of food and jars

of water, climbed several times a day between the pueblos and the croplands on the mesas above. One of the largest and most impressive pueblos, Mesa Verde's famous Cliff Palace, is sheltered in an enormous cave 325 feet long and 90 feet deep, with a rocky ceiling that arches to a height of 60 feet. It contains more than two hundred rooms and must have housed several hundred people. From the cave to the mesa above stretch 100 feet of vertical cliff; the canyon floor lies a dizzying 700 feet below.

PUEBLO BONITO

Floor plan

Pueblo Bonito, New Mexico. This Anasazi community, built during A.D. 900–1100, was four to five stories high, and contained about 800 rooms and 30 kivas.

The Anasazi diet was diverse. Among their domesticated plants were corn, squash, and beans. To these they added wild plants such as piñon nuts, mint, onions, and berries. Rabbit, venison, and turkey supplied meat dishes. Women made pottery for cooking and storing, and also for ritual containers. Men wove nets or baskets, made simple bows, and chipped arrowheads; they were cultivators as well as hunters, unlike the males in the woodlands, who left cultivation to the women. Fishing equipment and fish bones do not appear in the remains; archaeologists believe that although there were fish in the nearby streams, they were not used for food.

The Pueblos Abandoned.   Shortly before A.D. 1300, pueblo life abruptly ended in much of the Southwest. Dozens of communities were abandoned. The dwellings seem to have been designed for security, so their desertion suggests a retreat after a period of attack, but nowhere do we find evidence of widespread warfare. More people accept as explanation the long drought that gripped the entire Southwest for more than a generation toward the end of the thirteenth century. The evidence for that dry spell is unmistakable, recorded in the shrinking annual growth rings of trunks of ancient trees. This climatic change may have forced a migration to places with more water, principally the Rio Grande valley, where sixteenth-century Spanish explorers found many flourishing pueblos. But drought alone does not seem to be the answer—the settlements were never reoccupied after the drought passed. Perhaps the pueblo people did try to return to their former villages, but found the land occupied by other Indian settlers too formidable to be driven out.

If that happened, who were the new people? Quite probably they were typical Archaic desert foragers like the Utes, who had long lived in the Great Basin on the outskirts of the pueblo country. Some evidence in the form of pottery remains suggests hunters coming from the north—as far as Canada—Athabaskan Indians, the ancestors of the Navajo and Apache. These tribes are unrelated to their southwestern neighbors. Comparison of the languages suggests that their nearest tribal connections are to be found in the interior of Alaska and northwestern Canada today. For reasons still unknown, these northern hunting people began to drift into the Southwest perhaps as early as the thirteenth century and had completed their movement by about A.D. 1500. However, evidence for this early movement is scant, and many archaeologists believe the date of pueblo abandonment too early to have been forced by Athabaskan attacks.

A new theory about how the pueblos came to be abandoned is now more and more widely accepted. Many Southwest archaeologists and ethnologists believe the cause was an ecological crisis. The drought, combined with severe deforestation, soil erosion, and the resulting rapid runoff of rainwater, leaching crucial minerals out of the soil, forced the people into a more restricted territory. These environmental conditions brought about a sort of energy crisis: there was no longer enough timber for building and fuel, and the land could no longer support enough agriculture to feed the population.

In early America west of the Rockies, agriculture never spread beyond the Southwest. In most of the Great Basin, dry farming was impossible and irrigation was difficult at best, though we know of a few desert tribes who used crude irrigation techniques to encourage the growth of some wild plants whose seeds they gathered. In most of California, dry farming was no easier; summers were almost as dry as in the desert, and that region's most important food staple, the acorn, did not lend itself to cultivation. Foraging was so easy in California, though, that agriculture was not a pressing need. Natural food resources were plentiful and easily reaped. Incentives for agriculture were even less along the coast and in the Pacific Northwest, where wild food was even more abundant. East of the Mississippi, however, agriculture spread widely, producing societies that were true urban centers by the time Europeans arrived.

The Eastern Area
The Mississippian Tradition

While groups lived in small villages throughout the East, communities grew in population and complexity along the lower reaches of the Mississippi River. Their growth shifted the hub of prosperity through time and space away from the Woodland centers in Adena and Hopewell, which seemed generally to decline after about the year 900. The later tradition, called Mississippian, eventually spread over many of the tributaries draining into the great river, from Louisiana to Wisconsin and from Oklahoma to Tennessee, and by about 1200 had developed into one of ancient America's most remarkable cultures. By any criterion—wealth, population, social complexity, or technological and artistic sophistication—the Mississippians were the most advanced of any Indians living north of Mexico, and their vigorous societies lasted in one form or another long enough to be witnessed by Hernando de Soto and other early European explorers.

Those we call the Mississippians were neither a single society nor a single linguistic group. Although it is not always possible to connect historic tribes with prehistoric sites, archaeologists believe that at least three languages were represented within the Mississippian tradition: Muskogean, spoken by the Creek and the Choctaw among others in historic times; Siouan tongues as spoken by the Yuchi; and in the Midwest, some Algonkian.

Mound Building. Truncated pyramid mounds are the hallmark of the Mississippian. They are not primarily burial mounds, although some burials are found in them, but flattened pyramids that had structures, probably temples, on the top. The mounds were much larger than those of Hopewell and Adena construction. Their great size was the end result of additions over many years, perhaps eight or ten layers altogether. Many had log stairs laid up a ramp on one side for access to the temple on top.

Comparing these mounds with the huge pyramids raised by the ancient Egyptians and the people of Mexico and Central America, we see that the Mississippian structures were monumental by any standards. The largest mound, at Cahokia, in what is now southern Illinois, is a hundred feet high. It has a base several times larger than that of the Great Pyramid of Egypt, covering nearly fifteen acres. In the Americas it is smaller only than the Pyramid of the Sun at Teotihuacán and the great pyramid at Cholula, both in Mexico. And this monster mound is just one of eighty or so still standing in this area; probably another forty have been leveled by farmers in the recent past.

From the number of these temple mounds and their size, as well as information left us by the French who visited Mississippian centers in the sixteenth century, it appears that Mississippian society was strongly ceremonial. In fact, ceremonial items such as figurines, plaques, and headdresses found throughout the Mississippian area are so striking that they have a special classification: the Southern Cult, also referred to as the Buzzard Cult and sometimes as the Southern Death Cult. Cult artifacts are wrought from materials like shell, copper, stone, and clay, and include earrings, pendants, and pottery. A feathered snake, the weeping eye, sun symbols, and engraved representations of human sacrifice have been discovered. These motifs also appeared in the elaborate and often grotesque pottery.

Influence from Mexico. The ceremonial objects have to do mostly with death, and many scholars believe they show some contact with or influence from Mexican cult practices, with their human sacrifices. Many of the Mississippian designs appeared earlier, though, in Adena and Hopewell sites, most particularly the raptorial bird we have seen before, and the eye motifs. After 1200, however, Mexican influence is more noticeable, for carvings and pottery then began to be decorated with a feathered serpent resembling the Aztec god Quetzalcoatl.

In other ways the Mississippians were apparently influenced by Mexico far more than earlier mound builders had been. We are uncertain how that influence reached the Mississippians; perhaps it was the result of trading or raiding expeditions along the Gulf coast. Not only do their mounds resemble Mexican types, but the very basis of their advanced way of life—intensive corn, bean, and squash agriculture—may well have been imported. Their strains of corn were much more productive than any known before in the mound-building area and almost certainly were grown from improved seed that originated in Mexico. If, as we believe, there had been Mexican contacts of some sort as far back as Hope-well and Adena times, the Mississippian period can be called a peak of that trend.

Mississippian Cities. The heights of the great Mexican civilizations were never quite attained by the Mississippians, however. They failed to invent a written language, one of the essential signs of advanced civilizations. But in many ways they came very close, and who knows how high they might have climbed if these societies had not been disrupted, even destroyed, by the Europeans? Their largest settlements, among them Cahokia, were cities with populations of 30,000 or more, putting them in a class with such ancient centers of the Old World as Ur in Mesopotamia and Mohenjodaro in India.

Other large Mississippian centers were Etowah in Georgia, which may have been built by ancestors of the historic Cherokee people; Moundville in Alabama, probably early Muskogean speakers; and Spiro in Oklahoma, perhaps ancestral Caddo. Some of the Late Mississippian sites are considered early Creek, Choctaw, and Chickasaw communities, but it is difficult to match archaeological remains in the Southeast with known groups because of the way the population was dislocated after European exploration and settlement.

A shell gorget of the Mississippian period from Etowah Mounds, Georgia (diameter, 2½ inches). This type of chest ornament, suspended from a cord around the neck, was cut from conch shells by stone tools.

Populous communities and monumental mounds show how much the Mississippians achieved, but their specialized crafts and industries are equally good evidence. Their elaborate pottery, stone carvings, and metalwork—the latter still made from copper found in nuggets, not from smelted ores—suggest that some of this work was done by full-time craftsmen. Nor was manufacturing limited to luxury goods. One community near Cahokia mined chert, a flintlike rock, and converted it into knives and hoe blades. Another may have specialized in evaporating salt from the waters of nearby salt springs; the demand for this commodity grew among people who ate more and more bland plant food and less meat. And many large Mississippian towns seem to have been military as well as commercial centers. One Louisiana community was completely surrounded with a moat fed by the Mississippi River.

Cahokia.   The city of Cahokia was well fortified by a stockade of stout posts, foot-thick logs set close together and plastered over with clay. Every hundred feet or so a square bastion of similar construction projected from the palisade. Each had a raised floor from which the defending archers could shoot down on their enemies. The gateways of the city were screened with curtain walls, L-shaped projections of the stockades that forced attackers to approach an entrance from the side instead of head on, slowing the attackers down and exposing them to heavy fire from the main wall.

Within the stockade, everyday life of Cahokia had its center in the marketplace, presumably found in the western part of the city near the waterfront. Here came stone hoe blades, furs, hides, dried meat, and copper nuggets from 400 miles away in Wisconsin. Many of the wares offered in the market were made in workshops scattered about the city, where Cahokian craftsmen turned out goods for both local consumption and export. Not only toolmakers, hide dressers, potters, and weavers gathered here, but also craftsmen who hammered ornaments from imported copper, engraved designs on shells shipped from the Gulf, and manufactured beads by drilling shells with hardwood bits and fine sand. On special occasions the focus shifted from the market and busy workshops to the city's several broad plazas, for festivals, religious services, or games of chunkey, a sport in which the players tossed a heavy disk-shaped stone ahead of them and then, throwing their spears, tried to pinpoint the place where it would finally come to rest.

Cahokia's most striking feature was not its protecting palisade or its market and spacious plazas, but the many mounds, large and small, that rose above the city. Some of the smaller ones held storehouses for corn and other crops, while larger mounds served as platforms for the houses of the more important citizens. However, the biggest, most impressive mounds had less personal uses. One of them, a truncated pyramid not far from the city's southwestern entrance,

Facing page:
A reconstruction of
Cahokia, ca. A.D.
900–1100, a Mississippian city near
East St. Louis,
Illinois.

was the place for ceremonies and religious rituals. A conical mound looming beside it sheltered the city's illustrious dead.

Dwarfing all was the great steep-sided mound that was Cahokia's religious and political center. More than a thousand feet long and nearly eight hundred feet wide, it rose in several enormous steps. On its topmost level, one hundred feet above the city, was a temple built of post and wattle (poles interwoven with branches), with a sharply peaked roof of thatch. On the lower terraces were homes that appear to have been residences of high-ranking personages. These, like the larger building above them, faced the principal plaza and the avenue leading toward the pyramid and the burial mound.

From the top of the great mound another structure beyond the city wall could be observed, an immense circle of posts, more than a hundred yards across, which may have been used as a solar observatory and a kind of calendar. A person seated on a post set near the circle's center could keep track of the shifting seasons. The position of the sun in relation to the surrounding posts as it rose over the bluffs half a mile east of the city would tell when to plant crops.

The structure of Mississippian society can be pieced together from many kinds of evidence. Many facts can be deduced from the remains of wood and wattle houses constructed of posts interlaced with branches, whose sizes presumably depended upon their owners' rank—they ranged from huts to buildings thirty feet square. Burial goods found in tombs also tell much about the status of those interred. And we have eyewitness accounts of the life of the Mississippians from Europeans who observed the culture in its final stages among tribes of the lower Mississippi valley. Combining these sources, we have a fairly detailed picture of a complex, socially stratified society.

The Decline of the Cities. Why Cahokia and nearby communities were abandoned is uncertain. Scientific dating shows that the city was still occupied as late as 1550, but it was empty when the first French explorers passed that way a century or so later. One theory traces the decline to social disintegration and warfare brought about by increased populations. Unquestionably the intensive agriculture on which all Mississippian life was based would have sharply increased their numbers, which in turn would have forced them to expand the cultivated area. And that may have been the problem. Once the richest river valley lands had been thickly populated, the northerly Mississippian communities could have expanded only in two directions. One way was into the numerous islands of long-grass prairie around them, but there the compacted soil with its thickly rooted tough grasses was impossible to cultivate without iron plows drawn by horses or oxen. The other route for expansion was into the forests, where trees could be cut down and burned to create fields for crops. Forest soils, however, unlike those of the annually flooded bottom lands along the rivers, are thin.

Even with a top dressing of wood ash they can be farmed for only a few years and then must be abandoned for a generation or more. Thus the Mississippian communities would have had to push their cultivation ever farther into the forest—and away from the rivers on which most of their trade depended.

This change would have produced problems not only in transporting goods, but also probably in political control. Collecting taxes (as the Mississippian rulers must surely have done to keep up their elaborate standard of living) may have been simple enough when their subjects were scattered along a riverbank, but not so easy if the tribute-paying villages were forty or fifty miles deep in the woodlands. Expansion into the woodlands also would have brought them into conflict with the tribes who already lived there. Although some of these tribes continued to follow an Archaic way of life, others were beginning to practice agriculture, making them more formidable in numbers than they had been as mere hunters and collectors.

There is no mystery, however, about what destroyed the more southerly Mississippian communities. When the French trader De la Vente visited the Natchez Indians of the lower Mississippi valley in 1704, he found them, according to their own accounts, much reduced in numbers by the diseases introduced by Euro-

A Middle Mississippian house. The diagram shows the wattle-and-post construction—mud plastered over poles laced with branches.

peans. The Indians, because of their long isolation from the Old World, had little or no immunity to European germs, so that outbreaks of smallpox, influenza, measles, or even the common cold could wipe out a whole community. De la Vente himself wrote that thanks to smallpox, the Natchez population had dropped by as much as a third in a mere six years, and similar catastrophes must have overtaken many other tribes; germs as well as goods can travel along trade routes. A generation after De la Vente, the French finished the job that the microbes had started. In a war against the Natchez they killed most of the population and dispersed the remnant.

The Great Plains

The great plains of North America extend from the edge of the flood plains of the Mississippi River on the east to the Rocky Mountains on the west, and from the southern third of Alberta, Saskatchewan, and Manitoba to mid-Texas. They blend in gradually with the desert Southwest; nowhere is the change sharp. Moving from east to west, the general plains division has three zones: the low plains on the east, marked by tall prairie grasses, the sods of which are too tough to cultivate with stone equipment; the high plains, with shorter grasses and less annual precipitation; and the mountain foothills, driest of all. The gradual rise in elevation from east to west means that the rivers flow swiftly to the east, and each spring, as the mountain snows begin to melt, they flood, refertilizing the land around them with productive silts. The great rivers of the region are the Missouri, the Arkansas, and the Red, and their tributaries. The area from north to south also may be subdivided into northern plains, central plains, and southern plains, the difference here being one of temperature rather than altitude.

We have examined one tradition of the plains: Big Game Hunting. Between 5000 and 2000 B.C., probably because of the hotter and drier climate, that tradition had diminished and the large game, except for the bison, had died out. A generalized Archaic tradition followed, about which relatively little is known, and it in turn was followed by Woodland peoples penetrating from the east, bringing pottery and some knowledge of domesticated plants. This Woodland period, usually called Plains Hopewellian, was succeeded by a Village tradition, probably influenced by the Mississippian to the east and based on river valley agriculture.

The most westerly plains area never took on any sort of cultivation but remained stable in an essentially Desert Archaic way of life, with sparse population and little social or technological complexity. Although we may see a connection with the Desert Archaic in the ways of life that came along after Big Game Hunting fell off in the western plains, corn cultivation appears to have come in from the East rather than from the Southwest. The river system flowing to the East was an easier and more inviting route for the cultures of that region than a trek across the arid desert to the Southwest.

The river regions on the eastern plains show strong Hopewellian connections. From about A.D. 300 to 1000, or even a bit earlier, small groups of cultivators moved into the plains from the East. Those Indians hunted and farmed, made pottery, and lived in small, fairly permanent villages along the rivers and streams. The pottery styles alone showed Woodland characteristics, and mound burials of the Woodland type appear as well in some areas.

The Plains Village Tradition

Between about A.D. 1000 and 1600, or the time of European contact, the plains settlements along rivers and streams reached a climax. The inhabitants planted and harvested crops on the fertile river flood plains where they had some shelter from the bitter winds that whipped over the flat land in winter. Numerous storage pits much larger than any known from Plains Hopewellian also hint at more productive cultivation and larger population; crop yield must have been great.

The Plains Village settlements consisted of sizable earth lodges, partly underground, close to the cultivated fields in the river-bottom lands. Away from the river valleys, the plains were vacant of human population for most of the year, but during the spring, as tender grasses watered by early rains attracted the mating buffalo, the villagers moved out from their settlements to hunt. The men must have conducted bison hunts as in past centuries: stampeding the animals over cliffs, driving them into traps or swampy areas where they were disabled or mired down, using grass fires to supplement feeble human muscle, spears, and bows and arrows.

Influence from the East. We find even more evidence of eastern connections in this later period than in the time just before it: items of trade and commerce from the Mississippian peoples, and protective stockades and ditches. Here, in contrast with the Southwest, the principal cultivating tool was a hoe made of a bison scapula (shoulder blade), another sign that cultivation filtered in from the East. Grinding stones were not common; the villagers probably used wooden grinding equipment like the mortars and pestles of the East.

The Mississippian cultures probably spread to the West by migrations. Though such movements cannot be proven yet, the easy route the rivers offered makes the idea seem logical. No sharp break separated the new way of life from that of the earlier plains cultivators; the people continued many of their practices with-out noticeable change. Hunting, still important, was done mostly with the bow and arrow. Many people added the fish in the rivers to their food supply, much as in the general Eastern Archaic.

Burials. The Plains Villagers had many ways of burying their dead, starting with simple interments. They used secondary burials as well, waiting for the flesh to decay, then reburying the bones in communal pits called ossuaries, in natural hills, or beneath small artificial mounds. Some bodies were even buried under the lodges. These varied means of disposing of the dead might indicate that people from a number of eastern groups moved westward, or perhaps local tra-dition or environmental conditions caused the differences. By the time of Euro-pean contact, certainly, the Plains people had several linguistic divisions, though their styles of living were similar throughout.

Few sites where the Plains Villagers lived have been matched archaeologically to groups still in existence when written history began. On the upper reaches of the Missouri River were the ancestors of the Mandan and Arikara, and proba-bly those around the Lower Loup River in east-central Nebraska were ancestral to the Pawnee. The early Wichita settled in central Kansas and must have been visited by Coronado in 1541.

Summary: The Results of Cultivation

By 5000 B.C. in Mexico the warmer, drier climate led to a way of life like that in other desert areas, with a vital difference. The people, depend-ing more and more on plant foods, began to cultivate grasses native to the cen-tral Mexican region that were forerunners of maize. Between about 5000 and 2000 B.C., the Mexican Indians improved corn until it was very productive, its large ears filled with grains. Now that they knew about cultivation, the people could settle down in villages, no longer having to move about searching for food. However, until Europeans came to North America, no animals like horses, cattle, sheep, or swine had been domesticated. Hunting then was still the only source of meat.

The idea of cultivation spread from Mexico to the north. In the desert regions of the southwestern United States, along rivers and in the few spots where they could find water, people began to settle down and cultivate crops. Some of these earliest farmers were the ancestors of later Pueblo people. Elsewhere in the desert, people had to continue their life of wandering, for without a water supply they could not farm. The two ways of life went on side by side: farming where there was moisture, and nomadic hunting and plant collecting in water-less places. The wandering people probably raided the farmers, who may have developed their special type of house, the pueblo, to protect themselves from marauders.

In the East during the Woodland period, groups of Indians had already settled down to village life in river valleys, where they found they could encourage the growth of wild plants in a way that approached cultivation. They were thus ready to accept the new cultigens that filtered in from the south, and soon their steady diet included corn, beans, and squash as well as the wild plants they continued to reap. The Woodland populations increased and villages grew. Farming in the river valley lands was easy and productive because the soil was deep, rock-free, easy to work with primitive tools, and replenished each year when the river floods brought new silts. River-bottom farming along the Ohio and Mississippi rivers and tributaries was rich enough to support large populations. Between about A.D. 900 and 1500, cities such as Cahokia in Illinois grew to great size, and the larger populations organized into new kinds of social groups. Farmers produced enough so that some people could devote their time to crafts, government, religion, or trade, and not spend all their time seeking food. When the farmers were not busy in the fields, they could help build the mounds and temples, directed by some sort of leader.

This general Mississippian way of life penetrated into the river valleys of the plains, the only part of that vast grassland that could be tilled—elsewhere lay the densely rooted prairie grasses that defied cultivation with digging sticks and bone or stone hoes.

By the time Columbus bore news of the American continent back to Europe, Indian people already had true cities along the river systems of the Southeast and Midwest, and people led less complex village lives in the rest of the eastern Woodlands and along the rivers and streams of the plains. In the southwestern deserts, the Desert Archaic way of life continued, alongside settled agricultural communities where water made farming possible. In the Great Basin, in the far West, and in the foothill area of the plains, the Archaic ways also lingered as in the Subarctic and Arctic, except that by then the people in the Arctic were the Eskimo, not the Indians.

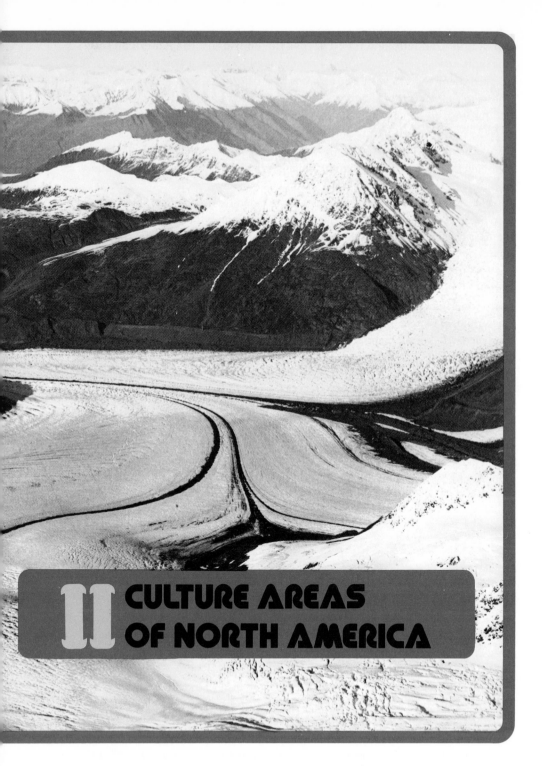

II CULTURE AREAS OF NORTH AMERICA

Spreading gradually down and across the continent, the American Indians built new societies wherever they stopped to settle. People slowly adapted themselves to each new environment, developing new ways of life. These collective ways of life are called *cultures.* The many kinds of environments and resources the Indians encountered inspired many kinds of *adaptations,* and thus the Indian societies were surprisingly varied. Differences among societies also came about through change over time, or *cultural evolution.* It would be astonishing if any of us in this country, Indians or non-Indians, lived today as our ancestors did centuries ago. Even if Columbus had never seen this side of the Atlantic, none of us would live now as people did in his time. Indian societies also grew unlike each other because of *cultural isolation:* tribes that lived by themselves, separated from others by great distances or bitter climate, changed little.

Other tribes settled close together, in more or less the same environment, with much the same resources, and developed similar adaptations. Often they borrowed useful traits from each other. Those who lived closest to the innovators would, of course, pick up a new invention earliest. This sharing is called *cultural diffusion.* People living close to each other, with much happening around them, exposed to novel ways of life, changed or evolved quickly.

All these ways in which cultures change—adaptation, evolution, isolation, diffusion—make it clear that no such person as a typical Indian ever lived. The people who adapted to coastal living were very different from those who learned to live in the desert, plains, or mountains. Because we cannot take the time to study each of the hundreds of Indian cultures, we will focus on groups of tribes within geographically distinct regions where similar ways of life developed. These regions are called *culture areas.*

The Culture Area Scheme

Notice that culture areas are indicated on the map inside the covers with no distinct definition of borders. That is because life in boundary areas was a cultural mixture, and tribes there could reasonably be classified in more than one area. After all, they too borrowed ideas from each other and lived in similar surroundings. Thus different anthropologists have come up with somewhat different dividing lines. Still, the culture area is a very useful device. Considering that there were at least four hundred distinct Indian groups at one time, most of which are unfamiliar to many of us today, the culture area scheme is a good way to study general similarities and differences.

The culture areas we will examine here are not historically equivalent. We will see most of them at their climax, just before European disturbance. The Plains

Preceding pages:
**Surprise Glacier on
the Chugach Mountains of Alaska.**

horse culture is an exception, since it was Europeans who introduced horses to this continent. Thus you will find some cultures described as they were generations or even centuries before others. People on the Atlantic coast of Florida, for example, were contacted in the early sixteenth century, yet some Eskimo groups were unknown to outsiders until the end of the nineteenth century. Remember this time difference, and realize too that these descriptions are no more true of American Indians today than a description of colonial Philadelphia tells us anything about that city today. We will treat contemporary Indians in a later section.

In discussing Indian cultures before the time of European contact, we often speak of them as aboriginal, native, or indigenous. Words like these carry no suggestion of inferiority or superiority: they simply indicate that the adaptations in question occurred before colonists, explorers, and traders came along.

Reconstructing Ways of Life

You may wonder how we can study societies that left no documentary records and boldly say that this or that was the way of life at the moment of outside contact or of climax. The answer is that we build our reconstructions on archaeological information and ethnographic analogy. We depend not only on present-day ethnographic descriptions, including legends that are still told, but also on earlier written data, like diaries of settlers, economic, political, and military reports of explorers, personal accounts, letters, and traders' records. We use such information carefully, always balancing it with what we know about geography, climate, plants, and animals. Sometimes we can come up with remarkably good reconstructions; sometimes we are not so fortunate.

Although it is reasonable to talk about cultures in terms of the areas where they occurred, that is not at all the same thing as saying that environment *causes* culture. It simply means that environment cannot be ignored: every society has to respond to it in one way or another. The same human ingenuity has invented many ways of responding to each environment. Responses that take the form of material culture naturally are easier to see than such things as social organization and religion.

The Culture Areas

In Part II we will consider nine culture areas, starting with the hunters and gatherers and going in the direction of increasing complexity to the agriculturalists: Arctic, Subarctic, Plateau, Northwest Coast, California, Great Basin, Southwest, Plains, and East. Each chapter begins with a legend typical of the area; this is one way we learn how people saw their world and nature's wonders. For those who had no written history, legends were an important means of understanding the world.

Population

All our figures on population at the time of European contact and earlier are estimates, and they vary enormously. We do not even have accurate, documented population records for later periods. Today, figures on American Indians are probably the least reliable of all census data. Estimates on the number of people north of Mexico before European contact range from 1 million to 10 million, and in California alone, from 100,000 to 1 million. There is no way of proving any of these numbers. However, we do know something about relative density. Aboriginal population was highest in California, the Northwest Coast, and the Southeast, and sparsest in the Arctic, Subarctic, and Great Basin areas.

Language

Many people have the idea that all Indians shared one language. Actually, at least three hundred languages were spoken north of Mexico at the time of European contact, though many of those are extinct today.

Phyla and Families

Linguists group all languages, including the hundreds of Indian languages, into major categories called *phyla* (*phylum* in the singular), and within each phylum into divisions called *families*. To give a familiar example, English is in the Indo-European phylum. It belongs to the Teutonic family, like Dutch and German. French is an Indo-European language too, but it belongs to another family, Romance languages. Just as speakers of English and French cannot understand each other without special training, Hopi and Paiute could not understand each other even though their languages were both of the Aztec-Tanoan phylum. Thus when we refer to Algonkian speakers, for instance, we do not mean they could talk together, but that they spoke related languages.

Linguist Carl Voegelin established the language divisions which we use in this book. He has proposed seven phyla for the languages north of the Rio Grande: Paleo-Siberian, Na-Dene, Macro-Algonkian, Macro-Siouan, Hokan, Penutian, and Aztec-Tanoan. There remain some language families for which the phylum affiliation is uncertain. After each culture area chapter a list of the cultural units and their major linguistic affiliations appears.

Tribal Names

Our names for Indian societies are not often the names they took for themselves. Most societies called themselves something like "we, the people," or "the men." For other societies they used descriptive words. Our word for Chippewa comes from another tribe's description of them, meaning "those whose moccasins have puckered seams." Creek was the name given that tribe by British settlers, referring to the location of their towns. Fox got their name from a misunderstanding: a French party asked a group of Indians who they were and they replied with their clan name, which in English is Fox. The name they called themselves was Mesquaki, meaning "red-earth people." The Pima got their name from another misunderstanding with Europeans: *pima* means "no." Ottawa is an Algonkian word meaning "to trade or sell," and was applied to the tribe because of their trading activities.

Bibliography

Kroeber, Alfred
1939   *Cultural and Natural Areas of Native North America.*
        Relates culture areas and environment, vegetation, and physiographic zones.
        The book includes many helpful maps and Kroeber's population estimates.

Murdock, George Peter
1970   *Ethnographic Bibliography of North America.*
        Bibliography by culture area and tribe. Every student should be familiar with this
        important reference book.

Oswalt, Wendell H.
1973   *This Land Was Theirs.* 2nd ed.
        Studies of twelve tribes from seven culture areas, giving ethnography and history from contact to modern times or to extinction.

Owen, Robert, James Deetz, and Anthony Fisher, eds.
1967   *The North American Indians.*
        Reprints of articles on many topics arranged by culture area, plus a listing of films on Indians and Eskimo.

Spencer, Robert, and Jesse Jennings
1965   *The Native Americans.*
       A comprehensive textbook of both prehistory and ethnology of North America,
       including Mesoamerica.

Underhill, Ruth
1953   *Red Man's America.*
       This readable book, arranged by culture areas, includes history and ethnog-
       raphy, but only for the continental United States.

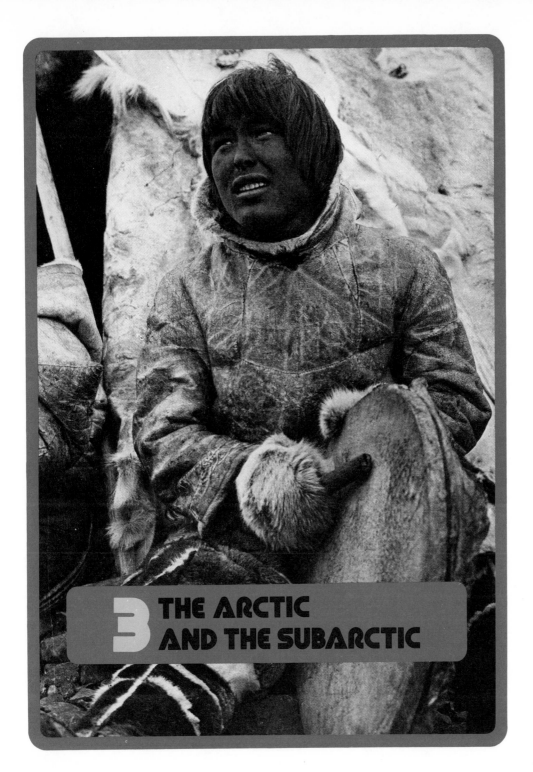

3 **THE ARCTIC AND THE SUBARCTIC**

VΛVΛVΛVΛVΛVΛVΛVΛVΛVΛV

Once upon a time a widower lived alone with his daughter, Sedna, who had grown to be a handsome woman sought in marriage by many young men. None of them pleased her, for she had lost her heart to a seagull who flew over the ice and wooed her with an enticing song. "Come with me to the land of the birds where there is never hunger, where my tent is made of the most beautiful skins. You shall rest on soft bearskins. Other gulls will bring you all your heart may desire; their feathers will clothe you; your lamp will always be filled with oil, your pot with meat." Sedna could not resist, and they went together over the vast sea.

When at last they reached the country of the gull after a long, hard journey, Sedna discovered that her new husband had shamefully deceived her. Her new home was not built of beautiful pelts but was covered with wretched fishskins, full of holes, that gave free entrance to wind and snow. Her bed was harsh, and she had to live on miserable fish which the birds brought her. In her wretchedness she called to her father to rescue her. "Oh, father, come to me in your boat and carry me home across the waters. Oh, come and take me back home."

When a year had passed and the sea was again stirred by warmer winds, the father went to Sedna, and, hearing of her woes, determined upon revenge. He killed her husband, the seagull, took Sedna into his boat, and they quickly left the country of the birds. But when the other gulls returned home and found their companion dead and his wife gone, they flew away in search of the fugitives. They were very sad over the death of their comrade and continue to mourn and cry until this day.

After a short flight, the gulls discovered the boat and caused a terrible storm to break out. The sea rose in immense waves that threatened the pair with destruction. In this mortal peril the father determined to offer Sedna to the birds and flung her overboard. She clung to the edge of the boat. The father then took a knife and cut off the first joints of her fingers. Falling into the sea, they were transformed into whales, the nails turning into whalebone. Sedna held more tightly to the boat, but her second joints fell under the sharp knife and swam away as walrus. Then the father cut off the stumps of the fingers, and they became seals.

Meantime the storm subsided, for the gulls thought Sedna had drowned. Sedna took up abode in the depths of the ocean whence she controlled the sources of nourishment. She sent out all the animals that served for food or sometimes withheld the supply, causing want and famine. When the people of the earth displeased her by their behavior or neglect of the taboos, she punished them with starvation.

ⱯⱯⱯⱯⱯⱯⱯⱯⱯⱯⱯⱯⱯⱯⱯⱯⱯ

In a nearly treeless land of cold, snow, and ice, with continuous darkness for three or four months each year, life offers few comforts and few products of the soil. Most of the native people of the northern land made their living from the ocean, and the ocean mammals also provided the raw materials for their clothing, housing, and tools. Small wonder, then, that the Sedna myth— in many versions—was told and retold by almost all Eskimo across 6,000 miles of Arctic coast.

The Environment

The landscape of the Arctic is rolling plains called tundra, with little vegetation other than mosses and occasional scrub bushes. It has no trees, for the Arctic lies beyond the northern tree limit. The Arctic Ocean freezes solid in winter, but in summer the ice cracks into pieces along the shores and drifts south with the ocean currents. Hunters can get trapped if the ice breaks up unexpectedly in the spring.

Cold is the outstanding feature of the Arctic environment. The Arctic winter is severe not only because of extreme cold, but also because daylight is so short. Surprisingly, snowfall is comparatively light; the winds build high drifts because no wooded areas are there to act as windbreaks. Summer winds are less violent than the winter gales that sweep with intense force across the barren land. The summer wind may even be welcome, because it blows away the insect pests— flies and mosquitoes—that appear with the warmer weather and mercilessly attack human and animal populations.

During the brief summer, temperatures do rise above freezing, and it can become quite warm, though never long enough for the sun's heat to penetrate far into the earth. This is the land of permanently frozen subsoil, called *permafrost*. When the topsoil thaws, it turns into a muddy mire over the frozen lower layer, through which water cannot drain away.

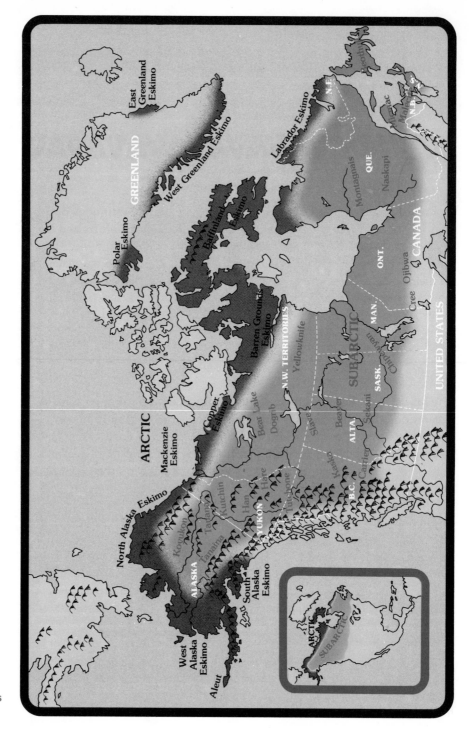

Arctic and Sub-
arctic culture areas
and their tribes.

Some Arctic areas, especially northeastern Canada, have hardly any soil where the land was scraped down to bedrock by the Ice Age glaciers. Because of this, the short growing season, the low summer temperatures, and the intense wind, the plants are small, tough varieties—dwarf willows, lichens, mosses, sedges, and low grasses. Limited though the vegetation is, it nourishes large herds of caribou and musk-oxen and tiny animals like the vole and lemming, which in turn support foxes, wolves, and weasels.

After spring thaw, the small lakes, the uncountable ponds, and the pools are full of fish and attract hordes of waterfowl. The sea ice melts, and ice floes break off. Fogs are frequent during the spring melting, and sunlight diffused through the fog can create a white-out, which may cause snow blindness.

At the North Pole the winter nights are the longest—six months—but even during that night the visibility is not as poor as one might expect. There is a good deal of twilight, and the snow reflects moon and starlight. Winter temperatures average below zero, dropping at times to 50 degrees below. Storms alternate with spells of quiet weather in which the little heat that remains in the earth radiates away into the clear, dark skies. Most herds and birds move south, and the remaining animals hibernate.

The Eskimo

The Arctic is one of the most unpromising and demanding environments inhabited by human beings. Probably the aboriginal population never reached 120,000 in the entire area. The people who settled this forbidding land, the Eskimo, spread from Alaska, where they had entered North America, across Canada and on to Greenland. Archaeology is difficult at best in the Arctic, but excavations indicate that the Eskimo population, a subdivision of the Mongoloid group, began entering North America between 3000 and 2000 B.C. By that time the land connection between Siberia and Alaska was again under water, so they must have crossed the strait over ice floes or in boats. The life they had led in northeastern Siberia appears to have been well suited to the new territory across the strait and all the way east along the arctic coast, for many Asian tools continued in use in the New World.

Over the great area inhabited by the Eskimo, just one language was spoken, though local dialects occurred, and linguists make a division between dialects south and west of the Yukon and all others. The Eskimo language has been classified with languages spoken in northeastern Siberia—Chukchi, Kamchadal, and other tongues—as belonging to the Paleo-Siberian linguistic phylum. It bears no resemblance to American Indian languages, and is the only North

American language that shows clear linguistic ties to any Old World tongue. Also within this phylum is Aleut, spoken by the natives of the Aleutian Islands, who were closely related to the Eskimo. The linguistic homogeneity suggests the relatively recent spread of the Eskimo across the continent.

Several other kinds of evidence also support the idea that the Eskimo reached America fairly recently. For one thing, the oldest artifacts identified as Eskimo are only about 4,000 years old. Moreover, the Eskimo resemble the peoples of northeastern Asia much more than they do other American aborigines. Their skin is relatively light, their profiles are almost invariably flattened, their cheek bones are wide, and their eyes are narrowed by the fleshy lids and epicanthic fold found in eastern Asiatic peoples.

Adapting to the Arctic

The bleak land occupied by all these peoples and their descendants was a tremendous challenge to their ingenuity. The way of life that existed among the earliest Eskimo arrivals and ultimately spread from Alaska to Greenland was regulated everywhere by the environment. People wore layers of fur and hide clothing, carefully tailored and airtight, because they would freeze if they did not. The women made undershirts of bird skins to be worn with the feathers against the body for added insulation. Babies rode naked in fur pouches on their mothers' backs; mothers packed the hoods with moss or used fur or bark diapers.

The climate forced the Eskimo to live, at least during the long winter, in well-insulated shelters—pit houses of wood and whalebone in Alaska, and igloos built of snow blocks in the central and eastern Arctic. As they entered their homes, the people carefully beat off ice crystals and snow so that their clothing would not become wet and heavy in the warmth. They had to dry all wet clothing carefully or it would freeze when they went outside. Drying was done on a frame over an oil lamp. Although some Eskimo hunted land animals the year around, most lived primarily off the sea by hunting seals, whales, and other marine mammals. The endurance of an Eskimo hunter is amazing to anyone raised in the temperate world. Almost never did they turn back once they got on the trail of an animal, and they learned to wait hours, motionless, for a seal at its breathing hole in the ice.

Eskimo wasted nothing, eating every edible part of animals and making bones, teeth, and antler into implements. They made sleds of antler and whalebone, wood of course being rare. Women rendered (melted down) fat into oil, and made hides into shelter, clothing, boat coverings, or other equipment. Sinew became the thread that held skins together.

Arctic survival required heat as well as food and shelter, and where timber was not available and driftwood was too precious to burn, the Eskimo burned oil from sea mammals. The best heating oil was rendered seal blubber, which burned with a clean, smokeless, hot flame. The Eskimo poured the oil into a soapstone lamp, a shallow stone carved with a depression, and added a wick of moss. The women could regulate the flame, which burned continually, and kept it low at night. For daytime, they fixed the wick to create more light and heat. The women cooked on the oil lamp and melted snow and ice over it for drinking water. (Water was rarely used for washing because it was too scarce.) It may be hard to believe, but Eskimo dwellings, both igloos and the semiunderground structures of Alaska, were comfortable, not drafty or too cold. Inside, the people went almost naked.

Regional Variations

The differences among the various Eskimo groups were slight. In Alaska where there were some trees and the environment was slightly less harsh, Eskimo built wooden dwellings and communal houses. For transportation they had two types of boat, the one-man *kayak* and the *umiak,* a large open boat made of hide stretched over a framework of lashed wood. They made some pottery and had complex trading relationships and ritual activities. *Labrets*—ornamental lip plugs—appear to have been confined to Alaska, as were a few other traits such as masks and basketry. These traits were also common to tribes of neighboring Indians and may have been derived from them and added to an older Eskimo culture.

Farther east, in the area called the Barren Grounds, the Caribou Eskimo severed all connection with coastal life. Geological data reveal that about six hundred years ago, in the central part of Canada, the earth's crust was uplifted, leaving the sea there too shallow for whales and other large sea mammals. To replace that main source of food, Eskimo there turned to the caribou and also fished in inland waters. Life there was so hard that they abandoned many cultural elaborations of the Alaska Eskimo in their struggle for sheer subsistence.

Another division of Eskimo, living around Coronation Gulf, followed the common Eskimo pattern of hunting sea mammals, but there nuggets of copper could be picked up and made into implements; thus these people became known as the Copper Eskimo. The Eskimo of eastern Canada in Baffin Land and Labrador also depended on sea mammals, occasionally including whales, as did the Greenland Eskimo. All these people used the kayak and umiak except the Polar Eskimo of North Greenland, who did all their transporting on their own backs, not even using sleds.

A kayak and a umiak, showing exterior views and framework.

Kayak

Umiak

Alaska: The Seasonal Pattern of Life

From our brief review of Eskimo life we can see that most traits typical of the Alaska Eskimo, except those taken from Indian peoples nearby, were carried east by the early people who spread in that direction. They seem to have abandoned a few traits as environmental conditions dictated; but on the whole, the people who moved eastward from Alaska, hunting both inland animals and sea mammals, were already adapted to life under all the conditions they met. The eastward migrants merely dropped some of their traditional ways, modifying others. Thus, if one way of life can be called typical and "purest Eskimo," it is the coastal, from which all the others developed.

Spring Whaling

The earliest Eskimo were the so-called Old Whaling People. Relics of their pursuit of whales, found on Cape Krusenstern in northwest Alaska, date from around 2000 B.C. These people left large flint blades which presumably tipped heavy-duty harpoons, and though no preserved bits of boats have turned up, Old Whaling sites have yielded plentiful deposits of whalebone, sure signs of the whalers' skill as hunters on the open sea.

By the end of April, when daylight stretches over nineteen hours each day, ice in the Arctic Sea begins to break up, leaving open lanes of water. The bowhead whales, huge animals sixty feet or more in length, move north through wide cracks in the ice in Bering Strait. As soon as the whales began their northward migration, Eskimo hunters rushed to load their umiaks onto sleds and moved out to the edge of the shore ice. Thanks to the long, sunlit days and vigorous tides, by that time of year the ice had broken up to within a mile or so of the village. Chanting songs urging the whales to come and be caught, hunters pulled on waterproof suits made of sheets of walrus gut.

A central Canadian Eskimo, painted in 1832, with his hunting and fishing tools and kayak and double paddle in the background.

When they sighted spouting whales offshore, they quickly launched the boats, each manned by the owner-steersman and six paddlers plus a harpooner in the bow. As the whales dived, the paddlers in the lead umiak paddled furiously while the captain steered toward the area where he expected the animals to surface. When a whale broke water, the paddlers, following the harpooner's gestured directions, edged the bow of the boat to within a few feet of the whale. Then the harpooner hurled his weapon at the animal. As the head of the harpoon sank in, the shaft fell away to be retrieved later. For the moment the crew was totally occupied keeping clear of the whale's thrashing. The line whizzed overboard, carrying drags of inflated sealskins to slow the whale's progress. The whale dived, the boat followed its underwater course, and the harpooner aimed a second harpoon and perhaps a third as the animal emerged. At last, tired by its wounds and the tug of the sealskin drags, the whale could no longer dive, but rested quietly on the surface.

Then came the most dangerous part of the whale hunt. Cautiously the whalers paddled up to the side of the great beast. The harpooner thrust his spear into the whale's side, searching for a vital spot. As the animal thrashed convulsively, he thrust again and again till the whale spouted not white but crimson. The paddlers had to backwater quickly to keep the boat clear of the animal's death throes.

In ten minutes or so, the whale floated dead, and the crew raised a shout of triumph. Hearing it, the other boats closed in to help with the slow job of towing the immense catch to shore. Long, steady paddling brought them at last to the shore ice, where the whole village joined in dragging the carcass, inch by inch, onto the ice for butchering. First the head was severed, and the wife of the victorious boat captain ceremonially offered it a drink of fresh water. "We thank you for coming," she intoned. "You must be thirsty." She then urged the whale's spirit, released when the head was cut off, to return to the land of the whales and tell its fellows how well it had been treated. Without this ceremony, the people feared, the whales would not return next year. After butchering, the heaped tons of whale meat were buried in storage pits for the coming period of cold. Also, blubber—whale fat—was made into oil or exchanged for furs and caribou skins with people of inland settlements.

Summer Activities

In early summer, whaling dwindled, and both groups and individuals began a variety of summer pursuits and outlets. Usually the winter village communities broke into smaller family groups or even into solitary hunters or traders. Some stayed on the coast, some moved to interior hunting grounds or fishing sites, and others trapped or traded. Interior Eskimo groups who had to depend on caribou rather than whales were always eager to trade with the whalers, and trading trips to the interior took long enough that hunting, trapping, and fishing could be done on the way. Meat, fish, and furs obtained during the summer travels were stored in pits cut in the subsoil, used as a huge freezer. If whole families moved together, they might stop midway at a convenient spot where the women and children stayed in a temporary camp in skin tents until the husbands and fathers returned. At these summer camps the women made clothing for winter, processing the furs and hides for the tailored garments no one could live without in the Arctic. The camp might also be a fishing station where a net was stretched across a stream to be emptied of the catch when the traders returned.

Dogs. The dog team accompanied the family and hauled the foods, supplies, and clothing obtained or made during the summer. If the journey was by stream, the dog team, walking along the bank, pulled the umiak. If snow was on the ground, they pulled a sled which, during warmer weather, was itself transported on the umiak.

Families rarely owned more than three or four dogs because food, even for people, was scarce, and a dog team could eat many pounds of meat each week.

A summer camp, showing an Eskimo group with their housing and cooking facilities.

However, dogs were important for hunting and transport. The tough, strong huskies—just one breed throughout the Arctic—could pull heavily laden sleds over great distances. Each dog was hitched separately to the sled, and the team spread out like a fan with the lead dog in the center, a short distance ahead of the others.

Solitary hunters often took along one dog, especially on seal hunts, for a good dog could smell out and locate a seal's breathing hole much more quickly than even the most skilled and experienced hunter. The Eskimo of interior Alaska and those of the eastern areas used their dogs during large hunts for caribou and musk-oxen. The dogs kept the herd at bay while the hunters shot arrows at a selected animal. Although dogs were work animals, not pets, the Eskimo often became emotionally attached to them and mourned the loss of a favorite animal.

Trading. Toward the end of the short summer, as signs of cold weather became noticeable, the family packed up the products of their summer activities and returned to the winter village. They usually traded with any groups they met on the way, exchanging seal and whale oils, hides, ropes of hide, birds packed whole in seal oil, driftwood, furs, and artwork such as carved ivory labrets. Exchanges were handled by recognized trading partners who had established formal, enduring trade relationships. Trading partners were usually not relatives because one already has a formal relationship with a relative; the wise thing was to spread out loyalties and dependence by forming non-kin relationships. In a world where cooperation was essential to survival, it made sense to create interdependence with as many others as possible, especially with those in another ecological zone, to obtain items not available in one's own area. It was usual to cement such partnerships with a sexual bond also. Partners had access to each other's wives, and these sexual relations made a quasi-kinship bond stronger than all other bonds except those of family.

Winter Life

Back at the winter home where the families once more congregated to form a small village community, there was a period of sociability as people told of their summer pursuits and prepared for the severe weather ahead. Boats were repaired, houses were caulked and readied for cold, traps were set, and perhaps men carved a piece of bone or walrus ivory into labrets or a hunting charm.

The Eskimo carved animal and human figurines as charms and toys and engraved geometric and naturalistic designs on many of their implements and utensils. Bone, stone, ivory, and horn took the place of wood. The Alaskan

Eskimo ivory objects from northern Canada (top to bottom): snow goggles (length, 4½ inches); comb (length, over 4½ inches); marrow pick (length, almost 8 inches); engraved comb bridge (height, 4 inches).

masks (almost no other Eskimo made them) were of hide, whalebone, fur, and, when it was available, wood, sometimes trimmed with shells and feathers. The masks were produced in great variety, representing the many Eskimo supernaturals.

The Seal Hunt.   Sometimes in the spring, when the seals and their pups were sunning on the coasts, several men would join to hunt them, but winter sealing was a different matter; it was solitary. In Alaska, seal hunters usually speared the animal as it rose to breathe. Seals swim under the ice, but they must have several widely spaced breathing holes through the floes, and keep these holes ice-free during the winter. The hunter and perhaps a dog searched for the holes, and might wait beside one of them many hours until the seal returned. The hunter often tried to attract one by scratching gently on the ice with a pointed strip of whalebone, imitating the sound of a seal's claws on the ice.

When the hunter found a seal's breathing hole, he would enlarge it with a flint blade mounted in an antler handle so that he could set a trap. He bored four

**An Eskimo seal
hunter waits at a
breathing hole for
his prey.**

small holes around the breathing hole and then lowered into the hole a tough net of thin whalebone strips, topped with ivory rattlers to warn, by their noise, when the seal had come. He attached the four corners of the net through the small holes he bored in the ice so that an approaching seal could swim over the net to reach the hole. Once the animal gulped a new supply of air, it dived, only to become entangled in the net that lay directly beneath. The rattlers shook and warned the hunter, who hauled up the net and killed the animal with a blow. Then he might take a drink of blood, perhaps his first fresh food for months. Wounds in the animal were plugged with a whittled stopper because blood was far too precious to waste. The hunter might set his net again or go home. To haul his catch home, he might form a coating of ice on the runners of his sledge by urinating on them, making the vehicle slide more easily when loaded. He lashed the seals and his tent on the sledge, and over his boots he slipped creepers—strips of corrugated carved ivory to give traction on the smooth ice.

Home Life.   In Alaska, home was a stone dome covering a pit about ten feet square and three feet deep; the stone was braced with whalebone or driftwood and topped with an insulating layer of earth. An Eskimo entered his house by stepping down into a passageway dug lower than the floor to trap cold away from the living quarters. There was no door, but a skin lashed across the entry could close it tight. On one side of the passageway was a small storeroom for harpoons and other bulky equipment. Inside, the walls were festooned with extra clothing, hide nets containing snares for trapping small game, and tools for working flint and hide. A sleeping platform situated at the back of the house, large enough for the whole family to stretch out comfortably on fox and polar bear skins, was only about three feet below the roof, where the warm air collected.

In the evening, the hunter might go over to the men's house. This building— common in Alaska, but rare farther east—was considerably larger than any family dwelling, but of the same construction. There the adult males of the village spent time eating, sleeping, repairing hunting equipment, and making new gear. At intervals, their wives brought in food, and from time to time work stopped for a wrestling contest or an insult match in which the men competed to see who could compose the most scurrilous songs about one another, to the uproarious delight of the listeners. These contests were only partly serious: the men were hunting partners and friends. Such competitions usually were a harmless way of working off grudges, relieving the tensions built up during the long, dark winter, or letting others know when they had behaved badly. Other amusements were quieter: telling tales of great hunters now dead or the clever exploits of Raven, the trickster spirit, or watching the shaman (a religious specialist) perform his feats, such as pulling a fur mitten from an empty tambourine.

Melting rack

Skylight

Ventilator

Sod

Clothing storage

Cooking area

Whale scapula
to control drafts

Whale
skulls

Pans

Bench

Frozen food

Food storage

Lamp

Well

PIT HOUSE: FLOOR PLAN

Whale ribs

PIT HOUSE: CROSS-SECTION

Cooking area

Snow blocks

Entrance tunnel

Sleeping
platform

IGLOO: FLOOR PLAN

Air vent

Clear ice window

Storage area

**Diagram of an
Alaskan pit house,
showing the floor
plan (top) and
cross-section. Sup-
ported by whale
bone or driftwood,
the house frame-
work was covered
with stone and
earth. Diagram of
an igloo (bottom),
showing similarities
in its layout to the
pit house.**

IGLOO: CROSS-SECTION

As long as the hunting remained good, the men spent much of their leisure time in the clubhouse, leaving it from time to time for another expedition after seals, a trapping trip for foxes or hares, or, after the spring's migrant birds had arrived, a hunt for eggs. And then again in April, the whale hunts recommenced.

Eskimo Life in General

Like the Alaskans, the central and eastern Eskimo made the seasonal change from winter communities to summer dispersement by family or individual. Whaling, although known on the Atlantic coast, was more typical of the northern and western Alaskan groups; interior peoples depended more on the great caribou herds. Indeed, the Caribou Eskimo, exploiters of the Barren Grounds, abandoned coastal adaptations entirely and lived off the caribou alone.

The main difference between the Caribou Eskimo and all other Eskimo groups was their restricted subsistence. Caribou herds migrated through the Barren Grounds twice a year, and human life there depended on those migrations. The scarcity of food produced among the Caribou Eskimo the simplest material culture of all Eskimo groups, and they had no mythology involving Sedna, the sea goddess, being far from the ocean and its supply of food. The only large mammals they hunted besides caribou were musk-oxen, which did not appear regularly. These Eskimo believed that caribou were the only good food, but fish could relieve the monotony and were important when caribou were scarce. Hunters did prefer, though, to spend time on an unsuccessful caribou hunt rather than go fishing. Eskimo usually hunted caribou communally by driving them into ambush or into water where men in kayaks killed the animals with stone-tipped spears.

The Caribou Eskimo did have some dwarf trees in their environment, so they made fire from wood, not oils. None of the Eskimo subdivisions used much of the plant life available to them, though, which is surprising considering how intensively they exploited the rest of their environment. Plant life in the Arctic has a short, but very flourishing, season. The long hours of sunlight in the arctic summer produce a brief burst of bloom, which the Eskimo thought important only as it affected the browsing and grazing animals that migrated northward for food. Caribou, moose, musk-oxen, and deer were hunted intensively by some groups and occasionally by others, but the plants on which the animals fed were not sought as nourishment by the people themselves.

Eskimo ate some fish and meat raw—the word Eskimo is Algonkian for "those who eat raw flesh"—but they cooked most foods as stews of meat chunks, blubber, water, and sometimes blood. Their cooking pots were usually ground stone vessels, but in Alaska might be poor-grade clay pottery. The cook suspended the "kettle" from a horizontal pole supported on a four-legged frame or from a tripod above the lamp.

Technology

Boats. Eskimo used two types of boats, the umiak and the kayak. The umiak, large enough to transport a dozen or more people, was used in whaling and hauling. It was often called the women's boat because it was the only kind they used. Kayaks were one-man boats, their framework covered with sealskin, except among the Caribou Eskimo, who used caribou skin. The opening fit snugly around the paddler so that with his waterproof jacket he was protected against the waves and could even right himself with his paddle if he capsized.

To the basic necessity, seaworthy boats, the Eskimo added a great array of special tools and devices specially invented or adapted for every requirement of arctic living. Their harpoons were often assembled from half a dozen parts. One widely used type had a detachable walrus ivory head fitted with a tip of flint or ground slate, in which a hole was drilled for attaching a line. The head was lashed not to the main harpoon shaft but to a flexible bone foreshaft. For still more flexibility, the foreshaft was seated in an ivory socket fitted onto the main shaft, and foreshaft, socket, and shaft were lashed together with hide or sinew. The shaft itself was further equipped with a bone or ivory thumb support for leverage in throwing.

The Igloo. Eskimo ingenuity also produced the *igloo,* one of the most unusual shelters ever devised by man. This house, built entirely of snow and ice, kept living quarters above freezing while outside temperatures dropped to 40 degrees below zero. We know that it was used in the central Canadian area, but we cannot trace its origin because when igloos melted they left no sign that they had ever existed. In prehistoric times they probably differed hardly at all from those made until recently by people of the central Arctic.

An Eskimo and his wife could build a family-sized igloo, nine to fifteen feet in diameter, in an hour or so. First the man drew a circle on firm snow to outline the structure. Then, with a spatulalike bone or antler knife, he cut the hard-packed snow inside the circle to make rectangular blocks about four inches thick. Standing in the circle, he trimmed the blocks and arranged them in an ascending spiral that gradually closed in to form a dome. Architects point out that this is the only type of dome that can be constructed without scaffolding, which was out of the question in the treeless northern Arctic. For a draftproof entry, he built a tunnel like the one used on a pit house, but made of blocks of firm snow.

The entrance was usually to the south, away from the north wind. Meanwhile, his wife, working outside the igloo, shoveled a plastering of loose snow over the walls to fill any cracks or holes. Children often helped close up the slits.

Once the shell was completed, the man built a sleeping platform of packed snow around the inside, covering it with furs and hides. The family used this area for dining and sitting as well as sleeping. A window of clear ice or seal gut in the wall near the entrance let in some light, and outside the window a large block of snow might be set to reflect light inside. Heat from the oil lamp transformed the inner surface of the roof into a smooth ceiling of ice that rarely dripped. Instead, a film of meltwater flowed toward the floor, where it froze. Often hides were suspended a few inches from the dome, creating a dead air space with great insulating efficiency. Three or more igloos might be built together, connected like rooms, one as a storeroom for equipment, another for clothing; the dogs often slept in the entrance tunnel.

More Tools.   Excavations at a north Alaskan site near Point Barrow, dating from around A.D. 500 and containing the remains of only about a half dozen pit houses, have turned up a large number of tools that helped the people adapt to their rigorous environment. The hunting gear included spear throwers and spears, nine kinds of bone missiles for bringing down birds, and half a dozen types of harpoon heads. Along with bows were implements to tighten bow strings, arrow shafts, and six varieties of bone arrowheads—some with multiple barbs for killing large prey. There were also mouthpieces for blowing air under the skin of a harpooned seal so that the body would not sink. Along with this hunting and fishing equipment, the Point Barrow site disgorged enough gear to fill an ancient hardware store: antler snow-shovel blades, probes for testing treacherous-looking stretches of snow or ice, whetstones, engraving tools, bow drills, whalebone digging tools, stone knives and adzes for working driftwood, needles and needle cases of bone, and dozens of other specialized tools.

Other ancient Point Barrow Eskimo had wrenches for straightening arrow shafts, hooks for hauling blubber off a whale carcass, and *gorges*. These last were double-pointed pieces of bone with lines attached to the middle—when a fish gulped one down, it jammed in the throat. For traveling over snow and ice, there were sleds as well as toboggans made of whalebone strips lashed together. The dog sled may very well have spurred the spread of Eskimo culture across Canada. Dog sleds not only would have given hunters greater mobility, but also would have made winter hunting much more efficient: seal catches, particularly, could be handled far more easily. And an abundance of boat remains showed that by 1,500 years ago, the skin-covered kayak and the umiak used in whale hunting had developed into forms closely resembling their nineteenth-century counterparts.

One anthropologist has called the Eskimo "gadget-burdened." They were well equipped to deal with the frigid zone in which they lived, but their equipment was not so much extensive as intensive. Although the Eskimo developed an almost unbelievably fine assortment of tools and mechanisms for adapting to the environment, their tool kit was not nearly so extensive as that of many Indians to the south.

Social Organization

Eskimo society was not complex. The family and the household were the basic social units; occasionally the two were the same. Most often, though, the household—those residing together at least in their winter homes—was some sort of extended family grouping. This meant that the nuclear family—man, woman, and their children—shared a home with grandparents, or grown brothers or sisters and their families, or another wife, or even combinations of all three. The closest ties were within the nuclear family, but the household was the most important economic unit for both production and consumption.

The division of labor was sharp and essential. Male and female tasks were complementary, and both were necessary. There were no unattached individuals, for no one could last long alone in the tough arctic conditions. If a woman's husband died, she expected to become the wife of his brother. If a man's wife died, he expected her family to send him another woman, usually a sister of his dead wife.

A very successful hunter might take a second wife to help with the domestic work, but few had more than two wives. Together a man and a woman were an efficient unit: the man was the provider with his hunting, fishing, and trapping, and the woman prepared the clothing from hides, cooked the food, and cared for the young and the home. The arduous life in the frigid zone gave little extra time for doing another's work; each took care of his own.

Beyond the nuclear family, any others in the household—grandparents, brothers and sisters, and more distant relatives such as cousins, aunts, and uncles—were expected to pitch in to accomplish any other domestic tasks. Within the household everyone lived with complete economic reciprocity: they produced together and consumed together; occasionally they starved together.

Partnerships. Some men's tasks, such as hunting, trading, or whaling, made it necessary to widen their circle beyond that of kinfolk, and to build up other loyalties and dependencies. A special relationship existed among the men in a whaling crew or the members of a caribou hunt. Those groups were semipermanent and formed and dispersed according to the seasons year after year. Only if feuds broke out, or if the leader of the crew or hunt seemed to have lost his powers, did those groups disband.

A man became and remained a leader only because he was competent, never because his father had been a leader before him. The owner of a whaling umiak persuaded his crew to remain with him because he was an effective whaler, not because he was anyone's relative, though he probably enticed the men to join him in the first place by giving them gifts. The relationship between the owner and his crew was like that between the leader of a caribou hunt and his hunting party. Each held his position by merit: the leader had demonstrated quite clearly that he was competent and wise, and men were willing to follow him because they expected success under his direction.

The trading partnership was another relationship that extended beyond kin ties. Those partnerships endured everything but a feud, and they were exclusive; one did not trade with just anyone, only with those who had entered into a special trading pact. Trading partners became a sort of pseudo-kin, and such associations usually carried with them a kind of bantering camaraderie; the partners were good buddies.

The Eskimo world, then, was divided into kinfolk—"us"—and non-kin—"them." Kin included blood relatives, traced through both maternal and paternal lines, and the sort of "secondary kin" of trading or hunting partnerships—those whom one could trust and count on. All others were looked on as at least potential enemies. For aid in daily activities, one called first upon close kin, next upon more distant relatives. For special assistance, as in trading or hunting, there were those in the specialized relationships. All these networks of association were practical; no government or system of laws decided who traded together or who would be in charge of a hunt. One man might dominate a household, just as the hunt leader or crew captain dominated his men—because of wisdom and competence. But outside of this tentative sort of leader position, social control was in the hands of society at large. Someone who misbehaved might be ridiculed gently or harshly in song, or scorned by his fellows. In extreme cases he might even be abandoned, his household packing up and leaving the undesirable behind. He then had to mend his ways, for otherwise he became truly a person without a country or even a house. Many people thought that supernatural forces would punish the wayward with sanctions too dreadful even to contemplate. These ways of promoting socially acceptable behavior usually proved effective, for it was through his social relationships that an Eskimo survived.

Marriage. Marriage was not formalized by any ceremony. It was an agreement between man and woman not only to live together but to take on their respective roles in the domestic economy, which in the Arctic was far more important than sexual union. Divorce was as simple as marriage; the couple separated. Sexual relations between men and women not married to each other were often used to cement relationships between men who were not related by kinship. That is, trading partners, members of a hunting or whaling party, or whatever, might exchange wives in recognition of their mutual bond. This special relationship between men who exchanged wives also extended to their children, making them, in effect, cousins.

A man who eloped with another's wife could expect to keep her only if he mustered more support from his kin and quasi-kin than the husband could from his. In many ways, might was right, but the result was endless feuding between the two kin groups, for most men were outraged to be cuckolded and sought vengeance. The two kin groups were then caught up in a very undesirable situation involving murder and further murder in retaliation, for they had no courts or policing agencies to settle such disputes. Consequently, families always tried to keep their own members in hand to avoid destructive feuding. Knowing that he lacked kin support, an Eskimo would think twice about any kind of wrongdoing.

Song Duels. When one Eskimo felt he had been injured by another, he composed a satirical song, which he sang at a public challenge performance. The target of the song responded, and the audience acted as judge and jury. When the decision on who was winner was announced, the contestants had to be friends again and not continue the quarrel. These song duels were both comic entertainment for the spectators and revenge for one of the participants. The duel stopped most physical aggression within the group and calmed hostile feelings and personal grudges; each party had his say in public and released his aggression and resentments vocally. No matter who was adjudged winner, each could then go about his daily business having had his day in court—the court of public opinion.

Abandoned Infants and Elders. The extreme conditions of life in the Arctic resulted in both infanticide and geronticide. Infants who could not be fed for any reason—their mother's death, food shortage, illness—and old people who could no longer make an economic contribution to the group might under some dire circumstances be abandoned. Such an act was never done lightly; infant mortality was already high, and children were greatly desired; old people were loved. If circumstances became severe, however, it was considered wisest to select those most apt to live and reproduce the community, and concentrate resources on them. The aged recognized the hardship and also the sorrow of such a decision, and they usually left quietly, unnoticed, to die rather than be a drain on supplies. All Eskimo grew up recognizing the possibility of such a fate.

Eskimo Religion

Eskimo religion, like other aspects of Eskimo culture, varied little from east to west. Eskimo everywhere believed in the existence of spirit powers in charge of the universe. In Alaska, male spirits predominated; elsewhere, the principal powers were usually female. Sedna, the sea goddess, for example, was less important in Alaska than in most other areas. The Caribou Eskimo, having turned to pursuing land animals, had for their principal deity Mother of the Caribou, a guardian of both human and animal life. In Alaska, a major divinity in charge of the universe was the Moon Man, who ruled the sky and the souls of game animals and human beings.

Eskimo relied on religion mainly for controlling subsistence and the forces of nature, preventing disease, and foretelling future events and conditions. Eskimo believed that nature was basically harmonious and that the supernaturals—all elements and beings that were "non-natural"—were either neutral or benign. They could be angered, though, by human negligence or disobedience. People thus were essentially responsible for their own problems and distress; their failure to behave properly and observe taboos and rules was thought to cause discomfort, disease, famine, and the other ills that beset mankind. Means of atonement were confessing sin and promising improved behavior.

Beliefs. Eskimo believed that humans and animals were in a special mystical relationship, the animals allowing themselves to be hunted and caught by man because they were sorry for him, though charms and other types of magical practices might force their capture too. Among the Eskimo, as well as most of the hunting peoples of North America, belief was strong that animals had souls or spirits that left the body at death to be reincarnated in another body. Hunters helped game animal spirits to reincarnation by offering them a drink of fresh water. Under no circumstance should a hunter offend the hunted animal, which might then withhold itself and all others of its class from man. Consequently, slain animals were addressed with words of esteem and requests that their spirits tell other animals that man had treated them well.

Proper etiquette toward the animal world required separation of land and sea mammals. Many taboos prohibited mixing flesh from the two types in meals or using the same weapons on them, and it was thought that whales were insulted if dogs gnawed on their bones or licked their blood. Among the Caribou Eskimo, it was taboo for dogs to chew the antlers or bones of caribou. If taboos were broken, the game animals, essential to the people's very existence, would be outraged and no longer allow hunters to capture them.

Human beings also possessed souls, according to Eskimo belief. A human soul might get lost or stolen, a situation that was a major cause of disease and very frightening to the owner, who then called upon a shaman (a religious figure and a curer) to locate the missing soul and return it to its proper place. Human souls were fragile things, especially when compared to animal souls, and that fragility symbolized the Eskimo feeling of helplessness in the face of capricious and inexplicable nature.

CHARACTERISTICS OF THE ARCTIC TRIBES

Clothing	Food production	Equipment	Shelter	Social and political organization	Religion	Warfare
Tailored skins (fur and hide)	Fishing	Harpoons	Igloo (central and eastern Arctic)	Nuclear families	Myths	Feuds between kin groups
Parkas	Hunting (sea mammals and land mammals)	Spears and spear throwers	Skin tents	Extended families	Spirits (control universe)	Song duel
Mittens	Some wild-plant gathering	Fishhooks	Semi-subterranean housing	Bands	Shamans	Warfare rare or unknown
Boots		Gorges	Pit houses of wood and whalebone (Alaska)	Social control in hands of society at large	Guardian spirits	
Undershirts of birdskin with feathers		Flint tools			Songs and other rituals	
Fur pouches for babies		Bone needles			Mother of the Caribou (Caribou Eskimo)	
		Nets and weirs			Souls present in both humans and animals	
		Bone and antler knives				
		Oil lamps				
		Sleds				
		Toboggans				
		Kayaks				
		Umiaks				
		Ground stone vessels				
		Pottery				
		Basketry (Alaska)				

In addition to the body and the soul, Eskimo believed each person had a third aspect, his name. A name was a very important thing, and when someone died, his or her name was not spoken until it was given to some newborn infant, who made the name come alive again. The Eskimo thought that the newborn cried at birth because it wanted a name. Eskimo names had no gender; they were used for males and females alike.

Eskimo belief included other categories of supernaturals: demons that were potentially dangerous because they could work evil, and a sort of psychic projection called the *inua,* which could come from animals, objects, and even places. In Alaska, inua were sought as personal guardian spirits that might be called upon for aid, good weather, good hunting, and good health.

Besides observing their many taboos, Eskimo performed magical rites to ensure welfare or success in their pursuits. Such rites included singing songs, reciting formulas, and carrying charms. Owners of umiaks, successful harpooners, and caribou hunt chiefs were semireligious figures, who all had special songs and charms to bring success to their expeditions. Eskimo songs, charms, formulas, and other magical activities can be compared to good luck charms like rabbits' feet, talking to dice, and lucky numbers. All people of the world have practices like these.

The Shaman.   The important religious figure was the shaman. He was only a part-time specialist in religious activities, also participating in the subsistence pursuits of his community and being a father and husband. All the people had ties with the supernatural world, but a shaman's were closer, and he could use those ties to cause good or harm. He was both respected and feared. He might be employed for the good of the community as a diviner to learn the cause of some misfortune or to predict weather conditions or hunting success. If game was scarce he might travel to Sedna to compel her to release the animals. On the other hand, he could unleash the fury of the supernatural world against others.

The shaman was also very important as a curer. The Eskimo were very anxious about disease, not only in the practical sense of broken bones, but in terms of disturbances we would classify as psychosomatic—responses to the tensions in Arctic life. Such disturbances were blamed on failure to carry out rituals, attacks by hostile shamans, soul loss, soul theft, and intrusion of a mysterious object into the body. Illness due to neglect of rituals was cured by confession and some prescribed atonement; a disease inflicted by a shaman was cured by going to a more powerful shaman. For the others, cures were done by the shaman, who located the soul and restored it or sucked out the object causing the illness. If a patient died, the shaman explained that he had been opposed by a shaman with greater power or by malevolent spirits. Though shamans could treat general injuries like broken bones and cuts, almost any adult knew how to care for those practical disabilities, and the shaman's real value was in psychological curing.

Most of a shaman's activities took place before an audience and included an element of entertainment. He used a variety of what we might call tricks to produce the required results: ventriloquism, sleight of hand, and human helpers or apprentices who gave the desired atmosphere by manipulating objects with strings invisible in the dim light. Some of the performances were spectacular, and it is no wonder that the shaman often worked cures on the psychological problems he encountered. The shaman was, of course, aware that he was using trickery, but he believed in his supernatural power, and his patient and audience believed in it too.

A person with potential for or interest in becoming a shaman either sought out spirit help on his own or apprenticed himself to an older shaman. Both men and women were eligible, but few women of childbearing age ever entered the profession; most women shamans were past menopause. Age seemed to be a factor in success, for it was generally thought that the most powerful shamans were old people, whether male or female.

It is hard for us to keep separate all the classes of supernatural and religious practices, and probably they were often confused in Eskimo thought. All of them symbolize the unreasonable and unpredictable aspects of nature that could be ignored only at one's peril. Life, nature, and the supernatural were uncontrollable and had to be appeased, pleased, and calmed with the many taboos of diet and behavior. The result would be an easier and more secure life, they hoped. The Eskimo took no chances; it was not a matter for debate.

THE SUBARCTIC

Northern
Athabaskan Legend

SZSZSZSZSZSZSZSZSZS

Long ago when the world was new, an Indian man was traveling in the wintertime. He had a long way to go, and the snow was deep and cold. It was so hard to walk that he could hardly go on. He asked aloud, "Why does the North Man do this? Why does he send such winter weather?"

Suddenly he saw a man all in white standing before him. At first he could not imagine who would be out in the winter cold, but as he drew near, he realized that it was a man made of snow. When the Snow Man saw the Indian and how cross and tired he looked, he asked, "What is the matter?" "Such terrible snow. It is so hard to travel. The North Man is no good." The Snow Man said, "I will try to help you; just keep on your way." And the Snow Man disappeared. The hunter went on with his journey.

Finally spring came and warmer weather. The lakes melted, and the hunter wondered, "What did the Snow Man mean when he said he was going to help me?" He began to hunt, and he saved all the fat from the animals he caught and stored it in bladders. He also cut lots of wood, which he arranged in deep piles. And he went on all summer and into the fall storing grease and piling up wood. He did not know why he did these things; something seemed to impel him.

As fall turned into winter, the snow began again. It snowed and it snowed, and there were great drifts around the hunter's camp and over his wigwam. The hunter built a fire, and one day the Snow Man came to the hunter's camp. "How do you like the weather this winter?" the Snow Man asked. "All right," replied the hunter. And the cold increased and the snow drifted higher. The hunter kept putting wood on the fire, and then he began to pour grease over the wood. The fire burned stronger. By and by the Snow Man asked again, "How do you like the weather now?" "All right," answered the hunter as before. He really had had enough cold weather, but he would not give in. He stood the cold better than ever before because he had plenty of grease and wood. He made the wigwam hotter and hotter.

At last the heat was too much for the Snow Man and he began to melt. Soon he went away entirely. As he left, he said to the hunter, "You are a stronger man than I am. You have conquered me, and now I must leave." Soon the cold began to moderate, and the winter continued just the way winters should be, not too cold, not too warm. It was a good winter, and the winters have been good since then.

SZSZSZSZSZSZSZSZSZS

Perhaps for the Subarctic peoples who told and retold this tale, it was an explanation of summer and winter, why winter was not eternal and how people learned to survive it. Certainly the intense cold and deep snows of the Subarctic must have been a constant concern for the people who lived there.

The Environment

As the name suggests, the Subarctic is the zone just south of the Arctic. It includes most of Canada and Alaska, except for the coastal regions. The boundary between Arctic and Subarctic shows up most clearly in the vegetation change from treeless tundra to forest, evergreens in the west and evergreens mixed with deciduous species (birch, elm, maple, oak) in the southeast. Subarctic animals include the small woodland types such as squirrel, rabbit, fox, beaver, and porcupine, as well as the larger fauna: caribou, musk-oxen, moose, deer, and bear. The region has many lakes and bogs, rivers and streams, filled with whitefish, salmon, pickerel, trout, perch, and sturgeon, and waterfowl make stops there in their yearly migrations. Along the Atlantic seacoast are shellfish. Plant foods throughout the area are limited, and the climate prohibits agriculture.

In the West, the Canadian Rockies are a powerful influence on weather, blocking the moderating force of the Pacific Ocean and letting polar air masses flow southward and spread out, circulating toward the East. Conditions reverse in the summer, when subtropical air masses move into the Subarctic across the prairies and lowlands of the Great Lakes by way of the Mississippi River system. The seasonal extremes are pronounced: winters are long and cold, and summers are relatively short but hot, with plagues of biting insects. Most of the precipitation falls in storms, snow in winter and violent rainfall in summer. In winter, the interior is even colder than the Arctic, which has the ocean to moderate its temperatures. In spite of the many game species, the harsh environment meant that food was seasonally scarce and famines were frequent for the native hunting peoples. Often severe winter cold and snow lying deep and forbidding were together almost unbearable. To leave home was to face agony; to stay home was to starve.

Aboriginal Population

We divide the Subarctic into eastern and western divisions by the languages spoken there. Algonkian was the language of the East and Atha-baskan of the West. Although the two language families belong to different phyla and have no more in common than English and Chinese, the cultural adaptations—the general ways of living—of the native peoples were very similar across the continent. There were regional variations in style and detail, but throughout, food was obtained by hunting, fishing, and some gathering.

Population was never great in the Subarctic—one estimate puts it at less than 60,000 for the whole area at the time of European contact. Perhaps that is on the low side; twice that is probably more accurate. When European intruders began to transmit their diseases to the natives, nearly half of those people died. One whole tribe, the Beothuk of Newfoundland, became extinct.

We know less about the Subarctic Algonkians than about almost any other aboriginal group in North America because of their small numbers and also because they were badly disrupted by early contact with European fur traders. The early European explorers had little or no interest in recording information about the northern Algonkians and have left us few descriptions. We know more about the Athabaskans because many bands still survive; in fact, their numbers seem to be growing.

Life in the Subarctic

The Subarctic hunters and fishers wandered in small bands. To the east there was a slight patrilineal trend, with brothers remaining together or close by, and wives moving into their husbands' territory. The Athabaskan area seemed to have a matrilineal preference. However, European contact and its disturbing influence altered the culture, gathering people into the composite band—a group formed by kinship, either maternal or paternal, primarily for economic expediency. One went where he thought he would have access to good hunting territory and fishing sites. Food was never abundant enough to allow a large population, and there was no political structure outside of kin organization or achieved leadership. A competent, wise man acted as group leader, deciding when to move on to new hunting grounds and generally seeing that the traditional customs and taboos were followed by the group. Only when hunting was extraordinarily good (and that was very rare) did a large number of people gather and feast.

Food

The lives of most Subarctic people revolved around caribou, their most important food. As among the Caribou Eskimo, caribou hunts were often communal: hunters surrounded a herd and drove it into a trap or enclosure, or perhaps a lake, where others waited in canoes to kill the floundering animals. In deep snow, a hunter on snowshoes could run down a caribou, and the Subarctic people also used snares for both large and small game. Game was supplemented with fish, especially salmon from the western rivers that flowed into the Pacific. Plant foods were sparse and contributed far less to the diet than among any native Americans except the Eskimo.

Subarctic dwellers stored food for lean months in caches (hiding places), sometimes pits in the ground, sometimes bags suspended from poles. In winter it was easy to preserve food by freezing, but summer heat was too high to keep foods frozen. To store meat, then, the women dried it, pulverized it, and mixed it with suet or other fat, making a classic Indian dish—*pemmican*—which remained edible for more than a year. In spite of their efforts at storage, however, most Subarctic bands were perpetually close to starvation in winter. Like the Eskimo, they sometimes had to abandon those who could no longer care for themselves.

Technology

Subarctic technology included many items to help people adapt to snow, although in general the tools were not so complex or ingenious as those of the Eskimo. The Subarctic people may have been the first to invent the toboggan and snowshoes, which they needed for swift movement over deep snow. The pattern or style of snowshoe varied from place to place. Some were round, some had a pointed heel, some had turned-up toes, but all were formed of a wooden framework, usually made pliable enough to bend easily by steaming, with a webbing or mesh of rawhide strips, called *babiche.* A thong of rawhide was woven into the netting and tied over the instep. These shoes kept the wearer from sinking into snow. They were not for speed, unlike skis. Different styles were adapted to different kinds of snow, and a tribe could usually be identified by its snowshoe style.

Another important item in the Subarctic snow was the toboggan made of bark, wood, or hide, pulled by human muscle—often by women. The word *toboggan* is Algonkian. The Subarctic people also used the bark canoe, a very important technological advance where waterways were plentiful. Birch bark made a lightweight canoe that could be carried over the portages, the trails between waterways.

A characteristic that set Athabaskans and Algonkians apart was the emphasis each placed on stone as a raw material. The Athabaskans used far more wood, horn, antler, and bone than the easterners, even preferring beaver teeth to stone for knives. The easterners made few utensils from animal products, preferring stone.

Although much of their territory was in the great northern conifer forest, the Subarctic people had no tools for hewing or working full-grown trees. They fashioned their wooden equipment from saplings, brush, and bark. In the West, the

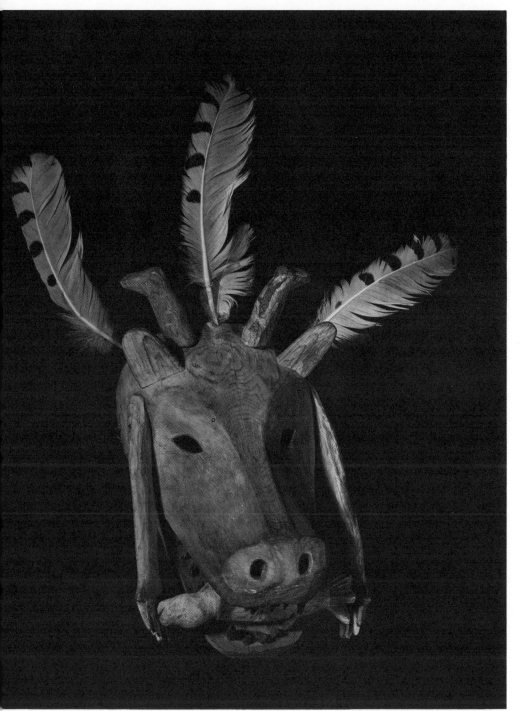

An Eskimo wooden mask from Good News Bay, Alaska (length, 11 inches). The mask depicts a wolf holding a seal in its mouth, with human feet protruding like horns and arms hanging down the sides of the head, presumably representing a spirit.

Athabaskans made containers of spruce roots and fibers as well as bark, and
bags, ropes, binding, and nets of babiche. The Algonkians made most of their
containers, even those for cooking, from birch bark. The women sewed the bark
with vines and made it watertight with pitch, and used bark containers not only
for stone boiling, but also for direct boiling—bark vessels actually can be hung
close enough to a fire to boil water inside without burning the bark. Women
used both the white outer layers and the light brown inner layers of birch and
heated them over fire or in steam to make them pliable, bending them to the
desired shape. Once the container cooled, the shape became permanent. Often
the women decorated the bark by scraping designs through the white layer, letting the brown layer show through, or they added moosehair embroidery, paint,
porcupine quills, and, after European goods became available, beadery. The
constant quest for food left little time for activities like art, but the women of
many tribes decorated not only the containers but also the clothing with porcupine quill or moosehair embroidery, and the Algonkian Naskapi painted geometric designs on their garments. The embroidery they produced was some of the
finest of its kind in North America.

**A quilled pouch
from Lake Atha-
basca, Canada
(length, 10½
inches). Before
European beads
were available,
porcupine quills
were the most com-
mon decoration on
leather used in the
Subarctic.**

Housing. All Subarctic peoples were on the move much of the year, following the caribou and other migratory game, going north in summer and returning to river valleys and deep forest in winter. They could not live in permanent villages and built shelters that were easy to put up and take down. The Naskapi of northern Quebec lived in conical *tipis,* some covered with caribou hides, some with birch bark. The Athabaskans also favored the tipi of skins or bark, and in both areas people built more temporary shelters of brush or spruce boughs. The Indians of interior Alaska and some of those in British Columbia built the most durable structures of the Subarctic—houses of logs or planks. Many tribes, among them the Naskapi, built domed sweathouses, primarily for ritual purification. The common form was a circular framework of saplings bent over to meet at the top. Bark or hide covered the framework.

Clothing. Women made semi-tailored clothing to protect against the bitter winter cold. Their sewing was not as fine as that of the Eskimo, and they probably borrowed some clothing ideas from the Eskimo, such as mittens, and leggings attached to moccasins. Men's leggings extended from foot to thigh and were held up by a thong attached to a belt. Along with leggings, men wore breechcloths, long shirts or hide coats, and fur hats. Generally women's leggings covered only the legs below the knees and were held by garters that were sometimes decorated with porcupine quills, or later, after European trade goods were available, with beadery. Women wore longer overgarments than men, and their loose, belted shirt-dresses kept their thighs warm. In cold weather both men and women wore fur robes as well as mittens and caps, and moccasins lined with furs for added warmth. Even in summer most Subarctic people covered their bodies as protection against insect bites.

   Women did the work of preparing hides. The furs used for hats, mittens, and other clothing came from hare, fox, muskrat, beaver, and mink. These furs were the object of the European fur trade in later times.

Religion

Subarctic beliefs were simple and ceremonies few. Across the continent people believed in a multitude of spirits and other supernatural beings such as monsters, giants, and demons. Both Athabaskans and Algonkians attributed misfortune and lack of success to witchcraft or to the supernaturals, and hunters normally sought supernatural aid in the form of a spirit helper.

   Like the Eskimo, the Subarctic peoples believed that animals had souls. Indeed, they believed that animals were more powerful than humans, that they had been the original inhabitants of the earth and could take human form if they wished. These powerful beings had to be treated with respect. They were appealed to and thanked for the good they bestowed on human beings in the form of food and raw materials. Although hunters were forced to kill animals, the souls or spirits of those slain returned to their spirit home, and the mortal remains, the bones, had to be treated properly or else the animal spirits would withhold others of their kind from other hunters. Among most caribou hunters, special rituals and beliefs were connected with the caribou. A "chief caribou spirit" lived in the mountains; unless proper respect was shown the slain caribou, the "overlord" would stop sending animals, and the people would starve. Often hunters would hang up the skull of a slain animal and offer it prayers and ceremonial smoke. Caribou bones were carefully kept away from dogs and also from menstruating women.

Every hunter hoped for a vision as a sign that he was under the protection of a spirit. Such a mark of favor helped him to face the perils of life, if not with complete confidence, at least with belief that he had support from the spirit world.

The fact of menstruation was overlain with fear that this female occurrence was dangerous to men and animals. During menstrual periods, childbirth, and for a while after, women were segregated from the male community. At such times, women were thought of as having almost an excess of spirit power—power dangerous to hunters and distasteful to the animals they hunted. At their first menstruation, girls were isolated and taught how to care for themselves and how to avoid men and animals taboo to them. The supernatural aura surrounding menstruating women was common to most Indians, but in some areas, including the Subarctic, segregation and taboos were very rigid.

As among the Eskimo, the sole religious practitioner was the shaman. Most of the Subarctic had no priesthood, although the Midewiwin society of the Ojibwa (to be discussed later) was an exception. The shaman's techniques included drumming, purifying people and objects with the smoke of tobacco (obtained by trade, since it could not be grown that far north), and in some areas, tent shaking. The shaman arranged the latter by techniques that we would call trickery, pulling slender cords to get the tent flapping as a sign to the followers that the spirits were present and listening. The drum was of great ritual importance to the shamans for divining the future and ensuring success in the hunt. Rattles were also used to catch the attention of the spirits who presumably advised the shamans and guided their actions.

The Windigo. Beliefs among the peoples of the Subarctic were inspired by their particularly harsh environment. One prominent and sometimes gruesome belief involved the Windigo, or cannibal monster. People's belief in the Windigo, and their resulting behavior, has been called *Windigo psychosis*. It occurred mostly among the Algonkian speakers, most particularly the Montagnais-

Naskapi, the Ojibwa, and the Cree. Since the food quest in the Subarctic was a constant struggle, the ever-present threat of famine gave a common character to all the cultures of the area. That pressure and the tensions it caused are central to Windigo psychosis.

The Windigo monster was a superhuman giant about thirty feet tall, who lived in the forest and preyed on human beings. The Algonkians believed many spirits inhabited the forest, but only this one was a cannibal. He was described as having a heart of ice, no lips, huge jagged teeth, and protuberant eyes rolling in blood. His feet were a yard long with pointed heels and only one toe. His hands were like claws. He hissed and made long-drawn-out thundering sounds, accompanied by gruesome howls. His speed and strength were enormous. The Windigo ate rotten wood, swamp moss, and mushrooms, but above all he loved human flesh. It was believed that he sought his victims hauntingly and relentlessly, but waited for darkness before he seized and ate them. Whenever a hunter failed to return from the forest, the Indians knew that he had probably fallen victim to the Windigo.

It was thought to be almost impossible to kill a Windigo. Some people believed that only a silver bullet could kill him—obviously a European addition to Windigo beliefs. A powerful shaman who could enlist the help of other supernaturals might be able to conquer a Windigo, but few ordinary mortals could.

The Indians had a number of ways of explaining this monster's origin. One explanation was that he had been a human being and was transformed by the spirits. Others held that he had been created out of a sorcerer's dream and sent out into the world to do malevolent deeds. Another belief was that the Windigo embodied all the people who had died of starvation. After contact with missionaries, some Indians came to believe that God had made the Windigo, presumably to punish evildoers.

Windigos and Cannibalism. The Windigo's compulsive desire to eat human flesh was his most fearsome habit. While such desire appalled the Subarctic people, cannibalism was a fact in their lives during times of famine. Because most people spent the winter in small family hunting groups, desperate hunger often meant eating a close relative, even a spouse or a child. A person who resorted to cannibalism became a Windigo. Consequently, anyone with a craving for human flesh—real or fancied—was considered a Windigo, possessed by the spirit of the Windigo monster. Once someone had tasted human flesh, he was thought to develop a burning appetite for more. Anyone who became a Windigo could not control his actions, and because he could not be cured, he had to be killed. It is reported that victims even asked to be destroyed.

The connection between cannibalism and becoming a Windigo could work either way. Among the Subarctic hunters, the search for a spirit helper was common, and some people acquired a Windigo spirit helper. A Windigo could select a person as his protégé, and if the individual did not reject the Windigo, he came to resemble his guardian in all respects, even to his heart of ice and his cannibal cravings. Or a shaman might send the Windigo spirit to an enemy to possess him or to become his spirit helper. A clever sorcerer could create Windigos by using his supernatural power to cause starvation, which forced the object of the sorcery to turn to cannibalism. Both males and females could become Windigos, which is surprising considering that it was the men who were the hunters, responsible for securing food and acquiring spirit helpers. Of the recorded cases, 40 were male, 29 were female, and the sex of one was not recorded. The records show that 44 of those cases involved an actual act of cannibalism; a family member was eaten in 36. Once a person had been designated a Windigo by others of his community, he probably turned to cannibalism even if he had not practiced it before because he believed it was futile for him to resist.

Other symptoms of the Windigo psychosis were deep depression and delusions in which other people were perceived as animals. The Windigo-bewitched individual withdrew from human society and did not eat, sleep, move, or talk—he sat preoccupied with cannibalistic thoughts. In this state of apathy he might still be helped, but once he had progressed to violence, his case became hopeless and he had to be killed for the good of society.

Seventy cases of Windigo psychosis are recorded in the literature, most of them back in the nineteenth century. The peak of the recorded incidents came during the greatest time of stress in Indian-white relations, which hints that extreme Windigo psychosis may have been a contact phenomenon, at least in its full-blown form, though cases recorded by Jesuits in the seventeenth century indicate that it was an aboriginal development.

The Chipewyan

Among the Athabaskan groups, the Chipewyan (not to be confused with the Algonkian Chippewa) were the most populous and spread over the greatest area. They were caribou hunters primarily, but they also pursued buffalo, musk-oxen, and smaller game, as well as waterfowl and fish. Their life was not easy, and did not vary much from the typical Subarctic ways of exploiting the environment. The one big difference was the very low status of Chipewyan women and their hard life compared to women of most other groups. They were so little valued that they were last to be fed and first to perish in times of famine. Female infanticide was practiced, and adult women are reported to have expressed the wish that they had perished in childhood, so hard was their lot in adulthood. Women took the place of pack animals, hauling the household goods on their backs during seasonal migrations. They were at the mercy of their husbands, whom they married in early adolescence and who were often middle-aged men. Women were considered inferior to men in all ways. They prepared food for men, but they did not eat until the men were full, when little food might be left.

The women did have one way of escaping the burdens their men imposed upon them. Like all Subarctic men, the Chipewyan men feared and isolated menstruating women. But they seemed not to understand the timing. Consequently, when a woman wished to escape her husband, she moved to the menstrual hut, as often as several times a month, where she could be sure no man would pursue or bother her.

That kind of abuse might seem to lead inevitably to broken marriages, but in fact divorce was not more frequent among the Chipewyan than elsewhere. The harsh life meant, as in the Arctic, that the male-female division of labor was complementary and essential. Neither men nor women could easily manage alone. Sexual exchange of wives, here as in the Arctic, bonded two men together in a quasi-kin relationship, and if one of the men died, the other would be responsible for the wife and children of the deceased.

The difficult life affected the elderly, the sick, and the disabled, who might be neglected or abandoned when food was scarce. The Chipewyan may stand out as inhumane, but their environment was harsher than anything most of us can imagine. Hardships in the Subarctic were so great that society had to give its few meager benefits to those most likely to survive. The central subarctic zone took a terrible toll among those hardy enough to live there.

The Ojibwa

Probably the largest tribal unit in the Subarctic were the Ojibwa, Algonkian speakers who lived along the northern shores of the western Great Lakes. They spread southward from the Subarctic into the agricultural district to the south. The name Ojibwa is applied to the group that remained in the Subarctic, while those who moved into territory that became the United States are usually referred to as Chippewa. Both names come from the Algonkian word meaning "those whose moccasins have puckered seams"; they were simply transcribed differently. If you say each one several times, you will notice that they begin to sound very similar.

The Subarctic Ojibwa got many benefits by living on the border between regions. Life was never so rigorous as farther north, giving many more options for survival. Winters were neither so long nor so fierce; people enjoyed a delicacy in the form of maple sugar; and trade with fully agricultural groups to the south brought foods and equipment unavailable to the more northerly Algonkians. Some of the Ojibwa even did some rudimentary cultivation, and others availed themselves of the grain now called wild rice that grew in abundance around Lake Superior.

CHARACTERISTICS OF THE SUBARCTIC TRIBES

Clothing	Food production	Equipment	Shelter	Social and political organization	Religion	Warfare
Tailored skins	Fishing	Bows and arrows	Skin or bark tipis	Nuclear families	Myths	War more frequent among Ojibwa than more northerly peoples
Hide coats	Hunting	Harpoons	Log or plank houses	Bands	Spirits (monsters, giants, and demons)	
Leggings	Gathering wild plants	Traps	Domed sweathouses	Patrilineal trend in the east	Shamans	
Skin dresses		Weirs		Matrilineal trend in Athabaskan area	Witchcraft	
Long shirts		Nets			Spirit helpers	
Fur robes		Toboggans		The Three Fires (alliance between Ojibwa, Ottawa, and Potawatomi)	Midewiwin Society of the Ojibwa	
Hats		Canoes			Windigo Spirit	
Mittens		Birchbark containers			Souls present in both humans and animals	
Breechcloths						
Moccasins						
Snowshoes						

At one time, the Ojibwa joined with their kinsmen, the Ottawa and the Potawatomi, in a loose alliance known as the Three Fires. Before that, all three had been bands or separate units within a larger tribal organization. Although the individual groups or bands were mostly independent, with their own hunting territories, they were connected by language, common customs, kinship, and intermarriage. Separation into the divisions Ojibwa, Ottawa, and Potawatomi probably was due more to European classification and treatment than any self-perceived division, but as the Europeans treated the groups separately, in time they came to think of themselves as separate.

The Ojibwa fought more wars than the more northerly peoples did, perhaps because their life was easier. They used bows and arrows, clubs, knives, and hide shields in war, and carried home scalps of vanquished enemies. After a victory celebration, conquering warriors who had slain an enemy wore an eagle feather indicating their success. Their war practices probably were adopted from their enemies, tribes of the Great Lakes and the eastern Woodlands, some of whom spoke Algonkian and some Iroquoian.

The biggest difference between the Ojibwa and most other Subarctic people was not their much greater use of plant foods and their warfare, but their religious organization. Ojibwa religion had a more social and organized form, an association known as the Midewiwin, the Grand Medicine Society.

The Midewiwin was a religious and curing organization to which both men and women might belong if they were willing to spend the time and pay the heavy fees. There were four grades of membership, and each required long instruction and high payment. The initiate was expected to have a vision and personal con-

An Ojibwa Indian on snowshoes traveling with his family, shown in a lithograph by W. Day after H. Jones. The toboggan, also pictured, was used as the transport vehicle from the St. Lawrence to the Mackenzie River.

Part of an Ojibwa incised birchbark scroll from Minnesota. Scrolls were used as memory aids in Grand Medicine Society ritual.

tact with the supernatural. At an annual ceremony new members were inducted into the lowest grade. Very few ever attained the highest grade.

The Ojibwa had shamans, who followed the individualistic practices we have seen, but in this tribe, shamanism was less important and had less prestige than membership in the Midewiwin. The members' primary function was curing, mainly of psychological disabilities. Yet unlike curing elsewhere, it is said that members had much knowledge of natural drugs and many herbal remedies for nonpsychological problems. Their power came from the group, not from the individual, and membership brought very high prestige. Ritual was extensive. As a memory device, birchbark scrolls were inscribed with symbolic figures; these could not be called writing, but were closer to it than anything other groups north of the Rio Grande produced.

Bibliography

Birket-Smith, Kai
1958   *The Eskimos.* 2nd ed.
         A general suvey of Eskimo people by a distinguished European anthropologist.

Boas, Franz
1888   *The Central Eskimo.*
         An older classic about the Eskimo of Baffinland with many excellent line drawings of artifacts.

Jenness, Diamond
1928   *The People of the Twilight.*
         Describes the annual round of the Copper Eskimo.

Jenness, Diamond
1955   *The Indians of Canada.*
         A comprehensive survey of the Subarctic tribes with much information hard to locate in any other source.

Mowat, Farley
1954   *People of the Deer.*
         A gripping narrative about the hard life of the Caribou Eskimo.

Spencer, Robert
1959   *The North Alaskan Eskimo.*
         Ecology and social adaptation in North Alaska.

Lantis, Margaret
1947   *Alaskan Eskimo Ceremonialism.*

Suggestions
for Further Study

Other
Pertinent Works

Leacock, Eleanor
1954   *The Montagnais Hunting Territory and the Fur Trade.*

Osgood, Cornelius
1936   *Contributions to the Ethnography of the Kutchin.*

Osgood, Cornelius
1937   *The Ethnography of the Tanaina.*

Speck, F. G.
1935   *Naskapi.*

Teicher, Morton I.
1960   *Windigo Psychosis.*

MAJOR GROUPS AND LANGUAGES
OF THE ARCTIC AND THE SUBARCTIC

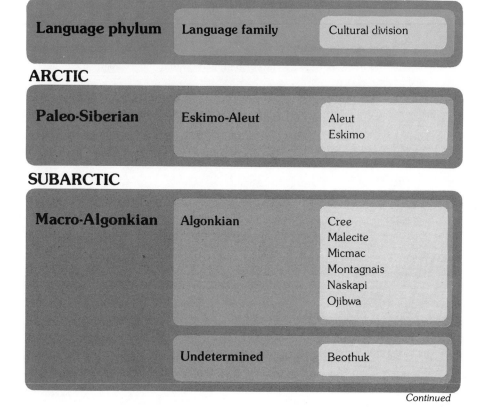

Language phylum	Language family	Cultural division
ARCTIC		
Paleo-Siberian	Eskimo-Aleut	Aleut Eskimo
SUBARCTIC		
Macro-Algonkian	Algonkian	Cree Malecite Micmac Montagnais Naskapi Ojibwa
	Undetermined	Beothuk

Continued

MAJOR GROUPS AND LANGUAGES (continued)

Language phylum	Language family	Cultural division	

SUBARCTIC (continued)

Na-Dene	Athabaskan	Bear Lake
		Beaver
		Carrier
		Chipewyan
		Dogrib
		Han
		Hare
		Kaska
		Koyukon
		Kutchin
		Sekani
		Slave
		Tanaina
		Tanana
		Tutchone
		Yellowknife

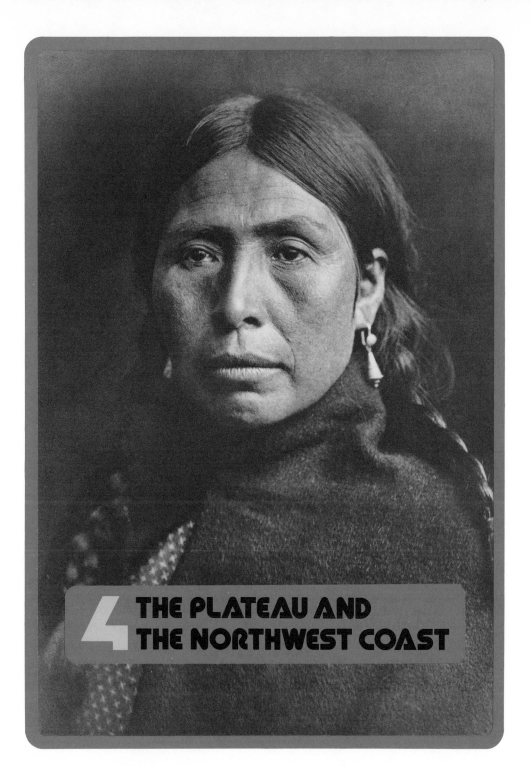

4 THE PLATEAU AND
THE NORTHWEST COAST

THE PLATEAU

YᏦYᏦYᏦYᏦYᏦYᏦYᏦYᏦYᏦYᏦYᏦYᏦ

Long ago Coyote tried to cross a flooded stream leading to the Thompson
River. He started across a log, but lost his balance and fell into the water.
He was in danger of drowning so he turned himself into a piece of wood
and was swept downstream to where the Thompson flowed into the Fraser
River, and on from there into unknown waters. He sailed along until he
was stopped by a fish weir owned by two old women. One of the women
picked up the piece of wood and said, "This is good wood. It will make a
nice bowl. I will take it and carve it."

When the old woman had made the bowl, the other brought a fresh
salmon to put in it. But the salmon disappeared before the women could
eat it. They put more salmon in the bowl, but each piece disappeared
quickly, and at last the women in anger threw the bowl into the fire. Suddenly from the fire came the sound of a baby crying. The old woman who
had carved the bowl pulled it from the fire and cried, "It is a baby, and I
have always longed for a baby!" She took the baby, a little boy, and
raised him as her own. But he was a difficult child, disobedient, stubborn,
and hard to manage. At first the women took him along fishing and gathering plants, but he became so headstrong they finally left him home.

Now Coyote, for he was the little boy, had never eaten salmon until he
came to the land of the old women. There were no salmon in his country,
and he acquired a taste for the fish. He determined to break open the weir
and lead the fish to his people up the rivers. When the old women had
gone, Coyote ran down to the weir, broke it open, and led salmon up the
Thompson and Fraser rivers; then he went over to the Columbia River
and led salmon up it and the streams that flowed into it. And all along the
rivers Coyote taught the people how to make the tools to catch the fish,
and how to cook and dry it for storage. That was how salmon came to the
land of the three rivers, and the people called Coyote their ancestor, the
ancestor of all tribes living between the Cascade and Rocky Mountains.
The people since that day have been known as Coyote people.

The Thompson, Fraser, and Columbia rivers, and others such as the Snake, the Okanagon, the Umatilla, and smaller ones, were the lifeblood of the Plateau. The rivers made possible a relatively large native population—maybe 200,000—for they teemed with salmon. It is not surprising that salmon and the rivers were often the focus of myths.

The Environment

The Plateau is an interior highland area bounded by the Cascade mountain range in the west and the continental divide or the eastern slope of the Rocky Mountains in the east. On the south it blends into the Desert Basin, and to the north its boundary is less well-defined, running roughly along the tributaries of the Fraser and Mackenzie rivers. It is an elevated basin with deep river canyons and mountain and hill zones. Much of the area is desert, so low is the annual precipitation, yet it is watered well enough by the river systems that the low rainfall is less important than in regions without rivers. Winters are cold, but not nearly so cold as in the Subarctic, and summers can be hot. The southern vegetation is dry land forms: cactus, sagebrush, scrub trees. The northern mountain slopes are covered with forests of conifers mixed with some deciduous forms.

Culturally, the Plateau is a transition zone. The cultures of most of its inhabitants resembled those of groups in neighboring areas: the Plains on the east, the Northwest Coastal peoples to the west, or the desert dwellers to the south. The differences are not strong, but the Plateau adaptations are distinctive enough to identify the region as a separate culture area. It includes the western quarter of Montana, southwest British Columbia, eastern Washington, most of Idaho, and northeast and central Oregon.

Prehistory

Remains of the earliest human occupations in this area show that salmon fishing was common among the earliest Plateau dwellers. Some of these people later moved on to the North Pacific Coast; the rivers offered natural passages through the Cascade and coastal ranges to the lowlands of the seaboard. Flint blades and fishbone debris at the Dalles, a series of rapids on the Columbia River, have been dated to 9000 to 7000 B.C. Other ancient remains,

The Plateau and the
Northwest Coast
culture areas and
their tribes.

of pit houses and earth ovens dating from early periods, indicate their long history on the Plateau. Long ago, as in historical times, the ovens were used to bake the vegetable staple of the Plateau, the camas bulb, a starchy root somewhat similar to the potato.

Another ancient form that lasted into historic times was a ground-level pole and mat dwelling. Its age is hard to ascertain because it is poorly preserved, but it may be very old. It seems, then, that the earliest people to move into the Plateau region made for themselves a way of life not really very different from that of their descendants who were visited by Lewis and Clark on their famous expedition from 1804 to 1806.

The Plateau is significant as a transitional area through which people passed in ancient times as they populated the continent. Here descendants of the original settlers coming from the Subarctic developed a new way of life, which would adjust and prepare their own descendants for the areas beyond—the Coast and California. It appears that people passed through the Plateau in small groups, not year by year but generation by generation. As they moved, they learned and invented new ways of adapting to new environments.

Life on the Plateau

As you read this quick description of the Plateau people, remember that the area they lived in was transitional. It had few clear-cut, unique characteristics and did not become a center of technological elaboration.

From ancient times, Plateau tribes moved seasonally to take advantage of many foods. Their winter villages usually were on the banks of one of the area's many rivers, where they served as fishing stations in all seasons, including the major fishing season from May to November. Groups left the winter homes to fish in new streams or to hunt in the hills in spring, summer, and early fall. Each community recognized a large territory as its own for gathering berries, roots, and other plant stuffs, and for hunting game.

Houses in the winter villages were permanent, large, and well-insulated. Many were pit houses built of logs and covered with sod. Light came from a hole in the roof, which also let out the smoke from the fire. With the addition of a notched log ladder, this hole served as an entrance as well. In summer, the people moved to lighter, less durable shelters. These usually were built of poles and covered with mats of rushes or cattails. Some of them were community dwellings, up to sixty feet long, constructed over shallow pits; others were made of the same materials but housed only one family. Openings in the roofs let smoke out and light in.

Salmon, a food staple of the Plateau tribes, was caught in a weir made of slender poles. Once the fish was entrapped, it would be speared through an opening in the top of the weir and withdrawn. A fish spear with two detachable bone points lashed to form a *V* (above) was commonly used.

Resources

None of the Plateau tribes practiced agriculture, for the region was too cold and too dry for cultivating the early corn species. The food important above all others was salmon, though other fish such as trout and sturgeon were eaten. Salmon was not only the favorite but the basic food, eaten fresh in season and dried for the rest of the year. Plant and animal foods filled out the diet of fish: camas bulbs, nuts, and seeds, and deer, elk, and mountain sheep, as well as smaller animals such as rabbit. Food was neither so scarce as it was in the north in the Subarctic, nor so bountiful as along the Northwest Coast or in most of California. The Plateau population was therefore denser than in the north, though sparser than in culture areas to the west.

The most important resources other than food were the plant fibers of grasses, rushes, reeds, and vines, which could be used in basketry. Basketry was important throughout the area from ancient times not only for containers and cooking, but for bedding, house covering, sandals, cradles, and shrouds for the dead. Justifiably famous for their fine work, the Plateau women made many forms: large cylindrical baskets of Indian hemp and bear-grass for gathering and storing roots; flat winnowing baskets of willow; mortar baskets of the same shape, but bottomless and fastened to a stone upon which the women pounded seeds or roots; cooking vessels of willow splints; flat bags or pouches for holding small personal possessions, and larger ones for holding clothing and family equipment. Matting was the principal house covering and also served as mattresses or tables.

Communities

With dependable subsistence from salmon and wild plants, the Plateau people could settle in stable, independent village communities. Villagers recognized ties between themselves and those in other villages in their common customs and dialects, not in any political unification. Varieties of four language families were spoken in the Plateau: Salishan (of uncertain derivation), Sahaptin (a branch of Penutian), Algonkian, and Athabaskan.

The village rather than the tribe was the main political unit in the Plateau. Among villages using the same language, people shared ceremonies, intermarried, and traded regularly. Each village set aside territories exclusively for those who belonged to the village, letting others use those resources only as guests; some groups would let others use their land only by invitation.

Some large and productive fishing sites were communally owned, and the catch was distributed among all members of the village. Fishing on such a large scale was done with the large traps or dams called fish weirs. Individual fishing spots were owned or controlled by small kin groups or even by individual fishermen. The large weirs were built and repaired by all the men in the community, while the small weirs and fishing platforms were built by their owners. Fishing rights were important and zealously maintained.

In most cases, the village was governed by a *headman,* sometimes referred to as a chief. He was chosen in some groups by the village adults and in others got his position by inheritance. Even the hereditary leaders, however, held power only by competence, and none was more than adviser to the community. If disagreement arose within the community, the headman negotiated a settlement agreeable to all. The position was his for life unless he displeased the village people, but his authority rested on their consent, and a council both assisted him and limited his power. In some groups women belonged to the council, and in a few cases they were chiefs.

The Plateau people were generally peaceful. Some had a reputation for making great efforts to avoid a fight. If raids or retaliation were felt to be necessary, the people chose a war chief or leader, but they rarely looked for prestige in warlike feats until after European contact. Then the Plateau peoples felt the influence of the Plains tribes, who believed a man's best way to success and prestige was in war. When Plateau people did any raiding, it was almost always against another linguistic group, and the raiding party was no more than a few volunteers. They occasionally took prisoners in the western Plateau, where influence from the Northwest Coast was strong. Those captives became slaves, but in time they were assimilated into the community.

Religion

Spirit Helpers. The Plateau Indians believed that success in life depended on the good will and aid of the spirit world, and that it was essential for every man to have a spirit helper. For a woman the helper was less important, but many women sought a guardian spirit anyhow. Having more than one spirit helper gave anyone a greater chance of success. Since so many of the people were in touch with the supernatural world, the line between shamans and others was not clear-cut in the Plateau country.

Indians believed that spirits took the form of animals, plant life, or even places, and that they often taught a song or a chant as a kind of talisman or charm to their devotees. Because spirits appeared only when someone sought them, a boy who wished to make contact with the spirit that was to become his guardian retired to an isolated spot to undergo what is called the vision quest. The spirit might take several nights before it appeared in a vision. After that the spirit would appear in time of trouble, or in dreams, or sometimes at a ceremonial dance given by those who had received it as a vision. Shamans found their guardians in the same way, but they had more helpers, and their helpers were more powerful.

Throughout life, people called on their spirits for help, but if the personal spirits could not or would not help, one could go to a shaman. As in the Arctic and Subarctic, shamans were curers of bad luck and unnatural disturbances brought on by broken taboos, unfriendly spirit contact, or intrusion by foreign objects. They might also be village headmen or leaders of fishing or hunting parties, because their ritual abilities were bound to give a better success than an ordinary man could expect. However, men whose guardian spirits were salmon or deer would lead the fishing and hunting, being especially favored by the spirit in control of the activity. Thus the position of headman or hunt leader had definite ritual and supernatural overtones.

Ceremonies.   Men who shared the same spirit helpers often joined during the winter to hold public ceremonies and dances. These gatherings renewed contact with the guardian spirits, and also with people from neighboring villages. They were also a welcome emotional release, breaking the monotony and working off anxiety and tensions during the cold and dreary months of the year.

Other public activities with ritual significance included the first-fruit ceremonies, celebrating the first catch or plants of the season. As the salmon began their journey to spawn in the inland waters of their birth, a salmon chief, who usually had a salmon spirit helper, thanked the salmon for coming and then caught and ate one, carefully disposing of its bones so that its spirit would not be offended. Such services were designed to placate the spirits of the animals and plants, thank them, praise them, and keep them plentiful in years to come.

Women's Taboos.   Another main focus of the Plateau people's supernatural interests was girls' puberty. Many Indian societies considered the menarche—the onset of menstruation—a time of supernatural importance, and the Plateau people regarded this period with particular awe. As in the Subarctic, it was an event heavy with spiritual meaning; the pubescent girl was supposed to be supercharged with power dangerous to males and their pursuits. Girls were taught never to touch their heads during the menstrual period because for the supernaturals the head was the most important part of the body. If her head itched, a girl learned to scratch with a special scratching stick. In some tribes, girls were taught to drink through straws or tubes, never allowing water to touch their lips. They were separated from the male community, living in a special hut while they were taught by older women to learn and observe menstrual taboos and to keep busy all day long. Such training prepared a girl for an industrious life as wife, mother, and plant collector.

Women did not usually think of menstrual taboos as a burden, but as a way to get out of daily chores and thus a welcome rest. Life for most Indian women was no less hard than that of the men, but they were given little prestige and honor. They were glad to be left alone.

The Nez Perce

Nez percé is French for "pierced nose," but the people of the tribe known by that name never did pierce their noses, as far as we know. Perhaps French explorers attached the name to a variety of tribes, some of which did have that custom. The name is no longer given a French pronunciation, but now is usually pronounced *nez purs.*

Seasonal Life.   The Nez Perce lived in settled villages in the southeast part of the Plateau area, the land that is now Idaho. They lived on fish and many varieties of plants, especially roots. In their food quest, as in other parts of their lives, they were typical of the Plateau Indians. In early summer they would leave their villages to seek the best plant grounds to dig starchy bulbs and tubers. As various bands met in the harvest areas, they found time for games and gambling and general festivities. It was good to be out in the open after winter boredom and isolation. At midsummer they moved on to reap other ripening plant foods, and by late summer they would be at favorite summer fishing sites, where they remained until October. The whole summer season was lived in the open with general freedom.

The return to winter homes in October marked the beginning of cold weather, when it was not so pleasant to be outdoors. The winter encampments or villages were the permanent Nez Perce homes, the place where they belonged, much as we might consider ourselves residents of one town, county, and state, no matter where we might travel during the summer.

Chiefs.   The Nez Perce group was made up of loosely bound villages or bands, each with its own headman or chief. This position of chief, though officially inherited, was really elective, for public opinion made the final decision in seating a new chief. The chief was assisted by an advisory council of important men such as warriors and shamans, who held their positions by prominence and recognized ability. Anyone who proved unworthy was soon replaced, and each village or band was independent of the others in choosing its representatives. The Nez Perce had no overall chief.

Guardian Spirits.   Young Nez Perce sought guardian spirits to help them win success in life. Both boys and girls hoped for a vision, and usually before age ten a child left home to go into mountain wilds and commune with the spirits. Parents decided when children were ready to set out on the vision quest, and told them about the land they would travel through. But outside of that advice, the child was alone. He had been told how he might expect to hear from the spirits, and that he should fast so that the spirits might come quickly. Expecting them to come in the form of an animal, the child, hardly more than an infant, hungry and perhaps frightened, would see an animal or a bird and be more than ready to believe that the supernatural had manifested itself to him. The child would usually find a symbol or fetish of his vision—a strangely shaped or colored stone, a feather, or perhaps a bone, something that seemed to show the spirit had just been there. That was his proof, to be carried whenever he needed spirit help. The spirit also might teach the initiate a song which, like the object, came to be a symbol of spirit power.

The child returned home secure in his vision. He usually sought other spirit helpers, too, making the vision quest a number of times. By adulthood, most Nez Perce thought they had made contact with many supernatural beings. It is easy to imagine what that must have meant. An Indian with many guardian spirits could hear them calling in the forest as trees whispered in the breeze, as clouds drifted across the sky, and as birds flew overhead. What a sense of confidence these signs from his guardians must have given him! The supernatural revealed itself in many ways every day.

Marriage. Parents arranged the marriages, the father of the young man visiting the girl's father, discussing plans, and offering gifts. The bride went to the groom's home when arrangements were complete. After a few weeks, the couple and the man's kinfolk took the gifts to her father's home, where they all partook of a grand feast. The groom's family then received gifts from the girl's family.

Only a few men had more than one wife. No ceremonies honored the later marriages, and no gifts were exchanged, for usually the other wives were sisters of the first. Divorce was simple, occurring at the wish of either husband or wife.

Plains Influence. By the time the Lewis and Clark expedition (the main source of our information) had reached their territory, the Nez Perce had taken on many aspects of Plains culture. They had horses, and were known by other Plateau tribes as rather aggressive. The Shoshoni and Bannock of the Great Basin were traditional Nez Perce enemies, and as competition for horses and buffalo grew, the Nez Perce came to consider the Atsina and some Blackfoot bands of the Plains their foes. The Nez Perce remained at peace with most Plateau tribes. They were in a favored economic position, being close to the buffalo-filled plains, and they took buffalo hides on regular trade excursions to the rapids on the Columbia River, the Dalles, to exchange for goods from the coast, especially shells.

The Klamath of Southern Oregon

Environment. The Klamath are difficult to place in a culture area. They were geographically and culturally transitional and showed traits of the Plateau, the Northwest Coast, California, and the Desert Basin. The isolation and separatism of the local groups were typical of California, as was the importance of seeds in the diet. Characteristic of the Basin were seasonal deficits in food supply and the absence of hereditary chiefs. The importance of fish in the Klamath diet, their simple first-fruit rituals, and their practice of head deformation show influence from both the Plateau and the Northwest Coast. Other Plateau characteristics were their house types and their linguistic affiliation. The Klamath probably took their armor of rods or tough hides from the Northwest Coast. The crude snowshoes that helped them move through the deep snows were ultimately derived from the Subarctic. The Klamath language belongs to the Penutian phylum, having its closest affiliations in the Plateau.

Klamath territory was mostly stream-watered marshland, and their greatest food resources were fish, mussels, and water birds. Compared to the Desert Basin, subsistence was bounteous for the Klamath; compared to the Northwest Coast, it was meager. Winters were long and cold with heavy snowfalls. Food was scarce at that time of year, and had to be stored in summer for the lean months.

Home Life. The winter settlement was a village of earth lodges and communal storage pits and a few domed, mat-walled huts. The earth lodges were excavated two or three feet down for better insulation and the entrance was a hole in the roof, which also let smoke out. Lodges were taken down each spring, because they became soggy from melting snows and vermin-ridden and smelly from the people and fires inside. Each fall when the families returned from their summer rounds they rebuilt the lodges.

The Klamath also built small semiunderground sweathouses, in which they

A reconstructed pit house. The roof, as seen from above, showing hatchway, rafter construction, sheathing of poles, and covering of earth (left); cross-section displaying pit, center posts, roof framework, and notched log ladder (right).

Top view   Cross-section

created steam by pouring water over hot stones. Both men and women used the sweathouses, though not at the same time. The men would sweat before a hunt to purify themselves ritually, but sweating was often just a relaxation as well. It was followed by a plunge in a stream, even in the cold of winter.

The Klamath's main social unit was the nuclear family, but the extended family was almost as important. They traced their kinship through both males and females, with slight emphasis on the male line. Most earth lodges were occupied by extended families, though the shaman might have one to himself, and the hamlet was governed by a loose council of respected men limited by group consensus. No leader had power without support of the community. In contrast with the social pattern of the Northwest Coast, wealth did not confer decision-making powers.

Clusters of hamlets or villages made up the group called a *tribelet,* of which the Klamath had six. They sometimes fought each other; the Klamath never had strong tribal identity, though they recognized themselves as related and a cultural unit speaking the same language.

Shamans. Shamans were the only specialists, serving as part-time curers and entertainers. With the guests supplying the food, their performances were given in midwinter and lasted five days and nights. For part of the time children were not permitted because the spirit power might be too dangerous for them. The shamans had assistants who helped summon the spirits and generally aided in the performance, which involved dancing and singing, calling the spirits, and tricks such as swallowing fire. It helped while away the long winter hours, and it was also an important ritual that demonstrated the shaman's spiritual competence and connections with the supernatural world.

The Food Quest. By late winter, food supplies ran low, and some years brought real hunger before fresh food became available. In March, the suckers, fish that were to the Klamath what salmon were to more northerly people, began their runs up the rivers. The Klamath observed a first sucker ceremony, and also caught salmon and trout. They had dugout canoes, which they submerged in the mud of the marshes and streams during winter to keep them from drying out and splitting. They also fished on the lakes at night by torchlight.

After spring fishing slowed down, the Klamath moved to flats and meadows to find camas bulbs and other edible roots and plants and cattail reeds for basketry. All summer, seed and berry gathering went on. Huckleberries, chokecherries, wild plums, and others were eaten fresh or dried and stored for winter. However, it was the use of water-lily seeds as a food resource that set the Klamath and the Modoc, their closely related neighbors to the south, apart from other tribes. In the thousands of acres of marshland and lake, pond lilies grew, and in August their seeds ripened. So important was this crop that the seeds were not harvested until a shaman had performed a simple first-fruits ritual. Women, children, and old men collected the wild pond-lily seeds from dugout canoes while the younger men hunted deer, elk, and mountain sheep. The summer encampments at the lily beds were a time of recreation and relaxation, but as summer came to an end, the Klamath returned to the winter sites to rebuild their earth lodges and prepare for the cold weather.

Work and Success. The Klamath philosophy of life was that hard work would be rewarded with tangible goods and respect from others. Poverty was the result of laziness. Headmen were those who demonstrated by their many

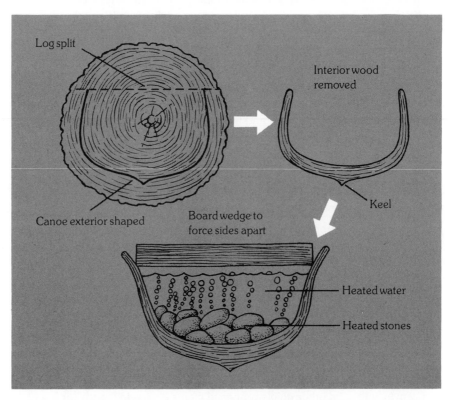

Dugout canoes were constructed by various steps. First a log was split, and the exterior of the canoe was shaped. The interior wood was then removed with adzes and fire. Next, the interior was filled with water heated by hot stones. The sides of the canoe were forced apart while heated and moist, and a crossbeam was wedged in to stabilize the shape of the sides. The water and stones were subsequently removed, the dugout dried, paddlers' seats installed, and a prow and stern might be added and decorated.

CHARACTERISTICS OF THE PLATEAU TRIBES

Clothing	Food production	Equipment	Shelter	Social and political organization	Religion	Warfare
Fur and fiber robes Leggings Tunics Skirts Sandals Snowshoes (Klamath)	Fishing Hunting Gathering	Spears Nets Hooks Weirs Traps Basketry Armor of rods and hides (Klamath) Dugout canoe (Klamath)	Ground-level, pole-and-mat dwellings Pit houses of logs and sod Earth lodges Sweathouses	Families Bands Villages —the main political unit. governed by headmen Chiefs and councils (Nez Perce)	Myths Spirit helpers First fruit ceremonies Shamans Vision Quest	Generally peaceful Small raids

possessions and their ability to support several wives that they had labored long and hard. The Klamath never amassed as much wealth as the Northwest people, but the idea of getting ahead was dominant, and even those born poor had a chance to work hard and make a success in life. The successful shared with their kinfolk and neighbors, of course, but it was considered demeaning to be dependent on others. It was a very individualistic philosophy, and everyone was expected to strive constantly to better his lot in life. Klamath believed it was good to work, and judged people by their industriousness and material achievement.

THE NORTHWEST COAST

Tlingit-Haida
Creation Myth

XXXXXXXXXXXXXXXX

Before the world came into being, a spirit ruled from the clouds. Beneath his realm was nothing but water. Raven was servant to the spirit. One day Raven was far from his home in the sky and became very weary. He flew on and on over the vast body of water, but could find no place to rest. Finally, he began to beat the water with his wings. He beat so hard that waves on each side of him rose up high, almost to the clouds. The waves suddenly became rocks that increased and spread into islands. Sandy beaches formed, and eventually plants grew from the sand.

Raven decided the land would be his, but after a while he grew lonely all by himself. He took two large piles of shells and from them he created two human beings, both women. Soon the women complained that Raven should not have made two women; one should have been a man. So Raven transformed one into a man, and that made everyone happy. That first pair was the ancestor of the Indians who lived on the islands.

Unfortunately, it was not long before the people began to quarrel, and they quarreled and quarreled. At last the spirit came down from his cloud kingdom and warned them that they would be destroyed if they could not learn to live in peace. And for a while, the quarreling ceased. It started once again, however, and the spirit decided to punish the people. He took the most obstinate and changed them into cedar trees. He then told the others, "If you can learn to live in peace, you will have these lovely trees for many things: planks for houses, trunks for canoes, bark and roots for

*mats and baskets. From inner bark you will make clothing." The people
had learned their lesson well, and from that time they have used cedar
trees for all those things.*

XXXXXXXXXXXXXXXX

The Environment

**The Northwest Coast culture area reaches more than 2,000 miles from
the panhandle of Alaska on the north to the northern tip of California on
the south.** It is called coastal because it covers very little territory east to west; it
is hardly a hundred miles at the widest, confined between the Pacific Ocean on
one side and the Coast Mountains of Canada and the Cascade Mountains of
the United States on the other. It includes a partly submerged offshore mountain chain forming many large and small islands, of which the most important
are the Queen Charlotte Islands and Vancouver Island.

The ocean, warmed by the Japanese Current, moistens and tempers the pre-
vailing westerly winds, and even in winter the mountains block off most cold air
coming from the interior. These geographic conditions cause intense fogs and
precipitation, for as the moisture-laden ocean winds rise against the mountain
slopes, the air is cooled to the precipitation point. The native people needed little clothing, and used it for protection against rain more than cold.

The western mountain slopes are covered with temperate-zone rain forest of
spruce, hemlock, cedar, and giant Douglas fir, some rising 250 feet above the
ground and fog to reach the sunlight. Firewood and building materials came
from these forests, and materials for basketry, cord, rope, mats, clothing, and
bedding, as well as canoes, boxes, implements, and utensils. The fringes of
these great forests are home to game animals, including deer, moose, elk, and
several varieties of bear. There are mountain goats and sheep, and fur-bearing
species like mink, beaver, and fox. However, the sea is a far richer resource, providing whale, porpoise, seal, sea lion, sea otter, and many kinds of fish. Halibut
may weigh up to a quarter ton each; sturgeon are twice as large. And there are
shoals of herring and smelt, cod, and the *oulachon*—the candlefish—so called
because, with a wick run through the body, it burns like a candle. Salmon were
once so plentiful that it has been said the people could have lived on them
alone. The tidal flats yield shellfish, one of which, the geoduck clam, is so large
that six of them might provide a meal for a large family. In spring and fall,
clouds of waterfowl fly by on their migrations, challenging hunters. This wealth
of food supported an estimated native population of 250,000.

Prehistory

Archaeology has been so limited along the Pacific coast that we do not know much about the region's prehistory. New excavations may change our tentative picture at any time, but it now appears that the classical Northwest Coast adaptations were produced by two cultural influences, one from the Plateau foragers and the other from the north, from the Eskimo or possibly even directly from Asia. These two traditions seem to have come together and evolved to suit the environment, producing the known cultures there. The evidence that the Coastal way of life developed from the hunting, fishing, and gathering adaptation of the Plateau people is fairly direct. Evidence for Eskimoid or Asiatic influences is indirect and rather tenuous, but certain whaling practices and myths indicate contact between Eskimo and Northwest Indians in late prehistoric times.

The specialized subsistence practice of the Plateau people shows up in Northwest Coast sites dated at more than 5,000 years ago, and this pattern extends down to the coastlands, where the major rivers empty into the Pacific. A simple basis on which later people could build appears to have been present from ancient times. Most prehistorians also see a veneer of Asiatic or Eskimo traits diffusing into the area, probably by way of the coast. The latter traits show up archaeologically in tools such as semicircular knives of ground slate and harpoons, and also in the physical anthropology of the region. The skin tone of the northern people was much lighter than that of other Indian peoples before contact. Alexander Mackenzie, the first European to reach one of the tribes, the Bella Coola, wrote in 1793 that he saw Indians with brown rather than dark brown or black hair, and with light-colored eyes. The Northwest Coast people also have much heavier facial and body hair than other Indians, and the epicanthic eye fold is more common among these people. All this suggests an infusion of Eskimo or Aleut genes.

Wherever the people came from, by 1000 B.C. they had established a genuine Northwest Coast tradition, and by A.D. 1000 that tradition reached the form and covered the territory in which the Europeans found it. How the spread occurred, though, is still a puzzle for archaeologists to solve.

Native Life

In aboriginal times, the richest providers of food were the rivers. As often as seven times a year, spawning salmon filled the waters so thickly, observers said, that one could walk across the water on their backs. Northwest fishermen speared, netted, or trapped them by the ton, and dried or smoked them for future use.

In terms of the food supply, the usual standard for wealth among nonindustrial people, the native peoples of the Northwest Coast were wealthy indeed. Food stocks of course must have varied from tribe to tribe, and were not always bountiful, yet the people of this area were so blessed with natural resources that they reached the limits of complexity attainable in a hunting and gathering economy. They built huge, durable houses; they made large dugout canoes that could carry sixty people or more; they were excellent craftsmen and artists, decorating nearly everything they made; they staged elaborate musical dramas and ceremonies; they engaged in intricate economic activities; and they developed a complicated system of social stratification.

We separate the ethnographic area of the Northwest Coast into northern, central, and southern divisions. Their basic adaptations were strikingly similar, but regional differences make the division useful. The best known northern groups were Tlingit, Haida, and Tsimshian; central groups were Bella Coola, Kwakiutl, and Nootka; and in the south were Coast Salish, Quileute, and Chinook. Near the present California-Oregon boundary, the culture areas blended, and we have to assign tribes to one area or the other arbitrarily. We place the Yurok, Karok, and Hupa in the California area, though others have put them in the Northwest Coast area.

Highest level/bedroom compartments

Middle level/sitting area

Lowest level

Fire

Chief's compartment

Door

Ocean

A generalized floor plan of a Northwest Coast house. On the lowest level this rectangular dwelling had a fire in the center, with a smoke hole above it. The middle level contained the sitting area, while the highest level provided spaces for bedroom compartments and the chief's compartment. The house contained no windows and usually only one door.

A Northwest Coast village, probably Kwakiutl, showing house construction, canoes, and totem poles.

The nature of the region's resources made it inevitable that all the inhabitants would settle on the coast or river banks and spend their lives near the water instead of the mountains inland. The topography meant that travel was easier and faster in coastal waters than overland. From Puget Sound northward, mountains rise steeply from the sea, and the coast is cut by deep fjords. With boats men could move among protected channels and exploit the marine life.

Technology

In this densely forested country, the main building material was wood, above all yellow and red cedar. It was durable, yet soft enough to work with stone or bone adzes and chisels. And because this kind of wood has long, straight, parallel fibers, great planks could be split off the logs with hardwood or antler wedges to make siding for houses. The planks were grooved or notched so that they could be joined without pegs. The result was rectangular dwellings sixty feet long and perhaps fifty feet wide, their gabled roofs supported on enormous cedar beams held up by massive cedar posts. The frameworks of most houses were designed to be permanent structures, but their siding was not part of the weight-bearing structure and could be dismantled whenever their owners had reason to do so, as when they set up housekeeping at seasonal fishing sites. At each site, the family maintained a house frame to which they attached the siding and roof planks. When moving time came again, the planks were stripped off and carried to a new site on the canoes that also moved the family. Sometimes the planks were lashed across two canoes, forming a useful deck.

Boats and Totem Poles.   The people stretched cedar logs, hollowed with fires and adzes, into canoe shape by partially filling them with heated water to soften the wood. They built canoes in many sizes, small ones for travel on streams, larger ones for ocean fishing and whaling, and great sixty-foot canoes for trade, warfare, and ceremonial visits. Cedar logs also were the medium for an important art form, now known as the totem pole. Elaborately carved with figures of animals and supernatural beings, the poles honored dead chiefs, marked the graves of important people, served as portals to houses, and generally were a sort of coat-of-arms indicating the owner's rank and title.

Boxes and Masks.   Cedar planks also provided the boxes that served as home furnishings, for storage, and for coffins. These wooden boxes were ingeniously made. Woodworkers cut a board to the shape of a cross, then scored it so that the side pieces could be folded up into place and pegged or sewn together. Fitted with covers, smoothed with abrasive sandstone or sharkskin, and usually

A carved and painted Tlingit food storage box (height 22 inches; width 13½ inches), whose sides have been made from one piece of red cedar. The design depicts a mythical sea spirit.

intricately painted or carved, these containers stored almost everything from whale, seal, or candlefish oil to sinew cords and spare points for arrows.

Wood carvers turned blocks of cedar into ceremonial masks, conventionalized yet vivid representations of men, beasts, and supernaturals, sometimes equipped with leather hinges and strings by which the faces could be opened to reveal another mask inside. Even cedar bark had multiple uses. Its tough fibers were woven into blankets, mats for covering walls and floors, openwork baskets for carrying fish, or baskets so tightly made that they held water. Woven cedar fibers also made hats and raincoats.

Other Materials. Though wood was the main natural resource, the craftsmen also used other raw materials. Various fibers were inventively used, such as strands of kelp, twisted into fishlines. Coastal people fashioned projectile points and knives from horn, bone, and stone, but in general they used far less stone than other Indians. Perhaps the most important stone implements were the axes and adzes for hewing wood. But craftsmen also used woodworking equipment with blades of bones and especially shell, honed to a fine edge.

Men made tambourine drums by stretching rawhide over a hoop, but hide was otherwise of little use in that humid climate: when soggy it stretched out of shape and tore easily, and when dried, it became stiff. Matting was far more use-

Kwakiutl woven matting used for clothing.

ful, and the women wove poncho-like rain garments and basketry rain hats. Another important raw material was mountain-sheep horn, which was carved into spoons or steamed and spread to make bowls. Deer hooves, goat hooves, and puffin beaks made rattles or jingles when attached to dance aprons, bracelets, or anklets.

Social and Political Organization

Tribes. It will be convenient to use the term *tribe* to refer to the linguistic groups of the Northwest Coast, but it is a term that must be used with caution, since it does not really correspond to the native unit. In fact, this English word has caused quite a bit of legal trouble in attempts to determine economic and political rights and claims. The anthropologist's use of the name Tlingit, Kwakiutl, or any other name really indicates a linguistic group that had no political unity in the people's minds. They saw themselves instead as villages or kin groups such as lineages, clans, or extended families.

The tribe—that is, the linguistic group—had no political figure with power or authority over the whole group. For instance, the Tlingit had no chief or leader who could speak for them as a whole. Those who spoke Tlingit recognized a relationship in their common language, and they had marital and kin ties in many communities, but their real loyalties were to the local group and not the linguistic group. While this is true of Indian societies generally, it applies especially to the peoples of the Northwest Coast, where villages speaking the same language might raid each other, a situation far from common elsewhere. The local groups were independent, and though they might form alliances with each other, the entire linguistic group never acted as one nation.

The northern tribes of the Northwest Coast were matrilineal, that is, they traced descent through the women. All the others reckoned descent through both mother and father, with some emphasis on the paternal side in matters of group membership and inheritance. In the north the local leadership was hereditary; in the south, wealth generally determined social rank and political position.

Social Rank. The northern and central emblems of rank were crests or coats of arms that showed the owner's ancestry; totem poles were one kind of crest. The system of social ranking among the Northwest Coast people was unique in native America. One anthropologist has called it rank without social class, because individuals were graded rather than classes of individuals. However, loose general groupings were discernible as chiefs, nobles, commoners, and slaves. Within each of these general categories, except for the slaves, there was a ranking of statuses from high to low.

The individual's social position was not totally rigid. One could raise his own rank or that of his children or heirs, sometimes by using wealth, sometimes by inheriting a higher position from another branch of the family that was in danger of dying out through lack of suitable heirs. Some promotion in social rank was in the chief's power—he could reward one of his group with a higher title.

Social position was certainly tied in with kinship, much as the rank and position of king is inherited in European societies. Yet inheritance was subject to limitations. The right to assume a higher position had to be validated formally at a potlatch (to be discussed in the next section), and the rest of the group had to approve the new heir. Consequently, social rank did not depend solely on heredity or wealth, but was a combination of the two, plus the individual's achievements. Even people with very low rank, however, still had basic rights within their local group. Only slaves were truly without rights, and even they could be ransomed (for most slaves were war captives) or could sometimes buy their own freedom. Slavery was often a temporary condition, but it was a shameful one. Occasionally an owner would kill slaves to show his wealth and power. Male slaves were killed more often than women and children, probably because they were harder to control.

The Potlatch

Events of social importance were proclaimed at the feast called a *potlatch* from a Chinook word. Potlatching took many forms within a group, and varied considerably from group to group. At the potlatch, social position was formally validated. For instance, when an old chief died, the new chief gave a potlatch to announce his new rank, and all the guests showed by their presence that they accepted his claim and supported him. A potlatch given for a position as important as that of chief always lasted several days, with singing, dancing, drama, and games as well as feasting. The hosts invited entire nearby villages and spent months on preparations for feeding the guests—sometimes more than a year. Large numbers of people were fed, and important guests were given valuable gifts. Among the Northwest Coast people, it was a virtue to distribute wealth, not accumulate it. One accumulated only to have something to redistribute.

The chief depended on his entire kin or local group to support him in preparing and building up supplies. Though much food was eaten and many presents were given, a potlatch was a kind of investment, for the givers were guaranteed a return potlatch in the future. The potlatch, then, was a type of social security regardless of its immediate purpose, because future return was assured. It was also a way of redistributing the community's wealth not only with food but with gifts, for everyone in the community came. The poor (even this area had some, orphans, widows, and people of very low rank) all got food, blankets, and equipment, and had an enjoyable time they could not have afforded on their own. The giver's kin group expressed its solidarity by helping with preparations and acting as co-hosts, and shared in the glory and esteem of giving a great potlatch. They too would be included in future potlatching when the guests repaid their obligations.

Other events worth celebrating had their potlatches too, but their style was far less lavish. The rites of passage when a boy came of age or a girl reached marriageable age, a new career, unusual success, even birthdays, all called for formal recognition. One could give only two or three really grand potlatches in a lifetime, but having lesser ones was a regular thing.

Potlatches also were given for services rendered, like help in a house-raising, and as a face-saving device. The guests would help to build the house, carve and raise the posts, and perform ceremonial offices—that is, guests of low rank helped with the hard labor while their chiefs visited with the host. But the host paid the guest chiefs in bounteous gifts, which they then distributed to their followers who had done the work. A high-ranking individual upon whom some misfortune fell or who suffered an embarrassment or an indignity might give a potlatch to wipe out his embarrassment, and at the same time demonstrate his right to high rank. The publicity following such a potlatch reestablished his self-esteem. He had acted the part of an important man and was recognized as one by the community.

In later times, when European disease had reduced the population, many titles fell vacant as whole family lines died out. A wild, sometimes quite destruc-

A Tlingit potlach. At left, a man wears an overgarment of cloth or canvas on which native designs have been painted. Several men are also wearing nose rings.

tive form of potlatching, the rival potlach, developed. Potlatching had always
been competitive, but in the last decades of the nineteenth century it seems to
have gone beyond any past extremes. People who had no inherited rights to
titles but who had become wealthy in trade goods beggared themselves giving
away presents, to gain the community's recognition for their assumed titles and
crests. Anyone who had the wealth could compete for these titles, and such rivalry produced some potlatches at which goods were destroyed, foods thrown
away, and occasionally houses set on fire (whether by design or accident is uncertain). These flamboyant potlatches have had a lot of attention, and were important in showing how the culture was changing, but they were not typical. They
were merely the way the newly rich tried to win the prestige of "old money."

With their potlatches the Coastal people confirmed their social positions,
distributed wealth to the community, and used food much of which was
not storable. Potlatches helped integrate social groups by making kinsmen more
dependent on each other, and were investments that would be returned, often
with interest, in the future. They probably also channeled aggression into a
harmless kind of rivalry that helped avoid more physical and socially destructive
conflict.

Northwest Coast Art

The Northwest Coast people produced what many consider the finest aboriginal
art north of Mexico. To see the Northwest style is to recognize it forever. Regional variations are visible, but the whole central and northern area did have
one recognizable style. It is highly conventionalized art, its stylistic traditions rigidly adhered to by the makers; it should appeal to those who enjoy cubism and
geometric designs. The style was applied in clothing, basketry, and the many
forms of wood carving: totem poles, boxes, masks, grave markers, and house
posts. It was a style unique in native America, resembling nothing in the art
forms of the Southwest, Plains, East, or other areas. Authorities who suggest
that the style shows influences from Asia or Polynesia have offered no evidence
beyond stylistic inferences of the sort that are suggested as proof for trans-
Pacific contacts.

Decorative art in the northern area was mostly two-dimensional, applied to
flat surfaces. Lateral symmetry was the hallmark of this art: the figures were
treated as though they had been split down the spine and spread out to either
side of it. Northern artists disliked bare space, filling all areas with their designs.
Central area artists had a style more like sculpture in treatment and use, and
stressed mass and movement. Southern art forms were less dramatic, confined
to simple tool embellishment, not large-scale design. Anyone who speaks of
Northwest Coast art normally has the central and northern areas in mind.

This Tlingit coat, woven from goat hair on a cedar-bark base, could be afforded only by the wealthy. The intricate geometric designs often indicated the genealogy of the wearer.

Northwest Coast designs depicted the supernatural or animal ancestors of lineage or kin groups, displayed as symbols of noble descent. Bear, Beaver, Eagle, Raven, Whale, and Wolf were the clan ancestors that appeared most often as crests or symbols. Artists followed the traditional ways of representing the animals by emphasizing one or two features: the whale was indicated by its large dorsal fin, the beaver by its large front teeth and broad, crosshatched tail, and the bear by its sharp claws. This was a thoroughly social kind of art, demonstrating, for all to see, the crests which were so highly esteemed.

The Chilkat division of the Tlingit tribe was famous for the fabrics they wove from cedar fiber and mountain-goat hair, used as ceremonial blankets, dance shirts, and skirts. The true loom was unknown on the Northwest Coast. The Chilkat blanket weaver twined horizontal threads with her fingers through vertical threads, suspended from a bar, and worked from top to bottom of the design. Like art applied to containers, houses, and crests, the Chilkat woven goods were designed as proof of prestige and wealth.

Copper brought from deposits at the Copper River in Alaska was beaten into one- to four-foot shield-shaped plaques called *coppers,* which were important in potlatch exchanges. Later artists engraved or embossed designs on sheet copper obtained from traders. Coppers were valuable and thus made gifts of great

Chilkat blanket (64 inches high; 54 inches wide) made of goat hair. Blankets of this size were usually worn as capes by the leading members of aristocratic families to display their family crests.

prestige and significance. Each time a copper was given away, its value grew; on extraordinary occasions, such as the succession of a major chief, one might be broken and thrown into the sea or the fire. In later times when potlatching became fiercely competitive, destroying a copper would challenge guests to give an even grander potlatch or sacrifice a copper of equal or greater value.

Tribes of the Northwest Coast
The Tlingit

The Tlingit language is related to Athabaskan. The most northerly of the Northwest Coast peoples, the Tlingit occupied the coast from Yakutat Bay in Alaska south to Cape Fox in British Columbia. They were divided into fourteen subtribes, the best known being the Chilkat, who made the blankets we have described. Being far to the north, the Tlingit showed traits also found among Eskimo groups. The two cultures probably were in contact, and borrowing moved both ways. The Tlingit also carried on trade with the interior Athabaskans of the Subarctic, getting from them copper, furs, and tools.

Like the Northwest Coast in general, Tlingit territory had high rainfall and mild temperatures. All the raw materials and vegetable foodstuffs of the lush, temperate-zone rain forest were available to the Tlingit. However, their northerly location meant greater snowfall than in the south. Consequently many artifacts of the Subarctic, like snowshoes, appeared in Tlingit territory.

Seasonal Life.   The Tlingit had winter homes in villages on the coast or at the edge of a river. A stockade ran around the winter village for protection from raiders. The dwellings were large plank houses of the sort described, each housing several matrilineally related families. Each family had its own apartment within the house, divided by partitions along the walls. The center of the house was on a lower level than the sides and contained the hearth. Fish were hung from the beams to dry. Outside, racks were set up for drying fish during sunny weather. Lean-tos against the outer walls of the dwellings housed menstruating women or those giving birth. At one side of the village was the community cemetery.

Summer encampments were more casual. Families built temporary houses (Tlingit did not bring sideboard planking from the winter homes), but they lived in the open too, moving throughout the territory that belonged to their kin group. Kin groups also owned the fishing sites and controlled the hunting and collecting areas. The people followed their summer pursuits only in the areas where their kin connections gave them rights.

In winter, the Tlingit caught halibut and trout for their main diet and collected

mussels along the coastline back at their "home" settlements. They also hunted
fur-bearing animals at that time because the pelts were in prime condition. In
spring the Tlingit women began their task of plant collecting, which lasted until
late fall. Men caught candlefish with dip nets and traps. Those fish were boiled
with hot stones in a wooden container, sometimes in a canoe, and the oil was
skimmed off and stored. Throughout the year animals were hunted and fish
caught and processed, some to be eaten immediately, some to be stored for
winter when food was less easily obtained. Drying was the common means of
preservation, although some food was stored in oil. As everywhere in this culture
area, salmon was an important food; the Tlingit caught many varieties, among
them coho, chum, and sockeye, from July through December. They took most
with weirs that directed the fish into a trap. The Tlingit also hunted sea mammals like seals, sea otters, dolphins, and sea lions.

Social Organization. Tlingit society was divided into two groups, each called
a *moiety,* from the French word for "half." The moieties were Raven and Wolf,
and every Tlingit belonged to one or the other. A man had to choose a wife
from the other moiety, and children belonged to the moiety of their mother because descent was matrilineal. That is, Wolf men had Raven wives, and all their
children, boys as well as girls, were Ravens. Each moiety was further divided into
smaller groups called lineages, or matrilineages, because membership in them
too was inherited from the mothers. One had to marry not only outside his own
moiety, but outside his lineage. The lineages had names, owned crests and ceremonies, and were headed by chiefs.

Moiety division, common among American Indian societies, often was a way
of giving mutual help. Among the Tlingit, a midwife assisted at births in the opposite moiety, never at births within her own, and the opposite moiety members
performed all tasks connected with death, such as care of the body and preparations for cremation, which was standard with the Tlingit. The opposite moiety
members mourned ritually and carved mortuary poles and mortuary boxes to
contain the remains. The moiety of the deceased gave a potlatch and presented
gifts to those of the opposite moiety who had taken part in the mortuary services.

Adult Tlingit of the higher ranks were expected to conduct themselves with restraint and dignity, and they encouraged their children to copy adult behavior.
Parents rarely punished children physically; instead they shamed them when they
behaved badly and praised them for good behavior. A regular part of childhood
training was in behavior suitable to their rank. At the tender age of six or seven,
boys moved to the home of one of their mother's brothers, where they learned
how to fill their positions in life and became familiar with the traditions of the
matrilineage.

The maternal uncle had authority over his sister's children. Because children belonged to their mother's matrilineage, the adult males of their lineage group were the uncles on the mother's side—never the fathers, who belonged to a different lineage. Usually one uncle took on the responsibility for a boy; the choice was expected to be mutual in that the boy took an interest in his uncle's calling (carver, hunter, shaman, or whatever), wished to be trained in that career, and expected to inherit his uncle's position. The important titles and their crests, however, usually passed to the oldest nephew if the child was generally competent.

Marriage.   Daughters of high-ranking families were carefully guarded, not only to secure their virginity but also to keep them out of the sunlight, for light skin was prized. At her first menstruation a girl of high rank was secluded for a whole year (a commoner, two or three months), during which the women of her matrilineage taught her about lineage traditions and also the behavior expected of her high estate. A female slave attended her during this seclusion. Soon after its end it was expected that she would marry. Her parents' wealth and position were known, and her own rank depended mostly on the *bridewealth* that had been paid for her mother. This bridewealth consisted of gifts the family of the groom gave to the bride's family, not as payment for her, but to compensate the family for her loss and because giving gifts was common at any social event in the Northwest Coast area. Just as individuals were graded, bridewealth followed rank, important parents receiving more for their daughters than low-ranking families. Parents hoped of course for a favorable marriage with a high bridewealth.

The bride had to marry outside both her lineage and her moiety. A mother's brother's son or a father's sister's son was the most frequent choice; that union kept wealth within a close kin group and between people of relatively equal rank. The bride's parents sponsored the wedding and feasting, but the groom gave a potlatch for his new in-laws, and the couple usually moved in with one or the other set of parents. High-ranking, rich men often had more than one wife, but the first wife held the highest position.

Aggression.   In spite of the mutual obligations binding members of opposite moieties, hostilities sometimes erupted between them, and even between matrilineages within the same moiety. To settle disagreements, feuds, or other conflicts, the hostile parties exchanged goods. There was a well-developed sense of "blood money," that is, payment for transgressions.

The Tlingit often conducted raids to take slaves or get revenge. Warriors wore armored jerkins or jackets made of rods or tough hide coverings, masks, and wooden helmets; they carried spears, clubs, and copper-bladed daggers. Warring groups took scalps, and sometimes impaled whole heads on poles and carried them home on exhibit. Warfare was glorified, and to be defeated was shameful. To restore peace, the combatants gave a series of potlatches at which hostages were exchanged and captives might be ransomed. Those not ransomed remained as slaves.

Tlingit Religion. Shamanism was the heart of the Tlingit religious practices. The shamans were thought by other Tlingit and by members of other Northwest Coast societies to be very powerful. They controlled supernatural spirits which

Tlingit carved wooden helmet (height, 9 inches; width, 10 inches) decorated with tufts of hair.

they inherited matrilineally: that is, shamans passed their spirits to their sisters' sons. The spirits were thought to leave the body at death and enter the body of the new shaman, who revealed that he had been chosen by going into a deep trance. The new shaman then had to demonstrate his power, after which he inherited his uncle's ritual paraphernalia. Shamans were distinguished from the rest of the community by their hair, which was never cut or combed. They identified the spirits they could contact with representative masks, and they also possessed charms, amulets, and rattles that they used in ceremonies. As in many other tribes, shamans were curers of unnatural afflictions, which they relieved by sucking or blowing out the cause. Women could be shamans, but very few were.

Like the Plateau peoples, Tlingit observed simple first-salmon rites as well as rituals to honor other species that supplied their sustenance, but none of these public ceremonials was as important to them as to tribes in the south. Tlingit men were expected to have spirit helpers, but might inherit them as the shamans did their powers. The vision that a man sought came from among the spirits associated with his matrilineage. An unimportant man of low rank could develop into a shaman by finding more spirits, and more potent ones, than ordinary persons had. Being able to contact the spirit world was a means of raising one's status and increasing prestige and wealth, for clients paid for shamans' services. No one, though, could accumulate enough wealth by shamanistic practices to rival a high-ranking wealthy man.

The Nootka of Vancouver Island

The Nootka occupied the western coast of Vancouver Island, a region buffeted by strong winds and heavy ocean waves caused by the violent southeasterly storms crashing into narrow bays. Fishing and whaling encampments were built on the seacoast, but the villages were sheltered on inlets some distance from the coast.

In most ways, Nootka life varied little from that of other tribes in this culture area. The winter village was the permanent community site, with houses of removable plank walls. As elsewhere, these planks were taken down and carried to the summer camps.

Social Organization. The Nootka had no moieties, clans, or lineages. They were organized *bilaterally:* their placement in social groups and inheritance ran through both men and women, with perhaps a slight preference for the paternal line. Extended families were the real units of society. They held land, including fishing grounds, berry and plant tracts, and shellfish beds, and also intangible property such as the rights to crests, titles, and ceremonies. Each extended family had a family head. Heads of the important families were the village chiefs. At a wedding, the father of the bride could bestow some of his family crests on his daughter, to be held in custody by his new son-in-law for his future grandchildren.

Among the northern Nootka groups, extended families joined into larger units, sometimes referred to as confederacies, but among the southerners the extended families and the village in which they lived remained the only social and political units. In the north, the highest-ranking chief (chiefs too had recognized grades) acted as representative of the confederacy under pressures from the outside, like war. Where the people did not organize in confederacies, each settlement was governed by the highest-ranking head of the extended families composing the community. A few noble families were the core of each local group, and they were responsible for its well-being, because they performed the rituals and saw that the taboos were obeyed. These were the privileged, but the commoners were related to them, usually being younger lines of the family. They owed the chiefs allegiance in return for participating in the rights to fishing and hunting grounds. Here again, social classes were not clear-cut; individuals, not classes, were ranked, and the chiefs depended on their non-noble followers and relatives for help in many pursuits, especially potlatching, which no one could manage alone.

Whaling.   The Nootka differed most from other tribes of the Northwest Coast in their way of pursuing whales, which suggested contact with Eskimo whalers. A whaling party set out in a dugout canoe large enough to hold a crew of eight and to stow lines and floats. The whalers and oarsmen wore nothing but oils and clay smeared on their skin and hats for protection from the sun. Sometimes their faces were painted in designs with ritual meaning.

The perils of whaling were recognized by the Nootka community and by the crew, who observed rituals and taboos before going out to sea. The canoe owners and harpooners, men of high rank, had contact with important spirits. Their positions were handed down in family lines, as were charms helpful in whaling. One charm might be the skull of an ancestor who had been outstandingly successful as a whaler. The charms and spirit tokens were kept in a box that was taken along on the canoe. The captain also spoke to the whale spirits, though without using the word "whale," which was taboo during a hunt. Whales were referred to as "noble ladies," and the captain spoke magic words to entice them to come and be caught.

While the crew was on a hunt, the captain's wife lay without moving at home. She symbolized the whale and by lying quietly she kept the whale quiet. Her husband had not slept with her for some time before the hunt, nor had any of the crew had sexual relations with their wives. Besides these sexual taboos, the crew observed dietary restrictions, and if any of the crew or the captain broke the taboos, there would be no kill or it would be a very difficult hunt.

When the captain's wife was informed of the strike, she began a chant asking the whale to come to the village, where it would be most welcome. After the exhausting battle, swimmers from the boat would tie the dead whale's mouth shut and attach tow lines to pull the animal laboriously to shore. The villagers greeted the crew joyously on the beach, and the captain's wife came to continue her ritual observances on the shore. She greeted the dead whale, welcomed it to the village, and brought it a drink of fresh water.

With blubber knives, the whale was cut up, a piece being carefully conserved for the captain for a special ritual. Women turned the blubber to oil by stone-boiling it in cooking boxes after cutting off pieces for guests, chiefs, and commoners in order of rank. The captain's own kinfolk received their shares in private, then everyone joined in a feast.

Dead whales sometimes drifted ashore, and the Nootka treated these chance events as another form of whale hunting. They performed rituals to make them happen more often, just as they did to ensure successful hunts by harpooning. Human corpses or skulls were used in the whaling ritual, not because the Nootka lacked respect for the dead—indeed, they feared and respected them greatly—but because remains were considered extremely potent magic. Whalers built a shrine away from the houses, where they placed the bodies, or sometimes carved images, around the figure of a whale. The chief, the harpooner, or the captain from families owning these rites (no one else could use them) was always a ritual specialist along with his other activities. He bathed, abstained from food and sex, and spoke his incantations and sang his songs nightly in front of his shrine.

Canoes. The Nootka also had a smaller sailing canoe that might hold three people. It was almost as long as a whaling canoe, but it was not nearly so wide. Captain Cook, the eighteenth-century explorer, fresh from his voyages to Polynesia, saw it and marveled that it did not roll over without a stabilizing outrigger. Large canoes were a specialty of the Nootka, who were admired for their craftsmanship by neighboring tribes. Nootka canoes had high prows and low sterns, both pieces separate from the main body and lashed on with fiber cords threaded through holes bored in both sections. The owner's crests were carved and painted on the stern and bow.

Only a wealthy man could afford a large canoe because of the amount of labor required to make one. The job took many days, and all workers had to be fed. A large cedar tree had to be felled and split in half. One half was selected and charred with fire and then chiseled out. Craftsmen who specialized in canoe building used adzes for the finer work of trimming the walls and finishing the

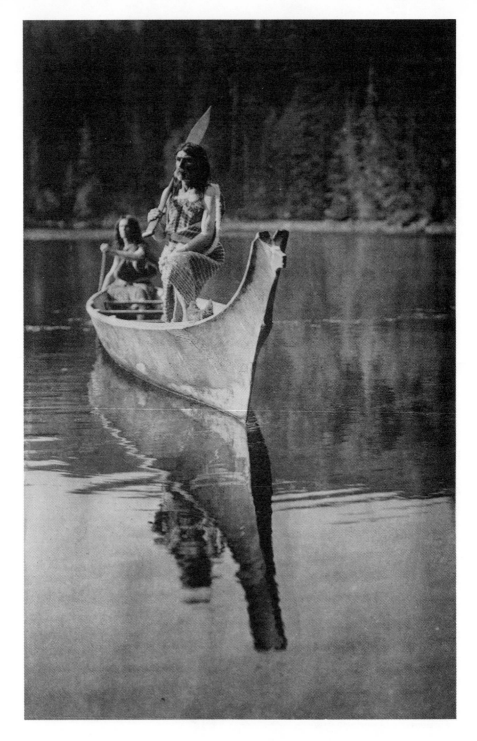

A Nootka canoe.

outside. When the hull was thin enough, it was filled with water into which hot stones were dropped, so the craftsmen could spread the hull, inserting cross-beams to hold the width.

Because cedar was easy to work, canoes could be made in about a month. The largest canoes, reaching sixty feet and carrying ninety to a hundred people, were used for war, transport to summer camps, and visiting. They were too large and clumsy to be safe whaling vessels. None of the canoes had rudders; the paddles were used for steering. Both men and women paddled; according to a European visitor of the late eighteenth century, women's paddles were blunt at the tip but men's were sharp for use as weapons in sea battles.

Dentalia. The Nootka controlled a resource greatly prized on the Northwest Coast—beds of shellfish called *dentalia,* named after their toothlike appearance. It was the shells, not the animal, that were valuable, and they were not easy to reap. A tool like a stiff broom was rammed down on them with just enough force to clamp a few of the long, thin shells in its points and hold them while the fisher pulled the catch back up. Dentalia beds were far enough offshore that shellfishing had to be done from a boat. Like fishing stations and berry tracts, dentalia beds belonged to families who kept their exact position a carefully guarded secret. The shells, divided into three sizes by length, were important in trade with the north, the interior, and down into California.

The Wolf Dance. The Nootka had an important winter ceremony, performed by a group called the Dancing Society. Because it involved a myth about wolf spirits, it is referred to as the Wolf Dance, and it was a kind of initiation rite. The elaborate performance lasted for days. Children and adolescents practiced their parts, and there were many feasts and dances, along with a lot of comedy and mirth, though the ceremony itself was serious.

The myth was about a Nootka ancestor, who intruded into the home of the Wolf Spirits. They taught him their songs and dances and ritual behavior, which he in turn taught to his people when he got back home. Each year the Wolf Dance taught these things to the initiates. Every child of the community partici-pated at least once. Children were given their family crests to carry, and high-ranking children went through the ceremony several times to receive all the crests of their distinguished line. This ceremonial taught and reinforced each child's place in society and entertained the community as well. The whole ritual ended with a potlatch.

The Nootka attitude toward the supernatural followed the usual pattern. They believed that spirit helpers were necessary to success and sought them in spirit quests, and shamans who had many spirit helpers were needed to relieve unnat-ural illness or bad luck.

The Chinook, Traders at the Dalles

At the Dalles, a series of rapids on the Columbia River, a rather small tribe called the Chinook built up a reputation as traders and middlemen controlling the flow of products up and down the river. All people coming along the river had to stop and carry their canoes around the rapids, and this portage took them through Chinook territory. Less is known about the Chinook than the other tribes we have sketched, but the information that has been recorded is a fine example of precontact trade.

Many items of their material culture as well as their language suggest that the Chinook were closely related to Plateau peoples. Yet in grasping the economic opportunity laid before them by their strategic location at the Dalles, they developed a unique adaptation. They were certainly in contact with the Plateau people, as well as with coastal societies and groups from the Great Basin. The rapids and waterfalls of the Dalles were swift, slowing both people and salmon as they traveled. The Chinook found the fish easy prey, and used their fortunate position to set up a sort of trade depot where people of varied tribal backgrounds met.

To the Chinook trading station at the Dalles, then, came peoples from areas of poor fishing to trade pelts of animals from the interior for dried salmon. Warring tribes brought captives, the Nootka brought valuable dentalia, and Basin peoples brought basketry and woven rabbit-skin robes. Candlefish oil was an important trade item, as was oil from seals and whales. Commercial interaction extended from Alaska into California and the Desert Basin and across the Rocky Mountains into the Plains. The Dalles was the hub of a wheel with spokes radiating in all directions, and the Chinook controlled the hub.

The first Europeans who saw these people left us little ethnographic description. The Lewis and Clark expedition passed through with Sacajawea, a Shoshoni woman interpreter; and an artist, George Catlin, visited the Chinook later. But they stayed just long enough to record the most obvious data. Consequently, reconstruction is difficult, and our picture of the Chinook is tenuous.

The Chinook language, belonging to the Penutian phylum, became the core of a trade language in historic times. The words *potlatch* and *hootch* (liquor) are derived from Chinook, which also gave its name to the desiccating wind that blows down the eastern slope of the Rockies. Chinook trade jargon was a combination of Chinook, words from other Indian languages, and some European words. With this tongue peoples who met at the Dalles carried on their business.

Although the Chinook subsistence basis—salmon—was typical of the Northwest Coast area, the rest of their culture was a modification of the Northwest culture. The Chinook had no totem poles, masks, or dramatic art; they lived in pit houses with only the gabled roofs above ground level, suggesting the Plateau much more than the Coast. Chinook obtained most of their canoes by trade as well as the box containers and the mountain sheep horn bowls they used.

Like some other people of both the Northwest Coast and the Plateau, the Chinook practiced head flattening, using a cradle that pressed down on the infant's forehead to produce a slanting or flat-fronted skull. The result was considered attractive. The Flathead Indians of the eastern Plateau got their English name from this practice, but strangely, it was not the Flathead people themselves, but visiting Chinook, or Chinook slaves, whom the Europeans saw; the Flathead did not practice head deformation.

The Chinook apparently had a social ranking system, but it was less rigid than those farther north. Their sociopolitical unit was the village, and kin lines were traced through both maternal and paternal sides, although paternal lines appear to have been emphasized. The eldest of the kin group became the headman if he was competent.

Chinook religion emphasized the vision quest and first-salmon rites; villages conducted their own ceremonies. Both males and females sought spirit helpers in visions, although guardian spirits were vital only for males because success in hunting and fishing depended upon supernatural contacts.

The Kwakiutl Warriors

The Kwakiutl, who lived on Vancouver Island and the nearby mainland, were much like the Nootka in their general way of life. The Kwakiutl had no tribal identity outside of their common language; they lived in villages that were essentially independent of each other. We consider them here because they were prominent in an area we have not previously discussed: warfare.

The Kwakiutl fought not for political power or economic gain, but for social prestige or to avenge the death of a kinsman or fellow villager. Kwakiutl wars were usually between villages of the same tribe; sometimes a few local groups joined together for an attack, but the resulting war could not be considered national. Most Kwakiutl wars were ceremonial in nature and did not involve massive killing or destruction: killing one individual usually satisfied the attacking party.

The most common reason for war was revenge for a death from warfare or murder, or even death from disease or accident. Death was considered a blow against the group, shameful and insulting as well as grievous, and it could be obliterated only by the death of someone else of equal social rank. The object of revenge might not have been responsible for the first death, and might not even have been a relative or a member of the same group as whoever committed the

CHARACTERISTICS OF THE NORTHWEST COAST TRIBES

Clothing	Food production	Equipment	Shelter	Social and political organization	Religion	Warfare
Very little clothing	Fishing	Spears	Large, gabled plank houses	Families	Myths	Exchange of goods to settle disagreements
Woven ponchos for rain	Hunting (sea mammals and land mammals)	Bows and arrows		Lineages	Spirits	Raids
Fiber shirts and skirts	Gathering (plants and shellfish)	Clubs		Clans	Spirit helpers	Warfare prominent among Kwakiutl
Furs		Copper daggers (Tlingit)		Moieties (Tlingit)	Shamans	
Basketry rain hats		Slate knives		Villages	Wolf Dance (Nootka)	
Tunics		Harpoons		Northern tribes matrilineally organized; others bilateral	Vision Quest	
Sun hats (Nootka)		Canoes		Social stratification: chiefs, nobles, commoners, and slaves	First Salmon rites	
		Mats		Extended families joined in confederacy (Nootka)		
		Weirs				
		Traps				
		Woodworking tools				
		Cedar boxes				
		Horn, bone, and stone projectile points				
		Sheephorn spoons and bowls				
		Armor of rods and hides				

initial act of violence. Even if death had resulted from sickness, revenge through another death was necessary. The attitude of those who had suffered a death, from whatever cause, was to make someone else mourn for a loss. A high-ranking man might get up a war party saying, "Why should I mourn? Let someone else wail."

Another reason Kwakiutl went to war was for social prestige. A man could acquire the social rank, privileges, and symbolic crests of another by killing him and taking over his position, usually keeping his women and children as slaves. Except for slaves, plunder was of little importance, and Kwakiutl never waged war to gain land.

Although a war party might include as many as two hundred men, only a few were specialists. Boys of the proper social position and disposition—younger brothers of chiefs, usually—were trained early for roles as warriors. They were taught to be cruel; they learned to use weapons, to run and swim to keep themselves physically fit, and to perform feats of endurance. These warriors were humorless and always ready to fight. Few married and raised families.

Kwakiutl weapons were bows and arrows, clubs, spears, and slings. The men wore body armor made of wooden slats, and war canoes capable of carrying fifty people bore them to the enemy village.

War parties attacked by surprise. Although no village knew exactly when attack might come, there was a conventional fighting season from about the middle of August to the first of October, when the water was not rough and frequent fogs helped conceal the approach of attackers. At that time of year, villagers moved to stockades, fortified hills, or other spots that could be defended easily. Kwakiutl also used trickery in attack, such as dressing as women and posing as harmless travelers or visitors. Kwakiutl always attacked at night, and killed and beheaded sleeping enemies. After a successful assault, they displayed heads taken as trophies on poles in front of their villages. The Kwakiutl had a reputation as ferocious fighters, and apparently they enjoyed that reputation.

Bibliography

Codere, Helen
1966 *Fighting with Property.*
      An analysis of the Kwakiutl economic system of the potlatch and its implications for social structure, as well as a study of the relationship between the potlatch and warfare during the period of acculturation.

Drucker, Philip
1955 *Indians of the Northwest Coast.*
      A general survey of cultures and aspects of culture.

Krause, Aurel
1956   *The Tlingit Indians.*
        A translation of a study made by a German in the last quarter of the nineteenth century.

Ray, Verne F.
1963   *Primitive Pragmatists.*
        An ethnography of the Modoc Indians based on the memories of native informants, discussing problems of change and the Modoc War.

Spier, Leslie
1930   *Klamath Ethnography.*
        The classic study of the Klamath tribe of the Plateau area.

Spinden, Herbert J.
1908   *The Nez Perce Indians.*
        A general study of the aboriginal society and change resulting from contact with Europeans.

Other
Pertinent Works

Boas, Franz
1966   *Kwakiutl Ethnography.*

de Laguna, Frederica
1960   *The Story of a Tlingit Community.*

Drucker, Philip
1951   *The Northern and Central Nootkan Tribes.*

Ford, C. S.
1941   *Smoke from Their Fires.*

Josephy, Alvin
1965   *The Nez Perce Indians and the Opening of the Northwest.*

Rohner, Ronald, and E. C. Rohner
1970   *The Kwakiutl Indians of British Columbia.*

Steward, Julian H.
1938   *Basin-Plateau Aboriginal Sociopolitical Groups.*

MAJOR GROUPS AND LANGUAGES
OF THE PLATEAU AND THE NORTHWEST COAST

Language phylum	Language family	Cultural division

PLATEAU

Language phylum	Language family	Cultural division
Penutian	Klamath-Modoc	Klamath Modoc
	Cayuse	Cayuse
	Sahaptin-Nez Perce	Klikitat Nez Perce Umatilla Wallawalla Yakima
Undetermined	Salishan	Flathead Kalispel Lillooet Sanpoil Shuswap Spokan Thompson

NORTHWEST COAST

Language phylum	Language family	Cultural division
Na-Dene	Haida	Haida
	Tlingit	Tlingit

Continued

MAJOR GROUPS AND LANGUAGES (continued)

Language phylum	Language family	Cultural division

NORTHWEST COAST (continued)

Language phylum	Language family	Cultural division
Penutian	Chinookan	Chinook
	Coos	Coos
	Tsimshian	Tsimshian
Undetermined	Salishan	Bella Coola Chehalis Klallam Lummi Quinault Salish Tillamook
	Wakashan	Bella Bella Kwakiutl Makah Nootka
	Chimakuan	Quileute

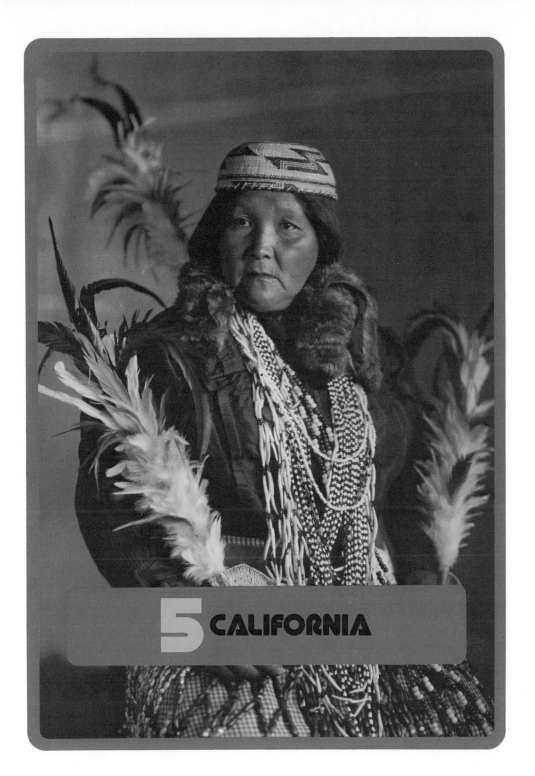

5 CALIFORNIA

Maidu
Creation Myth

YΛYΛYΛYΛYΛYΛYΛYΛYΛYΛYΛYΛ

Long ago there were no stars, no moon, no sun. There was only darkness and water. A raft floated on the water, and on the raft sat a turtle. Then from the sky, a spirit came down and sat on the raft. "Who are you?" asked Turtle. "Where do you come from?" "I came from above," answered the spirit. "Can you create some land for us?" asked Turtle. "We need dry land and some people to live on it."

Creator said, "To create land I must have some earth to make it from." So Turtle offered to dive to the bottom of the water and bring up some earth. He was gone a very long time, and when he came back to the surface, he had only a small amount of earth under his nails because the rest had washed away in his long swim to the surface.

Creator scraped the earth from under Turtle's nails and rolled it around in his hand. At first nothing happened, then the earth began to grow. It enlarged until it became as big as the world. The raft was grounded, and mountains stretched toward the sky. But it was still dark, so Turtle asked, "Can you make it light?" The spirit said, "I will tell my sister to come up," and to the east the sun began to rise. For a while it was bright and warm, and Turtle sat in the light, but then the sun went down, and Turtle asked the spirit to make more light. Creator said, "I will make my brother come," and the moon rose.

Then Turtle said, "What else are you going to do?" The Creator said, "I will show you," and he made a great tree grow. It had many different kinds of acorns on it. Turtle and the Creator sat for several days in the shade of the tree. They were pleased with the things the spirit had made. In a few days Coyote and Rattlesnake came up out of the ground. Then the spirit called birds from the sky and made more trees and animals to live in the woodland.

Then the spirit said that something else was needed, and he made people. He took earth and mixed it with water and made two figures, a man and a woman. The first man was called Kuksu, and the first woman was called Morning Star. And by and by there were many people on the earth.

For a long time everyone spoke the same language, but suddenly people began to speak in different tongues. Kuksu, however, could speak all the languages, so he called his people together and told them the names of

Preceding page: An early–twentieth-century photo of a Shasta Indian woman. She wears many strands of beads around her neck as well as an elaborately beaded belt.

the animals in their own languages, taught them to get food, and gave them their laws and rituals. Then he sent each tribe to a different place to live. Then he too left. He went to the spirit house that was up above.

YↃ᙭YↃ᙭YↃ᙭YↃ᙭YↃ᙭YↃ᙭YↃ᙭YↃ᙭YↃ᙭YↃ᙭

The Environment

The culture area called California has somewhat different boundaries from the state of California, though it includes much of the same territory The eastern edge of the state is part of the Great Basin culture area, while the southeast section fits best in the Southwestern culture area. In the north the transition from Northwest Coast into California is so gradual that border groups like the Yurok could reasonably be considered with either culture area. We have placed them in this chapter although, as you will see, they showed characteristics of Northwest Coast culture as well.

Within the culture area of California, three different geographic regions exist: northern, central, and southern. Set off by climate, altitude, and land forms, each region has different kinds of animals and plants; thus the people too adapted differently to each area. The native languages followed this geographic pattern as well, with one or two language groups dominant in each area.

All over California, the numerous streams, rivers, valleys, and mountains created secluded pockets where people could settle and flourish cut off from the other societies around them, and a denser population developed in California than in most other regions. This area, geographically only about 1 percent of North America, sheltered about 10 percent of the native population.

Because the California area shows so much diversity in such a small space, you may wonder why we think of it as a separate culture area instead of dividing it among the other culture areas around it. There are three things that unify California and set it off as a single area: people everywhere used wild foods, especially seeds; populations were dense and moved around very little; and elaborate death ceremonies and puberty rites were common. Of the three regions of California, the one most typical in these respects was the central area.

Northern California

In the northern region, the coast is rocky, battered by weather and waves into palisades and cliffs. Swift rivers rush down into valleys from the high mountains,

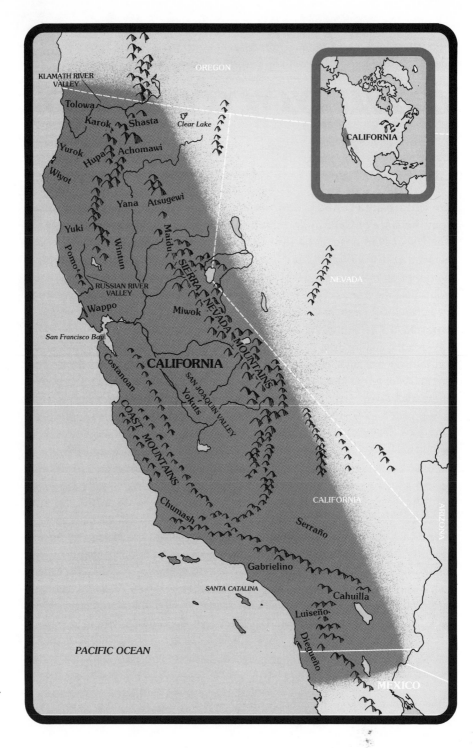

The California culture area and its tribes.

and rainfall is plentiful. The mountains are well-watered, and heavily wooded with tall sequoia, ponderosa pine, and Douglas fir. Some peaks are high enough to be snow-covered all year round; and both Mount Lassen and Mount Shasta were still active volcanoes in the early days of Indian occupation. In the mountains and forests, deer, bear, wildcat, coyote, and wolverine were abundant, and before the Europeans came the bighorn mountain sheep and wapiti were common. Many of these animals provided food, but even more important to northern Californians were the fish and shellfish along the coast, and the bass, trout, salmon, and sturgeon in the many rivers. Hokan languages were predominant in the north.

Central California

This is a land of contrasts and great diversity: inland lakes and ponds nestled among foothills, spectacular mountains with cascading rivers and streams, broad lush valleys, and coasts rich in shellfish. The variety of plants provided the California basketmakers with a wide selection of fibers, and the especially abundant oaks supplied acorns and hardwood. Fish and game were plentiful in the days before cities and industrial and commercial development. The climate is mild, except occasionally in the central valley, where temperature may go above 90 degrees in summer and sometimes drops to freezing in winter. Heavy fogs often blanket the coast, though rainfall is less than in the north. This region is larger than the other two and can be considered "classic" Californian. It was home for many groups of Penutian speakers, each having enough food and building supplies in its own rather small territory. They could gather plenty of one food or another in nearly every month of the year, and the acorns and seeds that were the staple part of their diet could be stored in anticipation of any shortage.

Southern California

Today, through extensive irrigation, southern California has become a major garden and agricultural area, but the land is naturally dry, and the mountains are less timbered than in the north. There are fewer rivers, and they flow through steep, barren canyons where fishing is difficult. The climate goes from warm to hot in winter as well as summer, though the mountains are cooler. The sandy beaches slope gradually to the water, without the high, abrupt cliffs of the north. Rainfall is scant, and lakes are rare. The tropical plants that grow in the area today survive only with artificial watering. Native forms are desert vegetation—such as chaparral, mesquite, and sagebrush—and oak, which is not as abundant as farther north. Indians of the area ate acorns and also seeds from plants like mesquite, which also provided wood for building, fibers for baskets, and a black dye. Animals of the region include kangaroo rat, horned toad, pronghorn antelope, squirrel, and rabbit, all hunted by the Indians. Great mounds of seashells from ancient times tell us that people lived on the coast even then and ate shellfish. Shoshonean was the dominant language.

California Peoples

Two mountain systems, the Coast Ranges and the Sierra Nevadas, run through California from north to south, roughly parallel to the coast. We have assigned the territory east of the Sierras to either the Great Basin or the Southwest. Between the two mountain systems lie fertile valleys where many small groups lived. Most of their names sound unfamiliar today: Maidu, Miwok, Yokuts, Wintun. California tribes were small, rarely larger than a few hundred people, and most stayed close to home. They had no need to travel, for wild foods were plentiful almost everywhere, and no one needed materials he could not find in home territory. Their society was simple, but they had economic security.

In the remarkably diverse California culture area, the people spoke more than one hundred languages, from every major North American Indian phylum except Aleut-Eskimo and Macro-Siouan. While some other culture areas had as many languages, none is so small. Why was California so rich in variety? Many believe the "fishtrap" theory explains it. The narrow coastal plain is blocked off from the rest of the continent by its north-south mountain ranges. The only way people could enter was by crossing the mountains, which have few passes, or by making their way over the southeastern California deserts. Thus, migrants were mostly small groups from diverse linguistic and cultural backgrounds who found their way into California from less desirable places. Once there, they found living conditions so favorable that they settled down and adjusted their ways to the pleasant conditions, like fish swimming into a trap.

The Promised Land

Our reconstructed picture begins, then, with people migrating from Asia, moving slowly southward over thousands of years. Most groups turned east, or continued south, or settled in intermediate territory. But splinter groups from almost all linguistic and social divisions must have made the trek over the mountains into a place that may well have seemed like the promised land.

Food Resources

What was the promise in this land? Anthropologists generally measure the wealth of a nonindustrial society by the amount of food available to the people. The early Californians had so much wild food within easy reach that agriculture held no appeal—even simple farming would have required more labor for less food than gathering wild plants. The climate too was agreeable, with almost no freezing weather except in high mountains, and temperatures rarely above 90 degrees outside the desert. Only the Northwest Coast was richer in easy-to-find food. California's aboriginal population must have been about 200,000.

So important were acorns in California cultures that they are worth describing. The many species of oaks there produce acorns big enough to amaze people from the East, who are accustomed to an inch-long nut. The western acorn is about three inches long and very plump and nutritious. It has one serious disadvantage: it contains tannic acid, which causes severe gastrointestinal disturbance and can kill infants. At some remote time, lost to both archaeology and ethnography, the California people learned to grind acorns to flour, which they then

Hupa Indian woman leaching tannic acid out of acorn meal.

leached with water by spreading it in a shallow pit in clean sand and pouring water over it. The water rinsed the acorn meal, washing away the tannin. The acorn harvest was reliable year after year, with little or no fluctuation, and the nuts and flour were easily stored for winter, which, indeed, was not severe.

Acorns were not the only means of subsistence. Pine nuts too were plentiful, along with mesquite beans, sage, and grass seeds. Also important were game—deer and many other species—and fish, particularly in the central and northern regions. With these resources, California developed the densest population north of Mexico in aboriginal times.

Technology

California people made almost no pottery, but they were among the best basketmakers in the world. It was the women who wove baskets, and they developed the craft into an art. Their raw material ranged from yucca fibers—used for sandals, straps, mats, and nets as well as baskets—to grasses, stems, and roots of ferns, bushes, and trees such as Douglas fir and the many species of oak.

The Californians made many kinds of canoes, from dugouts and planked boats in some areas to the common raft made of tule reeds (bulrushes). All

Tule-reed raft (top) and plank canoe (bottom); they are not drawn to scale.

Elaborately painted and feathered California Indians as rendered by a German artist who was traveling with a Russian exploring expedition.

were made for fishing, for the Californians traveled very little. Only the Chumash seem to have gone beyond their home grounds, exploring the ocean coastal regions north and south of what is now Santa Barbara. The Chumash built stronger vessels of planks to weather the rough coastal waters and the turbulent currents. Indians at the edge of the Northwest Coast made smaller versions of the dugout canoes typical in the northerly areas, while the inland tribes made tule canoes.

In the mild California climate people could get along with very little clothing, wearing nothing elaborate except perhaps on ceremonial occasions. Children went naked, older girls and women wore fiber or hide skirts, and men wrapped skins around their hips. When they needed footwear it was of hide or fiber, but many people went barefoot most of the time. A skin cape slung over the shoulder provided protection from rain and wind. Fancy apparel being unnecessary, the Indians often decorated their bodies with paints and tattoos, and wore shell, bone, wood, and stone necklaces and feathered hair ornaments.

The mild climate also made durable housing unnecessary. It was almost always simple, and often temporary, made of grass, tules, brush, or bark, occasionally covered with soil. The people lived outdoors much of the time. In the hot southern areas, shelter from heat and sun was far more important than protection from cold or rain. Some dwellings housed several families; some housed only a couple and their children. The Yurok and their neighbors in the north needed sturdier homes than those in the south, so they built plank houses that were similar to those of the Northwest Coast, though smaller.

Political Organization

Clan organization was largely lacking in California, the basic unit being the small village. Some villages were just a few families living together, but others had up to two or three hundred people. In the San Joaquin Valley, all the Yokuts villages together may have totaled 20,000 people, an unusual size for California.

The local groups, the villages, were really autonomous, though people from associated villages recognized their common customs and language. Such groups of independent villages made up the unit anthropologists usually call a tribelet. Villages almost never waged war against others in the same tribelet, and even between tribelets war was very rare. These were peaceful people, if for no other reason than that aggression brought no benefits.

The village leader, usually called the headman, governed the local group. Al-

**Yurok house made
of driftwood.**

Indian Hut

though he generally inherited his position, others obeyed him only as long as they respected his wisdom and experience. He had no police support or any other means of coercing his fellow villagers. Throughout California, no one, not even the headman, was considered above the others by birth, and there was little social inequality of any kind.

Religion

The shaman was often the most powerful and respected person in the community. He frequently played an important part in selecting the village headman by revealing the will of the supernatural. Some shamans obtained power from dreams, others from visions induced by hallucinogenic drugs. People believed shamans could control weather and cure disease, and often feared as well as respected them: the shamans' contact with the supernatural made them dangerous as well as powerful.

Ceremonies were most elaborate in central California, where long series of rituals took place every year. The people celebrated girls' puberty as well as boys' initiation into men's societies. Costumes for the dances that accompanied these rituals were often very elaborate. In the north, people honored the first salmon fishing each year and often had lavish death and mourning rites. The dead were usually buried in the north; in the south, cremation was the custom.

Indians in California had many kinds of cultures, yet within the three natural divisions the ways of adjusting to the environment and the styles of life had much in common. We will describe one society from each region, north, central, and south, to give some of the flavor of life in California in those early times.

The Yurok

The Yurok lived in the lower Klamath River valley, about two hundred miles north of San Francisco Bay. Situated in this transition zone between the potlatch-givers to the north and the "classic" Californians to the south, they blended a northwestern California culture with that of the Northwest Coast.

The Yurok built their villages near water—on the riverbank, at the river's mouth, or on the seacoast. From all the fifty or more permanent, year-round villages, people hunted deer and gathered seeds, acorns, and firewood in the hilly, heavily wooded land extending away from the rivers and the coast. The Yurok population totaled about 2,500, clustered into seven population centers. A typical village consisted of six or seven redwood plank houses—smaller and less

Karok, Yurok, and Hupa elk antler spoons.

elaborate than the Northwest Coast houses—and one wooden sweathouse for the men, which also served as their clubhouse and alternate sleeping quarters.

The Yurok shared their valley and their way of life with their neighbors upstream, the Karok and the Hupa. In fact, most of the three groups' material and nonmaterial culture was identical: legends, costumes, ceremonies, houses, and behavior. But there was one difference—the tribes spoke totally unrelated, mutually unintelligible languages. The Yurok language belonged to the Macro-Algonkian phylum, the Karok language to the Hokan, and the Hupa to the Na-Dene. The cultural similarities and the linguistic differences have led anthropologists to believe that the Yurok were there first, and that when the others arrived, they adopted Yurok culture.

Subsistence

The Yurok lived on salmon and acorns supplemented with deer, seeds, bulbs, and mussels. Very rarely they killed a sea lion or found a whale stranded on the beach. Food was abundant, at least enough to support permanent settlements, but it was never wasted. The Yurok felt two sparse meals a day were enough, and they ridiculed gluttony.

Men fished individually with nets, usually at privately owned fishing spots chosen for their productivity. When the salmon were running, one man could catch enough fish in a day to feed his family for a whole season. The salmon ran mostly in the spring and autumn, but since there were several species, there were fish in the river almost every month of the year. Men who did not own or share in a special fishing spot had to fish in the open river, where the catch was less bountiful.

The heart of Yurok life was the river. All nourishment and human contact, all transportation and communication, followed the watercourse. The Yurok reckoned direction not by north or south, but by words for "upstream" and "downstream," even along the seacoast. As one follows the river, upstream is at various times north, south, east, and west.

Prime deer-hunting lands were also privately owned. Wealthy men controlled large areas of good deer land where they could hunt with little effort, while poor men had to journey far from the village to the unclaimed lands. The Yurok concepts of wealth and prestige clearly came from the Northwest Coast, but without the accompanying crests and symbols.

Gathering acorns and seeds was women's work. After the women pounded the acorns and leached them to remove the tannic acid, they usually boiled the meal with hot stones in a basket to make porridge. The Yurok made no pottery, using instead wooden containers and baskets so finely made that they held water.

These Indians cultivated just one plant, a strong native variety of tobacco, which men smoked to make themselves drowsy before retiring.

Social and Political Organization

The Yurok, Karok, and Hupa all were so loosely organized that it is more accurate to call each an ethnic group than a tribe. All the Yurok shared a culture and a language, interacted and communicated, intermarried and traced relatives, but still they did not think of themselves as a unit. Each person saw himself as a village resident, not as a tribal member. Yurok folk tales are full of references to homesickness and love of one's birthplace. This kind of local attachment and loyalty to kin and lifelong friends are typical of all the California Indians.

Yurok leaders were the wealthy individuals; they drew power and status from kinsmen, followers, and semidependents and gave them back assistance, food, and protection. A village acted as a unit only if its entire population was one wealthy man's entourage. This was a transition zone, as we have noted, blending the rigid ranking of the Northwest Coast and the more democratic society of central California.

Besides having no chiefs, the Yurok had no priests. Each village ceremony was directed by the old man who knew most about it from his years of participation.

War and murder were the same thing for the Yurok, who undertook both for revenge, never for plunder or prestige. The revenge they wanted was retaliation for a death thought to have been caused by witchcraft. Deaths caused feuds that could have totally disrupted society if there had not been a means of settling them: blood money. When murder had been committed, wealthy men from both sides met to calculate the value of all property lost, injuries sustained, and people killed. They then set retribution to be paid in dentalia shells and other material. Representatives from each side met, examined the items offered for retribution, and danced over them. Once the payments were accepted, the conflict was settled; anyone who held a grudge after that was not behaving properly. Each side paid the other for losses and injuries instead of subtracting the lesser from the greater and paying the difference.

Compensation for the degrees of injury from insult to murder was finely scaled. How much was a man's life worth? The Yurok said it was worth as much as had been exchanged for his mother when she married his father, the bridewealth. A man whose mother had brought much bridewealth—dentalia, deerskins, other furs, and perhaps a canoe—was worth a great deal in blood money.

All Yurok rights were individual rights, and all crimes were committed against individuals. There was no state or township to administer punishment; compensation in a dispute had to be agreed on by the parties involved. The kin on both sides shared that responsibility, not as a group but as a succession of individuals; the closer the relationship to plaintiff or defendant, the greater the degree of responsibility.

Wealth and Property

The Yurok and their neighbors were obsessed with wealth, which they counted primarily in dentalia. These shells were used as a standard of value and a medium of exchange, the closest thing to all-purpose money found anywhere in aboriginal times. The dentalia were graded into standard sizes and strung on a measured string. A string containing ten shells was more valuable than one with eleven smaller shells, even though the strings were the same length; larger shells, especially without blemish, were more valuable. The Yurok graded the dentalia far more precisely than did the Nootka from whom they obtained the shells.

Being wealthy meant having a well-built house on a desirable site, with chests of treasure in its rooms. The finest houses had names, like English manors. Wealth meant owning good fishing and hunting lands that could be leased out, and paying high bridewealth for wives from other wealthy and prestigious families, thus increasing one's own wealth and status. It meant too that one's daughters would be sought after and would marry into wealthy families who would pay handsomely.

Only a few men were so wealthy. Most owned a simple house and some small share in a fishing place. They might take years to pay for their brides, partly with their labor. Any friendship, kinship, or other attachment with a wealthy man was a great security to the common man. A few were so poor or so deeply in debt that they had to give themselves up into debt slavery to a rich man. A slave or servant to a rich household often had a more comfortable life than a poor but free man.

Everyone wanted to be rich. They thought about wealth constantly, prayed for it, and behaved according to standards of moderation and good manners that were believed to bring it. But in fact they could do very little to become wealthy. A very few men were traders or built dugout redwood canoes that they sold to the neighboring tribes, but wealth generally stayed among the wealthy. The Yurok did not hold potlatches like the tribes of the Northwest Coast, and when a man died, his sons received most of his possessions, the rest going to his daughters, kinfolk, and hangers-on.

Being wealthy did have its obligations. A wealthy man paid for most of the World Renewal Ceremony (to be discussed shortly), often including payments to the mourners of the year's dead. Any transgressions he might commit cost him more than they would a poorer man, and his ownership of land was so absolute that trespassers who injured themselves while on his land could claim compensation—usually a share in the land involved.

The Yurok systems of laws and values depended on mutual agreement. Because of this flexibility and their concept of private property, they could accept contact with whites more easily than most other tribes did. They translated their shell money into American money (at one time a string of twelve shells was worth ten dollars). A few of their descendants still live today in their river valley, a wilderness not yet destroyed.

Religion

Guardian spirit quests were not very important among the Yurok. Their shamans were women curers who received powers in dreams with help from an ancestor. The shamans obtained their supernatural power in the form of "pains," which could enter a person and cause illness. Yurok believed that possessing one or more pains made the shaman able to cure or extract similar pains—sicknesses—from others. Those who became successful healers were respected and commanded high fees for curing, but they never gave up their duties as wives and mothers.

World Renewal. The Yurok placed more emphasis on ceremony than belief. Ethnographers give the name "World Renewal" to the cycle of about a dozen ceremonies the Yurok, Karok, and Hupa held every year. Each ceremony always was held in the same place, and each was different from any of the others. All, however, included the public performance of one or both of two distinctive dances, the Jumping and the Deerskin. This dance cycle was typical of the northern California area, as the Kuksu Cult performances were of the central and the Chungichnish of the southern areas. All these ceremonial cycles were meant to keep the world in order and running properly for another season and to ensure abundant food and prevent disaster.

Each ceremony in the World Renewal cycle had two parts, the esoteric or secret rites and the public performances. In the secret part, a long formula was narrated about the first performance of the ceremony by a member of an ancient, prehuman, half-spirit race, and its immediate beneficial effect. The recitation demonstrated the efficacy of the first and therefore of the current performance. It was spoken in sections by an old man, generally accompanied by a young assistant, before rocks and other places believed to be the abodes of the spirits. All the prescribed symbolic acts were performed by these two alone. They fasted and otherwise refrained from their ordinary activities, stayed in a house sanctified by tradition for this purpose, and spent a number of nights in a sweathouse.

Dances and Regalia. The public part of the ceremony was the dancing, which began after the secret rites had been completed. The dancing went on every day for five, ten, or more days. The dance outfits, songs, and steps were standardized by custom, and were neither symbolic nor sacred. The dancers, all men, were not impersonating spirits but displaying wealth in front of the audience. A large part of every rich man's wealth was dance adornment, and men came from miles up and down the river, bringing their treasures to show. Dance regalia was almost as highly valued as strings of dentalia. A wealthy man's dance outfits consisted of enough albino deerskins, red woodpecker scalp headdresses, and giant obsidian blades to outfit many dancers and thus display his worth to all.

On the first day the dance was brief and performed by a few young men and older boys, but as days passed, it built up in duration, intensity, splendor, and

The White Deerskin
Dance being per-
formed.

number of dancers, accentuated by competition among the rich men of the several villages involved. As days went by, they handed out more and more of their
own and their friends' valuables for their dancers to wear in the next dance. The
finest regalia, the most dancers, the longest dances, and the largest audience all
formed the climax on the last day.

The Jumping Dance and the White Deerskin Dance were different from each
other in costumes, steps, and songs. If both dances were performed, the Deerskin always came first, with costumes of deerhide or civet cat kilts, masses of
dentalia necklaces, and wolf-fur bands around the forehead. The dancers carried
poles with stuffed deer heads mounted at the end and white or light deerskins
draped below. Bright woodpecker scalps decorated the heads. A row of dancers,
each carrying skins thus displayed, was headed and followed by dancers holding
large ritual obsidian blades of fine workmanship. The dance step was very simple, merely a stamp of the feet, but the rhythmic swing of the mounted deerskins
was impressive.

The Jumping Dance was slightly more active, though it had only two movements, a high leap and a stamp. The costumes for this dance were elaborate: a

headdress, for instance, consisted of fifty large woodpecker scalps attached to a forehead band, topped with long white feathers. The dancers wore strings of dentalia around their necks, and deerskin robes around their hips.

Before the ceremonial dances began each year, some payment was made to grieving families of Yurok who had died since the last ceremonial cycle. The payment was to compensate for intruding upon the mourners' privacy and sorrow. Contributions might come from the villagers, or a wealthy man might donate the entire sum. Death brought mourning before and during burial. Among the Yurok, as everywhere in California, the names of the dead were never mentioned.

Kepel Fish Dam. The Yurok held one other large annual gathering that was both a ceremony and a cooperative food producing venture. Every autumn hundreds of people from several miles up and down the Klamath River gathered at the village of Kepel. There they spanned the river with a structure of logs, poles, and small stakes. The dam was really a fish weir: it did not halt the water flowing downstream, but its mesh was fine enough to keep salmon from passing upstream to spawn. It had ten sections, each with a gate and a pen behind the gate. Fish passed through a gate and were trapped in a pen, from which they were pulled out with nets and divided among the men who had built that section of the dam. For ten days the men pulled the fish out of the pens while the women split and dried them for storage. Each pen provided enough fish to last several families an entire year.

The Yurok never cooperated in nonreligious ventures, so it is understandable that they could build the dam only by associating it with religious ceremonies. Before work on the dam began each year, an old man, well-versed in the formulas, led a ritual for success, a young apprentice assisting him. After the fishing period was over, the people followed the dam's dismantling with a Deerskin Dance and then a Jumping Dance. Another rite, the first-fish ceremony, similar to the first-salmon rites of the Northwest Coast, was held many miles away at the mouth of the river. No fish were pulled from the dam until word arrived that the ritual specialist in charge had completed the first-fish ceremony.

The Pomo

The Indian peoples we refer to as the Pomo once occupied many villages over a large area of California north of San Francisco Bay. The population extended from Clear Lake on the east to the seacoast on the west; its center was in the Russian River valley, which runs roughly north and south. The

Pomo generally did not occupy the dense redwood forest of this region, but settled mainly along waterways and in the open valleys. The deep forest supplied only deer and acorns, while the valleys with their rivers and meadows provided an almost unbelievable variety of foodstuffs.

Abundant Food

Hunger was unknown to the Pomo. They had a liberal food surplus, not because of agriculture (for they had none) or methods of storing food, or an abundance of any one food (compare the Indians of the Northwest Coast, with their never-ending supply of salmon), but because of the sheer diversity of their wild foods. No one item was so necessary to their diet that its sudden disappearance could not be made up by other items. Exploiting so many food sources was time-consuming, however, and left the Pomo little leisure time.

Women gathered acorns in the fall and stored them in large baskets until needed. Then they ground the nuts with pestles in sturdy basket mortars, leached the flour, and stone-boiled the mush in watertight baskets or baked acorn meal bread in warm ashes. The acorn was not as important to the Pomo, however, as it was to some other California Indians. The Pomo relied as well on tubers and roots (arrowroot was popular), berries and bulbs (used for soap and fish poison as well as food), ferns, flowers, and leaves (some raw in salads, some boiled as we do spinach), and seaweed cooked into cakes. They made sugar from sugar pine sap, took salt from seaweed and natural salt licks, and used many plants for medicines. For meat and skins the men hunted and trapped deer, elk, bear, mountain lions, seals, sea lions, sea otters, rabbits, squirrels, and wood rats. They also caught birds such as quail, woodpeckers, pigeon, grouse, ducks, and geese, other animals such as turtles and lizards, and occasionally insects such as grasshoppers. Grasshoppers were caught and cooked in one neat operation: several Indians set a ring of grass on fire, and as the ring closed on the grasshoppers, they were confined to a smaller and smaller space, and finally toasted.

Fish, another main source of food, were caught from shore and from boats with hooks, traps, snares, nets, weirs, spears, and harpoons, and also by means of poisons that paralyzed the fish's breathing mechanism but were harmless to humans. Salmon, panfish, and many other kinds of fish were taken in the fresh water of the rivers and Clear Lake; abalone, many other shellfish, and octopus came from the ocean. Some residents of the Clear Lake area became professional fishermen, selling their catch for other necessities. These fishermen used boats of a type called the "balsa canoe" by anthropologists, which were neither canoes nor made of balsa wood. They were really rafts, made of loosely bound tule reeds gathered into a canoe shape, depending on the buoyancy of the individual reeds to keep afloat rather than a watertight hull.

The People

The meaning of the word *Pomo* is not clear. It is a native word, but not a name they used for themselves. It is reported to mean "red clay," used as a name because most of those people added a red clay to their acorn bread to give it color. All the Pomo spoke dialects of a language of the Hokan phylum. The dialects were so closely related that speakers of each could understand the others, but distinctive enough for linguists to group the tribelets into seven major divisions. None of these groups had political identity or unity, however.

The Pomo appear to have been in California a very long time, longer than most of their neighbors. White contact affected them rather quickly, so even though they were not all driven from their lands, we know little of what their culture was like in precontact days. The Russians encountered them in 1808, trading with them until 1847. The Spanish tried to convert them to Christianity beginning in 1823 with the mission at Sonoma. From 1834 to 1847, Mexicans moved into Pomo territory. In 1848, gold was discovered in central California, and the whole area was invaded first by gold seekers and later by settlers who ruthlessly took Pomo lands for their own. Those contacts and disturbances, added to the usual mortality from European diseases, make it hard to guess at precontact population. A figure often cited is 8,000 for all Pomo. At the time much of the ethnographic data were gathered, in 1910, there were 1,200 left. Of those that remain, the southwest Pomo, called the Kashia, have kept more of the old ways than the others.

Organization

During winter and spring, the Pomo lived in permanent villages along streams. Each community claimed its own territory, within which all its members were free to hunt, gather, or fish, though tracts on the shores of Clear Lake were family-owned. During the summers, which were always dry, the population spread out, some building temporary shelters like lean-tos away from the village, some sleeping out while on food quests, and some remaining at the village. The permanent winter quarters varied from small, single-family tipilike structures of redwood bark to circular or elongated multifamily houses of brush, up to fifty feet in diameter. Besides living quarters, each village had a men's sweathouse and a dance house. Both of these were round and half-buried in the ground, the sweathouse being small and the dance house the largest structure in the village. The men congregated in either of these—the home was for women and children and storing property, cooking, eating, and other domestic activities.

The largest unit of social organization was the tribelet, of which there were about seventy-five throughout the Pomo territory. Each consisted of one large village where the head chief lived and most of the ceremonies were held, and the surrounding small villages, each with its own lesser chief. The lesser chiefs inherited their positions, but social pressure could force their replacement if they were not competent. It is not clear whether the head chief was from a kin group in the main village or whether he was somehow selected from among the lesser chiefs. Those chiefs had little direct power but great influence as peacemakers, advisers, organizers, and, strangely perhaps, preachers on ethics and proper behavior to the assembled townspeople. They were not war chiefs; in fact no one could be described as a war leader. The society had no regular organization for war. A "battle" would sometimes start over a supposed wrong done to an individual or small group, but it ended as soon as an important man on either side was wounded or killed. When that first blood was drawn, the headmen or chiefs arranged a settlement and determined payments for losses.

Technology

Most of the material culture of the Pomo and other central California peoples conformed to the general description given early in this chapter. Their everyday clothing was typical of the whole west coast, women wearing only a skirt, men wearing a simple, short wrap-around skirt or, more often, just going naked. In cold weather both sexes wore rabbit-fur blankets.

Large carrying baskets with headstraps were also common to the whole area, and the Pomo shared most basket forms, sizes, and manufacturing techniques with other California tribelets. They were unique, however, in the elaborate feathered decorations that the women wove into their fine baskets, often acclaimed as the most beautiful in the world. The baskets were an item of some status and wealth; the finest were never sold but were given as gifts or kept in the family. The Pomo combined the coiling of basketmakers to the south and the twining technique of those to the north, added a greater variety of materials (at least twelve), and with great skill and care wove finely and tightly meshed baskets, beautifully decorated with bright feathers, shells, and beads. Their almost endless variety was rare among American Indians, a truly individual art, and the sizes ranged from those so small the weave cannot be seen to those large enough to hold a grown man.

Unlike the Indians in northwestern California, the Pomo had a rich musical

Pomo woman weaving a very large beautifully decorated basket.

life. They knew many songs and accompanied their songs and dances with flutes, whistles, drums, rattles, a musical bow, the bull-roarer (a sort of slat, whirled on the end of a rope), and a huge wooden drum that the dancers stomped on.

The Pomo made strings of shell beads and strung disks made of a mineral called magnesite, using these much like money. They did not hoard these things, however, or attach to them the value and status that the northwestern California tribes did. They were spenders rather than savers; a family might spend all its bead money on a visit to Clear Lake to feast and relax in the company of relatives and friends. Pomo were wealthy, but not obsessed with wealth. They did much traveling, using both the waterways and overland trails, and traded such items as bows, salt, woodpecker scalps, seaweed, beaver skins, shells, magnesite, baskets, and obsidian.

The Pomo developed an arithmetic and knew some astronomy. Special men learned such things and maintained the calendar, which not only kept track of the passing seasons, but also counted the passing years.

The Sexes

One gets the impression that the Pomo had an unusual degree of equality between the sexes. Marriage was accompanied by an exchange of gifts between both families rather than a one-way exchange of goods for a bride. Women could own and inherit personal property, and they won prestige as master basketmakers. Whether Pomo traced kinship *unilineally* (solely through males or solely through females) is not certain, but they do seem to have settled wherever they wished after marriage. A newly married couple could live with his family, her family, or in a new location.

Only men could become shamans, however. There were both good and evil shamans. The evil ones were the "bear doctors," who went about in bearskins and were greatly feared, though they probably existed as much in legend as in reality, and "poisoners," who could convince people that they were being poisoned. The good shamans were healers, some healing by sucking out the cause of illness, some by administering herbs and performing magic. The Kuksu dancers appear to have been healers also. They knew the medical properties of plants and herbs and used them for doctoring. A man became a shaman in one of two ways: either he inherited the paraphernalia from his father or some other shaman whose assistant and student he had been, or he received power directly from a spirit, often during an illness.

A Pomo feathered gift basket (height, 6½ inches). The rim is adorned with shell disk beads, and the decoration is completed with glass beads and abalone shell pendants.

The Kuksu Cult

Our information about the Kuksu Cult is scanty. We know that its ceremonial performances were of great importance to many peoples of central California, and we have some descriptions of the dances. However, we know little about the beliefs behind the practices. Kuksu ceremonies were shared by the Pomo with several other central California tribes, most notably the Wintun and the Maidu. This cult probably took form about a thousand years ago among these people, but no one knows where. Perhaps it was brought in by outsiders, like the modern Ghost Dance, and spread from tribe to tribe. Kuksu may be the name of the man who began the cult.

Among the Pomo, Kuksu was believed to be a spirit, but some of the other central California tribes, the Maidu, for instance, believed that he was the first man. (The myth at the beginning of this chapter is from the Maidu.) The Maidu performed the Kuksu ceremonials to dramatize the creation myth, but the Pomo performances carried other meaning, and they involved impersonating the spirit.

Kuksu Ritual. The Pomo form had a secret society to which all men belonged and into which all boys were initiated by older members, who symbolically killed the boys and then brought them back to life as members of the society. Cult activities, such as initiations, almost always took place in a ceremonial chamber, a large, earth-covered, semiunderground structure a little like a Pueblo kiva. Members of the cult may have used this building for leisure-time lounging or sweating in addition to the ritual observances.

The Kuksu dancers beat rhythm on a foot drum, a six- to ten-foot log slab on which they danced. The disguised and costumed dancers impersonated spirits: they did not dance to show off their costumes as the Yurok did. The Kuksu ritual was part of a cycle of dances and ceremonies that went on throughout the winter—the Pomo were dispersed in summer. A major ceremony was held in any one place only once in several years, which was just as well because it usually involved the expense and labor of building a new dance house. Between times, people visited and took part in their neighbors' ceremonies.

The whole cycle of dances was presumed to bring rain and nourish the earth, to bring a bountiful natural crop, and to ward off epidemics, floods, and earthquakes. The Kuksu dancers themselves brought renewed spiritual life to the community and took away sins and illnesses; the Kuksu was thus a world renewal ceremony.

Ceremonies began with social dances by men and women, though later in the presentations only men participated. Then came the "fire-devils," painted naked men who frightened the women and children, especially those about to be initiated. Finally came the true Kuksu, with painted bodies and huge, elaborate headdresses with radiating feathered sticks and a cover for the face such as a big red feather nose that hid the wearer's identity. The word *Kuksu* refers to both the dancer and the headdress. Each dancer danced separately about the dance house, moving in circles and turning his body in symbolic harmony with the universe. All the men of the village participated as dancers, drummers, fire tenders, or master of ceremonies. As the dancers left the village, the people believed they took with them all the community's sickness and sin.

During the ceremonial performances, the Kuksu danced in the assembly house at least once each day. The people spent the intervals eating, gambling, playing games, and watching other dances.

Ghosts and Spirits

There were other rituals in the cycle besides the Kuksu, such as the Coyote Dance and the Ghost Ceremony. The Coyote was the son of the creator who brought life to man, and the dance was a retelling of the origin myth. The ancient Ghost Ceremony—not to be confused with the Ghost Dance of the 1870s—was like the Kuksu in many ways. The "ghosts" were fearsome for the women and children, who were not allowed in the dance house to see the dance itself. The two kinds of ghost dancers were "ash ghosts" and "ghosts" proper, both having painted bodies and fancy head coverings. The ash ghosts had white ash on them and, it was believed, ate live coals. They probably were connected with the Pomo practice of cremating the dead.

The Pomo were unusual in that they believed in a creator god. However, their main religious concern was an ever-present fear of the spirits of field and woods. This dread kept them on good behavior, causing them to wash themselves, to take care of their children, to respect nature, to be honest and truthful, and to sing prayers day and night. Doing these things, they believed, kept the spirit world friendly. Boys and girls underwent a painful and frightening initiation to adulthood, which both scared and controlled the children and reminded all that fear and pain were a part of life.

Southern California Indians

On the coast, transitional between central California and the south, were groups we refer to as Costanoan, from the Spanish word meaning "coastal people." They lived to the south of San Francisco Bay in an area famous for many large seashell mounds, the result of mussel dinners on the same spot for thousands of years. From the little we know of the Costanoan culture, we believe that their food quest, material culture, death practices, and religious beliefs must have been similar to others of the central and south coastal areas.

The Chumash were another group who lived along the coast and on the islands just north of the present city of Los Angeles. Spaniards first arrived among them in 1542, but so little was recorded about their aboriginal settlements and subsistence that almost all we know about them comes from archaeology. We do know that they fished from and traveled in oceangoing boats made of planks sealed with asphalt from natural deposits in their territory.

The Mission Indians

The Indians who lived along the seacoast from San Francisco Bay south to the Mexican border were first disrupted by white contact—Spanish missionaries—more than two centuries ago. The missionaries took them over, reorganizing them into groups around the closest mission with little regard for tribal origins, cultural unity, or native languages. All had been hunters and gatherers; the missionaries forced them to become cultivators and cattle herders. So complete was mission control, backed up by Spanish soldiery, that old life-styles were lost within a generation or two. These tribes, known to us mostly by Spanish names (usually names of missions), are often called "mission Indians." Early descriptions of those Indians by missionaries and travelers relate their lives at missions, not their ways of living in native villages, especially not their "pagan" beliefs and ceremonies, which the Spanish were most eager to change. We are not likely ever to know all the original tribes and their distributions, populations, or cultures.

"Mission Indians" usually means the coastal tribes from Los Angeles to the Mexican boundary, though all the Indians from the Costanoans south have been given that name at various times. The cultures of these Indians were similar, and all but the Diegueño spoke Shoshonean languages. Their ways of life showed relationships with the Shoshonean speakers of the Great Basin to the east. They probably moved into California from the Basin relatively late, displacing other groups already in California, possibly the Diegueño and the Chumash, who moved south and north respectively. The easier food quest in California produced greater social and religious complexity and elaboration than the Great Basin tribes had. The southern Californians' own names for themselves and for each other were lost in years of mission living; today we know them only by the names of the missions where they settled in historic times.

Among the better known of these mission groups were the Fernandeño, named after the mission San Fernando, and the Gabrielino, after San Gabriel.

They appear to have been closely related and in pre-mission times probably were part of the same large ethnic group. The two tribes occupied most of the present area of Los Angeles and Orange counties, the islands of Santa Catalina, and San Clemente, most of the fertile lowland of southern California.

The Juaneño were named for the famous mission San Juan Capistrano, south of Los Angeles. Next in order south were the Luiseño, after the mission San Luis Rey de Francis, and the Diegueño, who occupied the last strip of coastline before the present Mexican border. They were named after the mission San Diego, as was the present city. They spoke a language of the Yuman family, and probably resembled the Yuma and other tribes to the east more than the other mission Indians did.

The Luiseño

The Luiseño lived mostly in the hills, not on the coastal lowlands like most of the other southern mission tribes. Perhaps that is why more of their old villages

In this earliest known view of California, Christianized Indians at the mission in Carmel are lined up to welcome a visiting French scientific expedition.

and ways of life lasted long enough for the early ethnographers to record. They spoke one language, with differences in dialect from the extreme north to the far south. They had no tribal name for themselves, but they did have names for local groups. Their pre-European population has been estimated at three to four thousand.

Life-style. The main part of the Luiseño diet was acorns and seeds; they also ate shoots, fruit, berries, and roots, and used at least twenty plants as household medicines. They ate some venison and lots of rabbits. Other supplementary meats were wood rats, mice, ground squirrels, quail, ducks, grasshoppers, mollusks, and fish. They hunted with the bow, but probably trapped and snared as much game as they shot.

If the early reports are accurate, the Luiseño used all three types of canoes found in California: the balsa or tule canoe like the Pomo, the dugout canoe like the Yurok, and the tarred plank boat like the Chumash. They built their houses in pits about two feet deep and eight across and often covered them with earth. Women cooked outside under a thatch roof shade, open on all sides. The men's sweathouse was small, used only for daily sweating, not as a clubhouse or sleep-

A Luiseño
sweathouse.

ing quarters. The dance and ceremony house was not a building at all, but a circular area ringed with posts and without a roof. Spectators could watch by looking in the entrances or peering over the posts. The Luiseño made big baskets, mostly for storage, but not the fine watertight ones, for, unlike most California Indians, the Luiseño (and the Diegueño) made pottery, probably having learned how from the Southwest. They also made pottery pipes in the form of tubes, which the men smoked lying down just before retiring.

Organization.   Little is known about the structure of Luiseño society before the Spanish, Mexicans, and Americans displaced them and reduced their numbers. They had patrilineal family groups, perhaps clans, which joined together to form ceremonial groups. Many of the southern mission Indians had a moiety organization, but we do not know that the Luiseño observed this dual pattern. Most kin groups were small, almost the equivalent of large extended families. Several smaller groups clustered about a large group and its chief or headman for the ceremonial grouping. The chief ordered the ceremonies, so a group without a chief depended on joining with other groups for religious activities. Chieftainship was hereditary; it was not wealth that brought honor, status, and leadership as in the Northwest, but the office that brought wealth. The followers supplied the wealth needed to carry out the ceremonies the chief directed, which were a cultural focal point for the participants.

Because we know so little about these precontact mission Indians, we tend to assume that they shared most traits, but it might be simply mission influence that made them seem alike. Some things about the Luiseño ceremonies do apply to the other mission and inland southern California tribes, some we assume were shared, and some are unique, or at least are recorded only for the Luiseño.

Religious Rituals.   Luiseño religious life focused on initiation rites and mourning rites. Both these basic tribal ceremonies involved the Toloache Cult, which the Luiseño shared with the neighboring tribes. Members of this cult used the narcotic, vision-producing Jimson weed or datura plant, and believed in a deity, Chungichnish, who gave the ritual to the Indians. The cult was centered on the boys' initiation into the secret society of the Toloache. In addition to weeks of fasting and physical and mental ordeal, the youths were expected to attain a new perspective on life in a "new vision," a violent mystical experience induced by the drug. The dreams a boy had at initiation he remembered all his life, and they determined much of his behavior and beliefs.

Songs, an important part of all Luiseño ceremonies, were unvarying myths and descriptions of rituals, though some were secular. Interestingly, some of their songs were in the Gabrielino language, which may mean that the Toloache Cult spread from the Gabrielino to the Luiseño.

The Luiseño had only two or three standard dances, which were used in most of the rituals. The most spectacular was the Fire Dance climaxing the Toloache initiation. It began with a huge bonfire and a ring of barefoot men dancing around it. By rhythmically closing in on and retreating from the edge of the fire, stamping on the hot embers, they snuffed it out.

Like the Pueblo and Navajo, the mission tribes made sand paintings by dribbling colored sands into designs three to twelve feet in diameter. They used these paintings in the Toloache initiation for boys, in the girls' adolescence ceremony, and in the death rites for members of the Toloache society. The circular sand painting was not quite representational, but had elements that stood for serpents, stars, and mountains—making a sort of picture of the world. At the center was a small pit or depression called the "Hole of the Dead" or the "Navel of the Universe," symbolizing death and burial of cremated remains.

The usual dance costume was a net skirt decorated with eagle feathers that swung out as the dancer spun around. Its simplicity compared to the dance regalia of northern and central California may be a result of the Jimson weed psychic effect; the dancers supposedly had their attention turned inward, recalling their own visions when they had been initiated.

Toloache Ceremony.   A Toloache initiation ceremony was held only once every few years, whenever there were enough boys of the right age. All the boys, plus any older boys, men not initiated in childhood, or men who had married into the tribe, were brought together and given the drug to drink. The potion was very carefully administered, for too large a dose could have been, and sometimes was, fatal. Only the initiates took the drug; no one ever drank the Toloache more than once in his lifetime. The boys passed out and dreamt while the adults danced all night around the fire. A boy usually dreamt about an animal, and never again killed that animal.

The ceremony ran for about six days, the boys dancing at night and sleeping during the day, fasting all the while. Even after six days of dancing, other rituals went on, the initiation tapering off slowly. For months the boys ate no meat and took part in occasional night dances. Older men taught them special knowledge during this time, such as the secret of the Fire Dance and other magic. The sand painting was made right after the fast. After a long lecture on proper moral behavior, a lump of meal was placed in each boy's mouth, which they all spat into the center pit of the painting. The painting was swept into the pit so that noninitiates would never see it.

As part of the ordeal of passing into manhood, the boys underwent a trial in which they were covered with biting red ants. They had to endure the pain sol-

A Luiseño circular sand painting made with lampblack and cornstarch.

emnly, without complaint. On another occasion they had to walk carefully through a trench on stepping stones laid out in the shape of a corpse; a stumble foretold an early death.

The other major ceremony of the Toloache Cult came at a society member's mourning anniversary. The members made a sand painting about Chungichnish, then swept the dead one's dance feathers and other ceremonial possessions into the pit and destroyed the painting.

The Girls' Ceremony. A girls' adolescence ceremony, though supposed to take place whenever a girl reached puberty, usually was not performed until several girls could undergo the rite at the same time. Probably a rich man's daughter celebrated her first menses and other girls participated, avoiding the costs or sharing them. The sponsoring parents were expected to feed the guests who attended the ceremony.

CHARACTERISTICS OF CALIFORNIA TRIBES

Clothing	Food production	Equipment	Shelter	Social and political organization	Religion	Warfare
Hide or fiber skirts	Gathering (seeds, acorns, wild plants, shellfish)	Bows and arrows	Simple dwellings of grass, brush, or bark	Families	Elaborate death ceremonies and puberty rites	Generally peaceful
Skin capes (in bad weather)	Hunting	Hooks	Gabled plank houses (in north)	Small villages	Shamans	Feuds settled by payment
Aprons	Fishing	Mats	Wooden sweathouses	Clans (occasionally)	Witchcraft	
Breechcloths	Grasshoppers (Pomo)	Nets	Subterranean shelters	Headmen	Women curers (Yurok)	
Rabbit-fur blankets		Canoes	Temporary lean-tos (Pomo, in summer)		Myths	
Hide or fiber footwear, sandals		Traps	Redwood bark tipi-like structure (Pomo, in winter)		World Renewal Ceremonies	
		Snares			First Fish Ceremony	
		Weirs			Kuksu Cult	
		Harpoons			Ghost Ceremony (Pomo)	
		Rafts (Pomo)			Toloache Cult (Luiseño)	
					Drug use in some areas	
					Creator god	
					Long series of rituals (central California)	

The girls' ceremony did not involve the Toloache drug. First the girls swallowed balls of tobacco. Anyone who vomited was thought to be unchaste. Then the girls were "roasted," laid out in a pit lined with warm stones and covered with more stones. They had to lie perfectly still for three days in the pit. During the night the men, and during the day the women, danced around them. They were let out once a day for bodily functions and given a light meal while the stones were being reheated. When they emerged, their faces were painted by the village chief's wife, and their bodies were decorated, sometimes tattooed. Exactly a month later, the girls gathered for a sand painting, after which their bodies were touched with balls of meal, which were then placed in their mouths. They spat them into the pit and the painting was destroyed.

Death Rites.   Most of the southern California Indians held elaborate death ceremonies. Luiseño ceremonies had two distinct parts: immediately after death the body was cremated and possessions were burned, then about a year later, images were made of the deceased and then burned.

When death was imminent, or immediately upon death, kinsmen dug a pit about two feet deep running north and south. They filled it with brush, erected a log pyre over it, and placed the body on top, face upward, head to the north. One kinsman supervised the cremation while other relatives sat nearby, weeping and wailing. It often took twelve hours for the flames to consume the body; if the heart were slow to burn, it was punched full of holes to speed destruction. When the body was consumed, the bones and ashes were gathered up and placed in a basket. Saving garments for a later ceremony, kinsmen burned all other possessions, while singing, dancing, and mourning went on all night.

The next morning, or as soon as enough food had been gathered, the dead one's clothes were washed, then they too were burned. This released the deceased from all earthly ties.

Usually only relatives were present at the cremation and the burning of possessions; that was a private ceremony and a time for grief. The effigy burning was a public ceremony which honored all the year's dead. All the neighboring people were invited, sometimes as many as five hundred, and food had to be provided for all for a week. Thus it was sensible to combine mourning for several people into one great public observance.

Mourners made the effigies of sticks and brush, with buckskin heads, and dressed them in men's or women's clothing. These images represented all the dead of the community since the last effigy burning. The ceremony lasted a week; on the last night all images and offerings to the dead were piled up and ignited as the assemblage mourned.

On the anniversary of a chief's death, his kinfolk held a night-long dance during which they killed, skinned, and cremated an eagle. Its feathers became part of a dance outfit.

Bibliography

Suggestions for Further Study

Kroeber, Alfred L.
1925   *Handbook of the Indians of California.*
An encyclopedic work on the cultures of the California area by an outstanding specialist. This book should be the starting point for all studies on California Indians.

Kroeber, Theodora
1961   *Ishi in Two Worlds.*
An account of the last surviving Yana Indian, who surrendered himself to the white world on August 19, 1911. A sensitive and fascinating book that conveys the heartbreak that comes from having one's way of life destroyed. Unforgettable.

Other Pertinent Works

Heizer, Robert F., and Alan Almquist
1971   *The Other Californians.* (Indian-White relations)

Heizer, Robert F., and M. A. Whipple
1951   *The California Indians.*

Strong, William D.
1929   *Aboriginal Society in Southern California.*

MAJOR GROUPS AND LANGUAGES
OF CALIFORNIA

Language phylum	Language family	Cultural division
Aztec-Tanoan	Uto-Aztecan	Cahuilla Gabrielino Luiseño Serraño
Hokan	Chumashan	Chumash
	Karok	Karok
	Palaihnihan	Achomawi Atsugewi
	Pomo	Pomo
	Shastan	Shasta
	Yanan	Yana
	Yuman	Diegueño

Continued

MAJOR GROUPS AND LANGUAGES (continued)

Language phylum	Language family	Cultural division

CALIFORNIA (continued)

Language phylum	Language family	Cultural division
Macro-Algonkian	Wiyot	Wiyot
	Yurok	Yurok
Na-Dene	Athabaskan	Hupa Tolowa
Penutian	Maidu	Maidu
	Miwok-Costanoan	Costanoan Miwok
	Wintun	Wintun
	Yokuts	Yokuts
Undetermined	Yuki	Wappo Yuki

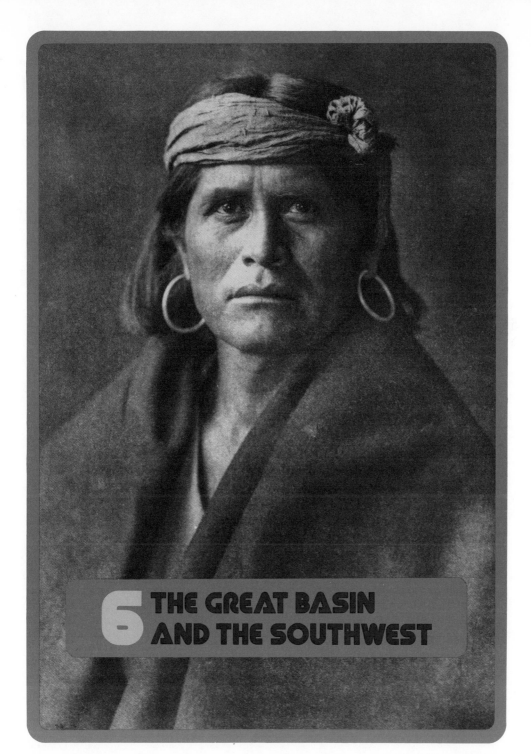

6 THE GREAT BASIN
AND THE SOUTHWEST

THE GREAT BASIN

SZSZSZSZSZSZSZSZSZSZS

There was a time when only animals and birds lived on the land, and they had no fire. Coyote knew that there was fire someplace, for he could see smoke in the distance. He did not know where it was coming from, so he sent the birds into the sky. Woodpecker went up and out of sight, but he returned without learning the source of fire. "Let me try," said Hawk, but he too returned without seeing it. Finally Eagle set out, and when he returned, he said, "There are flames on the other side of the mountain." They all decided to go to the fire, Coyote leading, followed by Woodpecker, Hawk, Bluejay, Rabbit, Roadrunner, and others. Coyote was very clever. He thought, "We must not let the fire-owners know why we are coming. We will carry firedrills to make them think we already have fire."

When they crossed over the mountain, they said to the fire-owners, "We have come to have fun, to gamble and play with you." The hosts gave them all food—to each bird a different kind of seed, to Coyote, berries. After they had eaten they began to gamble. This is what they did: they made three piles of dirt and hid a stone in one pile. Others had to bet on which pile held the stone. Whoever guessed right won the game. The hosts said, "You have not come to gamble; you have come to steal our fire." Then Coyote showed them the firedrills and said, "No, we have fire ourselves." Toward morning, they began to dance. Coyote wore a headdress over his hair and danced close to the fire. He danced closer and closer. Suddenly he bent over the fire and a spark caught in his headdress. The animals all ran toward home followed by the fire-owners. Before long, Bluejay was caught and killed by the pursuers. The animals were getting tired. One after the other they carried the fire. Finally Roadrunner said, "Let me carry it," and he ran making his feet point in many directions so the pursuers could not tell where he had gone. He escaped, and built a big fire back on the other side of the mountain.

That evening it began to rain. Coyote and his people carried plenty of wood to the fire, but the rain put it all out save one coal. Rabbit covered that with his tail until the rain stopped. But all the wood was wet then, and they could not find any tinder. Rat said, "I have a dry nest. We will use that." Soon they had fire again. Then Coyote dried his bow and arrow *and killed Rat and roasted him in the fire. After that he killed Rabbit, skinned him, and made a blanket of the skin. He said, "From now on people will do this."*

The Environment

201

SZSZSZSZSZSZSZSZSZSZSZSZ

The upland area known as the Great Basin covers Nevada, Utah, and parts of California, Idaho, and Wyoming. On the east, north, and west it is surrounded by mountain ranges, but its southern boundary is not sharp—one of many reasons to consider the Southwest and Basin as extensions of each other. Another is the desert conditions in both areas.

The foragers in the Basin and the cultivators in the Southwest, and the ways of survival both learned, reach back to a common base in the Desert Archaic period. Abundant milling equipment dating back to 9000 B.C. indicates that by then people were shifting away from big game hunting, depending more and more on wild plants for food. People of that period left behind other evidence of their way of life: wooden digging sticks, netting, and basketry. As thousands of years went by, these tools, plus leather, fur, and fiber clothing, remained vital for human adaptation to an environment that to modern people seems nearly barren of life-sustaining materials.

The Environment

The few streams in the Basin flow down from the surrounding mountains into the central depression rather than to the oceans. The area receives little precipitation and evaporation is high, so the water bodies in the Basin are quite salty. The Great Salt Lake of Utah is all that remains of ancient Lake Bonneville, which once covered an area about 350 miles long and 150 miles wide. Alkaline flats, the dry traces of old water beds, are common in the Basin. Those rivers that still carry water have cut canyons so deep that there are no flood plains to make cultivation easier.

Summers in the Basin and Southwest are hot, often over 100 degrees, and winters are cold, with temperatures sometimes falling to 20 degrees below zero. Precipitation there is never more than ten inches a year, and in many areas it is far less because the western mountains receive all the moisture brought by winds coming in from the Pacific. The streams depend on the mountain snows

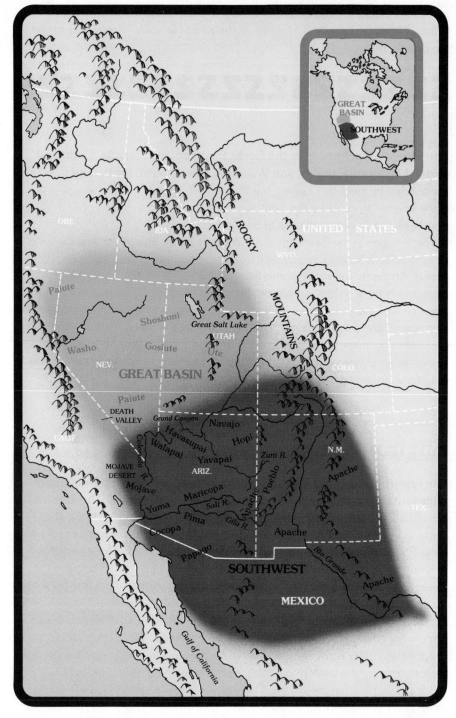

The Great Basin
and the Southwest
culture areas and
their tribes.

rather than rainfall. Patches of grass and clumps of desert vegetation like sage-brush are as much as the land can manage with so little rain. When Europeans first tried to cross the Basin, many died of starvation and thirst.

Though smaller areas within the bleak Basin varied in altitude and amount of available water, nowhere could people depend on a plentiful year-round food supply. Plant resources fluctuated yearly, each one being in short supply at least every two or three years. They also grew and matured at different times, forcing the Indian harvesters to move regularly from zone to zone. However, while no one plant was abundant enough to support people, many species could be eaten, and the people gathered every bit of the sparse vegetation: seeds, berries, nuts, leaves, and stalks, tubers, roots, and bulbs. So thoroughly did they exploit underground plant parts with digging sticks that they were called "Diggers" by Europeans, a term that later came to imply contempt for their poverty.

The animal food supply also fluctuated. Occasional antelope, and rarely a mountain sheep, were the only animals of any size to tolerate Basin conditions, so the people ate many species that others considered inedible—rats, snakes, and insects. Most of their meat, however, came from rabbits, whose populations exploded every few seasons and at other times became quite scarce. Where streams cut through the Basin, the people added fish to their diet—trout, salmon, and suckers—and also waterfowl and their eggs. When salmon were running, people could catch them in quantity, but since they did not know how to dry or smoke them, it was only worthwhile for them to catch what they could eat right away.

In the thousands of years between the Desert Archaic and European contact, Basin Indians did little to change their way of life, though survival became still harder as the climate grew drier. Indeed, studying the ways of life of modern Shoshoni and Ute has given us a reasonably good picture of the Desert Archaic.

Basin People

The harsh environment held the human population down and spread it thin; probably it never grew beyond 65,000 or 75,000 for the whole Basin area. All the groups in the Great Basin spoke Shoshonean languages of the Uto-Aztecan family, except for the Washo near the California boundary who spoke a Hokan language. As in so many other areas, people of the same linguistic group did not think of themselves as anything like a tribe. They lived in bands of perhaps fifty to a hundred people, and though they recognized common customs and dialects, they had only the vaguest notion of unity.

Exploiting the Environment

Bands occasionally came together to hunt rabbit or antelope or share a good crop of pine nuts and enjoy a bit of relaxation and sociability while there was enough for all to eat. Then they broke once more into smaller units—often individual families—to continue the never-ending hunt for subsistence. During winters people usually congregated in small settlements, separating into foraging bands and family groups again when the weather grew warmer.

Within the territory that belonged to the general unit we call a tribe, the bands moved in a fairly regular pattern over perhaps fifty to one hundred square miles. They took plant foods as they ripened, harvesting everything available in one small area and then moving on to another. Even with this diverse food supply, people suffered many lean years, and populations stayed small. The least productive territory was the southwest, the Mojave Desert and Death Valley. Life was not as hard in the mountain areas of California, Idaho, and Wyoming, where more water, game, and plants were available. But nowhere could people stop their search for food to settle down long, and with their simple technology, agriculture was impossible.

Housing.   In winter, a structure called a *wickiup* sheltered families in the central and northern areas of the Basin. This was a conical or domed hut of poles

A wickiup, used by
Basin families as a
winter dwelling.

covered with brush, matting, or bark strips, with a center fire pit and a smoke hole in the roof. Summer housing consisted of temporary huts or windscreens of brush, mostly for shade. Most housing in the very arid regions of the south was brush.

Some Basin people built sweathouses of brush or hides, making the interior steamy by pouring water over heated stones in a center pit. Sweathouses were built near a stream if possible so people could plunge into the water after sweating. As in other areas, sweating served as a kind of ritual purification, and it was also thought to have medical value. In some parts of the Basin, the heat for sweating came directly from an interior fire; this kind of sweathouse usually was a larger structure also used as a meeting house.

Food. As their ancestors had done for thousands of years, the Basin people held communal rabbit hunts when the rabbit population increased. Piñon nuts, grasshoppers, and antelope also showed a periodic spurt in numbers. Piñon nuts ripened in late fall, but like everything in the Basin, the crop was highly unpredictable from year to year. Women did most of the gathering, beating the cones that held the nuts from the piñon pines. In a good year, they might collect enough to store for a year or more, because the nuts kept well. When the grasshoppers swarmed, it was a joyous affair. People beat the grass, driving the insects into a pit, then boiled them, roasted them, or pounded them into a paste which was dried for storage.

Whenever antelope were available, the bands came together to hunt them communally, driving them into an enclosure of sagebrush and stone. Directed by an antelope shaman, who was believed to have supernatural power over antelope, the men, dressed in antelope headdresses, sang songs to lure the animals into the trap. Other hunters waited in ambush to kill them.

Women learned many ways of preserving plant food to help tide their families over the winter. They ground seeds, made them into cakes, and dried them to be consumed later. They dried berries whole or pounded them into a powder, and stored nuts in hide bags. All these provisions were kept in grass-lined storage pits at the site of the winter encampment.

Winter brought the best hunting, but even then animals were not plentiful. In the drier southern areas, game was so scarce that there was very little hunting at any season. However, Basin people used all food resources with such thoroughness that though they rarely feasted, they were rarely faced with starvation.

Technology. The Basin people's clothing and equipment stayed essentially the same for thousands of years: buckskin breechclouts and leggings in winter for men; aprons of shredded bark, fibers, or hide for women; and in cold weather, woven rabbit-skin cloaks and blankets and hide moccasins for both. Snowshoes made it easier to walk over deep snow. The most developed part of

Basin technology was willow basketry, as it was among most seed gatherers of western North America. Basin women made carrying baskets, seed beaters, trays, and bottles tightly woven and coated with pitch to hold water. They used natural vegetable stains to dye strands that could be woven in with the uncolored fibers to make designs.

Social Organization

In some parts of the Basin food was so scarce that people could gather into band-sized groups only once every few years. Between times they lived as isolated extended families, joining others only in years of rabbit hunts, good piñon harvests, or the like. Kinfolk on both the mother's and the father's sides were equally important. Anyone could marry anyone as long as no blood relationship could be traced between them. Marriages were made within the band and between bands, and the couple joined the family of one spouse or the other, often alternating as economic conditions changed. Among some groups, a man might have two wives (usually sisters), but monogamy was the rule, and divorce was simple: the couple merely separated.

These people had no tribal leadership at all. During band gatherings the temporary position of rabbit boss or antelope shaman provided an authority who could direct the hunt successfully. Those leaders acted while the group congregated and saw that people behaved during any recreation and dancing. When the group disbanded, their leadership ended, for it was no longer necessary. Individual families then followed the suggestions of the family elders.

Along with the help they gave in hunting antelope, shamans healed the sick and could appeal to the spirit world on behalf of the people. No one was a full-time specialist; shamans lived like everyone else, hunting, fishing, and so on. Each individual's relationship with the supernatural was his private business. There were no community rites, though the people enjoyed watching the shaman's curing activities as a moment of entertainment in a difficult way of life. People did seek spirit guidance, but the vision quest was much simpler here than in the Plateau and Northwest Coast.

The Paiute

All Basin peoples lived much the same kind of life, and the Paiute furnish a good example of it. Their territory spread from north to south over the western part of the Basin, interrupted only by the Washo. The Owens Valley Paiute, who lived just east of what is now Yosemite National Park, had the streams flowing

CHARACTERISTICS OF THE GREAT BASIN TRIBES

Clothing	Food production	Equipment	Shelter	Social and political organization	Religion	Warfare
Leather, fur, and fiber clothing	Foraging	Digging sticks	Wickiups (winter)	Nuclear families	Shamans	Warfare rare
Buckskin breechcloths and leggings	Hunting	Bows and arrows	Temporary huts or windscreens (summer)	Extended families	Simple form of Vision Quest	Short-lived feuds
Skirts	Fishing	Nets	Sweathouses	Bands	Spirits (animals, plants, and natural phenomena)	
Bark, fiber, or hide aprons	Grasshopper drives	Clubs			Ghosts	
Rabbit-skin cloaks and blankets		Hide bags			Witchcraft	
Hide moccasins		Basketry				
Snowshoes		Seed beaters				
Woven hats						

from the Sierras to make their lives a little easier; but most Paiute lived in very small groups, often just extended families, and never stopped moving in their search for food. They had no tribal organization, but several bands would get together for dances and feasts on the rare occasions when they had enough food.

Food and Clothing. The Paiute followed a regular seasonal pattern of food-getting within the band's traditional territory, knowing which roots and bulbs to dig in spring, where seeds and berries ripened in summer, and so on through fall, when the piñon crop came in. As they pursued plant foods, the Paiute also collected almost anything that walked, flew, or crawled—larvae and adult insects, grasshoppers, locusts, and ants. Men hunted for meat too, but in a land where plants were scarce, animals were scarce. With long sticks the men prodded rats,

An 1862 photo of two Indians and a white visitor. The Indians are wearing belted cloaks made of strips of rabbit fur woven together.

An Indian woman balances a basket in a conical carrying net, which is supported by a tumpline, or strap, across her forehead. Women were so accustomed to carrying heavy loads, that they actually found it difficult to walk unburdened.

lizards, and ground squirrels out of their burrows, and they set traps for rabbits. If rabbits were plentiful, the community held a rabbit hunt. A real windfall was an antelope or two.

The men could not catch enough animals to make much buckskin, and the people wore little hide clothing—only a loincloth for men and sometimes a skirt for women. Most of the time women wore fiber aprons, and sandals, if worn at all, were made of fiber too. Both sexes wore skin moccasins in winter, and woven rabbit-skin robes. To make these, the men cut each rabbit skin spiral-fashion into one long strip, which they twisted so that fur stuck out on all sides. The strips were twined with a fiber thread into a blanket or robe. Sometimes bird skins with the feathers still on were treated in the same way. Both kinds of robes were light and warm.

Baskets.   Paiute women were basketmakers of great skill. Working with reeds, grasses, bark fibers, or twigs, they made almost every implement except the men's hunting equipment: cradles, mats, seed beaters, hats, and above all, baskets. Baskets served as water jars, dishes, and containers. Large carrying baskets had vertical poles sticking through the bottom to hold them upright on the ground. The women carried those on their backs suspended by a strap called a tumpline across the forehead. To keep the tumplines from cutting into their skin, the women wore basket hats.

Dreams and Curing.   Men and women found spirit power in dreams, in which the spirit appeared as an animal or plant, mountains, clouds, or other natural phenomena. This power brought strength, skill, endurance, and good fortune, and to shamans it also gave the ability to cure. Dreams also could cause illness, not necessarily to the dreamer: a member of his family or a friend might become ill if a person dreamed it.

Ghosts too caused illness, for they attempted to steal souls. Witches sickened a victim by magically making some object like a small stone, worm, or lizard enter his body. Shamans cured the illness by sucking out the foreign object or going into a trance to retrieve the lost soul. Singing and dancing usually went on along with curing performances, providing entertainment for onlookers. Both men and women could become curers by getting spirit help, either involuntarily from dreams or by a quest in special mountain areas where it was thought the spirits would come to the seeker.

The Paiute never had enough of anything to make them targets for attacks by other Indians. Disagreements in the form of feuds sometimes erupted within the band, but they never lasted long, simply because the job of getting food left little energy for fighting.

THE SOUTHWEST

Keresan
Origin Myth

ⱯⱯⱯⱯⱯⱯⱯⱯⱯⱯⱯⱯⱯ

In the beginning, the earth was square and flat, and below its surface were four layers. All people, birds, and beasts lived in the bottom layer or world. Everything was in darkness. There was no sun, no moon. It was dark and it was crowded, but the people did not know how to get out. At

*last two boys pierced the roof of the lowest layer, making an opening. The
people tried all the plants that grew one after the other, hoping that one
would be tall enough to allow them to climb out. Finally after many trials,
they found a reed so tall that it grew through the opening. The people
climbed it to the second layer.*

*At first there was room for all, but that layer too became crowded, and
like the first world, it was dark. Again the people placed the plant under
the roof opening and climbed out. The third world too was dark. The two
boys found fire and set torches ablaze. In that light the men built kivas.
Things were not well, however. The women became crazed and neglected
their children. They danced all the time, ceasing only to sleep, and fathers
took care of the children. The men soon had enough of that and ascended
into the fourth world, this world. But it too was dark, and people worked
by the light of torches and fires.*

*Other beings of the world had come out with the people: one was
Spider. Spider tried to make it light. She spun a pure white cloth that
gave some light, but it was not enough. It was sent to the west and became
the moon. The people prepared a very white deerskin that made a bril-
liant light. From the skin they formed a shield and sent it to the east,
where it became the sun. Now there was light.*

*Now that people were living in the upper world, some of them began to
explore, and quarrel, and marry and beget children. Animals lived in the
world of light too, and some of them helped the people while others
played tricks on them.*

ⅤΑⅤΑⅤΑⅤΑⅤΑⅤΑⅤΑⅤΑⅤΑⅤ

**In many ways the Southwest is a continuation of the Great Basin, but
the river valleys are wider to the south, and some of the area has exten-**
sive plateaus. The plateau region is divided into flat-topped eminences called
mesas, and steep-walled canyons; the Grand Canyon of the Colorado is the
most dramatic. The mouth of the Colorado River, where it empties into the Gulf
of California, is much lower than the plateau region to the northeast; winters are
warmer there, and it is even drier than in the Great Basin. The Rocky Mountains, with peaks rising over 10,000 feet, have forests of firs at high altitudes,
with juniper and dwarf pine on lower slopes. In the valleys cottonwood trees, willow, and alder grow among bushes, vines, and other small growths. This non-
mountainous territory has scanty vegetation, poor grassland, low shrubs, many
kinds of cactus, and other plants adapted to dry conditions, such as yucca
and agave.

Early Peoples of the Southwest

The cultures of the Southwest, like those of the Great Basin, grew out of the Desert Archaic. Their diet too emphasized plant food, which predis-posed them toward using more and wider varieties of plant species. When farming techniques and corn spread north from Mexico, probably after 4000 B.C., some people in the Southwest added this new food to their diet.

Slowly the idea of cultivation spread around the Southwest, wherever there was enough water for it. Three typical early farming cultures were the Mogollon, Hohokam, and Anasazi. Descendants of the Anasazi and probably some Mogollon became the Pueblo Indians of historic times, and the Hohokam seem likely to have been the ancestors of the historic Pima and Papago. Then in the last quarter of the thirteenth century, many Anasazi settlements were abandoned. It seems likely that the reason was an ecological crisis resulting from drought, worn-out soil, and erosion, plus raids by nonfarming nomads.

By the time Europeans came, three distinct ways of life had developed in the Southwest. One of these was farming near the area's rivers. Settled along the Colorado River were groups speaking Yuman languages, and along the Salt and Gila rivers were Piman speakers, the Pima and Papago. The Yumans on the Upper Colorado were marginal cultivators, getting only a little of their food by farming. Downriver, cultivation was much more productive. The Piman speakers too mixed cultivation with hunting and gathering. The Pima emphasized domesticated crops, while the Papago found more food from wild plants and animals.

Living in what the Spanish called *pueblos* were a fully agricultural, settled people, the Pueblo. (*Pueblo* with a capital *P* refers to the Indians themselves; with a lowercase *p* it means their dwelling.) The Pueblo were true farmers, drawing at least 80 percent of their food from their gardens.

Latecomers to the Southwest, the Navajo and Apache, had a third way of life. They were hunters and gatherers and knew nothing about cultivation. The Navajo raided the settled Pueblo, taking from them some knowledge of farming, as did a few Apache groups. Other Apache remained hunters and gatherers, raiding cultivated fields. In fact both names, *Navajo* and *Apache,* come from a Zuni phrase meaning "raiders of the fields."

There was great linguistic variety in the Southwest. In addition to Yuman languages of the Hokan phylum, and Piman, of the Aztec-Tanoan phylum, there were those Athabaskan languages spoken by the Navajo and Apache, the Penutian tongues, and a few more languages of uncertain affiliation. Population in the Southwest was much greater than in the Basin, perhaps 300,000, but unevenly distributed. More people lived in farming areas than in the open land where hunting and gathering people moved.

The Upland Yumans

Beside the Colorado River, from the Grand Canyon to where the river empties into the Gulf of California, lived a prehistoric people whom archaeologists have labeled Patayan. This name comes from a Yuman word with the same meaning as Anasazi: "the old people" or "the ancient ones." Archaeologists know less about the Patayan culture than about the Hohokam or Anasazi, but they believe these people were ancestors of the Yuman speakers who lived there later.

The Yumans who lived farther up the Colorado—the Havasupai, the Yavapai, and the Walapai—are often called the Upland Yumans. These three groups probably were closer to the old Desert Archaic tradition than others in the Southwest; we include them in this area because they did practice some agriculture. Their simple social organization, religious practices, and material culture were typical of the Basin tribes. They had no unilineal descent groups (clans or lineages), and the family was the basic unit for producing food and making decisions. The Upland Yumans' territory was too dry for cultivation much of the time, and their settlement patterns and population density varied according to where and when they could find water.

The Havasupai. We cannot leave the Upland Yumans without a look at the extraordinary environment of the Havasupai. Their home was the floor of Cataract Canyon, an arm of the Grand Canyon. The gorge of Cataract Creek, a small tributary of the Colorado, widens for a little way, making room for banks deep in rich earth laid down by floods over the ages. Here the canyon walls tower several hundred feet straight up, with only two frighteningly steep trails to the top. The cultivable floor is less than half a mile wide, split by the clear blue-green stream that gave the Havasupai their name, which means "the people of the turquoise water."

The Havasupai combined a Basin way of life with some cultivation. They dammed Cataract Creek to force the water into irrigation ditches that ran to fields on the narrow canyon floor. During the summer both men and women cultivated the fields, then in the winter they shifted to hunting and gathering up on the canyon rim. The quantity and kinds of their basketry equipment, like their winter way of life, showed Basin connections.

After fall harvest, when the cultivated food was processed and stored, the families scattered. Women left the canyon seeking seeds and piñon; men hunted or went on trading journeys to the Pueblo or to the Mojave lower down the Colorado, where they exchanged skins for pottery, beads, and woven blankets.

In summer, the Havasupai built four-post, brush-roofed shelters without walls as a defense against the searing heat. These structures, often called *shades,* blocked the sun and let air circulate freely. In winter the people made dwellings of framework covered with brush or reeds, sometimes with an outer covering of earth. During the hunt in the upper canyon the men built wickiups of branches and bark to live in while they sought deer, mountain sheep, and an occasional bear.

The River Yumans

Leaving its steep-sided canyon, the Colorado flows south into a much flatter valley. Annual floods fed by melting winter snows and spring rains in the mountains spread over the lower Colorado plain and delta, dropping new, rich soils every year. This yearly inundation transforms the hot desert in the south into a green oasis along the river plain. Here along the lower Colorado lived the Mojave, the Yuma, and below them the Cocopa, close to the river's mouth. Together with the Maricopa, who lived along the Gila River near its junction with the Colorado, these tribes are called the River Yumans.

Exploiting the Environment. Native cultivation depended wholly on the yearly flooding of the Colorado. Besides leaving deep silts for farm plots, the flood waters also nourished a dense growth of wild food plants and cane, willows, and rushes for basketry and housing. The wild foods and the cultivated corn, beans, and squash could feed a population much larger than that of the Basin or even the Upland Yumans to the north. The Indians helped the wild plants along by scattering their seeds on the less fertile or less well watered patches.

Hunting provided very little food for the River Yumans. Game, even rabbit, was hard to find, so most of their nonvegetable protein came from the fish they caught in the river.

The river people's villages consisted of houses scattered along the river and its delta, high in the valleys or on steep slopes to escape flooding. In this hot desert land, protection from the sun was far more important than protection from cold or rain. Consequently, most housing consisted of open-sided shades with flat, slightly slanting woven roofs. There were also some more substantial structures, large earth-covered dwellings which, since there was so little rain, stood for years.

The River Yumans did not need much clothing. Their garments were simple: breechcloths for men, and for women a short skirt of the fibrous inner layer of willow bark, softened in water and woven into a coarse cloth. Both men and women wore rabbit-skin robes in cooler weather. Moccasins were unknown, but occasionally the people wore hide sandals. Both sexes painted and tattooed their bodies. Material culture, including basketry, was also simple and rather poor in quality and durability. Trade with other tribes brought in better goods than home manufacture could produce.

Social Organization. The River Yumans had loose patrilineal clans, which did little beyond regulating marriage. People married outside their clan. The family was the basic economic and social unit, and families moved freely from settlement to settlement. Perhaps because of this movement among villages the Yumans had a strong sense of tribal identity. They had a tribal chief, whose leadership was hereditary: a dead chief's nearest male relative was the next leader so long as he was satisfactory to the rest of the people. His main functions were to give advice and to be dignified and wise. Within each settlement, local leaders acted as advisers, but their authority was no more than general esteem. The tribal chief himself had no means of enforcing his rulings.

Unlike the Pueblo or the Indians of California and the Basin, warfare was frequent among the River Yumans. Usually they fought with one another, though the Mojave and Yuma were generally allied with each other. Battle among these people had an almost ritual quality; it was thought of as a spiritual necessity and was strongly mystical. Encounters were stylized: the opposing forces drew up in battle array, advancing close enough for hand-to-hand fighting with clubs. Warriors might also carry bows and arrows or spears, usually specializing in one type of weapon. Often leading warriors fought duels in front of the assembled fighters before the battle, and sometimes the "war" was won by the side whose champion won the duel. Renown as a warrior increased a man's social status. War also involved raiding settlements for captives, usually female, who were made slaves. During both raids and battles fighting could be fierce, and scalps were taken from fallen enemies.

Religion. Among the River Yumans, religion was very individualistic. Dreams rather than vision quests were the source of power and success. Dreaming about spirits gave men aid in curing the sick or success in war or other endeavors. Respected men and chiefs were thought to receive their inspiration and wisdom from revelations in dreams. Dreams were supposed to be destined for each person before birth, part of the Yumans' strong sense of predestination. They believed each life was already "set up"; one had merely to learn his lot from dreams. People made their dreams public so that their powers would be known to all.

Because dreams came naturally, the Yumans felt no need for the fasting, isolation, body punishment, or drugs common in many other societies. Dreams were not always of power, but all were felt to have supernatural content or symbolic meaning which could be used to predict the future. Except for the supernatural nature of dreams, the River Yumans had no developed religious theory or practices. The only religious specialist, the shaman, got his power like the rest of the people, from dreams. Women dreamed, but rarely had real power dreams and did not become either shamans or political figures. So strong was the belief in dream power that to wish a person good luck, one said "good dreams."

Like the people of southern California, the Yumans cremated their dead. The body was laid, face downward, in a trench filled with dry brush, and dry wood was piled high over the whole. To this were added personal belongings of the deceased and any offerings the mourners wished to make. After the fire had burned down, the ashes were covered with earth. No one ever again spoke the name of the dead person.

The Pimans

Both Piman tribes, the Pima and the Papago, occupied the southwestern section of what today is Arizona. The Pima lived along the Salt and Gila rivers, and the Papago lived in the desert along the Mexican border. Probably they were once a single group, almost surely descended from the prehistoric Hohokam. The two groups spoke the same language, differing only in dialects. Their only other cultural difference was that cultivation in Pima territory was easier than in the Papago, which had no permanent flowing water. Thus the Pima were sedentary, while the Papago followed the ancient life of seasonal movement, seeking new water sources as old ones dried up and exploiting the wild plant and animal life of their desert.

Subsistence.　Primarily farmers, the Pima depended on water brought from the rivers by irrigation ditches to their fields of corn, beans, and squash. They supplemented their diet with wild plants and animals, which they badly needed in years of drought and crop failures, and with fish from the rivers. With such a relatively stable food supply, the Pima lived in permanent villages led by a headman who had considerable authority in directing labor in the irrigation works. And the Pima had a tribal chief, elected by the combined village chiefs.

The Papago depended mainly on hunting and gathering and supplemented that food with a small amount of farming. Violent July and August rains soaked the Papago fields and ensured water in the flat plains and in the water holes and ditches they constructed to control runoff. Their farming was possible only because of this summer rainfall. Men did most of the cultivating of the maize, tepary beans, and squashes, while women gathered wild plant foods. When summer rains ended, the fields dried and even drinking water disappeared from the plains. Then families wandered to the mountains to hunt or went to trade with neighboring groups.

Fish, important to the Pima, were unavailable to the Papago, whose territory had no waterways. The Papago had no choice but a seminomadic life, and their villages were autonomous units with no tribal structure. One of their ceremonial practices, rare north of the Mexican area, was to gather the fruit of the giant cactus and ferment it, making a wine which they drank with solemn ritual until they were drunk. This was a symbolic drunkenness; the people were saturated with alcohol as the fields were drenched by the summer rains. Long ago, the Pima too followed this practice, but they appear to have abandoned it shortly after European contact.

In that desert climate, neither of the Piman tribes needed much clothing: men wore breechcloths, women wore wraparound skirts. Both went barefoot most of the time, putting on leather or yucca fiber sandals to cross rocky terrain. Desert trees such as ironwood and mesquite provided the Pimans with wood for implements, and the women gathered grasses and reeds to make the fine basketry for

A Papago grass house in the desert of Arizona.

which they were known. They also made some pottery in the ancient Hohokam style. For houses they had slightly domed structures, perhaps fifteen feet in diameter, with earth or sand piled against the sides, and roofs of brush thatching. They also enjoyed open-sided shades like the other Southwest groups during the intense summer heat.

Social Organization. The Pimans were peaceful and went to war reluctantly when faced with the need. Their principal enemy was the Apache who raided their fields. A warrior who killed an enemy had to go through rigorous purification. The enemy's ghost was greatly dreaded, and a man who had killed might endanger the entire village. Consequently, far from being honored and praised, any warrior who killed was put with his polluted weapons into isolation, far from the village. After a quarantine, observing strict dietary taboos and ritual behavior, he was allowed to come back into the community. Warriors never bragged of their exploits, and even the scalps they took were purified and ever after were given offerings of tobacco smoke.

Villages of both tribes were large groups of patrilineally related families. Men were expected to choose wives from villages other than their own and bring them back home to live. Girls were secluded at puberty and all later menstrual periods, and women gave birth in a hut away from the dwellings, remaining there for a month. Boys sought visions of spirits to help them in hunting. Like the River Yumans, shamans' power came from dreaming. They cured diseases (which were sent by animals or caused by failures in ritual), either by sucking out a foreign intruded object or by repeating the poorly performed ritual properly.

The Pueblo

The Southwest origin myth on pages 210–211 was recorded in many versions in the legends of the Keresan-speaking Pueblo. Some Pueblo myths strikingly resembled Judeo-Christian or Greek mythology in content and plot. In one of them, all the people of the world but two were destroyed for their wickedness, as in the Noah myth. In a kind of "Tower of Babel" story, two people quarreled so much that Earth Mother (one of the divinities) changed their language, causing each to speak a tongue the other could not understand.

Myths and legends carried a common theme: all the people should work together, behave properly, and respect ancestors and the supernatural, so that everything would go well and rain would come to water the crops and feed the people. From their many legends, the Pueblo developed their own cardinal points of the compass—six instead of four because they included up and down.

Each direction had a color, a god, an animal, a woman, a tree, a snake, and a warrior associated with it. In such a well-ordered world, there was always strong public pressure to do everything just right. Ingenuity and originality were not highly regarded; the "right" was the traditional way.

The people's critical problem was getting enough to eat. Game was rarely plentiful, and everyone had to work hard and pray for rain. With good hearts, powerful songs, prayers, paraphernalia, and proper ritual, the Pueblo believed they could accomplish anything.

The agricultural Pueblo were descended mainly from the prehistoric Mogollon and Anasazi, who had populated the mesas and canyons of the Southwest. They lived in the highlands of northern Arizona, in a valley in west-central New Mexico, and along the upper Rio Grande and tributaries on the eastern slope of the Continental Divide in New Mexico. The Pueblo usually are divided into two groups: the Western including the Hopi who live on the tablelands and promontories of northern Arizona, the Zuni in New Mexico close to the Arizona border in the valley of the Zuni River, the Acoma, and the Laguna—a recent group compared to the others, originating about A.D. 1700—and the Eastern or Rio Grande Pueblo. We speak of both the people and their village or pueblo with the same name: "The Zuni live at Zuni."

Three distinct language groups are represented among the Pueblo: Aztec-Tanoan (Hopi, and many Rio Grande people), Keresan (Cochiti, Acoma, and others), and Penutian (Zuni). See the table on pages 244–245.

The Environment

Although Pueblo settlements spread over a fairly broad territory, their physical surroundings did not vary much. Pueblos were built in high, semiarid country where temperatures went from intense heat on a summer day to cool summer nights, and cold winter days were moderated by weeks of unbroken sunshine. Summer storms were sudden and often violent, but some rain fell throughout the year. Rainfall was somewhat greater in the higher altitudes of the east, and the river systems there helped in dry periods, whereas the western area depended upon rainfall and seepage entirely. Wild plants and animals were sparse, although not so rare as in some areas to the south and west inhabited by other Southwestern Indians, or in the Great Basin to the north.

Pueblo farmers grew corn, beans, squash, tobacco, and cotton. Water for these crops had to come from several sources because rainfall alone was never adequate and was always uncertain, varying widely from one year to the next. In the west, the Hopi counted on small, intermittent streams running from the highlands to the valleys, and underground water that seeped through the sandstone of the plateau top southward, reappearing in small springs and pools close enough to the pueblos to be used for the crops. In July and August, a crucial time for corn, the land received enough water from rain and these other sources to ensure the harvest for most seasons. The threat of too little water always hung over them, however, and much of Hopi life was devoted to using the water as efficiently as possible and to performing ceremonies to produce greater rainfall.

Zuni also lived in arid country, but they had the advantage of a permanent though meager water supply, the Zuni River, as well as more springs and somewhat greater rainfall. The pueblo of Acoma, sometimes referred to as Sky City, sat high on a mesa which had only small springs at the foot; the people built large reservoirs on the top to trap rainfall and supply the town with water. Their fields were some distance from the town and were watered by both the springs and rainfall.

Eastern Pueblo could get water from the Rio Grande close by, and they dug irrigation canals to bring the water to their fields. Farming was far more risky in the west than among the Rio Grande Pueblo: besides the ever present threat of inadequate moisture, there was always the chance that violent summer storms would wash out the crop. To hedge their bets, the Western Pueblo planted in

Hopi women at a spring. They all are wearing elaborate squash blossom hairdos, signifying they are unmarried.

Zuni shaman grinding herbs for curing purposes.

many different spots, each receiving water from different sources, so that if one planting failed, they would have others to fall back on. They ensured against crop failure with magical precautionary measures, rites to compel the supernatural to help them obtain a successful harvest. The Rio Grande peoples also had elaborate ceremonial practices.

Men were the cultivators, and labor was clearly divided. Women were responsible for raising the children, general domestic duties, gathering wild plants, and making pottery. Men farmed, made their own equipment, built the houses—though women added finishing touches like plastering—and did the weaving. They also hunted, though hunting was less important than elsewhere in North America. Men from the Rio Grande pueblos ventured into the plains occasionally to pursue buffalo, and all hunted antelope, deer, and especially rabbit.

Religion

All Pueblo cultures had a complex ceremonial life. Ceremonial activities were communal, with curing societies, priesthoods, and ritual associations taking part. Especially in the west, personal crises passed quietly, often unnoticed. Vision quests were not important, and even shamans were considered suspect because of their individuality. The Pueblo ideal was to avoid individualism.

Religious societies performed their ceremonies exactly as their ancestors had done. And like their forefathers the people made prayersticks, lengths of wood with feathers and perhaps shells attached. Prayersticks were messages to the spirits to send rain and other needed things. People prayed to the gods and spirits for rain. Good spirits, called *katcinas* by the Hopi of Arizona, brought rain when they visited. They had come from the underworld with the people, and men were permitted to impersonate them. Dressing as katcinas, men danced to get the rain to fall. Cloud, rain, and lightning symbols were everywhere, even on the headdresses of the katcina dancers.

Ceremonial activities took place in the open for the benefit of all the community and also, in most pueblos, in kivas, chambers often partially underground, to which only members of the religious order or society were admitted. Religion was a part of almost all aspects of life, and government was a civil and religious combination of the type we call theocratic, although there was usually a war chief; his responsibility was confined to warfare, raiding, defense, and communal hunting.

When a Pueblo died, his body was buried, but his soul went back to the place of emergence to return to the womb of the earth. That was the way it had been, and that was the way the people thought it should be.

Inside a kiva in New Mexico's Zia Pueblo five shamans are practicing a cure on a young boy. The shamans hold plumes and straws in their left hands, rattles in their right. They are separated from the boy by a white line made of cornmeal.

Social Organization

The Western Pueblo were organized very differently from those of the Rio Grande. Westerners were matrilineal, belonging to their mother's clan, and new- lyweds moved in with or close to the bride's mother's household. Women owned and inherited houses and land, and clans controlled ceremonial activities de- voted to manipulating the weather. The Rio Grande peoples had greater variety. The Keresan-speaking people had matrilineal clans, but those were not respon- sible for performing ceremonies, as they were among the Westerners; associa- tions rather than kin groups usually had that responsibility. Relatives on the mother's side were generally less important than in the west. The father and his family had more authority over the young in the east, and the nuclear family was more important.

The other Rio Grande Pueblo did not have clans, but traced kinship through mother and father equally, and the extended family was the basic social and economic unit. An extended family might include a man and wife and adult sons or daughters and their spouses and children. Rights in lands passed through both sons and daughters, whereas under the matrilineal system those rights passed through women only. All Pueblo people were monogamous, but divorce was easy and common.

Technology

With timber scarce in the desert, the Pueblo turned to the raw material most abundant—stone. As their ancestors had done, they built flat-topped rectangular rooms side by side and often several stories high. Some of those structures they covered with a thin plaster of *adobe,* a kind of clay. Adobe formed into sun-dried bricks became a major building material after Spanish contact. Some pueblos were built around a square or plaza; others were built in a row. Often the first- floor rooms were entered from the roof, as in ancient times. Most rooms were dark, windows, if any, were small, and the people carried on most of their activi- ties outside—pottery making, preparing hides, preserving foods.

Women ground corn on a slab of stone called a *metate* (an Aztec word), using a smaller stone, a *mano* (Spanish for "hand") to pulverize the grain into meal. Women also made many pottery utensils: ladles, bowls, dishes, cups, pitch- ers. They decorated some of their pottery with painted designs, but containers used directly on the smoky fires were left plain. Shapes and designs varied from pueblo to pueblo, and a Pueblo could tell from looking at an item where it had been made.

The Pueblo made much of their clothing from cotton cloth: breechcloths, belts, skirts, and dresses that fastened over the right shoulder, leaving the left shoulder bare. They made sandals from plant fibers such as yucca, and moccasins from hide. Women wrapped strips of buckskin around their lower legs. Men and women wore rabbit-skin or turkey-feather robes in winter, and they decked themselves out gaily with beads and pendants of stone, shell, and minerals—turquoise was a favorite. Traders carried the handicrafts as far away as Mexico to exchange for shell and other raw materials.

The Hopi

Westernmost of the Pueblo people, the Hopi spoke a language belonging to the Uto-Aztecan family in the Aztec-Tanoan phylum. They lived in villages on mesas with their fields in the valleys.

Hopi housing was the usual pueblo structure of stone, several stories high, often terraced with the upper stories set back. Two hundred or so people lived

Two Hopi women, their legs wrapped in buckskin, sit weaving baskets.

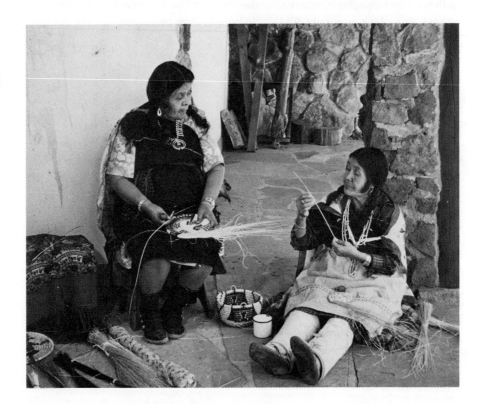

in each pueblo or village, grouped by clans. Sometimes the pueblo was built to enclose a courtyard. People got into the dwellings through a hole in the roof, using a notched pole as a ladder.

Cultivation.   Because they never got enough rain for their crops, the Hopi scattered their planting in many fields where runoff water and ground seepage supplemented the scant precipitation. In addition they had to face sudden summer cloudbursts that might wash out the crops or bury them under a load of mud. Consequently the farmers dug ditches around the fields and built protective barriers of brush and logs.

Most important of the crops was corn, followed by squash, beans, and cotton. Corn was planted earliest, in April and May. The young plants had to survive not only spring drought but also severe sandstorms. Squash was planted soon after the first corn, and then more corn and squash were planted with beans, spreading the planting so that fields were under cultivation at varying times, there were always plants in many stages of growth, and crops reached maturity and harvest at different times. Plants were widely spaced, sown in spots that had not been used the year before. Ten to twenty corn seeds were planted in the same hole, a foot or more deep to give the roots room to develop and protect them from drying out or being washed out. Sowing many seeds helped make sure that some plants would survive to maturity.

Cultivable land was allotted to each of the matrilineal clans, who marked off their plots with boundary stones. A clan's fields were never all in one place, nor was all the clan land under cultivation at any one time. Such dispersal improved the chance of a successful harvest—though some fields might fail, others would not. The men tended their wives' crops; women sometimes helped at harvest. Women were considered the owners of the land as well as of the houses.

Each stage of cultivation and plant growth had its ceremonial activity following the ritual calendar. The calendar was based on the sun's position at sunrise, which moves gradually from the southernmost point on the horizon at the winter solstice to its northernmost point at midsummer. The Sun Watcher, a religious functionary, took daily observations and announced the important dates. When the sun rose from behind a certain hill, he declared that planting time had arrived and all danger of frost had passed.

Katcinas.   At the winter solstice, all the adult Hopi men held the Soyal Ceremony. It was the responsibility of one clan, and was meant to force the sun, now at its southernmost position on the horizon, to return north so that the crops would grow. It was at the Soyal that katcinas appeared, staying until the summer solstice, when they presumably returned to their mountain homes.

The katcinas were supernaturals, cloud beings and bringers of rain, beloved

by the Hopi. Their appearance each year was portrayed by the katcina dancers, men in katcina masks who performed at ceremonials during the first six months of the year, when the katcinas were thought to live among men. Children were given small images of them, usually called *katcina dolls,* mostly to teach them about the many katcinas. All adult Hopi belonged to the Katcina Cult, though normally only men portrayed katcinas. For six months every year, the Katcina Cult members had to see that performances of ceremonies and rituals designed to summon the clouds and bring rain were done correctly.

In addition to their ritual performances, the katcina impersonators were a means of social control. They visited the houses, asking whether the children had been good for the past year. Children who had misbehaved were threatened with being hauled away in baskets the katcinas carried. Parents pretended to defend the children, who must have been terrified by the huge masked beings trying to snatch them from their homes. When children entered adulthood and were accepted as full members of the tribe, they were told that the katcinas were just their male neighbors and relatives. All this might seem to have been cruel to little children, yet katcinas were thought of as good and kind spirits.

Other Ceremonies. Another important ceremony, the Powamu or bean planting festival, took place in February at the new moon and lasted until beans sprouted in the kiva that belonged to the Powamu Society. Early in the ceremony, seed beans had been planted in basins of sand in the kiva. In the warmth from fires kept burning and with kiva members watering them well the seeds germinated quickly. These beans were considered omens of the year's crops—if they grew well, the yield would be good. Members of the Powamu and Katcina Societies had ritual duties, and their traditions, rituals, and lore were secret.

Every year in late summer, societies put on another ceremonial. The Antelope and Snake Societies performed together, alternating every other year with the Flute Society, conducting prayers and making offerings to bring rain to the crops and fertility to the women. But the best known Hopi ceremony is the Snake Dance, a nine-day ceremony. For the first four days, members of the society went out to the north, south, east, and west to collect snakes. The next few days were for secret rites carried on in their kiva. The ninth day brought a public dance in the square. Members of the Snake Society danced with snakes—both poisonous and harmless—held in their mouths or around their necks. After the dance, all snakes were released to return to the gods with messages asking for rain.

Tribal initiation in November was the year's last major ceremony. Men were initiated into the Katcina Cult, boys into one of four men's societies, and girls into women's societies. By this initiation they became full, functioning adult members of the tribe.

Facing page: This katcina doll carved from cottonwood is a representation of one of the various masked katcinas. Such dolls as this were presented to children as part of their education by katcina dancers.

These and the other ceremonials during the year, each one a series of dances and rituals, might last a few days and nights or a month or more. There was little time during the year when one ceremony or another was not under way. Hopi life was always and intimately tied to ceremony and religion. Most Hopi thought and endeavor were directed toward obtaining blessing and help from the supernatural. The main contact with the supernatural was the societies, who devoted their efforts to rain, fertility, crops, and good behavior.

Witchcraft. The Hopi explained crop failure, bad behavior, and all other undesirable happenings as having been caused by witchcraft. Witches might be either men or women; they could be recognized by their un-Hopi behavior—they behaved differently. A proper Hopi (*hopi* means "good") was cooperative, unassertive, generally undistinguished, and calm. Anyone who stood out as aggressive, ambitious, flamboyant, or offensive was suspected of being *kahope,* the opposite of Hopi, and probably was a witch. To call someone a witch was the worst possible accusation. Witches were referred to as "Two Hearts" because they were believed to have one heart of their own and another of the animal spirit that gave them their witch power. Witches were greatly feared as killers of people, animals, and crops. Although most Hopi religious activity was social, not individualistic, they did have some shamans, and it was to the shamans that the Hopi turned to cure illness caused by witches. However, shamans themselves were highly suspect, for they were too individualistic and might well be witches.

Cochiti

The pueblo of Cochiti, on the Rio Grande about thirty miles southwest of what is now Santa Fe, was inhabited by Keresan speakers. In climate and weather Cochiti was not much different from Hopi, but the river caused important differences in social organization. The work of irrigation required more political centralization than kin groups could provide, so Cochiti depended more on nonkin units.

Social Organization. The Cochiti did have matrilineal clans, but they were less important in religion and government than at Hopi. The matrilineal extended family brought up the children, but Cochiti fathers, not mothers' brothers, were the disciplinarians; the nuclear family was more significant here. The religious and economic functions taken care of by clans in Hopi were assumed by associations or cults at Cochiti, though the clan stayed in charge of marriage arrangements. Associations watched over village activities, disease, warfare, crop fertility, and communal well-being and harmony. Specific associations handled specific problems, seeing that the proper rites were performed. The Cochiti were much less absorbed by weather control such as rainmaking, and emphasized the importance of the sun.

Cochiti society was divided into moieties. Everyone belonged to either the Pumpkin (sometimes called Squash) or the Turquoise division, each with its own kiva. Children became members of their father's kiva, but a woman might transfer to her husband's at marriage. In fact, anyone could leave his father's moiety if he chose, though clan affiliation could never be changed.

The moieties had social, religious, and political influence. Some political officials were chosen from one kiva, some from the other, and those offices alternated between the two kivas. Each kiva was also responsible for putting on some of the ceremonials and dances, functions of the clan at Hopi. Cochiti also had a katcina cult, called Shiwana. Most of its ceremonies were secret, unlike the very public Hopi katcinas, but some of its dances were public, and the dancers' masks were as elaborate as the Hopi's. The Shiwana Cult was controlled by medicine societies.

Medicine Societies.   Cochiti medicine societies were very influential—the real basis of government, in fact. The head of the town, called by the Spanish a *cacique,* was always the head of a medicine society. He served as both government chief and head priest, and was constantly concerned with the general welfare, living a frugal life and fasting often to set a good example for everyone else. He was aided in the practical matters of government by a council composed of officers of the societies.

The village had four medicine societies, two in each moiety, which took charge of solstice ceremonies, performed cures, and destroyed witches. These societies were so highly organized that they have been called priesthoods. Joining a medicine society took up to four years of preparation. The head of the society saw to it that candidates spent that time observing the proper dietary and sexual restrictions, ending with a rigorous four-day purge. Then the candidate joined the other members in seclusion to be prepared for initiation. After songs, prayers, ceremonial whipping, and dancing, the initiate was given a new name. His was the lowest position in the society, and he moved up only as members ahead of him died. Medicine societies were never large.

Clowns.   Another form of association, besides the medicine societies and Shiwana Cult, was the clowns, called Koshare. They hid their identities not by masks and clothing, but with paint and hair: they were painted with horizontal black and white stripes from head to toe, black circles outlining their mouths and eyes in white faces, and their hair was arranged into two upright "horns" on each side of a central part. Koshare helped the cacique in communal activities.

The Koshare, or clowns, are those figures shown in this painting whose bodies are painted in stripes. The Koshare served to control the behavior of the tribe as well as to provide comic relief.

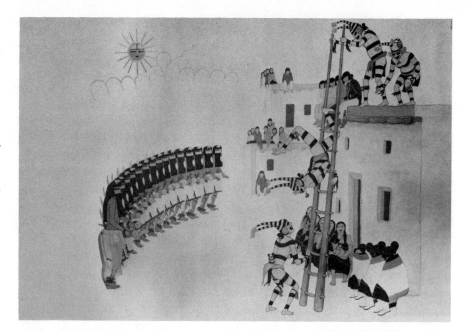

Both men and women could become members of the association of clowns, but women worked mostly on preparing food.

Social control may have been the clowns' most important job. Anyone behaving improperly could be sure of being publicly ridiculed or even humiliated by the clowns, and that was usually enough to make people conform. The clowns' antics also supplied comic relief, some of it bordering on the obscene. They behaved as other citizens could not, offering a vicarious experience in forbidden activity that greatly amused the spectators.

Cochiti had other associations, like the Warriors and the Hunters, that were less important than the medicine societies because they dealt with less significant parts of Pueblo life. These organizations duplicated some functions of medicine societies, but did not have their prestige or power.

Witchcraft. Fear of witchcraft was strong at Cochiti, and people were as afraid of being charged with witchcraft as they were of the practice itself. It was terrifying to think that you might be a witch and not even know it! Witches took many forms—human, animal, reptile, or even red fireballs with black centers. Members of the medicine societies could exorcise or cast out the witches, but sometimes it was hard to rid the community of sorcery. The tension would build up as each citizen wondered who might be a witch. Like the Hopi, the Cochiti blamed witchcraft for things that went wrong even when all rituals had been faithfully performed.

Pueblo Organization

We might call Cochiti, like Hopi, a small theocracy, combining government and religious functions in associations and individuals. The basic organizational difference between the two was their ways of recruiting people into the major public groups. The Hopi used kinship; in Cochiti it was membership in associations which cut across kin ties. Some anthropologists suggest that the non-kin organization made it easier to mobilize the community for the necessary public work in irrigation. Except for that, all the Pueblo people were much alike, especially in religion, which was the key to Pueblo life, and in their continuous ceremonial activity.

All Pueblo believed that their chiefs or caciques should set an example of the perfect Pueblo, keeping calm and remote from petty, personal squabbles. Chiefs should be above ordinary emotions such as anger, hate, or vindictiveness. Anthropologist Ruth Benedict described the desirable leadership quality as the golden mean—all things in moderation. Although such a personality served as a model for the average citizen, all knew that most people would fall short of it, and of course they did. Still, the societal standard the chief was expected to exemplify was very different from that of the Indians of the Northwest Coast, the Plains, or the East. The chiefs felt this pressure for perfection, and that is probably one reason why few men were interested in the position.

The Southern Athabaskans

Arriving in the Southwest later than other Indian groups were the Athabaskans, whose nearest linguistic relatives were the Athabaskan-speak-ing peoples of western Canada. Some anthropologists and archaeologists believe that advance groups of Athabaskans may have come to the Southwest as early as the thirteenth century, but most feel they probably were not there before the fifteenth. They were hunters and gatherers, more aggressive and less settled than the Pueblo; their raids on the farmers' fields and homes may have been part of the reason some pueblos were abandoned. Eventually they came to live in the area, and today their descendants are known as Apache and Navajo.

The Migration South

Probably the advance of these nomads from the north caused the settled farmers only minor problems at first—a few fields plundered, a few women stolen. The pueblos themselves, entered from the roof, were easy enough to defend.

However, as more of the intruders entered the Pueblo territory and preyed on the inhabitants and their crops, relations worsened, and it is easy to see how the invaders became more than a nuisance. One of their advantages was their superior weapon, the sinew-backed bow, which could shoot farther, straighter, and with more deadly effect than the Pueblo people's simple bow. The Athabaskans appear to have been enthusiastic and skillful warriors, and even today Zuni mothers frighten naughty children by telling them to behave or a Navajo will get them.

We do not know why the Athabaskans moved south into Pueblo country. Hunters and gatherers, they lived off wild foods as they moved, carrying their weapons and very little else. Probably their immigration continued over many decades. Some may have come through the Great Basin; others appear to have taken an eastern route along the foothills of the Rockies. By the time Europeans came, Athabaskans were living in the southern plains as well as in central Arizona.

As the Athabaskans moved, they not only raided the settled cultivators but began to take on some of the local skills and customs, modifying them to fit with their own traditions. Some groups of newcomers borrowed more of the Pueblo customs than others. Those who came to be known as Navajo learned to cultivate crops, as some western Apache groups did later, while eastern Apache remained hunters and gatherers, some of them later taking part in the thoroughly typical Plains way of life, which will be discussed in the next chapter. In spite of this mixing with a new culture, most of their dialects remained mutually intelligible at first, and the groups held onto a deep layer of common custom that stayed different from the Pueblo ways. As time passed, however, the Athabaskan groups became more and more differentiated.

The Apache

The southern Athabaskans probably did not become two groups, Navajo and Apache, until long after they wandered in from their northern homeland. They must have come in bands, which over the generations sometimes came together for a time, sometimes broke up. We have no facts about the Athabaskans before about 1600. By then Apache were clearly separate from Navajo. Though the Navajo mixed with the Pueblo and the Spanish, the Apache long remained aloof from both. To learn something about older Athabaskan practices and customs, then, our best source is the Apache.

The Apache had no tribal identity; their allegiance was to their local bands. Those bands have come to be known as the Chiricahua (the band of the famous leaders Geronimo and Cochise), the Mescalero, the Jicarilla, and an offshoot of

the Jicarilla, the Lipan, who moved into Mexico under pressure from the Comanche. All these bands ranged from southern Colorado to the Texas border,
and the Chiricahua also extended into Arizona. Other bands, collectively known
as the Western Apache, lived in east-central Arizona, where they grew far more
like the Navajo than the eastern Apache did. One eastern group joined the
Kiowa of the southern plains and was later called the Kiowa Apache. After the
horse appeared in the area, the Apache became raiders feared by all agricultural
neighbors; even the Western Apache raided, though they also did some cultivating.

Apache Life.   Among the Western Apache, the women tended the crops, and
collected the same wild plants favored by their neighbors on the west, the
Pimans. The Apache made a kind of beer from mescal, cactus fruit, or maize, a
practice they probably learned from Mexican Indians or perhaps the Pimans. In
the west, where it was too mountainous for horse transportation, horses were
more often eaten than ridden at first.

The nomadic eastern Apache had very little agriculture; they were hunters,
gatherers, and raiders. Before they had horses, they hunted buffalo on foot,
using dogs and *travois* to carry meat and equipment; the travois consisted of two
poles trailing from the animal's back and acting as shafts between which a net or
platform was constructed to bear the load. They were among the first Indians to
take to a mounted life when horses became available. It was from the eastern
Apache that the great Apache warriors came. Men had little trouble raising en-
thusiasm for a raiding party—that was a way of life and the means to success
and social recognition. Raiding and warfare were considered proper male occupations, and boys were trained to be aggressive and brave. Warriors collected
scalps of fallen enemies, but since all Apache greatly feared the dead, the scalps
had to be purified to make them safe. Then warriors often wore them on their
shirts as a sort of battle insignia.

Apache women were excellent basketmakers, but not very adept at making
pottery, which is of little value to people on the move. Clothing was of buckskin,
and most Apache lived in wickiups of brush-covered saplings; some plainsmen
built hide tipis.

Social Organization.   Apache bands were independent of one another and
had no overall leader. Each band had an informal chief who held his position by
his ability and the willingness of band members to follow him. Raiding parties
were volunteers who joined a war or raid leader they respected. The bands
themselves consisted of groups of extended families that had a strong sense of
band unity, especially when faced with external threats such as enemy raids.

The Western Apache's matrilineal clans probably grew out of their contact with the Navajo, who reckoned descent matrilineally; the other Apache bands traced their kinship equally through males and females. Almost all Apache practiced what has been termed *mother-in-law avoidance.* When he could, a man was supposed to avoid his mother-in-law; if he found that impossible occasionally, he should avoid looking at her. Men could have more than one wife, but the wives were always sisters.

Religion.   Every Apache had a horror of death, burying the dead one swiftly and burning his house and possessions. Then the mourning family purified itself ritually and moved to a new place to escape the ghost of the deceased. The ghost, not the body, was fearsome because ghosts might harm the living or take them away to their ghostly dwelling place.

A girl's first menstruation brought a four-day ceremony: a shaman sang songs, a woman instructed the girl in proper behavior, and masked dancers performed at night to bring the girl a blessing from the supernatural. This girls' puberty rite was one of the most important Apache ceremonies and may have been derived from the northern Athabaskan traditions in which the puberty ceremony was of great importance. Several Apache girls went through the ritual together, and the whole community participated at some time during the four days, if only as chanting spectators.

Masked dancers also appeared at ceremonies, for curing and to ensure success in hunting or warfare. Shamans got their powers from individual visions, but the dancers' rites and dance steps were learned.

The Navajo

Navajo land was and is desert with such typical desert vegetation as sage, piñon, and juniper. It is hot in summer and cold in winter, and drought is an ever-present threat; even in the mountains, rainfall never exceeds twenty inches per year. When it does come, the rain forms raging, land-eroding torrents. Over the centuries, rain and wind have carved the earth into spectacular mesas and canyons, fantastic buttes and skyscraping basalt columns.

Today the Navajo are the largest Indian tribe in the United States. They live in north-central Arizona, southern Utah, and western New Mexico. Little is known of them before 1600, when Spaniards entered their country. The Navajo are more like the Pueblo than the Apache are, perhaps because the Navajo were neighbors of the Pueblo Hopi for 600 years, and because many Rio Grande Pueblo refugees went to live with the Navajo after an unsuccessful war against the Spanish from 1690 to 1692. Though the Navajo took up the Pueblo dress, loom and weaving practices, and many ceremonies, they kept their distinctive

An old type of
hogan (top); a more
recent type of
hogan with stone
walls (bottom).

house. This was the *hogan,* a log-framed, earth-covered, circular structure with
the doorway always on the east. Later forms were often six- or eight-sided. Although many Navajo have moved into contemporary housing in recent years,
the hogan still is important for ceremonials.

Under Pueblo influence, the Navajo turned from their hunting and gathering
economy to farming, and after contact with the Spanish, to herding sheep and
raising livestock. Sheep gave wool for weaving, and all livestock was used for

food, because most of the wild game was gone and the sheep and other grazers ate whatever vegetation there was in the desert.

Special Patterns. The seventeenth-century Navajo way of life mingled Pueblo, Spanish, and ancient Athabaskan customs, adding cultivation from the Pueblo and herding from the Spanish to old traditions to produce a unique culture. Like the Pueblo, the Navajo developed matrilineal clans, but they kept their local group or band autonomy—often to the despair of the federal government agents, who tried to bind the Navajo with treaties, only to learn that no band felt obliged to observe agreements made by any other band.

The band was a scattered group, not a village, because to herd sheep in that environment people had to cover a wide area. They were bound by their common language, rituals, and kinship, which extended from band to band by marriage.

An outstanding contrast between the northern Athabaskan and the Navajo lay in the status they accorded women. As you may recall, the position of northern Athabaskan women was not high; among some groups, it was distinctly inferior.

A Navajo blanket weaver.

The Navajo woman held a strong and respected place in society. She was important economically because she controlled lineage property, which passed through women. As weaving paid more and more, the woman who did the weaving got the income from her work. She also owned the sheep, so that the proceeds from selling wool or sheep went to her. Socially, the woman was the center of the nuclear family. Newlywed couples generally moved into hogans near the wife's mother; if they divorced, the man returned to his mother's house. Children were closer to their mother's relatives because they usually lived nearby, and also because the matrilineal relatives formed the groups that did the daily chores and had most of the responsibility for rearing children. Like the Apache, the Navajo observed the mother-in-law taboo: a man was never to look at his wife's mother or even be in the same room with her, which must have kept in-law quarreling to a minimum but also inspired many Athabaskan mother-in-law jokes.

Kinship and Sociopolitical Groups.   Another group the Navajo formed was the *outfit,* composed of matrilineally related extended families living fairly close together. Each outfit farmed within a defined territory, clearing and planting new fields as old ones became infertile, and also herded within their own domain. The outfit was an organization cemented by kin ties and common land rights. It had a headman or spokesman who was an older, respected member of the outfit and who represented the group in disputes or dealings with outsiders.

Larger than the outfit was the clan, which was matrilineal (each member belonged to his mother's clan) and exogamous (each member had to marry outside the clan and also outside his father's clan). Clan elders were responsible for clan members' behavior and for training their children. Clansmen felt responsible for one another and supported each other in time of need or danger. The mother's brother was in charge of his nephews and nieces, disciplining as well as instructing them: his opinion had great weight in matters of marriage.

Social and political control thus was handled by the family, the clan, and the outfit, not by political or legal structure. Sometimes the outfits in a territory did gather into bands, under the leadership of a headman; these groups were territorial rather than based on kinship. As elsewhere, the headman's leadership depended on his wisdom and ability; he had no coercive power. Communities or bands made their decisions after discussion and unanimous agreement among the adults of the group, both male and female.

Navajo Sings.   As among the Apache, a girl's puberty was a time for ceremony, one among many in an elaborate cycle of rituals in which all adult Navajo took part. The girl's ceremony lasted four days and was intended to mold her into a virtuous young woman. While she was in seclusion, family and friends gathered to sing and ensure the girl's future.

Some of the ceremonials, called *sings,* were meant to cure ailments of any kind, from disease to laziness, from drunkenness to marital problems. A specialist often prescribed chants, songs, or rituals. Sometimes referred to as a Hand Trembler, he did part of his diagnosis by holding his hands over the sick one's body until they trembled where the disorder lay, then he recommended the ceremony that would work a cure. Then the sick person or a relative hired a singer who knew that ritual and was willing to conduct the sing, which would last from one to five days. To start the ceremony, the singer usually made a design on the ground by dribbling colored earths, pollens, powdered minerals, or ground charcoal between his thumb and fingers. Often referred to as sand paintings, these designs might better be called dry painting, because many substances besides sand were used. The singer then directed a continuous chant toward the patient; if it was not letter perfect, the ceremony would be ineffective.

The Navajo singer or chanter, sometimes called a medicine man, learned the sacred songs by being apprenticed to an older singer. Everyone sang sacred songs, but only the chanter could cure. Curing and chanting were part-time occupations, supplemented by tending flocks, farming, and hunting.

Community Ceremonies. Larger, public ceremonies, including whole communities, were like the family curing sings but more complex, and they often were meant for more than one patient. Social activities evolved around two of those ceremonies, making them something more than curing sings. The most famous and most often performed was the Enemy Way. *Way* is used as an English alternative for "sing." This ritual was designed to remove the evil influences from warriors returning from a raid. It was recently revived for soldiers returning from world wars and other military actions such as the Viet Nam conflict. Held in the summer months, the ceremony lasted four days. Anyone who felt he needed a ritual cure might decide to have the ceremony, though he usually confirmed his decision with a diagnostician. Enemy Way was performed to render the ghost of an outsider, an enemy ghost, ineffective. "Way" applies to the whole ceremonial, consisting of chants, rituals, and a dance. The dance part itself was social, having nothing to do with the ritual, and was a kind of courtship dance at which young unmarried women, dressed for the occasion, appeared each night to select male partners for the dance and as possible mates. That is why Enemy Way has in recent years been called the Squaw Dance.

Other dances, the Yeibeichai, took place in winter: nine days and nights of chants and rituals. This ceremonial was more spectacular than the dances of Enemy Way because the dancers were masked and costumed and, in the part called the Fire Dance, performed with firebrands. It was also a more powerful ceremonial, as evidenced by its greater complexity. Learning the necessary songs and paraphernalia took years of apprenticeship to an older singer. An ap-

In this sand painting of the Night Way Ceremony sixteen Black Fire Gods, eight on each side of a cornstalk, are shown. Zigzag lines on their arms and shoulders represent the Milky Way; the dotted Y on their masks, the Pleiades. In one hand, each carries a stick for making fire, in the other, strings of blue corn cakes. The black line at the bottom represents water, and the white line on top of it represents foam.

prentice paid for instruction in service, money, or livestock, which gave the younger singer the right to the performance. Stolen knowledge lost its power.

Ghosts and Witchcraft. Like other southern Athabaskans, the Navajo deeply feared the dead. They believed in ghosts, and believed that all ghosts were evil. Ghosts came back to cause trouble among the living, even to enter the bodies of the living, which was good reason for avoiding the dead. Anyone exposed to a corpse had to undergo long and expensive ritual treatment, and when someone died inside a hogan, it was abandoned. Often a seriously ill person was moved out of the hogan so that he would not die inside and force the family to seek a new home. As one would imagine, burial was quick, without much ceremony, and funerals and people near death were avoided whenever possible. So great was their dread that many Navajo would not go out at night when they believed ghosts were abroad. The Navajo were delighted when white undertakers took over the care and disposal of the dead.

The Navajo believed that just as some medicine men were good, laboring and paying to learn blessing chants, others did the same to learn evil chants. Those witches, both male and female, could bring illness and disaster, and the Navajo greatly feared them. Every Navajo believed that some people actually were initiated as witches and possessed evil power. They told many stories of "black Sabbaths," incest, nakedness, and murder.

Of all witches, the Navajo feared the Wolf-man and Wolf-woman most. Those beings could transform themselves into wolves or coyotes, and bewitch their enemies by sprinkling ground parts of human infants through the smoke hole into the hogan. Bullets could kill a Wolf-man or Wolf-woman, but kinsmen would seek vengeance against the executioner, and any kinfolk of witches were probably witches themselves.

Other Beliefs and Practices.   Navajo accompanied every one of their daily activities, no matter how mundane, with ritual. At sunrise the eldest male of the household began the day by singing a sacred song and dropping corn pollen, which was sacred, to the four directions, north, east, south, and west. Sacred songs were sung all day—in the fields, while driving the herds, as household tasks were performed—calling for blessings or protection for the family and herds. Men took sweat baths together in semi-underground rooms, combining cleanliness with worship. During the sweating, they sang songs that were mostly prayers, asking for good health, good crops, good herds, rain, and wealth.

Navajo religion was not so much a theological system as a means of keeping man in harmony with the universe and maintaining order and balance. The world was a dangerous place, and only ceremonials could bring security and serenity. Religion therefore was largely a guide to behavior from situation to situation and a way of atoning for neglect, ignorance, and errors in judgment, as well as countering the malevolence of others. Unlike the Pueblo, the many Navajo religious specialists did not form a body of priests, but were alternative sources of power or means of manipulating the supernatural. If one practitioner failed, a Navajo sought help from another.

The Navajo word for themselves, Diné, meant "people of the surface of the earth." Their creation myth is a key to the Navajo relationship with the Pueblo. Having borrowed from the Pueblo many ideas in myth and ceremony, the Navajo added their own special emphases and elaborations. The origin myth described their ancestors coming to the earth's surface and the happenings that ultimately produced the Navajo way of life. The Navajo believed that below the surface of the earth were twelve worlds, inhabited by powerful Holy People or Powerful Ones (Yei). Two of the Holy People, created from two ears of corn,

CHARACTERISTICS OF THE SOUTHWEST TRIBES

Clothing	Food production	Equipment	Shelter	Social and political organization	Religion	Warfare
Leather, fur, and fiber clothing Woven cotton (Pueblo) Breechcloths Fiber skirts Rabbit-skin robes Dresses Moccasins Sandals	Cultivation (corn, beans, and squash) Hunting Gathering Fishing Livestock-raising (post-contact Navajo and Apache)	Digging sticks Throwing sticks Basketry Nets Bows and arrows Spears Pottery Clubs Manos and metates Stone bowls and cups	Pueblos Kivas Wickiups Hogans (Navajo) Tipis (some Apache) Shades (Havasupai) Domed structures with thatched roofs Semi-subterranean houses	Bands Nuclear families Patrilineal clans (River Yumans) Matrilineal clans (Western Pueblo and Navajo) Patrilineal families (Pima and Papago) Bilateral extended families (Rio Grande Pueblos) Tribal chiefs (River Yumans and Papago)	Shamans Ghosts Spirits Witchcraft Dreams as a source of power Rituals for farming success Curing societies Priesthoods Ritual associations Katchinas	Warfare frequent among River Yumans (raids, duels, and battles) Warfare rare among Pimans Raids common among Apache

were First Man and First Woman, who, some accounts say, created the universe. They were the parents of Changing Woman, the most important person in Navajo mythology. She personified the earth, like Mother Nature; her "changing" was seasonal change. Changing Woman mated with the Sun and with Water and produced twin sons. They grew up and received from the Sun weapons and knowledge with which they killed the monsters that were on earth. The Navajo saw evidence of all this in natural land formations (mountains, lava flows, basalt columns) which they took to be the remains of the monsters. The Twin Monster Slayers' lives were a model for proper, traditional Navajo male behavior, just as witches were the model for improper, undesirable behavior.

There were many other Holy People—each associated with natural land features, other Yei, the weather, vegetation, mineral deposits, or animals. The Yei were not gods; their behavior was not perfect, and they could be controlled and persuaded by ritual acts, which were the guides for Navajo life. The whole Navajo mythology explained the otherwise inexplicable, creating traditions of knowledge, ceremonial practices, and proper behavior.

Bibliography

Suggestions for Further Study

Downs, James F.
1972   *The Navajo.*
        A study of Navajo sheepherding, describing the general reservation culture as well as the historical background.

Dozier, Edward P.
1970   *The Pueblo Indians of North America.*
        A general ethnographic and historical survey of Pueblo cultures by an eminent American Indian scholar and professor of anthropology.

Lange, Charles H.
1959   *Cochiti, a New Mexico Pueblo.*
        A historical and ethnographic study of one of the Rio Grande pueblos.

Ortiz, Alfonso
1969   *The World of the Tewa Indians.*
        Written by an American Indian anthropologist, this is a study of the Pueblo peoples of the Tewa linguistic group.

Simmons, Leo W.
1963   *Sun Chief: The Autobiography of a Hopi Indian.*
        A memorable study of the life of a Hopi man. This book puts the reader into the Pueblo culture as few others have done.

Basso, Keith
1970   *The Cibecue Apache.*

Beaglehole, E.
1935   *Hopi of the Second Mesa.*

Downs, James
1966   *Two Worlds of the Washo.*

Joseph, Alice, R. B. Spicer, and J. Chesky
1949   *The Desert People: A Study of the Papago Indians.*

Opler, Morris E.
1941   *An Apache Life-way.*

Steward, Julian H.
1933   *Ethnography of the Owens Valley Paiute.*

Stewart, Omer C.
1941   *Northern Paiute.*

Underhill, Ruth
1956   *The Navahos.*

MAJOR GROUPS AND LANGUAGES
OF THE GREAT BASIN AND THE SOUTHWEST

Language phylum	Language family	Cultural division

GREAT BASIN

Language phylum	Language family	Cultural division
Aztec-Tanoan	Uto-Aztecan	Bannock Gosiute Paiute Shoshoni Ute
Hokan	Washo	Washo

SOUTHWEST

Language phylum	Language family	Cultural division
Aztec-Tanoan	Kiowa-Tanoan TEWA DIVISION	Hano Nambe San Ildefonso San Juan Santa Clara Tesuque
	TIWA DIVISION	Isleta Picuris Sandia Taos
	TOWA DIVISION	Jemez
	Uto-Aztecan	Hopi Papago Pima

Continued

MAJOR GROUPS AND LANGUAGES (continued)

Language phylum	Language family	Cultural division

SOUTHWEST (continued)

Language phylum	Language family	Cultural division
Hokan	Yuman	Cocopa Havasupai Maricopa Mojave Walapai Yavapai Yuma
Na-Dene	Athabaskan	Apache Navajo
Penutian	Zuni	Zuni
Undetermined	Keresan	Acoma Cochiti Laguna San Felipe Santa Ana Santo Domingo Zia

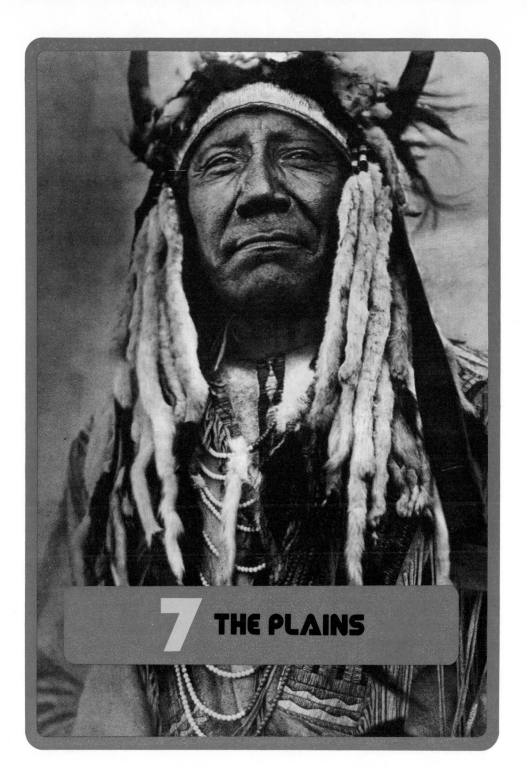

7 THE PLAINS

THE PLAINS

XXXXXXXXXXXXXXXXX

At one time there was nothing but a vast expanse of water. No earth existed then. Inktomi looked around and said, "If I had some soil, I would make some land." Muskrat said, "I can find soil for you," and he dived into the water. Many times he dived, and many times he came back to the surface without soil. Finally he took a very deep breath and plunged deep into the water. Inktomi waited for a long time before he saw Muskrat, but finally Muskrat came to the surface with a ball of mud in his paws. Inktomi took the mud and made the earth with grasslands stretching as far as the eye could see, and some streams flowing over the grasslands.

Muskrat and Inktomi enjoyed the earth. Besides the two of them, there were Rabbit, Fox, Coyote, Bear, Eagle, and Frog. Always the grass grew, and the weather was pleasant. Inktomi and his friends just sat around doing nothing or playing tricks on each other. Frog said, "It is always too nice. It is tiresome always to have weather like this." Inktomi thought Frog was criticizing, so he made it snow. And it snowed and snowed. Snow stayed on the ground for a long time. It was never warm anymore. Frog begged Inktomi to change the weather, and after a while Inktomi said, "When it was always nice, you complained, and I grew tired of your complaints. Now you are sorry; but I will make part of the year warm, and part cold. We will have ten months of cold, and two months of warm weather." But the animals begged Inktomi to make more warm weather than that, and he said, "Very well, we will have seven months of cold and five months of warm." And that is the way it has been ever since.

Then the animals said, "We are alone in the world. There ought to be some other beings." They talked to Inktomi. Inktomi thought, "I would like some other beings too." So he took some dirt and from it made a man and a woman. The new people asked Inktomi what they should eat. Inktomi did not want people to eat his friends, so he created buffalo. He told the people that they should eat buffalo. He said, "Everybody get ready. I will teach you how to hunt." He taught the men to kill the buffalo, and how to skin the animals. He showed them how to make knives to remove the skin, and he taught the women to make scrapers and how to scrape the skin so that it was soft and pliable. He showed the people how to butcher the buffalo and what parts could be eaten. He broke open a leg

Preceding page:
A 1910 photograph
of Two Moons, a
Cheyenne war chief
present at the battle
of Little Bighorn in
1876, when General
Custer's command
was destroyed by a
force of Sioux and
Cheyenne.

bone, and showed the people the marrow. Then he said, "From now on, this is what you will eat, all the parts of the buffalo. And you will make tools from his bones and horns."

After a while there were many people in the world. Inktomi's people hunted the buffalo as he had taught them, with bows and lances, and on foot. But one day his people saw that other men did not hunt on foot. They rode on the backs of large animals. The animals could go much faster than people on foot. On the horses, for that is what the others rode, the other people could keep pace with the buffalo, and they could kill more buffalo, and they could carry more buffalo meat. Inktomi's people begged him to get horses for them too. But Inktomi said, "I have given you all that I intend. You will have to learn to steal horses from the other tribes." And that is what Inktomi's people learned to do, and that is how they got their horses.

XXXXXXXXXXXXXXX

The Plains of North America stretch from southern Canada into Texas, from the Mississippi River to the Rocky Mountains. Treeless grassland except for wooded river valleys, the gently rolling territory was home to millions of bison, popularly called buffalo. In the valleys and hills other animals lived: deer, elk, antelope, bear, beaver, and, in the mountains at the western edge of the Plains, mountain sheep. In the rivers were fish, and waterfowl nested in trees, shrubs, and reeds along the banks.

This description of how Indians adapted to the Plains will be different from that of the other culture areas. For most areas we have tried as nearly as possible to recreate the aboriginal cultures, untouched by European contact. Plains Indian life, however, did not reach its climax (with a population of about a quarter of a million) until after Europeans introduced the horse to this continent. The Plains culture was not an aboriginal development but a contact phenomenon. We will see how life was lived on the Plains from about 1670 to 1870. After that the mounted nomads' flamboyant way of life slowly disappeared along with the buffalo they lived on. White settlers moving west from the Mississippi fenced in the land. No longer could Indians make their living on the open prairie; it belonged to ranchers and homesteaders.

To many people, the Plains life-style represents *the* American Indian, the Indian of the eagle-feathered warbonnet, galloping across a movie screen after buffalo or enemies. This Hollywood stereotype is not entirely imaginary: for about two hundred years, the Plains Indians did lead an exciting life focused on

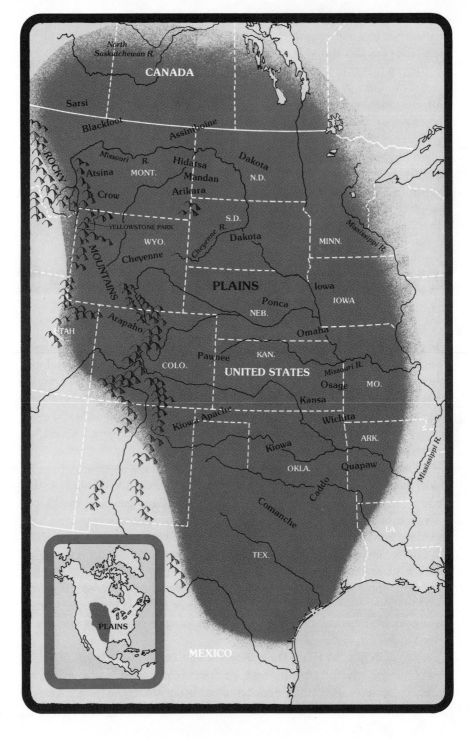

The Plains culture
area and its tribes.

masculinity and youth. The Plains way, however, though easy to romanticize, was just one of many Indian adaptations in North America.

Plains Prehistory

As you may recall from Part I, after about 8000 B.C., the climate of the Plains region slowly became much drier, and many of the animals sought by the early Big Game Hunters became extinct. Though some continued to hunt the buffalo, Plains people more and more turned to wild-plant gathering. Archaeological evidence suggests that human population in the Plains shrank greatly as the climate changed.

Much later, in the early centuries of the Christian era, Woodland people moved in from the east and settled in small villages along the Plains rivers. While they did hunt buffalo, as we know from remains of buffalo bones in archaeological sites, they also cultivated gardens of corn, beans, and squash. By the time Europeans came into contact with New World peoples, the Plains villages were good-sized. The villagers lived along the river systems, leaving their valleys only occasionally to hunt the bison. Few people dwelt in the grasslands of the Plains, for the tough, thick root masses of the vegetation there were almost impossible to penetrate with stone and bone tools, and cultivation was impossible.

When hunters ventured out on the Plains to chase buffalo, they did not go far from their villages, for they were on foot and had only their dogs to help them carry back the big, heavy carcasses. Like their mounted descendants, they turned the buffalo they caught into much more than food. They made robes, shields, and containers from hides; bones became implements like scrapers, axes, awls, and hoes. Women used the sinews for sewing; men used them for tying points to arrow shafts and for bowstrings. Horns could make cups, spoons, or ladles, and the shaggy buffalo hair was spun into cordage, woven into netting, or used for stuffing and padding. Even the dung, often called *buffalo chips,* was useful as fuel, as European settlers also found when they arrived.

Buffalo were as hard to hunt on foot as they were to carry, and the later hunters used the techniques developed thousands of years earlier by the Big Game Hunters. They stampeded the animals over cliffs or into pens, drove them into marshes, gulleys, or deep snow to disable them, and separated the weaker, young animals from the herd. Disguised with animal skins, the hunters crept close to the herd to drive in a lance or discharge an arrow. Buffalo were the biggest game these villagers preyed on, but they also hunted pronghorn antelope, deer, bear, and prairie wolves.

An effective method devised by Indian hunters to stalk buffalo was to disguise themselves as wolves and creep up on grazing herds. Buffalo in herds usually had no fear of wolves.

Buffalo hunting practices, with or without horses, changed with the Plains seasons. Men did some hunting in winter snow, but spring and summer brought great communal drives. Winter forage was scanty, keeping the buffalo in small groups. When the tender grasses sprouted and the mating season approached, the herd grew; mating went on from July to October. Calves were born in late winter and early spring, and the herds were slowed down by the less swift, more easily fatigued young animals. Hunting was good then.

In summer, women planted corn, beans, squash, and sunflowers, and men cultivated tobacco in fields along the rivers where the soils were deep, fertile, and free of the thick-rooted prairie grasses.

The Horse Comes to the Plains

A few times in history, technology has changed so sweepingly and dramatically as to alter a whole way of life. The invention of the automobile is one example. In the Plains during the seventeenth century it was the horse that changed Indian life.

Horses came to the Southwest with the Spanish, first appearing on the southern Plains around 1650, but the tribes in the northern Plains had none until nearly 100 years later. Having no word for horse, Indians called it the "mystery dog" or "big dog." One tribe, the Sarci, gave it the practical name "seven dogs," implying that one horse could turn out that much work. (When the machine came along we did the same, measuring its strength in horsepower.)

At first Indians used horses as food. The Spanish had tried to keep the animals from them, knowing that Indians on horseback would be hard to control. But the Spaniards could not hide their horsemanship from the Southwestern Indians, who learned by watching how the Spaniards broke and rode horses. Working for the Spanish, the Indians learned to care for horses and make bridles and saddles. From the Southwestern Indians the Plainsmen learned that horses were more useful for riding than for food. On horseback hunters could go farther and faster. A whole new way of life began, one that attracted people from surrounding areas and brought a wave of Indian immigrants to the Plains.

The Plains at the Time of Contact

As the horse began to spread northward in the seventeenth century, this is how tribes were distributed in the Plains: Along the upper Missouri River were agricultural village people, Siouan speakers—the Mandan and Hidatsa. Other farmers, also Siouan, were farther south—the Omaha, Osage, and Kansa. Caddoan speakers—Pawnee and Wichita—were in Nebraska and Kansas and the Caddo in Texas. The Arikara split off from the Pawnee and joined the Mandan and Hidatsa in the north sometime in the seventeenth century.

Few nonagricultural tribes lived on the Plains before horses came along. The Blackfoot, who were Algonkian hunters, lived in the northern Plains, and the Comanche, Shoshonean speakers, were then moving away from the Basin and into the southern Plains. The Kiowa originally lived near the headwaters of the Missouri; they moved south into the Plains on foot before the horse was introduced. The Blackfoot, Kiowa, and Comanche appear to have been the only noncultivators who lived there before the horse arrived. The other Plains hunters were latecomers, among them those familiar in cinema and legend: the Cheyenne, Crow, and Dakota. Some newcomers saw advantages in Plains life and moved there of their own accord. Others, from the east primarily, were pushed into the Plains by the struggles between the Iroquois and the white settlers.

People who came from the west, like the Shoshoni and Nez Perce, had never practiced cultivation as far as we know, but some newcomers had been farming people before entering the Plains. Cultivators like the Cheyenne, Crow, and Arapaho adjusted their ways and subsistence patterns, eventually abandoning settled life for hunting nomadism.

The Horse Culture

By 1700, the Plains Indians, old and new, had taken seriously to horsemanship. Though at first they got horses by trading with the Spanish to the south, later they commonly stole them. They never captured many of the horses that ran wild, nor did they breed horses much—except for the Comanche, who often did both.

The old Plains villagers changed their traditional ways after acquiring the horse, though not as drastically as others. They did not abandon their villages or their cultivated fields, but combined horsemanship with farming. The villages remained permanent homes; the village hunters left for long trips in summer, returning for the rest of the year. Old folks, women, and children mostly remained in the villages, where the women tended the crops, cured hides, and prepared food for winter.

Even the nomads were not constantly on the move. They camped for varying periods of time—longest in the winter—but they had no home base, and they carried their skin tent housing with them. The whole band moved—no one stayed behind. The nomads never thought of farming, for their hunters could supply more food in a day than the women could in months of cultivation.

The Plains, which were nearly vacant before the Indians acquired horses, quickly became a region of horsemen, fighting over territory, on the move most of the time (except for the villagers), creating the new way of life we have come to call the Plains culture. Though it was born and flourished quickly, it was so ap-

In this painting by George Catlin a Comanche struggles with a wild horse he has roped, while his companions carry on the chase. Indians usually pursued wild horses when they could not steal them from other tribes.

pealing and the changeover was so complete that the memory of past ways faded swiftly. The new Plainsmen came to believe that they had always been nomads of the Plains.

Changing Patterns of Life

The horse made a vast difference in the Plains people's ways of settlement, subsistence, and technology. It also caused changes in the social or-ganization of many tribes, and produced a new value system. Tradition already placed great value on the life of the warrior; the Plains horsemen expanded that tradition and elaborated it into a kind of military hierarchy with symbols of military distinction. They glorified bravery, individualism, and stoicism, and their whole way of life came to focus on manhood and youth.

Changing Technology

Housing. The villagers still lived in their traditional dwellings along the rivers. The Missouri River people (Mandan, Hidatsa, and Arikara) had large earth lodges of log framework over shallow pits, covered with poles, brush, and sod. Smoke from the fireplace found its way out through a smokehole in the roof. Entryways were large enough to let a horse through, and during severe winter weather, the people often kept their favorite and most valuable horses in their homes. The Pawnee and neighboring villagers built similar large, durable structures. The Wichita and Caddo, however, built thatched beehive-shaped houses with the hearth in the center of the floor, but with no smokeholes—smoke filtered through the thatching. These two tribes lived where winters were less severe.

The main change in housing on the Plains was the increase in size of the tipi, a conical building formerly covered with bark, brush, or deerhide, five or six feet high, with little space inside. But with horses to haul the tipi, packed on its own lodgepoles, Indians began to build their dwellings twelve to fifteen feet high with plenty of room for people and storage. The only housing the nomads had was the tipi, made with buffalo-hide covers. Villagers used the tipi too, but only while hunting away from home. The nomadic Plainsmen, always on the go, carried other belongings as well as their housing on the travois, an A-shaped drag with the narrow end over the horse's shoulder, the broader end dragging behind. This was a bigger version of the older, dog travois. Babies, children, household equipment, and aged relatives might also ride on the travois.

A travois used by Plains Indians to transport their possessions as well as their housing.

Equipment.   Pottery was far too easily broken to be useful to horsemen. Instead, possessions and even food went along in containers of leather. The fully nomadic people who had previously made pottery turned entirely to leather containers, but the villagers still used some pottery at home. The commonest container, known by the French name *parfleche,* was made by women from rawhide. Unpacked, it looked like a giant envelope; packed, it expanded to the size and shape of a small chest. It stored clothing and other belongings conveniently and often carried food, especially the dried meat and berry concoction called *pemmican.*

Much of the Indian riding gear was patterned on Spanish designs, modified for use on the Plains. While some riders, including most women, used saddles, many others chose to ride bareback. In style and decoration, saddles, bridles, and other horse trappings varied from tribe to tribe. Many Plainsmen made special saddles and horse decorations for dress occasions. Horse equipment was leather until trade with Europeans was well established; then metal parts, like bridle bits, came to the Plains. The Indians were very fond of good horses and took great pleasure in decking their steeds with gaily colored designs of bead or quill work.

Long after guns became available, Indians continued to use bows and arrows and lances for hunting and warfare. The early rifles, like the old one-shot muzzle loaders, were much too slow and hard to reload on horseback, and were less accurate than bows. In fact, guns were not used much on the Plains until the late nineteenth century. The horse did not make the traditional weapons obsolete, though the people did begin using shorter bows that were easier to handle on horseback. Eventually, as traders made metal available, Indians replaced their stone, bone, and horn arrowheads with steel points. In addition to bows and spears, warriors carried clubs of various styles and a protective shield of bison rawhide painted with magical symbols to make it more effective. Pectorals, large chestplates of bone, were more for adornment than protection.

Clothing. Clothing changed little, still being made of deerskin except for the great buffalo-hide robe people wore in winter and used for bedding. Men wore leggings and shirts or coats over breechclouts, and women wore skirts, jackets, or sometimes one-piece dresses. Moccasins, too, were made of hides, and were so distinctive in style that a good tracker could tell the wearer's tribe from a moccasin print. The main change in basic clothing was the addition of more decoration. Fringe trimming on the buckskin increased, and as Europeans brought beads in trade, women decorated garments with elaborate beaded designs as well as quill embroidery. Porcupine quills had been used for designs on the Plains in earlier days, but not so much as farther east.

The one really new piece of clothing was the tailed warbonnet, more a symbol of prestige than a garment. This feathered headdress with its long, flowing

A parfleche (left) was strapped to a horse's side and was usually filled with dried food, clothing, and other belongings.

Three Plains Indians are pictured wearing their feathered warbonnets.

streamers could hardly be worn except on horseback, it was so heavy and cumbersome. Plains warriors prized their bonnets. Only men who had done some brave deed were entitled to wear eagle feathers, and even those warriors wore them only on ceremonial occasions. Today not many people realize that only the mounted Indians of the Plains wore the feathered bonnet; now, tribes all over North America have taken the warbonnet as their trademark.

Most decoration done by Plains people consisted of geometric forms, except on shields and shield covers, men's robes, and tipis. Only men painted these, using representational designs that showed their feats, honors, or visions, or the year's main events. Women did the other decorating, the geometric art on the parfleches, and the quill and beaded work.

Communication

In spite of hostility among the Plains tribes as they jockeyed for good positions in hunting and war, there were many times when people of one linguistic group had to communicate with another. Even if they spoke varieties of the same language they might need an interpreter, and many of the groups who came into the Plains after the advent of the horse spoke languages totally unintelligible to

Painted tipis. The symbols could be painted only by men and represented important events, honors, or visions.

each other. To get along in this babble of languages, the Indians developed a standardized way of communicating, the so-called sign language. It belonged strictly to the Plains; Indians of California or Virginia, for instance, did not use it nor could they understand it without instruction. It could not express many abstract ideas, but it was enough for trade, parleys, and treaty making. White explorers, traders, trappers, and soldiers also came to use it.

Economic Change

The New Materialism. As men accumulated horses and buffalo hides, a new feeling about material wealth spread, and a kind of capitalism grew up on the Plains. Horses and sometimes hides were put to use as money, a medium of exchange. The value of other goods was counted in horses or hides, and even a man's bridewealth payments to his wife's family were determined in horses. Horses came to be traded for just about everything; they represented a man's accumulated wealth. Trade in stolen horses grew brisk, and horse stealing came to be much admired, a proof of manhood.

Until the coming of the horse, Plains Indians lived in egalitarian bands. No one had more than his fellow tribesmen, and sharing was part of life. Material possessions did not bring recognition or a commanding position; prestige came only from achievement. The horse changed all that. Men were ranked by wealth. With a large supply of horses, a man could be sure of having food, clothing, and other things for himself and his family. He could afford to add a wife or two—extra wives meant more hands to cure the hides that added to his wealth. An average family required a dozen horses just to move their belongings.

Sharing did not vanish, however. A wealthy man made himself bigger in the eyes of his neighbors and kinsmen by holding a give-away. This was a big affair, with feasting for the community and many gifts, even for enemies (to make them friends). Buffalo robes, decorated clothing, weapons, and foods were given away as well as horses, though horses were the real measure of stature. While the Plains give-aways were never so formalized as the Northwest Coast potlatches, both were investments in the future, for the recipients (except for the really poor) always repaid the generosity.

As a result of the economic abundance created by the horse, three loosely structured classes developed: a privileged class that was expected to be generous and responsible for the band's welfare, a middle class sharing most benefits of the upper class but with fewer possessions, and a lower, underprivileged class of people poor in horses and other possessions and dependent on the powerful upper class. Though these classes tended to perpetuate themselves by inheritance, a man could gain wealth as a warrior and hunter and change his class standing.

Trade.   For many centuries, Plains people had traded with each other and with those of other regions. After the spread of the horse, trading accelerated. The horse itself grew into a standard of exchange as well as a trade item, and special trading centers appeared. At Taos, in what is now New Mexico, the Pueblo Indians had long held trade fairs. The Indians of the southern Plains began to go to Taos to trade dried meat, animal skins, and other products for agricultural produce and European goods. Villages of the Mandan, Hidatsa, and Arikara became trade centers in the north. White traders also set up trade posts to deal in furs, hides, and other native commodities. Enormous quantities of buffalo hides changed hands for metal implements, and eventually for guns.

One wholly unfortunate item of exchange was liquor, which many Indians sought above all else. European traders later used it to cheat Indians, getting one warrior after another intoxicated and unable to manage his affairs. Eventually the government forbade the sale of liquor to Indians, but the liquor merchants evaded that law.

Social Organization

Kinship patterns were one aspect of Plains life that did not change much after the horse's arrival. Some Plains people, such as the Mandan, Hidatsa, and Crow, traced descent matrilineally. Some, like the Omaha, Oto, and Kansa, had patrilineal clans. But on the Plains, clans had little function except in the regulation of marriage: people had to marry outside their own clan. The family was most important everywhere. Often close ties among people of the same age also were essential for mutual help in hunting and warfare.

The major political unit was the tribe. The nomads broke their tribe into bands for much of the year but came together for communal hunts and ceremonies in the summer. Tribe members shared a common language and common territory, intermarried, and put up a united front to all outsiders. Some tribes were governed by a tribal council, like the Crow and Cheyenne. Others had no permanent tribal leader but would find leaders for specific events—to lead raids or direct hunts. Wealthy men commanded much respect, many of them gathering followers who obeyed them. Decisions that bound the whole community were made throughout the Plains by groups of tribal elders, that is, respected older men.

Associations.   Most Plains tribes had societies or associations for men, gathering members from many kin groups and bands within the tribe. Thus the associations were a cross-section of the tribe, not one kin or local group. Members were faithful to the tribe as a whole, making these organizations a strong unifying force. Members always felt great loyalty to the association and always stood united. Some of these associations were *age-graded*, with all members of one grade moving together to the next, much like our school system.

These brotherhoods are often called warriors' societies or military societies because of their policing and military functions. Members went on raids together; in fact, most warfare was carried on by the associations, though raiding parties smaller than the brotherhoods were also common. Rarely did the whole tribe engage in military action. The chiefs and elders, no matter how violent and aggressive they had been in their youth, were expected to be beyond the age of rashness and to strive for peace. Full-scale fighting, approaching total warfare, became more frequent when United States soldiers came to fight the Plains Indians.

Some of the warriors' societies were so renowned for bravery that it was a great honor to be asked to join. The most prestigious were the Dog Soldiers, a military society in several tribes. The Dog Soldiers of the Kiowa were especially famed for their bravery.

In addition to their military side, these associations had religious aspects, as we might expect among people to whom the supernatural was of vital importance in hunting and warfare. Many brotherhoods had their own ceremonials and sacred objects as well as the members' personal spirit power. In some tribes, all men belonged to an association; others left it to individual choice.

Some tribes also had women's societies, usually with strong magical or ritual aspects. They used their magic to summon the herd or make the crops more fruitful. Other women's societies were like craft associations—groups of hide workers or bead workers, for instance.

Status of Women.   Horses did not relieve women of much work, though they did carry the belongings women or dogs had formerly borne on their backs so the men would be free to fight or hunt. Horses even increased women's labors by helping the hunters bring in more hides for the women to prepare. Thus, as the hunters were more and more successful, *polygyny*—multiple wives—also increased. A good hunter needed several wives because they were the only source of labor. As hides and work piled up, the first wife might even suggest that her husband bring in another wife. Jealousy was never reported as being much of a problem among Indian women, probably partly because a man's second wife was likely to be a sister of his first wife.

Women were far less important in the Plains than they were among the Pueblo, Navajo, and Eastern agriculturalists. They were most valued for their services to males. Successful hunters needed women to cure hides, prepare meat for storage, and put up and take down tipis. The successful man was known not only by his emblems of accomplishment, but by the number of his wives, though few men, no matter how successful, had more than three wives.

A Comanche village painted by George Catlin. Women are preparing buffalo hides which, when sewn together, could cover tipis up to 25 feet in diameter.

Because women did help determine a man's wealth by their labor on his buffalo hides, they sometimes became influential, though not on a public or tribal level. A few women were able to become independently wealthy by accumulating horses in payment for their services.

Values and Beliefs

Though Plains Indians earned respect for their competence in hunting, glory came to them from feats of courage in warfare. Everyone in a war party helped each other, but honor gained in battle was individual. From the time they were boys, male Indians prepared for combat; at about fourteen they were initiated into one of the military societies. From then on their standing in the tribe depended mainly on their conduct in war. The sort of achievement that led to greatest prestige was an act of daring; we might call it foolhardiness. Helping a wounded tribesman to escape from the enemy was praiseworthy. Killing an enemy or stealing his horses also brought praise, but glory was reserved for the man who touched a live enemy without killing him and came home to brag about it. It was the custom to carry a small stick, a *coup stick* (*coup* is French for a "blow"), into battle or on raids, to touch the enemy. The warrior told about his acts of bravery on his return home by striking a pole with his coup stick each time he recounted an act of courage. That was called "counting coup."

The Vision Quest. The vision quest was of great importance to a warrior, who devoutly believed that he could win supernatural aid by fasting, prayer, and body mutilation. To communicate with the spirits was not a task for priesthood or communal religious effort—each man was on his own in appealing for the supernatural's pity and beneficence. Shamanism was played down in many tribes, and in some was even absent, for each person shared in sacred power. Other tribes, mostly those practicing some cultivation, did have shamans.

If no spirit granted him a vision after long fasting and isolation, a warrior would resort to self-torture, hoping the powers would take pity on him in his human helplessness. Torture could take many forms: chopping off a finger (certainly not one he needed for wielding weapons, however), cutting away strips of flesh, or driving bone pins several inches long through his back muscles, attaching a weight that he would pull until muscles and flesh tore, or until he collapsed. Trials like these, added to hunger, would call up a vision almost without fail.

Warriors kept strangely shaped stones, bones, or feathers—symbols of their visions or the animals that sent them power—in sacred containers called *medicine bundles.* The items were *medicine;* they had power. We could liken them to good-luck pieces, sacred talismans, or religious relics. Often a sacred song came with a warrior's vision, and it too became part of his medicine. Some tribes owned sacred tribal bundles, and the people believed that the tribe's well-being depended on the proper care and protection of those bundles.

The warrior had to make repeated contact with his source of power. Facing any important event, he could appeal for guidance and protection from the supernatural through another vision. If prayer and fasting did not bring contact, he would again try self-torture or perhaps stare at the sun for hours until he went into delirium or hallucination.

The Sun Dance. Warriors often sought visions during the big summer ceremonials, the best known of which is the Sun Dance. This was a ceremony put on for the good of the tribe, to keep the buffalo running and ensure a plentiful food supply.

Indians never took nature's bounty for granted. If people did not perform proper rites, the animals would withhold themselves from hunters, plants would wither, and the people would slowly starve. To prevent this ultimate disaster, twenty or more Plains tribes resorted to the Sun Dance. Its name came from the Sioux "gazing-at-the-sun dance," but the Cheyenne name for the structure in which the ceremony was held—translated "new life lodge"—reveals its purpose, which was to do no less than make the whole world over.

The Sun Dance took various forms. The most elaborate types were held by the Arapaho, Cheyenne, and Sioux, but its variations overlapped enough everywhere to make it one ceremony. It lasted about seven days and always took place in summer or early autumn when all the bands of the tribe had come together for the buffalo hunt. A pledger or sponsor gave the dance to fulfill a vow he had made at a time of danger or when the spirits had given him some special attention. It was his way of thanking the supernatural.

Sun Dance Ceremony. Although one person sponsored it, the Sun Dance was performed for the whole tribe, and almost everyone participated in some phase of it. The people put up their tipis in a circle with the dancing area in the middle. A large lodge, facing east, was specially built within the dance area for the ceremony. A group of renowned warriors cut down a straight tall tree, carried it to the dance site with solemn ritual, and erected it as a center post. The participants danced around and around the center pole for long periods, staring at sacred objects hung from it, perhaps sending themselves into hypnosis. Spectators sang and drummed, and both they and the dancers blew whistles.

Dramatic self-torture highlighted the Sun Dance. The warrior participants went without water and food, danced to exhaustion, and sometimes slashed their flesh to appeal to the spirits. In some tribes, a young man who had vowed self-mortification in the ceremony had a medicine man cut two small holes through the skin and flesh on each side of his upper chest. Sticking wooden skewers through the holes, the medicine man secured them to two ropes, the ends of which were fastened to the top of the central pole. The young warrior then danced, straining against the ropes until he broke free or the medicine man cut his flesh to release him. The pain and sacrifice of flesh was the ultimate proof of sincerity: he was giving up the only thing that really belonged to him.

When the ceremony was over, the Indians could again count on enjoying health, fertility, and food. The world was renewed, its complex harmonies restored, its many supernatural powers revived and ready once again to work for the tribe's welfare.

While the Sun Dance was underway, the tribal council or the elders usually met to make plans and decisions for the coming season. It was also a time for festivity and feasting, when marriages were made and friendships renewed. It caused some social strain, however, and the great size of the gathering could bring trouble. Social control was difficult when hot-blooded young men were whooping it up and trying to go on raids, and overly eager hunters could endanger the tribal food supply by stampeding the herds before the men were ready to hunt. During the summer a special police force was created to keep order just for the dance season. Usually one of the men's associations did the policing.

The Misfits. What of the man who had no taste for the life of a warrior, which, after all, was very dangerous? There was a socially acceptable way out: a man could choose to become a *berdache* and lead the life of a woman. A berdache was not necessarily a homosexual; he merely chose a way of life other than the ideal masculine pattern. He was denied honors, but he did not suffer public scorn or ridicule. In some tribes, notably the Blackfoot, women who found the average female role dull and uninteresting had a similar choice: they could become "manly-hearted" women and hunt and raid with the men. They were far fewer, however, than the berdaches.

How Plains Culture Developed

Although it was the nomadic horsemen who created the Plains culture, the villagers too found their lives reorganized by the horse and buffalo. Plains culture from north to south, both the cultivating and the hunting tribes, was remarkably homogeneous. The Plains became a melting pot of American Indian cultures, since without natural geographic barriers there was no way to maintain physical or cultural isolation among such mobile societies. The Plains area shows how people of widely different backgrounds living in the same environment (the Plains and the buffalo) came up with very similar adaptations when they encountered new technology (the horse).

In the Plains culture too we can see how quickly major cultural change can come about when people are willing to accept transformed subsistence patterns, value systems, and social organization. Contrast with that the change forced on the Indians in the late nineteenth century. By then, overkill and the encroaching frontier had wiped out the buffalo herds; proud warriors were debased into government wards. That cultural change is still being fought.

Although the Plains culture was strikingly similar everywhere, there were enough differences to support tribal individuality—a few examples of which we shall now examine.

The Blackfoot

The Blackfoot of historic times included three independent divisions with a common origin: the Siksika, the Blood, and the Piegan. Their territory was almost all north of today's Canadian–United States border in the province of Alberta. That makes them, along with the Sarci and the Plains Cree, the most northerly of the horse nomads.

The Blackfoot spoke a variety of Algonkian. Most authorities think they were pushed out of the East by tribes that were themselves pressed by Europeans. The Blackfoot reached their Plains home about 1720 or a little later, on foot.

The Pedestrian Blackfoot. The pre-horse Blackfoot were hunters and gatherers. They hunted buffalo by using the *surround,* men encircling the herd and killing as many of the outer animals with lances and arrows as they could before the beasts broke out, or by luring the bison into a corral or pound. Women followed the hunters and skinned and dressed the carcasses on the spot. Meat and hides were carried back to camp on dog travois. Buffalo hunting on foot was so difficult and dangerous that the Blackfoot hunters settled for occasional buffalo kills, supplementing this source of meat by trapping wolves, foxes, and badgers, and hunting deer and antelope. The Blackfoot especially valued deer and antelope hides for clothing. They would drive antelope into a pit at the end of a high brush fence, where concealed men clubbed the animals to death as they fell or tried to escape. Blackfoot also hunted mountain sheep, which were prized for their meat and horns. Meat from one animal or another theoretically could be had all year round, but in the northern Plains the intense winter cold and deep snow made hunting difficult and very uncomfortable. Consequently, in those pre-horse days, women dried all the meat they could during the short summer for use in winter.

Meat was the favorite Blackfoot food, but they also used the many nourishing plants available to them. Women gathered all sorts of roots, tubers, seeds, and berries. In preparation for winter scarcity, they dried plant foods and stored them like meat. The Blackfoot never ate fish, though fish were in the rivers. The only cultivated plant was tobacco, which the men planted each spring and harvested in the autumn. They smoked tobacco ritually and for pleasure.

The Blackfoot religion of pre-horse times probably grew from common Algonkian beliefs. One belief was that animals had supernatural power, which they would share with those who sought it by praying and fasting. Another was the Shaking Tent Ritual. A bound shaman was placed inside a tent, which soon began to shake; this meant the powers were communicating with the shaman, giving him the ability to predict where game could be found or to foretell the band's future. Religious beliefs and practices were simple in pre-horse times, and there were no large community ceremonials.

Even before the horse appeared, people won prestige from personal courage and achievement and from the supernatural power they might attain. A woman's status was the same as her husband's unless she had supernatural power of her own.

The Equestrian Blackfoot.   Horses spread slowly to the northern Plains, both because it was so far from the source of supply in the Southwest and because of the difficulties of bringing a string of horses across the great rivers, such as the Missouri. In the early days, the Blackfoot apparently got their horses from Plateau peoples to the southwest, rather than more directly from the south.

The Blackfoot alone among Plains Indians received the horse and the gun at the same time. They were among the last of the Plains people to get horses, in about 1740, and by that time the Cree, whose territory was just to the east, were trading guns to them. Whites stayed outside Blackfoot territory until about 1780, leaving the Cree as middlemen for the gun trade.

The Seasonal Pattern. With spring coming late in Blackfoot territory, and a semidrought settled in by midsummer, the grass was in prime condition for only about two months. Horses, buffalo, and other grazers feasted on fresh grass in spring, but after a summer of scanty forage, they rarely entered winter at their strongest. Blackfoot horses had a hard time, especially through the winters when fodder was short. Bison stayed in the area only as long as grazing was good, scattering to better pastures for the rest of the year. The people too broke into bands in winter to seek the protection of valleys and woods.

During the spring and early summer, when bison formed great herds on the northern Plains, the Blackfoot bands united into larger groups for a communal hunt. The rest of the year, people traveled in smaller units within their own territory. Each band was usually based on the *patrilocal* family—brothers, their wives, and children—but unrelated individuals or families might also form bands. Though wealthy men (that is, successful hunters) had more than one wife, most men were monogamous. Only economic expedience determined who combined into groups of kin or held territory in common.

The summer encampment that followed the concentrated hunting season was a scene of feasts and dances. Medicine bundles were sold (a Blackfoot practice; not all tribes sold them), as were robes and horses. Brotherhoods performed their ceremonials, initiating boys into the first stage and transferring some members to the next rank. After they acquired horses, the Blackfoot also began to take part in the Sun Dance, the culmination of summer activity. The tribe dispersed soon after and moved to winter camps.

Organization. Band leaders were chosen for their competence. There were no inherited political positions. The outstanding men from all bands formed a tribal leadership, but they had no coercive powers and they depended on the rest of the population for support.

Most Blackfoot men belonged to associations that took turns controlling the larger gatherings formed for the summer hunts. The association in charge was responsible for keeping the peace and regulating individual hunting; its members also had ritual duties. Blackfoot societies were age-graded: about every four years one grade moved or graduated to another level, taking that level's rights and rituals and transferring its own practices to the next junior rank. Junior members paid with horses or goods for the position they took in the next grade. Because payment was required, it was possible to skip a grade or to remain longer than normal in one grade. The oldest or highest grade formed a sort of council of wise men, a senior rank called the Bull Society.

Religion.   The Blackfoot Sun Dance was a display of wealth and self-torture. It probably came to them from the Arapaho, and it became their major tribal religious ceremony. The Blackfoot Sun Dance was unique in that women had a big part in it. A medicine woman pledged the dance and was responsible for its success. Women as well as men mutilated themselves for blessings from the supernatural, though the women's torture was milder—at most they would cut off bits of flesh or chop off a finger joint.

Along with the Sun Dance, the equestrian Blackfoot adopted the vision quest and the medicine bundle. The search for power from animal spirits of pre-horse days became more intense and more complex once they had horses. The warrior expected the spirits to reveal sacred items to him which he would then keep in his sacred bundle. Selling a medicine bundle was an important commercial transaction, for the bundle was always worth at least what was paid for it, and if it brought the buyer success, it became worth more.

Shamans or medicine men often became wealthy by charging high fees for successful cures. Many of the curers were women, who found this a way to buy horses of their own. Blackfoot women were valuable and influential not only as curers but as laborers. Good hunters depended on their wives for curing buffalo hides and other skins. Women were respected too as childbearers.

Warfare: Ambush and Battle.   Once the Blackfoot had horses, they became distinctly expansionist, taking over territory from neighboring tribes and profiting by a geographical position which allowed them to control the spread of both horses and guns. By 1850, Blackfoot territory stretched from the North Saskatchewan River to what is now Yellowstone Park. They also changed their war tactics, from infantry to cavalry. Before the horse, the Blackfoot pattern of warfare had been either ambush or battle. In an ambush, a few armed men fell upon a small group of unsuspecting enemies, capturing the women and children and killing the men. The women and children were married or adopted to replace killed Blackfoot, or taken as slaves. The battle was more complex. Opposing warriors chose the battleground by mutual consent. Then the two forces formed long lines facing each other, just within arrow range, and warriors fired arrows from behind large shields. Dancing and singing went on both before and during the conflict. Most of these contests were indecisive.

Mounted warfare swept away the large-scale battle, replacing it with the raid. Warriors of one band or age-grade formed the war parties, and stealth and maneuverability were crucial to their success. Casualties went up immensely. War became commercial, aimed at accumulating horses, and prestige came to be counted in numbers of horses, not courageous deeds.

Raiding for Horses.   Only one path led to wealth and social standing for the male Blackfoot—raiding. Many in the raiding parties were poor but ambitious young men, willing to risk their lives to get horses. There were also a few who loved the excitement. The raid leader, an older, proven warrior, chose his volunteer party of eager, competent men, and refused anyone he thought unreliable. Raiding parties rarely were larger than twelve men, for larger groups were hard to conceal and control. Sometimes young childless wives went along with their husbands.

Raids were less common in winter than in spring and summer because of the severe cold and deep snow, but some winter raids did occur. The blown snow covered tracks quickly, making it hard for the enemy to follow. Often the raiders covered themselves with white Hudson's Bay blankets, not only to ward off cold but also to help them blend in with the snow. In warmer weather they wore only the bare essentials: breechclout, leggings, and sometimes a shirt.

Though he trained to be skillful, resourceful, and swift, the Blackfoot warrior credited his success in raiding not to his physical prowess but to the power of his war medicine. No people relied more on war charms than the Blackfoot, who wore their personal medicine in buckskin bags hung around their necks or as hair decoration. In the bags might be herbs and a bear claw representing strength, a weasel skin for speed, or a bone disk symbolic of the sun. Feathers were commonly the hair ornaments. Men learned the formula for their medicine and battle songs from dreams, in which a dream spirit would take human or animal form. They might also buy war medicine from old men who had been successful warriors.

The Raid. The raiding party might travel several hundred miles, the first part on horseback, the last on foot. Along with their war medicine, the men carried pemmican, ropes to control the horses they expected to steal, and knives, often butcher knives made in Sheffield, England. The Blackfoot got these knives from Canadian traders and used them to butcher animals for food, cut firewood, or lift an enemy scalp if an opportunity presented itself. Raiders also carried a bow and quiver of arrows or a gun.

When they came close to enemy territory, they hid by day and traveled by night. Near the target they built a shelter, a bark- or brush-covered tipi or lodge where they would prepare for the assault, using it as a base camp for scouting and concealing supplies. From the camp, scouts located the enemy encampment and studied the layout and how horses were pastured.

The raiders scheduled the attack for daybreak. Creeping stealthily into the enemy camp, they tried to cut horses from their picket lines or to steal range horses without waking the enemies. If dogs barked, they could be pacified with chunks of meat. With their stolen horses, the men took off for home so that the enemy could not catch up. If they were caught, they had to fight for their lives. For the first day or day-and-a-half the raiders rode without stopping, except to change horses as the animals tired. Bringing back fifty or so horses was considered very good, and each man was entitled to the animals he had run off. If any arguments broke out, the leader settled them, and might even give up horses he had captured to those who had taken none. Such generosity increased his stature as a leader. After three or four days of travel, the party slowed down to a more leisurely pace. Near home they painted their faces as a sign of victory before they entered camp, where people greeted them with shouts and drumming.

The Cheyenne

The Cheyenne were once typical Algonkian agriculturalists of the upper Mississippi valley west of Lake Superior. Late in the seventeenth century they began slowly moving into the Plains, probably driven by pressure from dislocated Indian peoples to the east and white traders and settlers closing in. They came to the Plains still practicing cultivation, but probably also hunting buffalo like the traditional Plains villagers. By 1700 they were living along the Cheyenne River in North Dakota, and by 1800 they had enough horses to become fully nomadic horsemen, abandoning all agriculture.

As equestrians, the Cheyenne controlled a region of dry grassland on the high plains where trees grew only along watercourses in the mountain foothills. Most precipitation came in early summer, often in severe thunderstorms. In late spring and early summer, the grass grew luxuriantly, and great herds of buffalo gathered in Cheyenne territory. As the weather grew hotter and drier, the herds broke up into widely scattered foraging groups.

This pattern of animal life in turn controlled the Cheyenne seasonal rhythm of gathering into a tribe and dispersing in bands. In winter the mounted hunters left the unwatered upland because too little grass grew there to feed the horses, and they set up smaller camps in sheltered spots near watering places. In small groups the Cheyenne could find enough forage for the horses, and the hunters could cover a wider area in the foothills to search for deer, elk, antelope, and other game.

Most bands included a number of related families, led by men of proven ability who might also be tribal chieftains or leaders of one of the brotherhoods. Labor was strictly divided. Women gathered wild plants, tanned hides, cooked the food, and brought up the children. Men were hunters and warriors, making the weapons and performing all the rituals. Subsistence techniques generally were well adapted to the environment and provided a balanced diet in good times. Famine was always a threat in winter and early spring, though, so appeals to the supernatural were part of every aspect of procuring food.

The meat drying in this photo of a Cheyenne summer camp is most likely beef. A woman, at right, works on unprepared entrails.

The Council of Forty-four. During the spring and summer, when Cheyenne bands joined forces for communal hunting and ceremonials, the tribe was governed by the Council of Forty-four. Four headmen from each of the ten bands and four general chiefs formed the council, each having tenure for ten years. Their decisions and tribal rules were backed up by the Cheyenne military societies.

The council was concerned with internal affairs, the general public good, and external relationships like treaties. (War was in the hands of war chiefs.) Although it was the only body with authority to make decisions affecting the whole tribe, the council recognized that without public support those decisions would be meaningless, and held debates and discussed issues thoroughly. Decisions had to be unanimous, thus ensuring support from the whole society since the council was composed of representatives from all the bands.

Ceremonials. The tribal gathering in summer, when food was abundant and easy to find, was a time of spiritual renewal. It was then that rituals were performed to regenerate the tribe's vitality and bring success in hunting and warfare. Very important for tribal well-being was the Arrow Renewal Ceremony, a dance pledged by an individual to thank or praise the spirits, or perhaps because one Cheyenne had murdered another. (Murder within the tribe was considered very bad luck for everyone and required expiation.) There were four Medicine Arrows: two held power over buffalo, two over people. They were very sacred and were kept under the protection of an official appointed for that purpose. The Medicine Arrows stood for the tribe's collective existence; as long as they were cared for, the tribe would flourish. This supernatural power covered all Cheyenne, controlling both people and buffalo. The arrows, then, were the Cheyenne's greatest resource against severe anxiety, failure of the food supply, and extermination by enemies. The Arrow Renewal Ceremony brought the whole tribe together in sacred observances, after which all the hunters joined in a communal buffalo hunt. Anxieties relieved, the hunters went off confident that they would be successful, and certain that the whole earth and all therein had been revitalized in their favor.

Another ceremonial was the Cheyenne version of the Sun Dance, which they called the Medicine Lodge, or New Life Lodge, for its world renewal function. Usually the Cheyenne Sun Dance and Arrow Renewal Ceremony did not occur in the same year, but if they did, the Arrow Renewal Ceremony was more important and was given first. In the eight-day Sun Dance, warriors went through self-torture, suspending themselves from the central lodgepole by skewers through their chest muscles.

Religious Beliefs. Apparently the Cheyenne had no theory about how the world came to be; creation did not matter to them. They saw the world as composed of related parts, each governed by a kind of generous spirit. While the spirits had not created the world, they did know how to keep it operating properly, and they would give that knowledge to men who sought and listened respectfully. Human beings could not control nature, but they could learn to control themselves and know their place in nature. Careful self-control and the performance of exact symbolic rites would keep a man in tune with the environment, rejuvenate the earth, and maintain good health, good hunts, and victory in warfare. Self-discipline thus played a large part in Cheyenne conduct, from extreme sexual repression to bravery in the face of impossible odds.

The Cheyenne sought supernatural power through a vision quest, and shared the belief in guardian spirits common to many tribes, calling them "spirits who told me in sleep." To seek personal healing power or safety in a coming raid, a man would find a lonely place to fast and pray to the spirits. If a spirit was inclined to grant his requests, it appeared as a vision and told him how to prepare special charms, paint himself, and sing to summon his guardian. He was also given taboos to protect his new power. Under stress such visions came unsolicited, but they could also be called forth by the same sorts of gifts, offerings, or sacrifice used elsewhere in the Plains.

Prestige and Self-control.   Like all the nomadic tribes of the Plains, the Cheyenne were relative newcomers. Because they were constantly having to defend their hunting territory against other groups that might deplete the buffalo supply or stampede the herds, they placed much emphasis on military prowess. Prestige in war was socially important; counting coup against the enemy established the warrior's place in his people's eyes and gave him great psychological satisfaction. Dozens of ritual occasions allowed an outstanding warrior to count coup, receiving public acclaim each time.

The Cheyenne have often been described as sexually repressed because of their attitude toward sex and self-control. They believed that long-term continence gave a man great endurance and ability in warfare and hunting; it was not unheard of for a man to vow to abstain from sexual relations for years. Women were just as sexually constrained, and their virginity was very highly valued. Adultery was rare, and sexual continence was highly praised even for married couples. Ten years was the ideal spacing between children, bringing praise to men for abstinence and self-restraint.

Boys had no puberty ceremonies, but a girl's first menstruation was an important event. The girl's father would give away horses if he were rich, while her mother gave her a chastity belt to wear until she married and then whenever her husband was away.

The Comanche

The Comanche differed in many ways from the other Plains groups we have discussed. Their warfare was very individualistic, they never developed the military societies other Plains people had, and they did not perform the Sun Dance. What made them true Plains people was their total focus on horses: their superb horsemanship surpassed all others. They had been Basin foragers who apparently moved onto the Plains before horses came, an unimportant group speaking a Shoshonean language.

How They Got Horses.   By the time the Comanche came into history they were already horsemen. They were among the first Indians to acquire horses,

A coup stick. It was used by some warriors to touch an enemy during combat.

though no one knows exactly how it happened. We know where they were in the mid-seventeenth century, though, and that gives us a clue. The eastern groups of Apache had come by some horses while the Comanche were settled nearby, around what is now Amarillo, Texas. The Comanche must also have come into contact with Spaniards, who, of course, were horsemen. In any event, by 1700 they were raiding the Spanish not only for horses but for mules and making a reputation for themselves as extremely skillful equestrians and clever traders. Once horses became common on the southern Plains, they spread quickly northward, and the Comanche benefited from being strategically located middle-men between the supply in the Southwest and the demand to the north. Most other tribes had to trade through them, at least in the early days, so it is not surprising that the Comanche had more horses than any other tribe.

As time went on, the Comanche got their horses from many sources: trade with the Spanish and with other tribes, theft, raiding, breeding, and capturing wild mustangs. Even the poorest Comanche had at least one horse; the wealthy might have hundreds. It is said that some Comanche had more horses than did whole tribes in the northern Plains. Eventually the Comanche ceased trading *for* horses; they traded horses for other things.

Horse stealing was prestigious, fun, and easier than breaking wild horses. The Comanche built quite a reputation for clever horse theft, inspiring many stories about thievery taking place despite "impossible" conditions: under the noses of guards or soldiers, or in stables where men were sleeping. The Comanche also stole mules, using them for backpacking and carrying war captives, since mules were slow.

The Comanche also bred their horses, unlike most other Indians. They castrated all stallions but those chosen for their fine qualities to breed the mares; riding horses were almost always gelded. The most desirable horse was wiry, swift, and easy to turn and train. Comanche did not shoe their horses, but toughened the hooves by walking the animals near a fire. Sometimes they made a sort of rawhide boot for a horse with a sore hoof. To break a wild horse, a Co-

Frederick Remington's painting captures the drama of a Comanche horseman racing through gunfire to swoop up a fallen comrade.

manche usually rode it into water for the first few attempts so that when he was tossed by the bucking animal, he would land safely.

Skilled Equestrians.   The Comanche were described as such fine horsemen that they looked like part of the horse. They rode both with saddles—modified from Spanish originals—and bareback, controlling their mounts with their knees and a simple rein. Babies on their mothers' backs became accustomed to riding before they learned to walk, and at four or five a boy had a horse of his own. Girls were as accustomed to riding as boys, though girls did not ride in hunts or raids. Boys were so competent that they were really trick riders, practicing daily like an athlete or dancer. They learned to pick up things from the ground while riding at full speed, and by adulthood they could swing a man up from the ground onto a horse. They often used this trick to rescue fallen comrades in battle; leaving a wounded Comanche to his enemies was about the worst thing another rider could do. Usually a pair of riders made the rescue, one on either side, leaning down to grasp the prone man at the same instant and raising him onto one of the horses. Men and horses practiced that feat until their timing and coordination were perfect.

Training Horses.   A superior animal would be trained by its owner as a war or buffalo horse or both. A war horse had to be able to stand the whooping and screaming of the fight, and to respond alertly to commands the rider gave by pressing with his knees or shifting his weight while his hands were busy with weapons. An attacker galloped in a straight line, hanging over one side of the horse with only one heel showing over his mount's back. In that position he could loose arrows from under the horse's neck, shielded by its body. The rider was supported by a loop of horse or buffalo hair woven into the animal's mane and slung around one of the man's shoulders. He locked one leg over the horse's back and the other under its belly.

For buffalo hunting, a horse had to have many of the characteristics needed in battle—speed and fearlessness to enter the fringes of a nervous, thundering herd without guidance from his rider's reins, quickness to avoid the charge of a wounded bull, and deep wind to stay with the herd for miles. Comanche ponies were perfect machines of the hunt. They were trained to ride up to a fleeing buffalo, then veer aside as soon as they heard the twang of the bow. The hunter approached a buffalo from the rear, coming up swiftly and shooting an arrow into the soft, vulnerable area between the rib cage and the pelvis. At such close range, the arrow did tremendous damage. The hunters also killed with lances, but success in either case depended as much on the steed as the rider. It is not surprising that races and other contests on horseback were favorite Comanche sports.

A Comanche had great esteem for his favorite horse. He combed it and petted it, and for safety's sake usually picketed it at night near his tipi. To kill a man's favorite horse was about the same as committing murder.

In this painting of a buffalo chase the beauty and rhythm that made horse and rider one is dramatically rendered.

The Crow

Old age is evil; it is far better for a man to die young in battle than to live to comfortable old age. So believed most of the Plains Indians, among them the Crow of southern Montana. Consequently boys trained young to become warriors, learning from games that imitated adult war conditions. Boys counted coup on animals as their elders did on enemies, and girls danced with the hair of a wolf or coyote as though it were an enemy scalp. On his first war party, a youngster might find himself the butt of practical jokes, and he was expected to carry the meat, do menial tasks, and locate water for the older men. But all such incidents prepared a young man for the time when he would be on his own, facing an enemy with only his meager weapons and his wits.

Warfare and military feats were the way to gain social standing and a chieftaincy among the Crow. War was a focal point for all Crow, not just those of one class or sex. Women's social status came from their husbands' military feats: they danced wearing scalps their husbands had accumulated, and proudly displayed their weapons. Nothing was more effective in whipping up emotion for a raiding party than a woman's grief over a fallen son or husband. There were even a few women warriors, one of whom was reported to have struck a coup and scalped a fallen enemy Blackfoot.

Crow warriors carried home scalps as evidence of a killing, but scalping in itself had no special merit. Cleaned, dried scalps were displayed as trophies at the end of a long stick.

Raids. The most frequent type of aggression was a raid organized by one man, consisting of a small party under his personal care. Men followed him because they expected success—the winning of horses and glory. As among the Cheyenne, the tribal leaders were expected to keep the peace and might veto the raid if it looked ill-advised, so they were not usually informed of plans for raids. The leader found all the approval he needed in a dream or vision giving him full details on where to go, whom to raid, and what loot to expect. A man who could not get the right kind of vision could go to someone known to have war medicine for direction from his dreams. Skeptics did not follow a raid leader if they doubted the power of his vision. Members of the party observed taboos during the raid to make sure it would be a success, and carried along the leader's sacred bundle for its medicine.

Raiding parties usually set out on foot, after dark. Bivouacking in simple shelters, they would send out scouts to find the enemy. Once the enemy was sighted, rituals were begun: men sang around a pile of buffalo chips, and one of the scouts announced the sighting by kicking over the chips. On the raid each man wore sacred objects on his body and designs painted on his face. The sponsor would pray to the sun for a safe and successful raid. Their goal was to steal or free enemy horses, and if they were able to do so the party returned home satisfied.

Enemy camps often caught the intruders at their work, and would try to fight them off or pursue them on horseback. If a member of the raiding party was killed, someone would go ahead to tell the camp by firing a gunshot and signaling to the people with a blanket. Those in camp went into mourning while the unlucky raiding party stayed in isolation for ten days. Then they would try again. If they were able to steal horses on the second attempt, the grieving ended, though the dead warrior's family would continue mourning until an enemy had been killed.

Although death in battle was considered glorious, the war party always tried to avoid losing people. Any man who got a reputation for leading raids on which men were often killed began to have a very hard time finding followers.

Winning Glory. A man could do four things in battle to win glory; when he had accomplished all four, he won the title of chief. The deeds were: (1) striking coup by touching a live enemy (the first coup of battle was ranked higher than any later blow), (2) snatching away an enemy's weapon in a hand-to-hand encounter, (3) stealing or freeing a horse in the enemy camp, (4) leading a successful raid.

Warriors wore symbols telling about their brave deeds. A coup striker might wear wolf tails on the heels of his moccasins; a gun-snatcher might decorate his shirt with ermine skins. Any warrior also had the right to picture his deeds on his robe and to recite his own praises on public occasions.

Other Reasons for Raids. Aside from the honor and social status warriors could win in battle, the desire for loot, horses above all, was motive for raiding. Although gaining horses from any source was profitable, the Crow felt it showed more valor to cut loose a picketed or hobbled horse than to make away with many that were wandering free; and of course a picketed horse was more apt to be valuable. Whatever loot the raiders got the leader theoretically could claim for himself. In practice he always shared it, not only with others of the raiding party, but often with those who had remained at home.

Another reason for raids was revenge: avenging a slain tribesman, or replacing Crow horses that had been stolen by taking as many or more from the enemy. If they killed an enemy, the warriors returned with blackened faces. They might take prisoners, often marrying captured women into the tribe. Male captives might also be spared, but not so commonly as women and children. If the Crow had suffered losses during the raid, or the enemy had put up great resistance, prisoners might be tortured and killed. It was a custom everywhere to adopt captured children.

An interior view of
a Mandan lodge.

The Mandan

A Siouan-speaking people, the Mandan had settled on the upper Missouri River
long before Europeans reached the New World. By the time European explorers
met them, two other sedentary tribes lived close by, the Hidatsa, also Siouan,
and the Arikara, a spin-off of the Caddoan-speaking Pawnee. All lived in settled
villages on terraces or cliffs along rivers. Archaeological ruins indicate that in
prehistoric times these villages were not fortified, but by the nineteenth century
the Mandan had built stockade fences on the sides of the villages not naturally
protected by cliffs.

Mandan villages had sturdily constructed earth houses fifty to eighty feet or
more in diameter, large enough to house an extended family and a few horses
during cold weather. Ground was excavated about two feet deep, above which a
superstructure of heavy center posts and cross-beam logs was raised, walled with
poles and roofed with rafters, over which branches were entwined. The entire
building was covered with earth and sod, leaving only a center hole for smoke to

escape. A short tunnel with a wind baffle of planks just inside the lodge was the entrance. People often sat on the roofs, where many foods were spread to dry before the women moved them to storage pits sunk into the lodge floors. These houses were warm in winter and cool in summer. They were built around a central area used for ceremonies and sports, a sort of village plaza or square. On the summer communal hunt, the Mandan lived in hide tipis.

Cultivation and Hunting. The Mandan participated in the mounted life of the Plains, but they also cultivated gardens. Cultivation was mostly women's work, but men helped clear the fields, and old men and children did some of the cultivating. They planted their gardens in fields along the river, after clearing off the trees by cutting them down and burning them or saving them to use for building houses. The women planted corn, beans, squash, and sunflowers in the rich river-bottom land, which they turned up and cultivated with hoes, digging sticks, and rakes. Tobacco, much used for ritual, was cultivated by old men. Unlike the fully nomadic tribes, the Mandan lived on their crops and had well-developed ceremonials for agriculture. They also traded corn to nomadic people for horses and hides. Village tribes ate nearly as much buffalo as corn, but the mounted Indians had only whatever corn they got by trade.

Fishing too was more important for Mandan subsistence than it was to most other Plains tribes—not surprising, since they lived on the river. Large numbers of bones in the village garbage heaps prove they were especially fond of catfish.

After the major spring planting came a lull in farming. Then the Mandan hunters turned from elk and deer, which they hunted all year, to the bison and the great summer communal hunt. They rode out onto the plains, sometimes for long periods, leaving their villages to be cared for by old people, some women, and the youngsters. Other women went with the hunters to process their buffalo meat and hides. Though the Mandan had hunted buffalo before they had horses, it was far more important later because, like the other Plains tribes, the horse made them more productive hunters.

Religion: The Okipa. The Mandan had no Sun Dance, but they had a midsummer ceremony for tribal well-being called the Okipa that was much like it. The Okipa was sponsored by an individual to fulfill a pledge; if several people wanted to sponsor one, several might come in one season, both before and after the buffalo hunt. Much self-torture went on during the Okipa, more than in many versions of the Sun Dance. An Okipa society directed the ceremony and guarded the sacred Okipa bundle that ensured the tribe's safety. The ceremony was for the good of the whole tribe. During its performance, the Mandan creation myth was acted out; it was much like the myth at the beginning of this chapter. The first part of the ceremonial celebrated the subsiding of the flood, then dancers, costumed or painted as mythical personages such as First Man, acted out the coming of the buffalo. The final parts of the ceremonial—the torture—were initiation rites to induct young men into manhood and ordeals to harden warriors for extreme trials of endurance.

Social Organization. The Mandan tribe was divided into two moieties, each with a part in the political organization. In each village, the peace leader came from one moiety and the war chief from the other. Within the two divisions were matrilineal clans, which controlled the fields, allotting them for cultivation to individual families in the clan. Women were important in land use and inheritance of rights in this matrilineal system, belonging to age-graded associations like the men. Membership in the grades was purchased. One rank of young men, the Black Mouth Society, was responsible for social control during tribal hunts. The Mandan also had a tribal council of leaders from the villages, which had no coercive powers but led by example and persuasion.

Raising Corn and Hunting Buffalo. The Mandan are typical of Plains villager life, though villages varied, of course, in customs, environment, and particularly climate. But the village tribes kept the pre-horse cultivation practices at the

George Catlin's
portrait of a Man-
dan medicine man.
Catlin's paintings
provided the
first visual record
of the tribe.

CHARACTERISTICS OF THE PLAINS TRIBES

Clothing	Food production	Equipment	Shelter	Social and political organization	Religion	Warfare
Buffalo robes	Nomads: hunting, gathering, fishing, some cultivation of tobacco, and trading with villagers	Bows and arrows	Skin tents	Local bands	Shamans	Warfare—the most important source of glory for men
Leggings		Spears	Large tipis	Matrilineal and patrilineal clans	Spirits	Frequent raids
Shirts		Scrapers	Earth lodges of log framework over shallow pits	Tribes	Guardian spirits	"Coup" counting
Coats	Villagers: cultivation (corn, beans, and squash), hunting, and gathering	Awls	Thatched beehive-shaped houses	Tribal associations	Vision Quest	Scalping
Dresses		Hoes	Sweathouses	Age grades	Sun Dance	
Breechcloths		Clubs		Moieties (Mandan)	Arrow Renewal Ceremony (Cheyenne)	
Skirts		Shields		Council of Forty-Four (Cheyenne)	Okipa Ceremony (Mandan)	
Jackets		Pectorals				
Moccasins		Axes				
War bonnets		Pottery (villagers)				
		Parfleches				
		Basketry				
		Buffalo horn spoons and cups				

same time that the new, swift transportation enriched and elaborated their hunting activities. The two ways of getting subsistence meshed without strain. Before the buffalo hunt, the fields were prepared and sown. Women with children old enough for the occasion and all able-bodied men moved onto the plains to hunt bison, the women curing meat and tanning hides as the men killed the animals. Though matrilineal at home, hunting parties generally shifted to patrilocal or patrilineal arrangements, because brothers preferred to work together. When they had killed as much game as they could haul, the people returned to their permanent sites to harvest crops and process food for winter storage. Belief and ceremony among the village tribes included both rituals for good hunting and success in warfare (including the Buffalo Dance and the Okipa Ceremony) and a Rain Dance for good crop-growing weather.

Bibliography

Lowie, Robert
1954   *Indians of the Plains.*
        An excellent survey of the Plains Indians after they acquired the horse.

Nabokov, Peter
1967   *Two Leggings: The Making of a Crow Warrior.*
        Good biographical and ethnographic information about the Crow during 1840–1920, and one man's quest for leadership.

Neihardt, John G.
1961   *Black Elk Speaks.*
        A description of a Sioux medicine man's dreams and the influence they had on his life.

Neihardt, John G.
1951   *When the Tree Flowered.*
        A compilation of the life stories of many real Sioux into one fictional man. This excellent ethnographic work should be more valuable to students than the more esoteric *Black Elk Speaks.*

Ewers, John
1955   *The Horse in Blackfoot Indian Culture.*
1958   *The Blackfeet.*

Fletcher, Alice, and Francis LaFlesche
1906   *The Omaha Tribe.*

Grinnel, George B.
1923   *The Cheyenne Indians.* 2 vols.

Lowie, Robert
1922   *Plains Indian Age Societies.*
1935   *The Crow Indians.*

Mishkin, Bernard
1940   *Rank and Warfare among Plains Indians.*

Secoy, Frank R.
1953   *Changing Military Patterns of the Great Plains.*

Wallace, Ernest, and E. A. Hoebel
1952   *The Comanches, Lords of the South Plains.*

Wilson, Gilbert L.
1924   *The Horse and the Dog in Hidatsa Culture.*

MAJOR GROUPS AND LANGUAGES
OF THE PLAINS

Language phylum	Language family	Cultural division
Aztec-Tanoan	Kiowa-Tanoan	Kiowa
	Uto-Aztecan	Comanche
Macro-Algonkian	Algonkian	Arapaho Atsina Blackfoot Cheyenne
Macro-Siouan	Caddoan	Arikara Caddo Pawnee Wichita
	Siouan	Assiniboine Crow Dakota Hidatsa Iowa Kansa Mandan Omaha Osage Ponca Quapaw

Continued

MAJOR GROUPS AND LANGUAGES (continued)

Language phylum	Language family	Cultural division

PLAINS (continued)

Na-Dene	Athabaskan	Kiowa Apache Sarsi

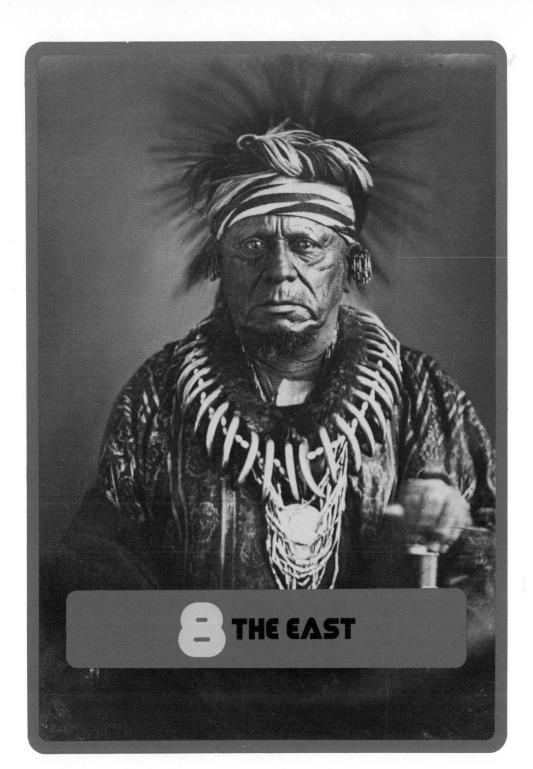

8 THE EAST

THE EAST

VΛVΛVΛVΛVΛVΛVΛVΛVΛVΛVΛV

Many years ago a young Indian man built a small lodge away from the home of his family. He had arrived at the proper age to undertake a fast and learn what kind of spirit would be his guide and guardian through life. He entered his little lodge where he would not be disturbed, and prepared himself to receive a spirit.

He sought to clear his heart of every evil thought, and to think only good, beautiful, and kindly things. He ate nothing and he meditated for two days. Nothing happened, and the young man felt despair. On the third day, weak and faint, he wondered whether any spirit would come to him. He lay on his bed, and suddenly saw a bright light at the lodge door. At first, the man was frightened, but then he saw that a beautiful woman had entered his lodge. She was richly and gaily dressed in many flowing garments of green and yellow colors. She had a plume of waving feathers on her head, and she had long, light hair, very different from Indian hair.

She spoke in a soft, musical voice. "I have come in response to your fasting." The man tried to approach her, but she seemed to move away. He told her he was lonely and he wanted her to stay with him. She told him that if he did just exactly as she said, she would be with him always. She would return to him the next day and tell him what to do.

When the woman returned, the man was very faint in body, but strong at heart. He said, "I have continued my fast to show you my good heart. Now you have promised that you will never leave me." "You have won your desire," she said, "and your fast will soon be over. This is what you must do." And she took the man by his hand and led him from the lodge.

Outside, some distance from the lodge, was a meadow of dry grass. The woman told the man to rub two dry sticks together quickly, holding them in the grass. Soon sparks flew, and the grass caught fire. Then the woman said, "When the sun goes down, you must take me by my hair and drag me across the field. After that you may eat." The man did not want to drag her, but she told him he must, and if he did, he would never again be hungry. When evening came, he did as he had been told. The woman disappeared, but wherever he had dragged her, a tall and graceful plant arose. On it were golden clusters of grain, and on each cluster the man

Preceding page:
A photo of Keokuk,
a Sauk war chief
who fought against
the British during
the War of 1812.
He is wearing a
James Monroe
Peace Medal,
awarded because of
his efforts to pre-
serve peace be-
tween whites and
Indians.

could see the light, silky hair of the woman. It was corn, the friend of all mankind, and every spring it grows again as the Indians plant the kernels in the ground.

The Eastern culture area stretches from the Mississippi River to the Atlantic Ocean, and from the Gulf of Mexico to the Great Lakes and slightly north of the Canadian border (as far north as maize can be cultivated). In this very large area with its many regional variations, most Indian groups adapted themselves to woodland living. All practiced agriculture, but though corn was very important in the diet (as in the myth introducing this chapter), nowhere did cultivation make up much more than half the diet. Game, fish, and wild plants were abundant and could be taken with little effort. In two parts of the East, farming was not done at all: the Calusa area of south Florida, where the people lived entirely on wild foods, and the extreme northeast, where the growing season was so short that crops very often failed. Yet even there people had corn, getting it in trade with more southerly neighbors.

Early Life in the East

The East had three distinguishable subareas, which we can call the Northeast, Southeast, and the Western Great Lakes regions. Though cultures in all three areas shared woodland living and corn cultivation, a number of differences in environment and cultural adaptations make the three regions distinct.

Languages, however, followed a different pattern. Algonkian speakers lived from the western Great Lakes to the New England coast and down the coast into North Carolina. Piercing this expanse of Algonkians was a wedge of Iroquoian speakers, concentrated around the eastern Great Lakes and spreading into the Appalachians. Separated from this northerly Iroquoian group by Algonkians was another set of Iroquoian speakers around Virginia, eastern Tennessee, and North Carolina. Some Siouan-speaking tribes lived south of those Iroquois, and a few isolated Siouans had established themselves along the Gulf coast. By far the most common tongues of the Southeast were languages of the Muskogean family, and Muskogean is limited to the Southeast.

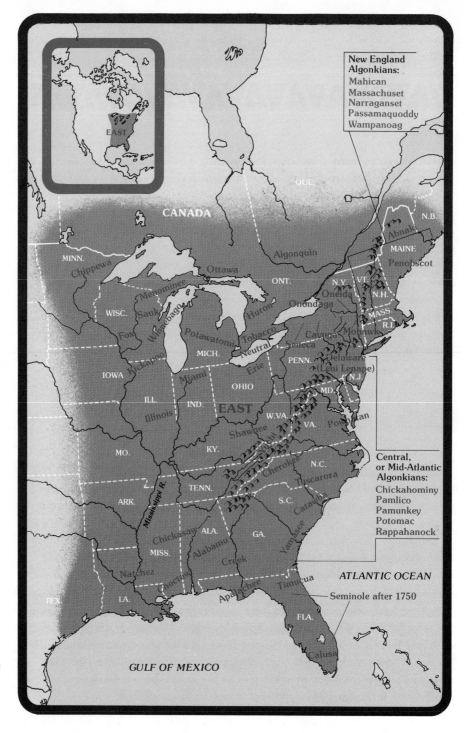

New England
Algonkians:
Mahican
Massachuset
Narraganset
Passamaquoddy
Wampanoag

Central,
or Mid-Atlantic
Algonkians:
Chickahominy
Pamlico
Pamunkey
Potomac
Rappahanock

The Eastern culture
area and its tribes,
showing the subcul-
tural divisions.

Estimating aboriginal population in the Eastern Woodlands is difficult, but the area was large and life there was fairly easy, so as many as 750 thousand to a million people may have lived there.

Prehistory

The early Easterners hunted large game animals like mammoth and bison. Around 5000 B.C. they started to shift from big game to smaller animals, exploiting many local environments such as lakes, rivers, coastlines, and especially forests. We call this time of growing local diversity the Eastern Archaic.

About 1000 B.C. groups in the northern part of the area began to build mounds of earth, usually over burials. They also started to use some plants intensively, corn among them, and to make pottery. These new adaptations marked the beginning of the Woodland Tradition, which held on nearly unchanged in some places until the Europeans came.

Another group of mound builders began their own tradition after about A.D. 1000, mostly in the Southeast. Their mounds held temples, and some were part of real urban centers like Cahokia in Illinois. They also farmed intensively along fertile river flood plains. The greatly improved corn they grew must have come from Mexico, though how it came we do not know.

The East at Contact

The Atlantic seaboard was the scene of the first European colonies, and consequently of the first and most complete damage and destruction to Indian societies. Native American life was so disrupted that little was left to be recorded by the time scholars realized what had happened. By the nineteenth century, the coastal tribes were gone; unlike the Plains, Southwest, or other areas, no one was left to preserve any of the old traditions. Most of our information about the seaboard tribes at the time of first contact comes from a few early observers who wrote down their impressions. Even these records are not as complete or as competent as we might wish. After all, these English, French, and Spanish observers were not ethnologists. They did not always understand what they saw, and often they misinterpreted what the Indians were doing: one described an initiation ceremony as a sacrifice of young boys. Sometimes references are made that excite our curiosity, but no descriptions come with them. Much of the time we have to reconstruct the aboriginal life by leaning heavily upon ethnographic analogy, archaeology, and general anthropological theories of kinship and political structure.

Tribes in the Southeast and around the Great Lakes lasted longer than those of the coast, and we know more about them. However, our picture of European-Indian contact is one-sided; almost everything we have is from European sources. Indians recorded very little, and nobody seems to have cared much about what Indians thought of it all.

Ancestors and Descendants.

Often we cannot connect historic tribes with prehistoric sites; all we can do is make reconstructions from language comparisons, and even those often defy explanation in detail. For example, the northern speakers of Iroquois were culturally similar in many ways to the Southeastern peoples. In fact, northern Iroquois were much more like the Southeasterners than their own northern neighbors. Northern Iroquois were matrilineal, lived in large dwellings with extended families, practiced intensive agriculture, and tortured war captives, all Southern traits. Their nearest linguistic relatives were southern Iroquoian speakers, the Cherokee and Tuscarora, from whom they were separated (at the time of contact) by a solid block of Algonkians.

Comparing language and other cultural relationships, we might guess that some Iroquois speakers moved north and settled around the eastern Great Lakes not too long before Columbus. Yet archaeological findings indicate that the Iroquois of the north had been there much longer than that. The connection over time, then, between southern and northern Iroquoian speakers is not at all clear; we have too little information.

The same is true of the relationship between Southeastern Siouans and Algonkians. The Siouans built their villages and sowed their fields in the broadleaf forest of the Piedmont, while the Algonkians lived on the sandy soil and marshlands of the tidewater zone. We have no doubt that the Algonkians pushed down from the north where most Algonkian speakers lived long before Europeans came to North America. Did the Algonkians come before the Siouans? Or did they invade the Siouan people and drive them from the coastal plain? Or did the Siouans come from the west and drive the Algonkians onto the coast? No one knows for sure.

Ohio and the Mound Builders.

Where Adena-Hopewell people had lived, in and around Ohio, an abrupt decline in population appears to have struck just before the Europeans arrived. In fact, the population fell so sharply that some maps of tribal locations in the early historic period show that region as uninhabited. Soon, however, people driven from their homes farther east by the many European-Indian struggles filled that void. Cultural hybrids, groups composed of Indian-white mixtures as well as remnants from many fragmented tribes, made their temporary home around Ohio.

A somewhat clearer relation between history and prehistory is found between some of the historic Southern tribes and the prehistoric temple mound cultures of the Southeast. Some archaeologists are convinced that the people who lived at the Etowah site in Georgia were ancestors of the Cherokee, and sites in the lower valley of the Mississippi were probably prehistoric Natchez towns. In general, the inland tribal groups in the Southeast are thought to be descendants of the late pre-European cultures in their area. Moundville in Alabama probably was prehistoric Apalachee, and other mounds in Alabama and Georgia were probably Creek.

Resources and Technology

Indians of the East had natural resources in abundance: the great forests, which provided wood, game, and wild plant foods; the rivers, coasts, and lakes, which had fish and shellfish; and the rainfall which came at the right season and provided enough water for farming. Men hunted, fished, fought, and made equipment for those pursuits. Women gardened, gathered wild plant foods, cared for the home and the young, and made utensils for those tasks.

Food. We still eat many of the dishes Indian women made from corn. They made succotash by boiling beans and corn with a chunk of fat. Hominy was made by boiling corn with wood ashes: lye from the ashes loosened the hulls, then the plump corn kernels were washed free of ash and hulls and boiled some more. From corn meal, made by pounding corn kernels to a fine flour, women produced corn cakes, bread, and a corn porridge. Sometimes they added nuts or berries to their corn bread. Corn soup was a favorite all over the East. Parched corn could be brewed into a drink something like coffee.

Other foods, of course, were also important to Eastern Indians. Eastern Indians ate berries, both raw and cooked, and dried them for storage; they also steeped them in water to make fruit drinks. Other beverages came from sunflower seeds and roots of the sassafras tree. The Woodland Indians had several seasonings, though most of them did not use salt. Indeed, among the Onondaga, a tribe of Iroquois speakers, salt was taboo. Instead, the women added wild onion, ginger, and maple sugar to their dishes.

Shells and Pottery. The Indians who lived along the seacoasts and rivers used shells for many kinds of utensils, like spoons, cups, cutters, and scrapers. The men even used bivalve shells as pincers or tweezers to remove whiskers. (Fortunately for Indian men, they had very scant facial hair.) Eastern Indians had raw materials for just about anything they needed from food to construction to adornment.

Almost all Eastern Indians made pottery. Before shaping and firing it, women mixed clay with fine bits of stone, shell, or fiber (called *temper*), which kept the clay paste from splitting and cracking as it heated. Shell-tempered pottery was a hallmark of the Southeast. Indians could tell the tribe of the potter from the shape and temper of the pottery.

Clothing.   Garments varied with the climate and season. Indians in the colder parts of the Northeast wore fitted skin garments most of the year. Women's dresses were made from two skins, one hanging down the front, one down the back, from the shoulders. In the winter were added sleeves for extra warmth. Men wore breechclouts, and put shirts, coats, and leggings over them when it was cold. Leggings were made in pairs, but not sewn together; each leg was separate. They were held by a cord fastened to a waistband, usually the waistband holding the breechclout. Farther south, people wore little more than breechclouts and skirts. Women there made their skirts of plant fibers. Most moccasins throughout the East came up to the ankles, where they were tied. Women often decorated the clothing with flattened porcupine quill embroidery.

Hair Styles.   Women usually wore their hair in braids, and men often did too. Another common male style was the *roach,* a stiff ridge of hair two or three inches high, running from the forehead to the back of the neck and sometimes

An Eastern Indian whose scalp lock has been styled into a roach to which deer's tail hairs have been fastened.

padded out with red-dyed deer hair. The rest of their hair they plucked, shaved, or burned off with hot stones. A popular arrangement for men left only a *scalp-lock,* a lock of hair grown long as a challenge to enemies to "come and get it." Both sexes sported many hair ornaments of shell, feathers, stone, and copper. Bear fat was a common hair dressing for both men and women, sometimes mixed with soot to make the hair blacker.

The People

Warfare.   It may be impossible to explain why some people seem more belligerent than others. Whatever the reason, warfare in the Northeast and Southeast seems to have been almost continuous at the time Europeans arrived, and the Europeans provoked the hostilities still more. Even before contact, many of the tribes quarreled and feuded constantly—Iroquois against Algonkian, Algonkian against Algonkian, Muskogean against Muskogean—seeking revenge for injury, theft, or trespass. The renown and glory that war honors brought throughout the East were no help in keeping things peaceful.

Fighting was by ambush and hit-and-run raiding. Warring groups were seldom large; one or two dozen men made the usual war party. Bows, stone and bone knives, and stone- or wooden-headed clubs, called *tomahawks* by the Algonkians, were their weapons. After Europeans introduced metal, tomahawks had iron heads.

Warriors had rituals to perform before going to war, and they observed taboos while fighting. If they returned victorious, the community celebrated with a victory feast or dance. If the war party lost a man, the warriors and villagers observed mourning rites and vowed revenge.

Religion.   Eastern warriors, like those in western culture areas, sought guardian spirits and supernatural help. Most found their spirit help in dreams or visions after fasting and isolation. Like Indians elsewhere, the Easterners looked not to one god but to spirits and natural power. They felt themselves to be a part of nature, certainly not superior to it, and religion was a powerful factor in their lives. They held elaborate ceremonies and carried out detailed rituals to thank, placate, or appeal to the supernatural.

Shamans were curers who had much spirit help to cure disease. In the East, curing was often combined with an ability to bring good weather, foretell the future, and ensure success in warfare and hunting. But Easterners also had medicine societies, and in the Northeast and Western Great Lakes regions shamanism was secondary to medicine societies.

The Indian character is often painted as silent, unsmiling if not sullen, and generally aloof or unfriendly. This portrait probably came from times of oppression or was painted by people who made no effort to be friendly. Early reports showed Indians to be eager to meet newcomers and generally interested in and delighted by European goods. Bitterness and hostility grew as their lands were taken away.

The Northeast

The Northeast subarea includes what is now New England, the Atlantic states as far south as Virginia, the Ohio valley, the eastern or lower Great Lakes (Erie and Ontario), and Canadian territory about one hundred miles north of the lower Great Lakes. It is a region cold in winter, with deep snows, and often hot in summer. The Appalachian mountain ranges extend southward from the northeast into Alabama, and include the Catskills, Alleghenies, Blue Ridge, Cumberland, and other ranges. The Appalachian is an old, worn-down mountain system with no very high peaks. Two ridges run north and south parallel to the coast, and the valley between them is very fertile. On the east the primary rivers draining the Appalachians are the St. Lawrence, Hudson, Potomac, and Dela-

Indian encampment on Lake Huron.

ware, and on the west, the Ohio and its tributaries. Many lesser rivers also drain the area, which gets enough rainfall for agriculture everywhere.

The forests are a combination of deciduous trees—elm, oak, ash, birch, and maple—and various needled evergreens, such as the hemlock. They provide a home for many woodland animals like squirrel, deer, fox, and bear. Nuts and berries of many species are everywhere, and many varieties of fish fill the lakes and rivers. The climate is suitable for farming, and the ground is fertile. Thus subsistence for the Northeastern tribes was varied, combining corn cultivation, hunting, fishing, and wild-plant gathering.

Women were the cultivators, but men helped in cutting and burning the trees to prepare the fields. The fields were farmed until they were no longer fertile, then new fields were cleared while the old lay fallow—a practice known as *slash-and-burn agriculture*. After a generation, the fertile fields were often some distance from the village, and whole communities moved to be closer to the garden plots. Some groups, especially the Iroquois, got more food from cultivation than others; the Algonkians of New England found winters severe and the land rocky and hard to cultivate.

New England Algonkians

The earliest European colonists landed on territory belonging to the coastal Algonkians. What thoughts passed through the minds of those Indian New Englanders when they saw such strange ships and strange people land on their shores? We can only guess. But during the early years of European settlement, relations between European and Indian were most often friendly. The New England Algonkians of the vicinity kept the Pilgrims alive, in fact, for European wheat and other grains could not be sown in the rocky soils. An Algonkian of the Wampanoag tribe, Squanto, taught the newcomers to plant maize in little hills and fertilize each mound with an alewife, a species of fish. Much American literature on the early settlers is about the Atlantic Algonkians, including *The Last of the Mohicans* and other works by James Fenimore Cooper. Few descriptions, though, give accurate ethnographic information. Since the way of life of those Eastern tribes has long since disappeared, we must flesh out our attempts at reconstruction with analogy, theory, and some guesswork.

Algonkian Village Life. The Northeastern Algonkians fought off heavy snowfall and winter cold with many of the same techniques the Subarctic Algonkian folk used. The great difference between the two was their way of handling the food quest: the New England Algonkians could grow maize. And this led to another difference: they were also more settled. They lived in villages among their fields in *wigwams,* domed structures of bent poles or saplings tied together and covered with sheets of bark, hide, or woven matting. Wigwams usually housed small families, just the parents and their children, instead of extended families, though some New England Algonkians made wigwams large enough for two or three families.

Like their Subarctic cousins, the New England Algonkians treated animal bones respectfully. Also, they segregated women at their first menstruation, during menstrual periods thereafter, and at childbirth. They traveled the streams in bark canoes, gathered wild plant foods, hunted and fished, and cultivated corn, beans, and squash. New Englanders exploited coastal resources such as clams and lobsters, and, like their northern Algonkian relatives, tapped sugar maple trees for the sweet sap. From them we have taken into English the words *succotash, hominy, moccasin, squaw, papoose,* and *wigwam,* and many place names such as Massachusetts, Narraganset, and Allegheny. The words *podunk,* referring to a small, provincial town, and *mugwump,* a renegade in politics, both came from Algonkian.

Political Order. Algonkian tribes of the Northeast were divided into villages that had their own names, and the tribes also formed alliances that have often been called confederacies. But these relationships probably were too temporary and limited in power to be true confederacies. Our information is so scant that it is hard to tell just what aboriginal politics were like. Probably the confederacies were alliances among independent groups speaking the same language with differences only in dialect. Such alliances probably formed and broke up quickly in a generation or less, depending mainly on the personal magnetism of a leader from one of the member tribes. When he died or lost power, the alliance would fall apart. However, some authorities do think the connections among the New England and Atlantic seaboard Algonkians were real confederacies, somewhat lasting, with some kind of supreme leadership, usually a council made up of leaders of the member tribes. It is a futile debate, for the Atlantic Algonkians were so disrupted by European settlement that we have no records to decide the issue. Early in the colonization by European powers, though, leagues of some sort existed among many Indian societies in the Eastern area. In fact, most of the names by which we know the seaboard Algonkians are not their tribal names but names of the alliances.

After Europeans interfered with aboriginal life, such alliances grew more structured in defiance of the common enemy. They never quite developed into a potent adversary force, though, for the member tribes always ended up fighting each other as much as their foe, the Europeans.

Some of the Algonkian groups known as confederations during the historic period were the Abnaki of Maine, including the Penobscot and the Passamaquoddy; the Massachuset, around the present city of Boston; the Narraganset in

Rhode Island; the Mahican of the upper Hudson Valley and in Connecticut (where they were known as the Mohegan); and the Leni Lenape or Delaware in New Jersey, Pennsylvania, and Delaware.

The Abnaki. Tribes in the Abnaki alliance were at the northern limits of cultivation and resembled people of the Subarctic in many ways. Though they had a reputation for being peaceful and gentle, they went in for the raiding typical of the Easterners. They often tortured male prisoners, but women captives were absorbed into the tribe and treated kindly. The Abnaki lived in multiple-family bark- or mat-covered wigwams in stockaded villages. Each village was governed by a council of elders that met in a council house much larger than the dwellings. Each tribe had both a peace chief and a war chief, and corresponding tribal councils, one in charge of civil matters, the other of warfare.

The Abnaki favored the French over the English in the colonial struggle in the Northeast, but after the French lost power, they made peace with the English. Most of the Abnaki moved to Canada, although two subdivisions, the Penobscot and Passamaquoddy, remained in Maine.

The Leni Lenape. The Leni Lenape, or Delaware (as the English called them, after the river that ran through the territory), once were a very important and respected tribe. Many other Algonkian tribes called members of the Lenape tribe "grandfather," a title of honor; the Shawnee and Mahican believed that they were descended from Lenape. In the early eighteenth century the Iroquois assumed control over the Lenape, then both Iroquois and white pressure pushed the Lenape out of their traditional lands. They settled in Ohio and Indiana and eventually lost all cohesiveness, some groups ending up in Arkansas, Texas, Kansas, and Oklahoma.

The Mahicans. The Mahican or Mohegan confederation extended from the Hudson River valley in New York as far north as Lake Champlain, and east into Massachusetts and Connecticut. Conflict with the Iroquoian Mohawk to the west, coupled with inroads by settlers, forced them to the south. They joined with the Lenape, finally losing their identity in the emigration to lands west of the Mississippi River. One of the tribelets of the Mohegan, the Stockbridge (named after the village in Massachusetts), moved to Wisconsin, where their descendants still live near Lake Winnebago. One of the Lenape groups, the Munsee, also set up a home there.

All these peoples seem to have lived much like the Northeastern Algonkians. Their clothing was of deerskin, with leggings, shirts, dresses, and robes in cool weather, and loincloths alone for men in warm weather. Leggings were often worn as much for protection against underbrush as for warmth.

Resources in the Northeast.   A settler in the mid-seventeenth century described Northeastern food as a stew of maize and kidney beans boiled with fish or game. The fish included eels, shad, herring, and alewives, and the game was beaver, bear, venison, moose, raccoon, or otter. Other wild foods that might be boiled with meat were groundnuts, Jerusalem artichokes, and several kinds of nuts: acorns, walnuts, and chestnuts. Algonkians also ground nuts into flour, which they used to thicken their stews and soups. Corn was ground into meal and made into johnnycakes or porridge cooked in clay pots and spooned out with a wooden ladle. They made containers of bark and basketry as well as pottery.

Leaders in Peace and War.   Eastern Algonkian leaders are often called *sag-amores* or *sachems,* English versions of two Algonkian words for "chief." Generally the position ran in families, though competence was always considered. Leaders served only with the people's consent and were guided by a council of respected elders. Some of the leaders were quite autocratic, but generally the tribal council tempered such tendencies. Sagamores were not monarchs, although the colonists, used to kings where they came from, often referred to Indian leaders as kings, princes, and so on.

Older men were honored for their wisdom, but war was the young man's way to prestige. War took the form of raids and ambushes, not large-scale battles. Tomahawks, shields, and scalping knives were used, along with the bow and arrow. It is from the New England Algonkians that we got the expressions "to bury the hatchet" and "to take up the tomahawk."

Warfare increased as conflicts arose with the English settlers. Tribes often broke up, and new groups might contain members of several tribes. Others fled west or into Canada, where the French were friendly. Refugees made new alliances with the tribes in the areas they fled to. All this changed the aboriginal political picture so rapidly that it is now impossible to know how formal the alliances were before Europeans arrived and how much the European onslaught forced the Indians into confederation in the face of a common enemy.

The Iroquois League

Iroquois speakers spread as a block across the lower or eastern Great Lakes territory and the southeastern shores of Lake Huron, wedging into the eastern Algonkian territory. The major Iroquois tribes were the Huron, Erie, Tobacco, Neutral, and a group that came to be known as the League of the Iroquois: Seneca, Cayuga, Onondaga, Oneida, and Mohawk. These latter five were often called "the Iroquois," but Iroquois is *not* the name of a tribe or political unit; it is a *language.* We shall refer to the five nations collectively as "the League."

The Legend of Deganawidah. How the League got started as a federation is not clear. Some have claimed it really was an aboriginal development, while others believe it was formed because of European pressures. A legendary tradition involves a folk hero, Deganawidah, who lived in the sixteenth century and may have been a shaman. Deganawidah was distressed because the five tribes fought so much among themselves when they were all oppressed by the Huron, who were far more powerful at that time. (Deganawidah probably was a Huron by birth but a Mohawk by adoption.) He persuaded Hiawatha, a Mohawk chief (not the fictitious Chippewa Hiawatha of Longfellow's poem), to help him create an alliance among the five tribes. This alliance became the League of the Iroquois, whose object was to end intertribal war and promote peace and well-being among the five tribes and any others who chose to join them. The legend varies depending on when it was recorded and which tribe was telling it.

For decades after the League was formed, the five nations were greatly feared as aggressors by the Huron and by the Algonkians as well. The League never did really halt internal strife. In 1722, one group of southern Iroquoian speakers, the Tuscarora, joined the League, which became known as the Six Nations. Eventually some tribes of the League joined the colonists while others allied with the English during the Revolutionary War.

Iroquois Village Life. All Iroquoian speakers had a subsistence similar to the Algonkian. Their foods were cultivated crops, game, and wild plants. Farming and wild-plant gathering were women's tasks, while men took care of fishing, hunting, and warfare. Material culture too was much like the Algonkian in weapons, tools, and utensils. Like the Algonkians, the Iroquoians lived in villages, usually behind *palisades,* fences of sharp, pointed poles, but their homes were multifamily longhouses, not the wigwams of the New England Algonkians or the Quonset-shaped houses of some other Algonkian tribes. An Iroquois village might have several hundred people or as many as 2,000 to 3,000.

All tribes of the League used the *longhouse,* a building fifty to one hundred feet long and about twenty feet wide, which housed several related families. It had a door at each end and was gabled or vaulted, rather like a long, narrow barn. Down the center ran a corridor, in which each longhouse family had its fire. The families lived in separate compartments on either side of the corridor. Platforms against the walls were both beds and seats. The League symbolized itself as a vast longhouse, stretching from west to east. The Seneca were "Keepers of the Western Door," and the Mohawk "Keepers of the Eastern Door." In the center were the Onondaga, "Keepers of the Council Fire" and "Keepers of the Wampum Belts."

Wampum. Both Algonkians and Iroquois of the Northeast made beads of white and purple shells, stringing them into strands and weaving them into belts.

Those beads were called *wampum,* an Algonkian word. Strung beads were sometimes used as adornment, but the woven belts took on greater importance, their symbolic white and purple designs representing treaties and agreements, records of events, and public accounts. One Onondaga sachem kept the treaty wampum for the five tribes; he had to remember what all the symbols meant and interpret them when necessary. Eventually wampum came to be a medium of exchange, a sort of money, after Europeans began using it. The beads were hard to make, and wampum disappeared when trade beads from Europe became available.

Warfare. The almost constant warfare among the Eastern tribes was broken by peace only for practical, beneficial reasons, such as trade. All the people of the area were aggressive, but the Iroquois got a reputation as particularly bellicose, even vicious, warriors.

Iroquois generally went to war for one of three reasons. First, warfare could bring a young man personal recognition, because the highest ideal of manhood was the warrior's life. Second, it was the way to avenge someone killed in battle

An Iroquois warrior wielding his tomahawk.

or taken prisoner and tortured to death, a habit among all Iroquoian tribes of the Northeast. Third, warfare supplied prisoners for sacrifice to the supernatural.

Most captured males were taken to the home village to be tortured to death. Women and children might be killed at once, but often they were taken back to be adopted by a family that had lost a member in warfare. Such adopted prisoners apparently received emotional as well as physical welcome, and they seem to have accepted their new positions faithfully.

Male captives also might be adopted, but not until they had been tortured. Algonkians also tortured captives, but Iroquois torture was more severe. Sometimes the Iroquois stopped short of death, either adopting or enslaving the captive. It was the Iroquois women who made that decision. Women often were the principal torturers, too, perhaps an indication of their importance among the Iroquois. Many dead captives were eaten, the heart usually by a privileged person and the rest shared by all. Cannibalism, torture, and killing were looked upon as a form of sacrifice. They also have been explained as psychological release for people under tension from much warfare and many deaths among their own people. Whatever the explanation, these practices made the Iroquois not only feared but hated.

Social Order. The Iroquois diverged most from the Northeastern Algonkians in social organization. They were matrilineal; children belonged to their mother's clan. Iroquois life centered on the longhouse group, a subdivision of the matrilineal clan, sisters with their husbands and children living in a common dwelling. The women owned the fields and the houses and worked together farming and doing domestic chores. Husbands moved into the longhouses of their wives and returned to their mothers' homes if divorced.

Political Structure. Women were important not only because they were cultivators and property owners, but also because they nominated the leader who represented their clan in the tribal political structure and could recall him if he were unsatisfactory. Each tribe was governed by a council of chiefs, usually called sachems. Families within the clans held the rights to clan leadership positions, but competence settled which man would become a sachem. When an old sachem died, the women of his clan nominated his successor. The tribal council and the rest of the tribe had to approve the selection, but approval was almost automatic.

The League had nothing to do with internal affairs within each of the five tribes, but dealt with intertribal, external problems. The League was led by a council of fifty leaders, all sachems of the member tribes. Their titles were taken from the names of the first fifty leaders, except for Deganawidah. In his honor, a title in the League council was replaced by an honorary position called the Pine

An Iroquois
sachem. The word
sachem was de-
rived from the
Abnaki word for
"chief." The Iro-
quois sachems
represented the
tribes on the
League council. The
office was heredi-
tary in certain
clans, but the indi-
vidual filling the
position was
elected.

Tree Chief, which could be held by any distinguished person, male or female (sachems were always male). There was no set number of Pine Tree Chiefs. New League sachems were installed in winter, and the League met during the summer in Onondaga territory. One of the Onondaga sachems was chairman of the League.

The League council made decisions on common defense and offense, arbitrated disputes among the member tribes, and discussed common problems. For its members the League meant internal peace, but for its neighbors it usually meant war. Pine Tree Chiefs often tried to push the League council into hostilities, frequently with success. Most Pine Trees were young warriors, who gained power as conflict with Europeans increased.

All Iroquois might attend League meetings and listen to the deliberations. If they wished to express an opinion, they asked their sachem to speak for them, though Pine Trees spoke for themselves. Only sachems voted, each tribal group voting as a block; that is, though the Onondaga had fourteen sachems and the Seneca only eight, each tribe had just one vote. Only unanimous decisions were considered passed, so it might take many votes, interspersed with debate, for a measure to pass.

Ceremonies and Societies.   The Iroquois observed agricultural ceremonies throughout the year, each one usually lasting four days. In the early spring, a maple syrup ceremony was followed by other rituals like the planting ceremony, wild strawberry ceremony, and green corn, green bean, and harvest ceremonies. Most important was the midwinter festival, which was a new year ceremony, a time of ritual cleansing and new beginning. The Iroquois celebrated many lesser rites, dances, and small ceremonies of thanksgiving. Religious officials (both men and women), called Keepers of the Faith, organized and managed these ceremonials.

Another organization of religious practitioners was the False Face Society, a group of curers who wore masks carved into grotesque grimaces as part of their curing ritual. A man became a member by dreaming that he had joined the society. All False Face members were men except one woman, who was Keeper of the False Faces. Anyone who was ill reported to the Keeper, who sent the masked dancers to that person's house. There they danced, shaking turtleshell rattles and sprinkling ashes to effect a cure. Anyone who dreamed he had joined the society also went to the woman, who directed him to carve a mask for himself. The initiate always carved his mask from a living tree, for that was more powerful than one carved from a block of dead wood. False Face Society members also performed spring and fall ceremonies to frighten evil spirits away from the villages. Another curing group was the Huskface Society, whose members wore cornhusk masks to represent harvest spirits. The Huskface Society performed at the midwinter ceremony and the green corn festival.

A mask of the False Face Society, worn in the ritual to eliminate evil spirits. The grotesque carved face shows an intriguing combination of skill, sense of humor, and sense of horror.

Many Iroquois sought out shamans for help when all else failed or to be sure they had skipped no possibility of spiritual help. Shamans were less important among the Iroquois than in tribes without organized religious societies.

Supernatural Power and Spirits. The Iroquois believed that all supernatural power came from *orenda,* an invisible power that flowed through nature and could be tapped or drawn upon through dreams. Orenda was a great impersonal force that filled the world, the sky, and all of life; it was not a spirit or deity. It is like the Polynesian concept of *mana,* and also has been compared to electricity. It exists in the natural world, but must be captured and harnessed to be useful for mankind. Some other Indian groups had an idea similar to *orenda;* the Algonkians called it *manitu* and the Siouans, *wakonda.*

In addition to this general power, the Iroquois believed in animal spirits and other supernaturals, one of which was called the Master of Life. Europeans, especially churchmen, seized upon the concept of Master of Life and transformed it into a great single god. But the precontact Iroquois had no such religious classification; the Master of Life was merely one among many supernatural entities.

SZSZSZSZSZSZSZSZSZSZS

*Before there were human beings on the earth, the animal fathers lived
there. They were kept busy making parts of the world; different animals
created different parts. Beaver and his family made the Great Water
(Lake Superior) by building a dam at the eastern end. Manabozho, the
Great Hare, saw what they had done and he said, "That is not what I
wanted. I do not want a dam there." So he stamped on the dam. But
Great Hare did not stamp hard enough. He did not destroy the dam completely, but left rapids, waterfalls, and whirlpools.*

    *Great Hare lived in a land called Michilimackinack, with islands, rip-
pling water, wide-spreading shade trees, and leaping fish. Manabozho
made the first fish net after watching Spider weave her web. He knew that
nets could help catch fish. Wild rice grew in the land of the Great Hare.
He discovered it, and taught the Indians how to use it. Manabozho showed
the Chippewa the islands of wild rice in the lake, and he showed them
how to cut paths through the wild rice beds, and how to beat ripe heads of
grain into their canoes. The Indians then taught the white man about wild
rice.*

SZSZSZSZSZSZSZSZSZS

The Western Great Lakes

Early Life around the Great Lakes

**The subarea called Western or Upper Great Lakes covers roughly what
we now call the Midwest. It stretched from the eastern borders of Lake**
Huron to the western edge of today's Minnesota, and from about one hundred
miles north of Lake Superior to where the Missouri and Mississippi rivers meet.

    The Western or Upper Great Lakes (Superior, Michigan, and Huron) are con-
nected by many smaller lakes and rivers, either directly or by short overland
trails called *portages.* Cultures around the Western Great Lakes were very similar because communication and transportation among them was easy, and the
same natural resources were plentiful everywhere. All the Upper Great Lakes
tribes were Algonkian speakers except for the Siouan Winnebago and the Iroquoian Huron.

    Indians of the Upper Great Lakes lived in a region where woodland alternated
with areas of prairie. All were cultivators, but the grass that today is called wild rice

gave them a nutritious and plentiful substitute for maize. It grew on the shores of the Great Lakes and throughout the lake regions of Minnesota, Wisconsin, Illinois, and northern Michigan. There it was so abundant and so greatly used by the people that some authorities make a special culture area of the wild rice region. In addition to gathering wild-plant foods, the Indians also hunted woodland animals and even the bison that came into the nearby prairie.

Migrations and Changes. Tribes must have moved around the Great Lakes in prehistoric times, but slowly and without much disruption. Change speeded up when Europeans in the East began pressing westward. As Eastern tribes shifted under European pressure, the less powerful were driven from their lands. Some woodland tribes ended up in the prairie grasslands of the Midwest, others where their tribal range included both woodland and grassland environments.

Naturally, those changes forced adjustments in traditional ways of life. Where birch trees were scarce or altogether missing, people had to use something besides bark for housing or equipment like canoes. Consequently, dugouts were the water transportation through the prairie area. But life on the prairie had advantages, too, for the growing season there was longer and the winters were less severe.

Woodland tribes of the Western Great Lakes were the Menominee, Chippewa, Potawatomi, Huron, and Ottowa; the Great Lakes tribes of the prairies were the Sauk, Fox, Miami, Illinois, Winnebago, and the Prairie Potawatomi (sometimes called Mascouten). Tribes of the two ecological niches, woodland and prairie, traded and interacted regularly. Rivers and lakes made transportation easy, and most tribes spoke languages within the Algonkian family, so communication was not difficult. Differences that we can see in looking back at these groups probably were not noticeable to the people themselves.

Food and Technology. The peoples of the Upper Great Lakes grew maize, did much hunting and gathering, and made wild rice an especially large part of their diet. Except for wild rice, the culture of the Western Lakes was not very different from that of the Eastern Algonkians. Tools, equipment, and clothing were similar, and the houses were barrel-vaulted rectangular buildings or domed mat- or bark-covered wigwams. People used bark canoes on the lakes, and dugouts to travel the prairie streams where trees with suitable bark did not grow. East was like west, probably because the Lakes tribes had come from the north and east where most of their Algonkian relatives lived. When they moved into the Midwest, they did not need to make much change, since the new environment differed only in degree from their old homes.

Kinnikinnik. Men grew tobacco in the Lakes region, but more often smoked a substance called *kinnikinnik* (an Algonkian word meaning "mixture"). This was made from several plants, usually sumac, dogwood, and willow bark, and often tobacco too. Kinnikinnik was smoked in pipes, some of them very elaborate. Bowls were carved from an easily worked red stone called *catlinite,* quarried in Minnesota, and were fitted to long, often fancy stems. We call such pipes *calumets* or peace pipes, although men smoked them before going to war or on trading expeditions as well as at peace councils. Calumets were also used to burn tobacco as an offering to the supernatural. Travelers going through foreign or hostile territory carried them to prove their peaceful intentions. The calumet of historic times probably evolved from the platform pipes of the Hopewellians, and spread into the prairies, Plains, and the lower Mississippi Valley. Men who smoked a calumet together were bound together for a purpose (not necessarily peaceful); to break faith with fellow smokers, whatever the endeavor, was a serious breach of trust.

Social and Religious Organization. Algonkian kinship organization was somewhat different among these midwestern tribes. Most of the Western Great Lakes peoples developed a clan system tracing relationship patrilineally through males, whereas the New England and Middle Atlantic Algonkians traced their descent bilaterally, through both parents.

The northern Ojibwa Midewiwin or Grand Medicine Society penetrated south around the Lakes and into the middle Mississippi River area. This association of curers performed its most important rite, the Medicine Dance, once or twice a year. The dance or ceremony varied from tribe to tribe, but it always included curing and initiation rituals and entertainment.

Like other peoples with ceremonial organizations, the Great Lakes tribes occasionally found that they needed a shaman to cure some difficult illness. Shamans had special power from the supernatural, which they demonstrated in their ritual tent-shaking performances. They would retire to a small skin- or bark-covered structure to contact the spirits. Observers on the outside would hear voices coming from the tent, and could see the tent move or shake, clearly indicating to the faithful that the spirits had come. A shaman's spirits helped him cure disease and bring good fortune to those who consulted him. Some people, however, felt that shamans were practitioners of evil because they had such power; shamans were respected, but they were often feared as well. Men of middle age or older were almost always the shamans in the Lakes region. For success in life, each young man expected to find his own guardian spirit.

The Prairie People

Midwest prairie Algonkians shared most of the Lake people's customs, though they had to trade for wild rice, which did not grow in their territory. Their housing, clothing, and equipment were different only in emphasis. In fact, some peoples, like the Potawatomi, extended into both environments. This group apparently migrated from the Northeast Atlantic coast, if we can believe their legends. Some stopped in the spot where Chicago later grew up, while others moved into prairie lands. The two divisions are distinguished by the names Potawatomi and Prairie Potawatomi, though the latter also have been called Mascouten.

Other Midwest prairie tribes, the Sauk and closely associated Fox, probably were pushed there by aggressive Iroquois and Eastern Algonkians in pre-European times. They apparently lived in wild rice country for a while, but were driven out by Menominee and Chippewa, settling in Illinois among the association of tribes known as the Illinois (Cahokia, Kaskaskia, and Peoria, among others).

These prairie tribes cultivated corn extensively, besides growing squash, beans, and tobacco and hunting the buffalo. Around 1800 they obtained the horse, and after that their subsistence was like that of the Plains villagers in most ways.

The Menominee

When Europeans first met the Menominee in the seventeenth century, their territory was the land of forest and lakes around the Menominee River, the boundary between today's Wisconsin and Michigan. Menominee now live on the Wolf River in central Wisconsin.

Menominee society was divided into patrilineal clans that formed moieties of Earth People and Sky People. Moiety division here had little function except to regulate marriage (one married outside one's moiety) and to act as undertakers and mourners for each other. It was an egalitarian society, though Menominee chiefs all came from the Great Mythical Bear clan. As usual, however, only men who proved their ability became chiefs. The chief, a civil figure, was mainly responsible for keeping peace and order and taking action necessary for the tribe's welfare. A tribal council aided him in his deliberations. Shamans or members of the Medicine Society (the Midewiwin) often had greater influence than the chief, because they had supernatural power behind them.

War Customs. War leaders directed hostilities, holding their leadership only as long as the conflict lasted. To gather followers, they relied on their reputations as warriors and their charismatic personalities. Menominee war leaders owned war bundles believed to have supernatural powers that would lead their owners to successful exploits. Gathering for a pre-raid ritual, the war party watched the leader display what was in his war bundle. They did a war dance and sacrificed, then ate a dog (a practice probably taken over from the Huron).

Then all went off toward their objective. Just before the attack, the leader distributed items from his war bundle to the rest, covering them all with spirit protection.

Warriors fought with clubs and bows, wearing no protective armor. Any warrior who killed an enemy won the right to wear an eagle feather, and the first to kill on a raid got a wampum belt. Warriors scalped the fallen, stretching the piece of flesh with its hair on a small hoop. In the victory dance the warriors displayed their scalps on poles, then gave them to female relatives. Menominee warfare usually stopped short of the extremes reached by the Plains or more easterly tribes.

Religion.   Besides their simple shamanistic practices and the ceremonials performed by the Midewiwin Society, Menominee had other society and cult observances. With the Chippewa, the Ottawa, and the Potawatomi, they practiced bear ceremonialism. They regarded bears with special respect; whenever a man killed a bear, he treated the body reverentially. It was carefully disjointed, not hacked apart, and the hunter and his family gave a feast for invited guests. With the food he served the people, including the bear meat, the host spread out food that bears enjoyed, like maple sugar. The bear's head was decorated with ribbons and beads, and the skin was spread out on a mat. A speaker called upon the spirits of all bears, saying that they were respected by the Menominee, who always treated them well, and inviting other bears to come. After the meal, the host carefully gathered and disposed of the bear's bones, never leaving them thrown about for dogs to gnaw.

The Menominee believed in forces unfriendly and dangerous to people as well as in well-disposed supernaturals. They shared most of the beliefs of other Algonkians, though apparently not the Windigo phenomenon, perhaps because the Menominee had no fear of famine. The tribal culture hero was Manabush, their version of the Chippewa Manabozho. He was the Earth Maker who created the world and its beings and taught the Indians how to live. His earthly home was Mackinac Island. Stories about Manabush livened up long winter evenings and taught the children tribal lore.

Wild Rice.   Though the Memoninee practiced agriculture, it was largely the abundant wild rice around the Great Lakes that allowed their population to grow so dense that many European explorers remarked on it. Rice even gave them a name—*Menominee* means "wild-rice people." Today that same wild rice is popular as a luxury food. It is still harvested by Indians, now mostly for commerce.

Wild rice is hard to reap because the grains scatter at a touch. The harvester has to catch the grain as soon as it matures, for it quickly falls into the water and is lost. The Menominee reaped the grain from canoes, usually with one person guiding the boat and another bending the stalks over the gunwales, lightly beat-

An old print show-
ing Indians reaping
wild rice.

ing the grain heads so the ripe kernels would fall into the canoe. The prickly
hulls irritate the skin, forcing the gatherers to wear protective clothing.

To separate the edible grain from the hulls, the Menominee first parched or
toasted the kernels, then trod on them in hide-lined pits in the ground or, in later
times, in big containers. This "dancing the rice" was done by huskers wearing
high moccasins in historic times, though it is said that long ago they danced
barefoot. Men, women, and children danced the rice, separating the grain from
the shucks, then winnowing the inedible portion by throwing the grain in the air
and fanning the hulls away. The edible grain, heavier than the hulls, fell to the
ground. After all the work was done, everyone joined for a big feast.

Muskogean
Trickster Tale

YꓘYꓘYꓘYꓘYꓘYꓘYꓘYꓘYꓘYꓘ

*Wildcat Elder tried for many days to creep up on Wild Turkey to catch
him for his dinner. He tried and tried, but he was not successful. Then
Wildcat got a bag, crawled into it, and rolled himself along. He rolled
right up to Wild Turkey.*

Wildcat said, "I'm having fun. See me roll around. If you would like to roll around, you can get into my bag."

Wild Turkey crawled into the bag. Wildcat quickly tied up the end and rolled the bag for some time. After a while, he stopped and untied the bag. "Yes, that was fun," said Wild Turkey. "But I don't want to have all the fun. Let me out so those young turkeys over there can have some fun." Wildcat let Turkey out of the bag, and Wild Turkey ran away. Wildcat was angry because he had planned to have Wild Turkey for dinner. So he said to the young turkeys, "Elder Turkey had a good time rolling in the bag. Would you like to try?" One young turkey got in, but he could not roll. Wildcat said, "It won't roll because it's too light. There is only one small turkey in it. Let some other young turkeys get in."

Finally some other young turkeys stepped in, and Wildcat tied the bag, threw it over his shoulder, and ran home. At home he gave the bag to his mother and said, "I have brought something home for dinner. Be careful how you untie the bag." His mother was curious, and she untied the bag too quickly. One young turkey flew out, but she managed to keep the others. Though Wildcat scolded his mother, they had enough for a feast.

YKYKYKYKYKYKYKYKYKYKYK

The Southeast

Running from Virginia and Kentucky south, the Southeastern subarea includes the territory we generally speak of as "the South." Along the coast is a low plain of barren soil, sand dunes, and saltwater marsh and grasses. Stands of cypress thrive with aerial roots that allow growth in the stagnant, oxygen-poor water. Many rivers and streams cross the plain, but they flow slowly and are filled with disintegrated rock and silts that build up soil deposits at the river mouths.

To the west of the coastal plain is the Piedmont, a plateau 100 to 150 miles wide, edged by the southern Appalachians. Like the North, the Piedmont and Appalachian areas are forested with deciduous and evergreen trees that shelter many kinds of forest animals. Beyond the mountains is an area of deep, fertile soil stretching to the Mississippi River, almost entirely occupied by Muskogean-speaking tribes. Throughout the Southeast the climate is mild, in some places approaching subtropical, though snow falls in the higher elevations and frosts have been known as far south as middle Florida.

Early Southeastern Culture

The Muskogean-speaking peoples of the Southeast had distinctive traits which they shared with the Cherokee (Iroquoian), the Southeastern Siouans like the Yuchi and the Catawba, and the Central Atlantic Algonkians. Many of the Southeastern Indians descended from the prehistoric mound builders, but the Algonkians and Siouans appear to have arrived later. Connecting specific historic tribes with archaeological sites is difficult and often impossible, because tribes moved so much even before contact; after that, movement increased immensely. Some tribes, like the Shawnee, moved all over the East, from Pennsylvania and the Ohio River valley through the South, ending up in Indian Territory—today's Oklahoma. The Seminole tribe did not even exist until the middle of the eighteenth century, when it was formed by refugees of half a dozen Muskogean-speaking groups.

Southeastern Customs. From the accounts of early French explorers, we know that the most complex social development in the Southeast arose among the Natchez of the lower Mississippi Valley. The Natchez had a society that was unusually stratified. Their practices included torture of war captives, ritual cannibalism, the Green Corn Dance, and keeping perpetual fires burning in sacred buildings. From these traits, it is easy to see cultural connections between the Southeast and the Iroquois in the North.

Most Southeasterners shared in the customs of the Black Drink, an emetic brewed from a shrub, *Ilex cassine,* which caused vomiting. Men drank it to purify themselves during ceremonies, before going on a raid, or before a council meeting.

Towns in the Southeast. Almost all Southeastern people lived in towns along rivers or streams. The towns were arranged in much the same way: residences and public buildings around a plaza, with farmlands in all directions on the outskirts. Their sturdy thatched-roof houses had mud-plaster walls over poles interwoven with reeds or branches. Some houses were circular, some rectangular. Summer structures were open-sided to let cooling breezes through. Stockades of upright posts surrounded many towns, and moats or earthworks often added protection.

As elsewhere in the East, women were the farmers, but men helped clear the fields. Men hunted woodland animals and also alligators. Nearly all Southeastern people counted descent through women; after marriage, couples generally moved to the wife's village. Polygyny was allowed, but only wealthy men and chiefs had many wives.

Some Southeastern tribes had centralized political structures and definite social classes. Some even had a nobility formed of war leaders, priests, civil chiefs, and their families, and chiefs often wielded considerable authority. Such people expected and got special treatment. They wore clothing exclusive to their rank, and servants or slaves carried them around in litters, protecting them from the sun with sunshades.

Warriors.   Warfare was the path to prestige and success. A warrior's adornment—feathers, body paint, and tattoos—told his feats in battle. As in the North, tribes were in a constant state of hostility with one another. Men about to go on the warpath fasted, danced, and smoked ritually. The warriors brought back scalps of the enemy, but scalping in precontact times was apparently far less frequent than later, when Europeans paid a bounty for Indian scalps. Warriors protected themselves with wicker armor and bark shields, but wore little else: only breechclouts and moccasins.

Religion.   Warriors performed their own religious rites for success in war, but the major religious observances in the South were for planting and harvest. The new year started when the first crops ripened and was celebrated by a festival called the *busk* or Green Corn Dance. People threw out old goods and put out old fires. A new fire was ritually kindled by a priest, and women took flames or coals from it to light the new year's fires in their homes. A highlight of the festival was the Black Drink, which cleaned out the drinkers as they had cleaned out their houses. Toward the end of the busk, the first corn of the season was gathered, cooked, and eaten. The new year had started, and the people forgave every crime and misdeed of the past season, short of murder.

Only the Calusa, an alliance of small tribes in south Florida, differed from the Southeast subsistence pattern of agriculture. They were a hunting and gathering group, using a starchy tuber (kunti) which grew abundantly in their tropical land instead of corn.

The Central Atlantic Algonkians

In 1607, English settlers established a colony on the river they named the James in Virginia. Those colonists were in intimate contact with a now famous group of Indians, the Powhatan, whose chief was also known as Powhatan. The group's fame stems from the daughter of Powhatan and her part in colonial history: she was Pocahontas, the woman who, according to legend, saved Captain John Smith's life.

Powhatan, whose personal name was Wahunsonacock, was chief of six tribelets, a position he inherited from his father. Under his leadership at least two dozen others were added to the group. Consequently the Powhatan usually are

A 1612 map of
Virginia showing
Powhatan, wearing
a crown of feathers,
inside the royal
wigwam.

considered a confederacy, although, once again, the alliance depended on one man's control and organizational ability, not a tradition of federation. Some of the tribelets in the confederacy were Pamunkey, Potomac, Rappahannock, and Chickahominy, whose names have been given to rivers of Virginia. South of the Powhatan, in what is now North Carolina, were other Algonkians, the most prominent being the Pamlico. The North Carolina Algonkians are not very well known, though they were recorded in pictures by John White and in writing by Thomas Hariot, an early colonist. We know the Powhatan from the writings of Captain John Smith, William Strachey, and some later authors.

Village Life.   The Central Atlantic Algonkians lived in villages. Some groups, like the Pomeioc, are known only by the names of their towns instead of by tribal affiliations, because they became extinct as cohesive cultural units before much information had been gathered about them. However, we can use accounts written by the early explorers and settlers to recreate something of the life of those southern Algonkians.

Villages contained up to fifty multiple-family dwellings scattered among gardens of corn, tobacco, and other common crops. The people created their fields out of the forest by felling and burning the trees. Some of the towns were protected by palisades; others were open. A typical house was domed and rectangular, with removable matting over the framework, not unlike a longhouse. During hot weather, sections of the wall-covering were removed to keep air circulating. Rivers and streams were favorite sites for villages, which may explain why so many of the area's rivers came to be named after Indian tribes. The waterways allowed communication and transportation into the Piedmont by dugout canoe. They also provided drinking water.

The Temples.   Within the towns were structures the early colonists called temples. These were no different from other village buildings except that they were used for mortuary, storage, and religious functions. They contained wooden posts carved at the upper end in a likeness of a human face and sometimes draped with shell and copper beads. What these images meant to the villagers we do not know because the early records are inadequate. Presumably they were idols representing spirits.

The temples also held surplus produce, the chief's wealth in foodstuffs, furs, and other goods stored for hard times. But their most exotic function was to hold the mortal remains of chiefs. Most bodies of the villagers were buried, but those of chieftains were disemboweled and skinned; the flesh was sun dried, and the skin was cured. Then the skeleton, clothed in its own treated skin, was placed inside the temple beside those of other chiefs on scaffolds near the idols or images. The flesh or muscle tissue was wrapped in mats and placed at the

Their rype corne.

Their greene corne.

Corne newly sprong.

Their sitting at meate.

The place of solemne Prayer.

The howse wherin the Tombe of their Herounds standeth.

SECOTON·

A Ceremony in their prayers wth strange restures and songs dansing abowt posts carued on the topps lyke mens faces.

A painting of an Algonkian village showing the interesting domed rectangular construction of their houses.

mummy's feet. A religious official, living under the mortuary platform, watched over the remains. What all this meant to the inhabitants must forever remain a mystery to us. All we have to go on is interpretations by European observers, who were hardly unbiased scientific investigators.

Shamans. We do know that the Central Atlantic Algonkians had a class of religious practitioners, priests or shamans. They performed cures with herbs, emetics, and laxatives, as well as by bloodletting and scratching. They must have practiced in much the same way as Algonkian shamans of the North. People in this area seem to have taken sweatbaths for spiritual and physical purification, and shamans too purified themselves by sweating. They doubtless performed other purification rituals as well which we know nothing about. Shamans distinguished themselves from other people by shaving their hair into unusual patterns, painting their scalps, and rubbing the uncut hair with fat to make it stand up. They also sported hair decorations of snake or other animal skins, or even whole stuffed birds.

Clothing. Here on the coast (from Virginia to Carolina) the climate was generally mild the year round, and clothing was usually deerskin loincloths for men and aprons for women. Some apron-skirts left the buttocks exposed; others dipped down front and back. If the weather turned cool, both sexes wore robes of hide or fur or sometimes of feathers, perhaps decorated with beads or painted designs. Body and facial tattooing was common on women, less so on men, who usually adorned themselves with body paint, necklaces, and earrings.

The Chief. Tribes were warring all the time when the Europeans first arrived. That hostility may have been normal, but many experts believe Chief Powhatan aggravated it as he conquered neighboring tribelets and brought them under his dominion. He was an unusually powerful chief, a true autocrat, collecting tribute from subject tribes and keeping his wealth in special storehouses. He had several wives, though polygyny was not common, and the English reported that he had a sort of bodyguard of fifty select warriors. Such authority and centralization of power were far from usual among Algonkians and probably came from Powhatan's own qualities and charisma. The only power equal to his was found far away among the Natchez in the lower Mississippi Valley. But for the Powhatan group it was an innovation rather than tradition, the product of conquest by a powerful chief rather than voluntary confederation.

Chiefs generally had their land prepared, cultivated, and harvested by the people. Women did most of the farming, but men helped them clear the land. The chieftain's harvest was stored not only for his personal use, but for times of public need and for trade.

Food.   Along with crops, shellfish of the coastal flats contributed to the diet; they also yielded shells that could be traded or made into beads and utensils. Plant foods included wild tubers, seeds, nuts, and greens. Central Atlantic Algonkians also caught fish with snares and weirs, spears, hooks and lines, and even by shooting them with bow and arrow. Meat, too, was a part of the diet. Hunters went after game individually or in group hunts, in which women and children joined to drive elk and deer into rivers or surrounds where the hunters could kill them in quantity. Then women roasted, boiled, and dried the meat for storage.

Initiation Rites.   The practice the English settlers completely misunderstood was the boys' initiation ceremony. We do not have a good description of it, but it

Algonkian fishermen at night. The Indians in the foreground are bringing in their catch with a multipronged spear and dip net. In the center of the canoe in which they are sitting a fire is blazing on a clay hearth to attract the fish. Note the weirs in the background.

seems to have been a rite of symbolic death for the child, who was then reborn as an adult. Captain John Smith called the custom child sacrifice, believing the boys actually were put to death. The initiation appears to have been a ritual beating of the boys by adult men while the mothers wept and mourned as though the boys were really being killed. The boys, painted white, then lay in a depression or pit in the ground as though interred and spent the night there while some ritual was performed. Then they stayed in the woods, probably with an elder or shaman who taught them the tribe's sacred customs. When the boys returned, they were accepted as adult males. It is easy to understand why the English were mystified, especially since the boys surely could not reveal the secrets of initiation to the colonists or anyone else. It probably seemed another of the "savage ways."

The Natchez

The Great Sun.   When French explorers came upon the Natchez in the lower Mississippi River valley, they were particularly struck by the strongly centralized Natchez government and the stratified social classes. There was nothing else like the Natchez society north of Mexico. Their hereditary ruler, the Great Sun, was a monarch in the European style. He was in charge of the chiefs of Natchez villages, and his word was law. He was assisted by a council, however, so that other members of the nobility and the town chiefs limited his despotism somewhat. He was treated with reverence, his subjects remaining some distance from him and walking backward when leaving his presence. He and his representatives and close relatives were carried in litters on the shoulders of warriors or slaves. Small wonder the French were impressed! Unlike the Central Atlantic Algonkians, the Natchez political and social complexity could only have been built over many years, not put together by one unusually powerful personality.

The Great Sun lived in a large house facing a plaza in the main town of the Natchez. On the other side of the plaza was a temple which, like the Sun's house, stood on a mound. Also facing the town square was the house of the Head War Chief, a brother of the Sun. The plaza was a ceremonial center, and the rest of the villagers lived in houses scattered some distance away. Other Natchez towns also followed this pattern of plaza and temple, surrounded by dispersed dwellings of the townspeople, with the farmlands beyond. When a Great Sun died, his house and its mound were destroyed, and new structures were built for his successor.

White Woman.   The Great Sun's mother held the title of White Woman. She too was very powerful. At her death her title seems to have fallen to her oldest daughter, but the early accounts are ambiguous and contradictory. In any event, the White Woman was never a wife of the Great Sun. Since the descent system was matrilineal, the successor to a Great Sun was never his son, but his sister's son. An early French explorer described the succession: "At [the Great Sun's] death his children are only nobles. . . . On the other hand, of the sons of his sister, who was herself white woman or female Sun, the eldest will be great chief or Great Sun, the second little Sun, chief of war. . . ."

The Natchez Class System.   All Natchez filled some position in a system of social stratification that has been called both a class and a caste system. It included two major social divisions, the nobility and the commoners. The nobility too had gradations, from the Suns through the Nobles to the Honored People. The commoners have come to be known as Stinkards from the French name for them, *Puants.*

Marriage customs required that members of the highest class marry common people. Suns were children of Sun mothers and Stinkard fathers; Nobles were children of Noble mothers or of Sun fathers and Stinkard mothers. Honored People were offspring of Honored Women or of Noble fathers and Stinkard mothers, and Stinkards were produced by marriage between two Stinkards or between Honored Men and Stinkard mothers. In other words, children of women of the upper three classes took the rank of their mothers, but children of Stinkard mothers were one rank below their fathers unless their fathers were Stinkards. The Great Sun, of course, was from the Sun class, the child of a Sun mother and a Stinkard father.

People could move up in the ranks by meritorious service or war exploits. The important political and religious positions went to males of the Great Sun's matrilineage, his brothers and maternal uncles. At his death, the Great Sun's wives were expected to sacrifice their lives, and parents often offered their children for sacrifice, thereby raising their own rank. Sacrificial victims were strangled, but they first swallowed pills of strong tobacco, which made them unconscious.

Other Customs.   As agriculturalists the Natchez grew the crops common to all American Indian cultivators: corn, beans, and squash. The women also gathered wild-plant foods, berries, nuts, and greens. Men helped with harvest and field preparation, and their hunting and fishing added animal protein to the diet. Domesticated dogs helped in hunting, and occasionally they were eaten.

As in other Southeastern societies, shamans performed cures and were also responsible for weather control, making rain or bringing fair weather. They did not manage public religious activities; those were the responsibility of the Great Sun and his officials. The Great Sun was in fact the tribal high priest as well as the ruler, and the government was thus a sort of theocracy.

Temples in each village held relics and holy images. They were sacred places before which a fire was always kept burning. The Great Temple of the tribe

Natchez Indian in winter costume.

stood in the town of the Great Sun, and in it the bones of former Great Suns were preserved. Only White Women, Great Suns, and a few other special individuals might enter that temple. The Great Sun and White Woman performed rites there daily, people made offerings in front of the temple, and at the first-fruits ceremony each year, everyone presented seeds as an offering before planting. Produce was offered at harvest. The Natchez also had an annual cycle of agricultural rituals, thanksgiving and harvest ceremonies, and feasts of the hunt. The Great Sun presided over all these.

Our information about the Natchez is unusually good all the way back to early contact times, thanks to the records left us by many interested French explorers. We know less about neighboring tribes, yet we have good reason to believe that the Natchez social stratification was not unique; other tribes of the area probably had similar social classes. We have no indication, though, that any other group had marriage customs like theirs. Those practices set them off from tribes like the Tunica, Chitimacha, and Timucua, who appear to have shared many features of a social class system.

The Seminole

Throughout the East, Europeans caused dislocation, fragmentation, and realignment of Indian societies. In the Southeast most of the disruptions ended with the Indian peoples being pushed westward, but some groups of Creek found refuge in Florida. There they were joined by remnants of other tribes, mostly Yuchi, Apalachee, and Yamasee. Together they became known by the Muskogean title Seminole, which means "separatist" or "wild," implying that those people refused to be pushed around and broke away from the main body of Creek.

It was in the 1700s that the Seminole became recognized as a unit. Most of them came from two Creek segments, often called Upper and Lower Creek. Both were Muskogean speakers, but they spoke different languages within that family, Muskogee (Upper Creek) and Mikasuki (Lower Creek). They still have that linguistic duality today. The Creek remained dominant among the Seminole, and all other members learned to speak one Creek tongue or the other.

Meat was a staple of the Timucua diet, and deer meat was especially favored. In this sketch by Jacques le Moyne deer are shown being hunted.

This mixture of people moved into Florida while it was under Spanish control. The Spanish had established missions in northern Florida, and enthusiastically tried to convert the Indians, but they were not colonizing as the English were doing in the North. Consequently the Florida tribes did not have to defend their lands.

Timucua and Calusa. The major tribes at the time of contact in the sixteenth century were the Timucua in northern Florida and the Calusa in the south. About the Calusa we know little more than that they were nonagricultural hunters and gatherers. Our information about the Timucua is better because a cartographer, Jacques le Moyne, left sketches of them. Le Moyne was in Florida in 1564 and 1565 during the French Huguenots' brief attempt to settle there. The French colony was destroyed by the Spanish in 1565, but le Moyne escaped with his art. He pictured the Timucua as typical of the Southeastern Muskogeans: agricultural, sedentary, and well organized under a stratified, centralized government. Their houses were circular, not rectangular, but in other ways their material culture resembled the Natchez. Le Moyne probably did most of his sketches from memory when he returned from Europe, though he may well have made notations while he was still in Florida. His finished engravings made the Indians look like the exotic savages Europeans expected.

Refugees Rebuilding. At the time the Seminole mixture came to be considered a distinct unit, there were few if any Timucua left. Both they and the Calusa had been ravaged by European disease, against which they had no immunity. Any people from either tribe still alive must have joined the Seminole, who settled in north Florida and quickly re-established their old way of life. The hybrid character of the Seminole group made little cultural difference because the people all had similar backgrounds.

The new union was successful, and the Seminole, now free of English aggression, built villages and started anew. Some escaped plantation slaves fled into Spanish Florida as well, and they were either absorbed by the Seminole or established villages near them, following much the same subsistence practices. From the Spanish the Seminole acquired some new plants, like fruit trees, which they cultivated along with the traditional corn, beans, and squash, and they also began to raise horses and cattle. Their life was not very different from that of the English settlers north of Spanish territory. Recognizing their "civilized" way of life, Europeans began to refer to them, along with the Cherokee, Creek, Choctaw, and Chickasaw, as the Five Civilized Tribes.

The Seminole War. But the new nation, the United States, cast envious eyes on the peninsula. In 1817, Andrew Jackson entered Florida, supposedly to re-

CHARACTERISTICS OF THE EASTERN TRIBES

Clothing	Food production	Equipment	Shelter	Social and political organization	Religion	Warfare
Fitted skin clothing	Cultivation (corn, beans, and squash)	Bows and arrows	Some skin or bark tipis	Nuclear families	Shamans	Warfare continuous in Northeast and Southeast
Dresses	Hunting	Traps	Wigwams (Northeast and Great Lakes)	Patrilineal clans (Great Lakes)	Spirits	Raids
Skirts	Fishing	Weirs	Longhouses (Iroquois)	Matrilineal clans (Northeast and Southeast)	Guardian spirits	Ambushes
Aprons	Gathering (plants and shellfish)	Tomahawks	Barrel-vaulted, rectangular or round buildings (Southeast)	Bilateral groups (Northeast and Central)	Medicine societies	
Breechcloths		Shields	Sweathouses	Moieties (Menominee)	Agricultural ceremonies	
Shirts		Stone and bone knives		Village and tribal councils	False Face Society (Iroquois)	
Coats		Canoes		Tribal chiefs	Orenda (Iroquois source of supernatural power)	
Leggings		Bark containers		Confederacies	Temples (Southeast)	
Deerskin robes		Basketry		Social classes (Southeast)		
Moccasins		Pottery		Centralized government (Southeast)		
		Hoes		The League of the Iroquois		
		Wicker armor and bark shields (Southeast)				
		Spoons, cups, cutters, and scrapers of shell				

This lithograph of a Seminole village shows some of the different house styles of the Indians. In the warm climate buildings were often constructed without walls; others were raised on stilts above the marshy ground.

cover runaway slaves. In 1821, the United States annexed the territory. At that time, all the Indians in Florida were called Seminole, and once again they became the objects of military aggression as European settlers found their lands appealing. Then came the Seminole War of 1835 to 1843, after which most Seminole were removed to Indian Territory in Oklahoma. A few hundred, however, fled down the peninsula to the sawgrass everglades and cypress swamp region where soldiers and guns could not follow. There they established a new home in former Calusa territory. Unlike the Calusa, the Seminole remained agriculturalists, cultivating crops on high, drier areas in the swamp.

Displaced People. South Florida's environment was quite different from the Alabama and Georgia Creek territory or even the north Florida country, and the Seminole had to abandon many traditional ways when they moved into it. They did keep their matrilineal clans, their two languages (Muskogee and Mikasuki), and their housing, which they modified by leaving off the walls to keep air moving in the tropical climate, and by building the flooring as a platform about three feet off the swampy land. Dugout canoes became more popular in that area of high ground water. But the complex political organization typical of the South-

Billy Bowlegs, a Seminole war chief on the warpath. He is rendered here without war paint for purposes of portraiture. The paint on his two followers is not merely decorative but also serves to some extent to camouflage them.

east was forgotten, and they could not pasture their herds of cattle in that undrained region. The Seminole groups became small autonomous camps without any political centralization or overall leadership, and slowly their observances of community religious ceremonials like the Green Corn Dance deteriorated, leaving all religious practices in the hands of the shamans.

Bibliography

Lurie, Nancy O.
1966   *Mountain Wolf Woman.*
        The life of a Winnebago woman in Wisconsin during the period of culture
        change after European contact, giving the so often ignored woman's point of
        view.

Morgan, Lewis H.
1851   *League of the Ho-De-No-Sau-Nee or Iroquois.*
        (Several editions.) A classic ethnography by one of the first American scholars
        who studied Indians.

Ritzenthaler, Robert E., and Pat Ritzenthaler
1970   *The Woodland Indians of the Western Great Lakes.*
        A very readable and informative survey of Midwestern Indian cultures.

Swanton, John R.
1946   *The Indians of the Southeastern United States.*
        This encyclopedic compendium of the Indian societies of the Southeast gives a
        list of tribes from the mid-Atlantic states south as well as general aspects of
        Southeastern culture.

Thwaites, Reuben G., ed.
1896–   *The Jesuit Relations and Allied Documents.*
1901   Seventy-three volumes of priceless information recorded by the first literate Eu-
        ropeans to come in contact with many Northeastern tribes, from 1611.

Garbarino, Merwyn S.
1972   *Big Cypress, a Changing Seminole Community.*

Gearing, Fred
1962   *Priests and Warriors: Social Structure of Cherokee Politics in the 18th
        Century.*
1970   *The Face of the Fox.*

Hickerson, Harold
1970   *The Chippewa and Their Neighbors.*

Hoffman, W. J.
1893   *The Menomini Indians.*

Landes, Ruth
1970   *The Prairie Potawatomi.*

Radin, Paul
1926   *Crashing Thunder, the Autobiography of a Winnebago Indian.*

Trigger, Bruce G.
1969   *The Huron.*

MAJOR GROUPS AND LANGUAGES OF THE EAST

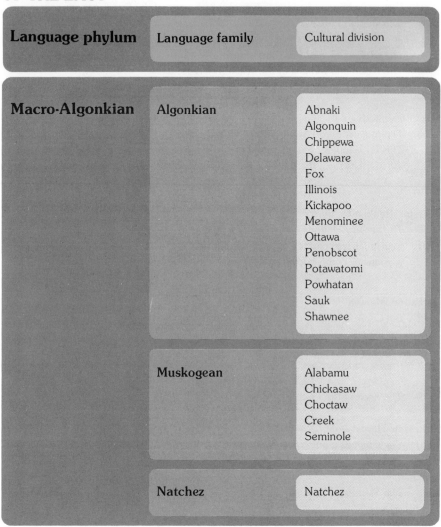

Language phylum	Language family	Cultural division
Macro-Algonkian	Algonkian	Abnaki Algonquin Chippewa Delaware Fox Illinois Kickapoo Menominee Ottawa Penobscot Potawatomi Powhatan Sauk Shawnee
	Muskogean	Alabamu Chickasaw Choctaw Creek Seminole
	Natchez	Natchez

Continued

MAJOR GROUPS AND LANGUAGES (continued)

Language phylum	Language family	Cultural division

EAST (continued)

Macro-Siouan	Catawba	Catawba
	Iroquoian	Cayuga Cherokee Huron Mohawk Oneida Onondaga Seneca Tuscarora
	Siouan	Winnebago
	Yuchi	Yuchi

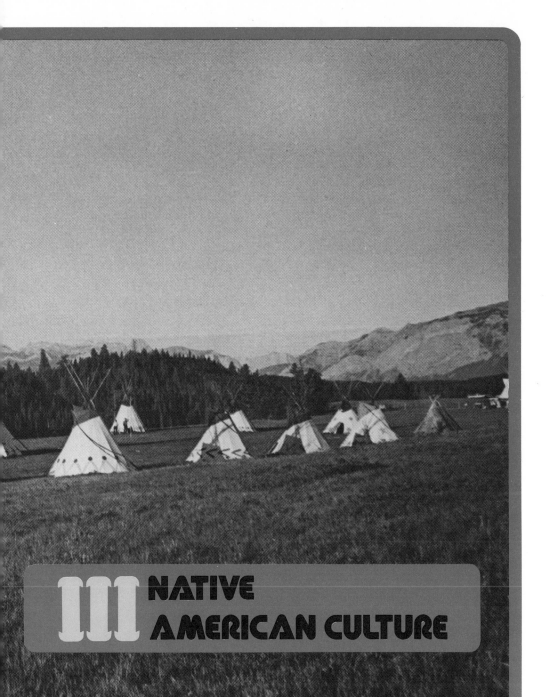

III NATIVE AMERICAN CULTURE

In Part II we have examined native American societies in a geographic framework, noting similarities and particularly contrasts from one area to another. We have seen that even within a fairly small region, groups often adapted to their environment in quite different ways. Now we will approach Indian cultures from another point of view by looking at general aspects of native American life as a whole—technology, art, religion, political and social organization, economics and trade, and warfare. For in spite of the tremendous regional variations, in many ways Indian societies followed the same basic pattern, one much different from our own.

Incredible as it may seem, as recently as the nineteenth century some European social scientists still denied that tribal peoples had the institution we call marriage, or that they followed any ethical or religious precepts at all. Europeans were fond of describing non-Europeans as childlike and emotional and themselves as rational and scientific. Stereotypes born of misconceptions like these can best be laid to rest by information organized topically. This arrangement makes it easier to see the real differences between European and Indian ways, and also to see the many similarities.

Preceding pages: A
Plains scene. Tipis
are spread in a
circle framed by
trees and mountains.

Motion pictures have found sources in American Indian sagas, but they rarely gave a full or fair treatment to Indian societies.

Even today, people tend to ask for general information about Indian life rather than about Indians of specific areas. What kind of marriage customs did Indians have? What was their religion like? How did they rear their children? How did they make political decisions? What kinds of tools did they use? While answers to these and other questions must vary from area to area, there are, nevertheless, many general statements we can make about Indian life. Though some of the data of this section may repeat information in earlier chapters, Part III is included to make cross-cultural comparisons and contrasts clearer and more precise.

Bibliography

Astrov, Margot, ed.
1946 *American Indian Prose and Poetry.*
        Songs and stories from the major culture areas.

Bandelier, Adolf
1890 *The Delight Makers.*
        A fictional account of precontact Pueblo Indians. Gives a real feeling for the fear of witches and witchcraft.

Driver, Harold E.
1969 *Indians of North America.* 2nd ed.
        A major textbook, the only one arranged by topics of culture. Every student should be acquainted with this work.

Hodge, Frederick
1906– *Handbook of American Indians North of Mexico.*
1910   An encyclopedia of topics and tribes. An older work that should be better known.

Underhill, Ruth
1965 *Red Man's Religion.*
        The only general text on Indian religion. Very easy to read.

Benedict, Ruth
1923 *The Concept of the Guardian Spirit in North America.*

Densmore, Frances
1926 *The American Indians and Their Music.*

Douglas, Frederick H., and René D'Harnoncourt
1941 *Indian Art of the United States.*

Dunn, Dorothy
1968   *American Indian Painting.*

Feder, Norman
1965   *American Indian Art.*

Gifford, Edward W.
1928   *Pottery Making in the Southwest.*

Morgan, Lewis H.
1965   *Houses and House-life of the American Aborigines.*

Radin, Paul
1956   *The Trickster: A Study in American Indian Mythology.*

Speck, Frank G.
1919   *Functions of Wampum among the Eastern Algonkian.*

Spier, Leslie
1921   *The Sundance of the Plains Indians.*

Thompson, Stith
1971   *Tales of the North American Indians.*

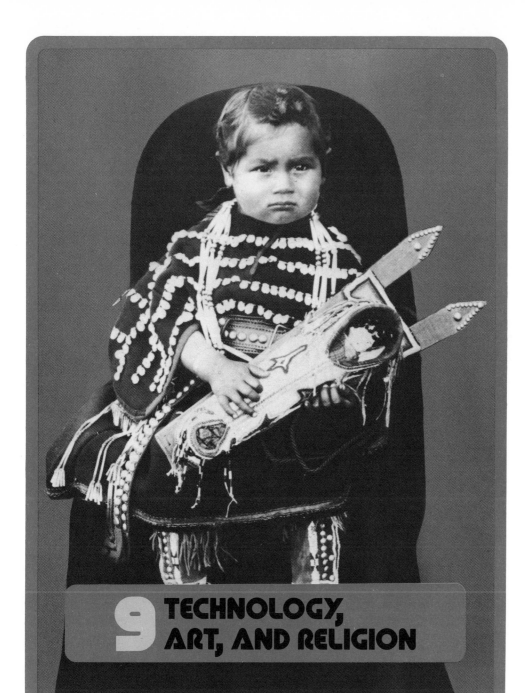

9 TECHNOLOGY, ART, AND RELIGION

A society's practical arts—the way its people make and use the tools they need to sustain and reproduce life—constitute its technology. A human group provides itself with food, shelter, and protection with its technology. And beyond simply satisfying those physical needs, technology includes the means to satisfy intellectual and aesthetic needs: the performing arts, such as music and dance, as well as the graphic arts, such as sculpture and painting.

Preceding page: A Kiowa child. Her cloth dress is decorated with elk teeth, which many tribes considered treasured ornaments. She is holding a cradleboard containing a porcelain-faced doll.

Eskimo demonstrating a sinew-backed bow and ivory-tipped arrow at Chicago's Columbian Exposition of 1893. He is wearing a coat made from squirrel skins.

Throughout the New World, people created all the tools and utensils they needed from the natural materials of their environment. Though archaeologists have shown that long-distance trade existed long before European contact, that trade was highly specialized in luxury or exotic goods such as mica, obsidian, and shells. Implements of daily living, the common household tools and building materials, had to come from the immediate vicinity. Thus, as we examine native technology, we find that the major variations in housing, transportation, weapons, and clothing arise naturally from the environmental differences and the availability of various resources. Still, many raw materials were available over nearly all of the continent—stone and bone, for example—so we can generalize about the manufacture and use of many implements.

The Food Quest

The food any human society eats depends upon what is available. We have already pointed out the abundance of food in the Northwest Coast culture area and the scarcity in the Subarctic. But no society can eat without first doing some work to obtain food. The kinds of food-getting work American Indian societies did were hunting, gathering, fishing, and cultivating. Later, after the Europeans introduced domesticated animals, Indians added stockraising.

Gathering

In the Great Basin and California, people ate more wild plants than any other food. Everywhere else except for the Arctic, wild plants were important even where the cultural emphasis was on hunting or agriculture. American Indians ate a vast variety of wild vegetal foods, from roots and tubers to greens, fruits, seeds, and nuts. Even fungi added to the diet: Indians of the Southeast made one fungus, tuckaho, into bread.

Everywhere the gatherers were women, often aided by their children. For most gathering they needed no implement other than containers; going to pick berries or greens, they usually carried baskets. To reach tubers and roots, they used digging sticks, and for seeds, simple beaters to knock the ripe grain into containers. They knocked down nuts too, reaching into the trees with long poles. To gather the hard-to-reach fruit of the prickly pear cactus, which was protected by sharp spines, women made tongs. Most of these looked like large clothespins, a piece of wood with a slit, but sometimes they were two pieces held together like chopsticks or paddles. Tongs also were used to handle hot stones for stone boiling or sweatbaths.

To gather maple syrup in the Great Lakes, eastern Subarctic, and Northeastern regions, Indians cut into the sugar maple tree and inserted a tap or spout, catching the sweet sap that oozed from the wound, usually in bark containers. Then they cooked the sap by stone boiling, stirring it as it cooled with wooden paddles, and sometimes pouring a little on the snow to make chewy taffy, which they ate immediately. After cooking and cooling the sap, which crystallized into sugar, they stored it in bark containers and used the maple sugar as a seasoning.

Hunting

Though much of their diet came from wild plants, Indians considered the hunt more important. People of the Plains gave so much prestige to hunters that other food resources got little attention, even though it was plant food that often staved off starvation in lean seasons. Game was the favored food almost everywhere. Through the years, Indian hunters developed many ways of trapping, disabling, and killing animals. They studied each animal's ways and learned how to get close to it without warning, stalking against the wind, wearing disguises of animal skins, and waiting for prey at water holes.

The large game animals Indians hunted were bison, moose, caribou, elk, antelope, deer, and bear. Deer were the most widely hunted, but the Plainsmen preferred bison, and the Subarctic people went mostly after caribou. The Eskimo and Indians of the Northwest Coast hunted sea mammals as well as land animals.

The people generally preferred hunting large game animals over small animals, simply because they had more meat on them, though small animals filled many a stomach when larger game was not to be had. One bison meant at least half a ton of meat, one deer a hundred pounds, and a large rabbit ten pounds or less. The many by-products made the big animals even more desirable: hides for clothing and shelter, hair for embroidery and padding, antlers for handles and projectile points, hooves and horns for glue, sinew for thread and string, bones for needles and other tools and for ornaments, and guts for containers.

Deadfalls (traps with heavy weights that fell on animals, disabling them), surrounds, and impounds (the confined areas where animals were driven and killed), used in ancient times, remained important in hunting herd animals. Antelopes' great speed might have kept them safe from hunters except for the animals' great inquisitiveness. Indians knew how to attract their curiosity by waving strips of hide or feathers from long poles. As the antelopes went to investigate the flapping objects, the men could get close enough to shoot them. Dogs often went along to hold animals at bay while hunters closed in for the kill, and hunters sometimes would try to lure the animals by imitating mating calls.

Hunting Weapons. Indians depended on two basic devices for killing: spears and bows. Spears, as we know from archaeology, were the oldest implements of the hunt. With the spear thrower or *atlatl,* hunters gave their spears added thrust and accuracy, but because atlatls were unwieldy on horseback, mounted Plainsmen rarely used them. Hunters of the Big Game period in American prehistory used spears, but we still have not determined the earliest use of the bow and arrow in North America. Nor do we know whether Indians invented bows here independently or ancient hunters brought them across the Bering Strait from the Old World. Sure evidence—preserved prehistoric bows—demonstrates their existence by A.D. 500, but many archaeologists believe that hunters used bows far earlier, by 1500 B.C. Bows and arrow shafts decay rapidly, of course, so we do not have any very ancient remains. Stone arrowheads might seem likely to show the date of introduction conclusively, but they do not because many stone points small enough to be used on arrows might also have been points for small spears, such as fishing spears. We know too that arrows for small game such as birds and squirrels usually did not have stone tips. By the time of European contact, though, all Indians and Eskimo used bows.

Hunters made four basic kinds of bows: the self-bow, the sinew-backed bow, the sinew-wrapped bow, and the compound bow. Indians chose springy wood, bone, or horn for the compound bow, put together in several layers and glued and lashed together. Plains Indians favored this style. In the Eastern woodlands the self-bow was the popular form, made of a single length of wood, often four feet long or more. The sinew-wrapped bow was an Alaskan form, brittle wood wrapped with sinew. Hunters made sinew-backed bows from self-bows by backing them with sinew to give extra spring. Some Eskimo made their compound bows of whale ribs, with a wooden grip. Plains bows were usually short for easier shooting on horseback.

Indians selected reeds, canes, or light wooden boughs with great care for arrow shafts. They dried them to season the wood and straightened and smoothed them with stone or bone implements. Feathers for arrows came primarily from hawks, eagles, and turkeys. Properly attached, the feathers made the arrow twist or spiral in flight. Indians usually split the feather before attaching it with glue, but Eskimo usually used the whole feather.

The men made bowstrings from rawhide, sinew, or twisted fibers. Glue came from animal tissues, hooves, sinew, or horn, boiled for several days to produce a jelly-like substance that was a very effective adhesive. Indians also used gum resins or pitch from some trees and shrubs.

Indians formed arrowheads not only of stone but of bone, horn, antler, shell, wood, and copper, and in many styles and shapes. Some arrows had points loosely attached so the point would stay embedded in the flesh when the shaft was withdrawn, but most hunters bound their arrowheads firmly to the shafts so that they could recover both. The heads were attached with sinew, cording, or

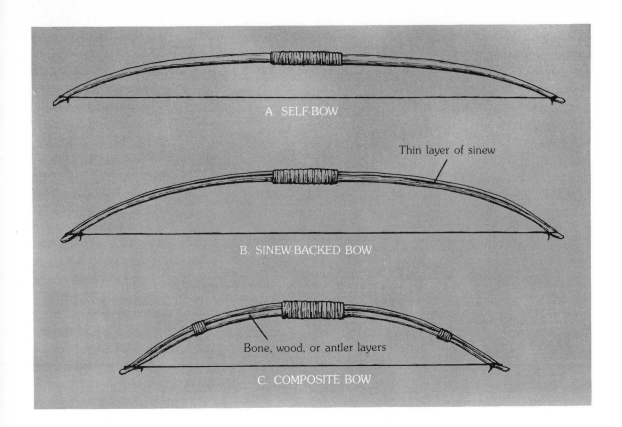

A. SELF-BOW

Thin layer of sinew

B. SINEW-BACKED BOW

Bone, wood, or antler layers

C. COMPOSITE BOW

The three basic kinds of bows used by hunters: the self bow (A); the sinew-backed bow (B); and the compound bow (C).

rawhide slipped around the notches, or lashed firmly in an over-and-under pattern if they had no notches. Hunters used the same techniques to attach spear and knife blades to shafts.

Hunting Methods. Often, when an animal had been wounded but not killed, hunters clubbed it to death with anything from a simple knobbed stick to carved stone or wooden implements to clubs set with spikes, stone heads, or copper blades. Pueblo hunters used missile clubs, called rabbit sticks, which were thrown to bring down rabbits.

Hunters of the Southeast and the Iroquois in the Northeast used blowguns to kill small animals and birds. They hollowed long stalks of cane or straight pieces of wood, then fashioned a projectile or dart from a splinter of cane or wood, padding it with thistledown, cotton, or other soft material at one end. The other end of the dart was sharp. The padding provided resistance which the hunter blew against. With practice, a hunter became skillful in bringing down small game with a blowgun.

Indians caught many smaller game animals such as foxes in traps. Some traps killed the animals, while others imprisoned them alive. One simple trap used a morsel of food as bait. One end of a heavy stone was propped up by a stick above the food. When the animal tried to take the food, the stone fell, stunning or killing the animal. Another trap was a pit in the ground, covered with branches. When the animal stepped onto the branches, it fell through into the pit. Some pits had a sharp stake at the bottom to impale the animal; others merely imprisoned the animal until the hunter killed it.

A clever way of catching eagles and hawks, which were prized for feathers, was for one man to lie concealed in a pit over which brush had been laid. On the brush another man would put a dead squirrel or rabbit. When the bird, attracted by the prey, alighted, the hunter in the pit would grasp its feet, then crush or strangle it.

Hunters set snares for rabbits, birds, and other small game. Along animal paths to watering places or feeding grounds, a trapper suspended a loop of sinew or hide from the tip of a springy sapling bent over and lightly set into a notch on another tree. An animal stepping on the loop released the bent sapling, which sprang up, catching the animal in the noose.

To butcher and skin animals, Indians used knives of stone or almost any material that would take and hold an edge: wood, reed, antler, shell, bone, and copper. Beaver teeth made very good cutting implements. Indians usually hafted the knife point to a shaft exactly as though they were fashioning a spear or arrow, but the knife shafts were much shorter, only four to six inches long.

Fishing

In much of native America, fishing was not very important. People of some tribes (notably in the Plains and the Southwest) even thought fish were not fit to eat. But fish was the most important item in Northwest Coast and Plateau diets and was also vital to the Arctic and Subarctic folk.

Aboriginal fishing implements included nets, weirs, hooks, spears, and traps of many styles and designs. All across the continent fishermen built the traps called weirs, wickerwork dams that let water flow through but trapped the fish. Indians constructed many other styles of fish traps, but the principle was the same: fish entered an enclosure in which they could not turn around to swim back out. The people fished with hooks and lines as well as spears, and especially in the Southeast and California they used fish poisons. These worked only in still water, diluting too rapidly in moving streams. The poison, made from plants like crushed walnut bark or soap root, caused temporary paralysis of the fish's breathing mechanism, but was harmless to anyone who ate the fish.

Fishers dipped nets lashed to poles into water where fish were plentiful and also stretched large nets all the way across streams. A group of men working together could sweep a lake or pond with a large net, holding the lower edge of the net on the bottom with sinkers.

Fishhooks were made of bone, shell, ivory, wood, or copper. The gorge, much like the hook except in shape, was a straight sharp pin at the end of a line. When a fish swallowed a gorge, it stuck in its throat, and the fisherman could haul the catch from the water. People also shot fish with bows and arrows and caught them with pronged spears. In northern areas, the men chopped holes in ice to fish in winter with hooks, gorges, spears, or bows. People of the Northwest Coast caught large fish with harpoons.

Along the north Pacific coast, the Indians relished fish eggs, collecting them on evergreen branches held down with weights in water where fish spawned. Once the eggs were deposited, the branches were removed and the eggs dried for storage. Around lakes and ponds, men learned to attract fish at night with torchlights and then spear or shoot them with arrows. Wherever shellfish could be found, women dug them from the sand.

Cultivation

Native peoples of Mexico and South America developed many domesticated plants, but Indians north of Mexico cultivated only three in quantity—corn, beans, and squashes—though they grew many varieties of each. Some societies used sunflowers and amaranths, which we consider weeds today; those "weeds" added important amounts to the food stock.

Everywhere except among the Pueblo Indians, women were the cultivators of everything but tobacco, which was the other major cultigen north of Mexico. Men grew tobacco to smoke for ritual purposes as well as for pleasure, planting it even where nothing else was cultivated, as in the northern Plains. All the cultivated plants except the "weeds" had originated in Mexico or farther south in prehistoric times, and much archaeological investigation today is aimed at pinpointing where they started and by which routes agriculture diffused to tribes north of Mexico.

Planting and cultivating were simple throughout North America, involving digging sticks, hoes, and rakes. Farmers punched holes in the ground with the digging sticks and dropped seeds into the holes. They usually planted corn, beans, and squash in the same field, often using cornstalks as supports for the squash vines. Indians had no draft animals or ploughs, but fields for the native plants did not require or get the kind of preparation associated with Old World plants like wheat.

Some digging sticks were no more than pointed branches, but others were made with a toe rest and one end broader and flatter than the other, like a narrow spade. Occasionally the cultivator slipped a ring of stone over the stick as a

This engraving shows how beans and corn were sown. Men, using fish-bone hoes, broke up the ground while women dug evenly spaced holes into which they dropped the seeds.

weight to give more thrust. Hoes had heads of flaked stone, wood, and also bone; the scapula or shoulder blade of a bison made an excellent hoe. People also made rakes of wooden prongs attached to a handle, but just as often used an unmodified antler. Both rakes and hoes were used for weeding and breaking up the ground, though nowhere was much weeding done. In fact, Indians did not look after their gardens very diligently, putting most of the effort into planting and harvesting. Where fields were rocky, they just planted around the rocks.

Indians did not need to design special tools for harvesting, for corn, beans, and squash required no implements not already in use for gathering. The men picked rather than cut tobacco leaves, and the harvesters moved the produce from field to home or storage in large baskets.

Preparing Food

People have always eaten some foods without preparing them in any way, but other foods have to be treated before they are eaten. Most grains or seeds are easier to digest as flour or meal, and people generally prefer cooked meats to raw. Cooking food also makes it easier to preserve and store for the future.

Grinding and Pounding

With stone or wooden equipment, Indian women of North America pounded and ground maize, acorns, other seeds and nuts, leaves, stalks, and dried meats, making them more edible or preparing them for storage. Grinding was the main technique for turning nuts and seeds of all species into flour for gruels and breads. In the West, women usually used stone grinding equipment, while wood was more popular in the East, but both were distributed widely.

A woman ground grain by rubbing it between two stones, using the larger as a base and holding the smaller in her hand. Today, the smaller stone is called a mano (especially by Spanish-speaking people) or pestle, and the larger stones are termed metates or mortars. Anthropologists often speak of this equipment as milling stones or grinding stones. Grinding stones might be oblong, round, or irregularly shaped. Usually the metate is an oblong stone; the pestle is shaped like a rolling pin, while a mano usually is rectangular.

Women of the East did their grinding by pounding rather than rubbing, and they used wooden equipment. Their mortars were sections of tree trunks about eighteen inches in diameter, hollowed to a depth of about two feet. Into the mortar they poured the grain, then pulverized it with a wooden pestle, a large pole with thickened ends. Women stood while using a tree-trunk mortar.

Food Preservation and Storage

Indians dried both animal and plant foods in strong sunlight, or by the fire in regions that had cloudy weather. Strips of dried meat called *jerky* might be stored in containers without further processing, but often women pulverized jerky into pemmican by mixing it with mashed berries and suet, then packed it away. Women made many varieties of pemmican with different meats and berries, occasionally adding bone marrow, and in some places using dried fish for the base.

People had many ways of storing dried meat, fish, plant foods, and pemmican, always choosing storage places where the foods would stay dry and safe from animal scavengers and vermin. To keep food from predators, they hung it from tree branches in hide or basketry containers or hid the filled containers in cache pits. Some people, like the Mandan, dug these pits in the floor of their lodges, but many pits were outside and unprotected, covered only with stones to keep animals out. In the Arctic, it was impossible to dig into the permanently frozen ground, so food was simply left on the surface. Covered with a pile of stones, it kept very well in this natural deep-freeze. The Mandan and many

This Indian woman is using a stone mortar and pestle to pound wild cherries, including pits, into a mush to be used in making pemmican.

others lined their large pits with clay, rawhide, and grasses to keep out burrowing beasts and insects. To conceal caches from enemies, Indians often built fires over them so that the ashes would hide the traces of digging, or else they carefully removed and replaced the sod or poured water over the soil to even out any evidence that something had been buried there.

For more immediate use, people braided shucks of corn together and suspended them from the roof poles of the house. Southeast people built small corncribs near their houses, plastering the insides to discourage vermin and animals. Women might store full ears of corn in the cribs, or just grain. Inside their homes they kept daily food on shelves or ledges in containers of natural materials like bark, pottery, basketry, skin, or wood.

Cooking

Women did all the cooking: roasting, broiling, boiling, and baking. The only cooking technique common today that the Indian women did not use was frying.

To boil foods, women used fireproof containers of pottery, or even bark that could be hung close enough to the fire to bring water to a boil without burning through. Or they might drop very hot stones into liquid in containers of skin, basketry, wood, or viscera (like stomach pouches). Heat from the stones would eventually bring the liquid to a boil, but stone boiling was much slower than direct boiling.

Women roasted or broiled meats and some vegetables, especially ears of corn in their own husks. In the Southeast they broiled fish on a grill of green sticks over the fire; elsewhere meat or fish was put on a long stick stuck in the ground at an angle toward the fire. Often people roasted meat and whole small game in the coals and hot ashes, first encasing the food in clay or leaves. In addition they cooked many foods in earth ovens, which were holes in the ground with hot coals or stones at the bottom. The cook put wrapped foods on top of the stones or coals, covering everything with soil to keep the heat in long enough to cook the food. The New England clambake is a direct descendant of these earth ovens.

The women baked breads directly in warm ashes or by laying the dough on "baking stones" over a flame or coals. In very early Spanish times, the Pueblo began to use simple beehive ovens with draft holes, probably copied from the newcomers. Pueblo women baked their corn bread, something like tortillas, on flat hot stones.

Fire-making

Indians used fire not only for cooking, but also for warmth and protection from wild animals. Fire-making was important in many ceremonies we have discussed, such as the Creek Busk and other new-fire and world-renewal rituals.

Indians had two techniques for starting fires. Striking a spark with flint and pyrites (iron-containing rocks) was common in the Arctic, Subarctic, Northwest Coast, and New England areas. The other way was to produce heat by rubbing wood on wood. The firedrill was a favorite way of creating friction: spun rapidly, it heated tinder or wood powder at the point of contact to combustion temperature. The Onondaga appear to have been the only group to create friction by rubbing a stick over a wooden plane surface, sometimes called a *fire plough*. Keeping coals alive was a necessity everywhere because it was quite difficult to start a fire.

Housing

All over the continent people needed shelter from cold, rain, or heat. Some types of house were specific to tribes or regions: hogans, pueblos, and plank houses. General structures appeared in several areas, including wigwams, wickiups, tipis, and earth lodges. Indians also built cruder structures for temporary shelter. No one name covers such buildings, but we would call them huts, lean-tos, or shacks.

General Forms of Housing

Wigwams and Wickiups. The word *wigwam* is Algonkian for "dwelling," but Algonkian speakers built other house types too, including the barnlike structures of the Central Atlantic people. We have no word for these houses, but they were much like the Iroquois longhouse. Wigwams had circular or oval floor plans and domed roofs; they were covered with sheets of bark, woven mats, or skins. The framework was of saplings imbedded in holes about two feet apart with tops bent over and bound to make the arched roof. Some wigwams housed only one family; others were much larger.

Wickiups looked something like wigwams, and people often have confused the two, but there were differences. Wickiups housed Apache, Basin, and California peoples, while wigwams were Algonkian. The wickiup floor plan was often irregular, though sometimes oval. Wickiups were less permanent than wigwams, and generally cruder. Instead of hides or sheets of bark, they were covered with brush. They were favored by nomadic people unwilling to spend much time on buildings they would soon abandon.

Tipis. Tipis appeared in the Subarctic, Northeast, and Plains areas, small conical structures covered with hides or bark. In the Northeast and Subarctic, the buildings never were very large, but after horses appeared on the Plains, tipis there became much larger.

Women put up and took down the big Plains tipis and made the buffalo hide covers for them. Men cut the poles for the framework. Once all materials were gathered, two women could erect a tipi in an hour.

Most tribes used a tripod of especially strong poles for the tipi's main support, but some tribes used four poles. The women tied these poles together at the top and raised them, planting the untied ends firmly on the ground. Then they leaned more poles against the original group and tied them in place. The frame was not a true cone but was tilted slightly to give more room at the rear and better ventilation through an off-center smokehole.

When the poles were all in place, the women fastened the hide cover to another pole, hoisted it over the frame, draped it around the poles, pegged the bottom edge down, and closed the open seam with large wooden pins like skewers. They attached a door flap that could be adjusted for ventilation. Finally, they inserted two lighter poles outside the tipi in the smoke flaps at the top of the cover. By moving the poles, the women could adjust the flaps to compensate for changes in wind direction or close them completely in rain or snow. When finished, the average Plains tipi was about fifteen feet in diameter at the base, providing ample room for a family and their equipment.

Good poles were hard to find on the grasslands, so people took along the framework of the tipi as well as the cover when they moved. Often the poles formed part of the horse travois.

Earth Lodges. Earth lodges were permanent homes for semisettled people, most common among Plains villagers, in the Plateau, and in southwest Alaska. They varied somewhat in floor plan, but most were circular, and almost all were dug two or three feet below the surface of the ground before the framing was put up. Lodges were large, some having room for prized horses as well as several families.

The earth lodge is named for its insulating covering of soil or sod that kept the interior warm in winter and cool in summer. Indians constructed the lodge framing with sturdy posts, for it had to support not only the heavy soil on top, but the pressure of its own size as well (see page 280).

Many of the Plateau lodges were entered at the top, with a ladder through the central smokehole, but the Plains villagers built their lodges with tunnel-like vesti-

A sketch of a Mandan village showing their circular earth lodges. The boat on the roof of the nearest house was placed there to cover the smokehole during heavy rain. The village is surrounded by a simple palisade of stakes.

bules and entries large enough for horses to pass through. Dwellings of the Pima and some California tribes were like the earth lodge, but smaller, less sturdy, and relatively impermanent. The Navajo hogan was like an earth lodge in that it was slightly underground and often covered with a layer of soil, but it too was much smaller.

The Wattle and Daub House.   In the Southeast, rectangular and also circular houses were made of pole frameworks intertwined with tough vines or flexible branches. The Southeasterners then covered the framework with a mud plaster called daub. Most such houses had peaked or gabled roofs. In hot weather, the people built similar shelters from the sun, leaving off the siding of branches and daub to improve air circulation. Such structures were found in all hot regions, with minor differences in style.

Specialized Forms of Housing

Pueblos.   The pueblo structure evolved from the early Anasazi pit house. The early domed houses, built over saucer-shaped depressions, developed into straight-sided buildings with upright posts supporting a flat roof. People entered these either through the smokehole or through a side passageway. It was during this early transition period that the residents also began to build rooms side by side. The pit house continued on as a ceremonial room (kiva), while the above-ground rooms were built up of wood and stones, often with an adobe clay plastered over the stone, into the pueblo of several stories. Logs spanned the pueblo walls, creating a flat roof; over these, the builders laid brush and poles, plastering them with more clay. In time, they built more rooms over the first, and the roof of each room became the floor of the room above.

   In later times, probably because of Spanish influence, people began to make the adobe clay into sun-dried brick, which they used in place of stone. From the Spanish, Indians also learned to build indoor fireplaces with chimneys, and to build more doors and window into the pueblos. Taos, a pueblo still occupied today, shows not only these additions, but television antennas on the roofs.

Hogans.   The Navajo house, the hogan, gradually changed in floor plan and construction. The early form was cone-shaped, with forked logs as its main structural support. The builders set the logs upright and placed poles or branches crosswise, supported by the forked ends of the logs. Over this basic framework they laid brush, and covered the whole with earth, leaving a smokehole in the center roof and a doorway on the east. The later form of the hogan was six- or eight-sided, made of horizontal timbers, and was usually much larger than the earlier.

Plank Houses of the Northwest. Woodworkers felled tall, straight cedar trees, trimmed off branches, then split planks from the trunk by driving wedges in a straight line from end to end. They used the planks for both siding and roofing over a framework of heavy cedar posts with rafters or crossbeams also of cedar. Entryways into homes of high-ranking individuals were elaborate, many with totem poles in front. Sometimes the carved pole formed the doorway. A post with a hole large enough for an adult to pass through was set flush against the front of the house. Often woodworkers carved the crests of the owner on the major structural house supports as well.

Iroquois Longhouses. Upright posts formed the main supports for the longhouse, and horizontal poles lashed to the vertical posts created rafters. Though the longhouse roof was peaked, it had no ridgepole. Instead, the builders slanted roof supports toward each other from the two sides, crossing the ends at the top and lashing them together.

Large slabs of bark covered the framework. Often women prepared strips of bark by laying them on the ground, slightly overlapping, and lacing them together with cords of plant fiber. Then the men lashed the sheets to the sides and roof of the building. Single slabs of bark were often lashed directly to the structure.

Interior of Oneida longhouse.

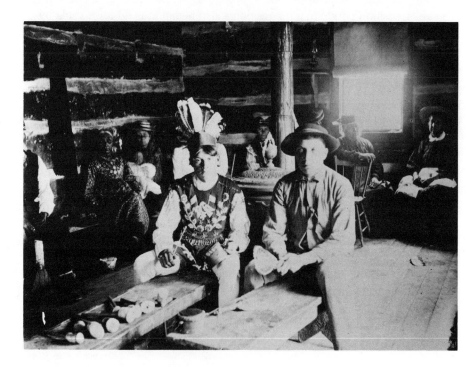

Sweathouses.   Sweathouses of one sort or another appeared in pre-Columbian America from the Arctic to Mexico. The most common form was a small wigwam, its framework of flexible poles bent and fastened into a domed structure and covered with skins, bark, or matting. Inside, a shallow firepit contained hot stones on which people sprinkled water to make steam. Ordinarily one person at a time used this small sweathouse, though once in a while two might use it together.

Some areas, like Alaska, had large, fairly permanent sweathouses dug into the ground. Such buildings almost always doubled as men's clubhouses when they were not being used for sweating. In the large structure, men built fires inside and sweated from the direct heat. Everywhere, a dip in a stream followed sweating.

Building either kind of sweathouse usually involved ceremonial observances, for sweating had to do with ritual purification. In some areas women availed themselves of the sweathouse, but never at the same time as men.

Housing is an interesting example of the impact of environment on culture. But it is also excellent evidence of people's inventiveness and creativity. Natural resources determine the building materials, but people turn those materials into many varied styles. Clearly, environment is never deterministic. Even in the two most difficult regions, the arctic and the desert, human choice and creativity led to many and diverse results.

Transportation

It may seem surprising that although many Indian groups were constantly moving themselves and their possessions from place to place, they had no knowledge of the wheel. Actually, wheeled transport would not have been much use to them, for they had no draft animals to pull vehicles. They did need transportation for such daily tasks as moving food and materials, and larger jobs like hauling raw materials and goods long distances for trade, and transporting the young, aged, and sick to new homes or village sites. Before Indians had horses, their transportation depended almost entirely on human endurance; they had only dogs to help with light loads.

Water Transportation

Though Indians made other kinds of boats as well, canoes were their most common means of water travel. The bark canoe was broad and sat high in the water, so that it could be paddled in very shallow places. Tribes developed their own styles, but most bark canoes had similar framework: lightweight wood sheathed with bark, preferably birch. Where birch did not grow, people learned to use other barks, especially elm. Men sewed sections of bark together with root fibers and waterproofed seams with melted pitch or tar. These light boats were fairly easy to carry overland between waterways.

Dugout canoes, differing only in style, had wide distribution, from the Northwest Coast to the Southeast. To make one, men set fire to a suitable tree, carefully limiting the blaze, and then cut it down with stone axes; charred wood cut more easily than green wood. With adzes and gouges, the canoe maker removed wood, making a depression in the log, which he filled with water. By dropping hot stones in the water, he softened the wood enough to spread the sides, which were propped apart with boards. He then emptied the water, and when the dugout dried, the spread was permanent (see page 132). With more trimming and perhaps separate pieces added on for prow and stern, the canoe was ready to try out. Because dugouts were carved from such large trees, they were rarely portable.

Eskimo boats, the kayaks and umiaks (see page 82), were skin covered, and so was the *bull boat* made by villagers of the Upper Missouri. The bull boat was like a cup, with a framework of saplings; it had no prow or stern. Villagers used it only to cross rivers, not for travel, for its circular construction made it very inefficient for speed. Peoples of the California area made boats with bundles of reeds, and the Chumash of California made plank canoes. Indians propelled all types of canoes with paddles. Whether people of the Northwest Coast used sails before European arrival is not certain, but they were reported to be sailing shortly after European contact, the only Indians known to have done so. Only the whaling Northwest Coast peoples went out to deep ocean waters. Others kept to inland waters or ventured not far off the coast.

Land Transportation

Human backs carried most of the loads on land, over the network of trails that covered the continent. Backpacking moved items of trade, personal belongings, food, and babies. To ease the burden, Indians often placed a strap called a *tumpline* across their brows and connected it to the bundles on their backs. Mothers often carried their babies on their backs in cradle boards suspended from tumplines or straps over their shoulders (see page 209). In the Arctic, women carried babies in their hoods or pouches in their clothes.

Before horses arrived in America, the dog-drawn travois carried many goods. Once they had horses, Indians enlarged the travois. Horse travois held household goods (see page 256), and often old people and infants, too. Sometimes a simple top or shade was added to keep off sun and rain, and some Plains Indians even made a cage travois for transporting puppies.

Travel over snow required sleds and snowshoes. Eskimo and Indians of the North used sleds drawn by dogs and by people, made in many shapes and styles depending on the materials available and the use they were meant for. Sleds had runners, with a deck or platform. Subarctic people invented toboggans without runners, the bed or deck running directly on the snow.

With snowshoes people could walk over snow without sinking, moving much faster than without them and cutting fatigue. Indians made more styles of snowshoes than sleds, all with the same basic parts: a wooden rim with toe and heel crossbars of wood or rawhide, netting across the framework for the feet to rest upon, and thongs to attach over the instep. On snowshoes the traveler walked with long strides, raising his toe at each step and letting his heel drag. Indians did not have skis.

The Ojibwa snowshoe dance was performed at the first snowfall of winter. It was not so much a ritual performance as the result of sheer exuberance for the return of the snow when the men could hunt on snowshoes again.

Clothing

Indians wore clothes as climate dictated, not for modesty or to conceal their bodies, for the nude human body aroused no shame or embarrassment. In fact, Eskimo, who wore far more clothing than any other North American natives, went about entirely or nearly naked in their homes. Clothing was worn for more than protection, though: Indians decorated themselves with objects and paints they found pleasing, and some groups indicated social position or religious office by the clothing or ornamentation they wore. Men generally dressed differently from women.

Kinds of Apparel

Of all the people on this continent, the Eskimo stand out as skillful makers of protective garments for cold weather. They tailored their clothing fully and knew how to make waterproof seams. Their garments were tight at the wrists, neck, and ankles, but loose over the rest of the body. Clothes had two layers, creating a dead air space between the inner and outer layers that kept body heat in and arctic cold out. Eskimo used both furs and dehaired hides of sea mammals, caribou, polar bears, and foxes for their apparel, and insulated their mittens and boots with feathers, down, and moss. The women sewed with sinew thread and needles and awls of bone.

Much of America's aboriginal population dressed in animal skins, though people in warmer climates made fabrics of plant fibers. For most of the continent, people favored deerskin. Where buffalo were available, people used their skins for robes and blankets; but whatever animals the hunters brought home contributed furs or hides for clothing. For the most part women made the clothing, though in a few California and Basin tribes, men and women each made their own.

Clothing Styles. Men usually wore breechclouts (loincloths or breechcloths), with shirts and leggings for more protection. Northeast and Plains women wore skin shirt dresses, and in the Northwest and Plateau they had woven plant-fiber skirts. In California and the Southeast, women wore only fiber or skin aprons. Both men and women added robes of fur (buffalo, wolf, rabbit—the animals of their environment) in cold weather.

Pueblo Indians grew cotton, spun it into yarn, and made their clothes from cotton cloth into which the yarn was woven. Pueblo men wore a kiltlike garment, and the women draped dresses over their right shoulders and under their left.

The rainy, foggy Northwest Coast climate made some rain garment useful there. Indians of that area made basketry hats (much like Chinese coolie hats) and a kind of poncho of basketry matting. Despite the rain, however, the coast was not cold; the Indians often wore nothing, which was better than keeping on clothing that got wet and stayed wet.

Footwear. Footwear of leather appeared everywhere except among some prehistoric Southwestern groups, who wove or braided plant-fiber sandals. People of the Southeast usually went barefoot. In the rainy Northwest, people found footwear a nuisance much of the time. Leather becomes stiff when it gets wet and then dries; bare feet were far more comfortable.

Indians made two types of moccasins: those with rawhide soles separate from the soft upper leather parts, and those made of a single piece of soft leather. The two-piece moccasins were favored by Plains and western Indians and the one-piece style by Northeast and Great Lakes peoples. Some groups also made long or "boot" moccasins. The Pueblo women wore these with strips of leather wound around the calves of their legs like bandages.

Body Decoration

Hair. Indians had little body hair and scanty beards. While a few Indian men were reported with mustaches, most carefully removed facial hairs with tweezers made of bivalve shells or two small pieces of bone, shell, or wood. They decorated the hair of their heads in enormously varied ways, even within one culture area or tribe. Men and women decided for themselves how they would wear their hair. Some men shaved their scalps, leaving a ridge of hair, called a roach, from forehead to the nape of the neck. Men of many areas also made artificial roaches from animal hair, especially from stiff deer hair (see page 296), and wore them to pad out their own hair or placed them over their unshaven heads as a kind of headdress, tied under the chin, or under braids, or pinned on. Braids were popular all over the continent for both men and women, and people of all areas also allowed their hair to flow loose. Among the Pueblo, many men and women cut their front hair into bangs. A Pueblo woman's hair style told whether she was married: elaborate buns of hair over each ear meant she was single (see page 220). To groom their hair, Indians made combs of wood, bone, horn, and stiff straw, and porcupine tails were their brushes.

In many tribes a baby's first haircut was an important event, and parents often saved the hair from that first cut to give the child later. Hair was important; it was connected with life. Many believed that an enemy who got hold of hair clippings would have power over the one the hair belonged to, so hair clippings were disposed of carefully and secretly.

Where it was available, bear fat was a favorite hairdressing, sometimes mixed with pigments to color the hair—soot to make it blacker or ground red ochre to make it red. Many Indians also padded out their braids, not just their roaches, with animal hair. After European contact, horse hair became very popular for false hair. Indians often used animal fats and oils to groom their hair, and in the Southwest the Pueblo made shampoo suds from the pounded root of yucca.

Paint and Tattoos.   People sometimes painted their faces and bodies with symbols of clan relationship, bereavement, or intent to make war. They also decorated their bodies with paints to protect against sun and wind, or just because body paint seemed attractive. In warm areas where clothing was scant, Indians were particularly fond of body paint for decoration (see page 171).

Indians of the Southeast used body paint lavishly, and tattooed their bodies too. Someone skilled in tattoo design perforated the skin with sharpened shells, stones, or bones, and rubbed in soot to make the design permanent. We have sixteenth-century paintings by Europeans of Southeastern Indians, showing people with every inch of exposed skin covered with tattooing.

Jewelry.   All across the land men and women enjoyed wearing earrings. Mothers usually pierced babies' ears when they were one or two years old. Earrings might be quite elaborate, made of bones, colored stones (like turquoise), and copper. People of the mound builders' period often inserted large copper spools in their pierced earlobes, stretching the lobes by inserting bigger and bigger ones until they could fit spools two or more inches in diameter.

Earrings were just one form of jewelry that Indians everywhere liked. From bone, claws, colored stones, shells, and indeed any attractive material they made necklaces, headbands, and armbands. Hair decorations of feathers, down, and other colorful items were universally popular too. On the Plains, a necklace of bear claws was a sign that the wearer was very important, and women sewed elk teeth onto clothing for another impressive type of decoration. Plains warriors strung long tubular bones called *hair pipes* into breastplates. After contact, Indians sought imported glass and china beads to sew onto garments or to weave into belts or necklaces. The period of great beadwork was the last half of the nineteenth century.

Arts and Crafts

Indian art is applied art, a practical thing, not a purely aesthetic exercise done for enjoyment. We do have some sculptures with no known func-tion: ivory carvings from the Eskimo, a deer head from Key West, stone images by the mound builders. Perhaps their creators intended them as hunting or health charms, but they might also have carved them just from artistic impulse. Most often it is impossible to separate Indian art from craft. Probably the artists themselves thought of their work as decoration rather than art. But we do not have to distinguish between art and craft to appreciate the results.

The Indian artist was essentially a conservator, not an innovator, trying to preserve cultural traditions and values with his art. Even when he used a new material, like glass beads, he applied it in culturally established ways. However, new ideas and new materials brought change over the years. Some elements of prehistoric art still appear today, but contemporary Indian art is quite different even from that of the generation just before it.

Indians decorated both utilitarian and ceremonial objects: containers, weapons, clothing, masks, ritual headdresses. Styles varied from one culture area to another—it does not take a specialist to spot a mask or totem pole from the Northwest Coast or a katcina mask or doll from the Southwest. However, neither portraits nor the use of perspective appeared anywhere in the art of native North America.

Woodworking

Indians in forested areas were skilled woodcrafters, and Northwest Coast woodworking was the highest development in carving north of Mexico. In pre-European times Indian carvers used adzes and knives of shell, stone, copper, and animal teeth. They chopped down trees that were not too large with axes and set fire to the base of larger ones, charring them for easier cutting. They also used drills, chisels, scrapers, and sanders or smoothers. Pueblo people made dolls, figurines, and other objects of wood so soft that they could shape it entirely by rubbing or sanding it with coarse rock. After iron knives became available, woodcarving flourished, especially on the Northwest Coast.

Indians bent or straightened wood by steaming or soaking it. They carved knots of trees into dishes and small bowls by gouging and scraping them, and fashioned some spoons and ladles of wood.

Bone and Horn

Surrounded by man-made materials as we are today, few of us think of bone and horn as useful raw materials. To the Indians, though, they were a valuable source of spoons, cups, ladles, and other utensils. To work horn, the craftsman first rid it of fatty deposits by heating it. Then he boiled it in water until it was pliable and could be worked with stone or bone knives or bent to the desired shape. After he had formed it into the utensil he wanted, he let it cool and harden. It would then hold its shape permanently, needing only to be polished with sand or sandstone, and perhaps rubbed to a gloss with animal fat or oil.

To work bone, the craftsman followed much the same procedure. After heating or boiling it, he let it lie in sunlight to dry and bleach, then fashioned it into beads or pendants or even combs.

Pottery

The Eskimo, northern Indians, and those of the Pacific Coast and Basin had little pottery, and the mounted Plainsmen abandoned pottery because it was too fragile to transport. All other groups gathered, mixed, and tempered clay to form pottery, a women's craft throughout North America. Each region showed its own style, but the major technique was the same across the continent.

First the potter obtained a clay and fine sand. She washed the sand and ground the clay to a fine powder, carefully removing any foreign matter, and mixed them in just the right proportions. Sand acted as a temper, keeping the

Zuni water jar (height, 10 inches) decorated with deer.

pot from cracking while it was being fired. But if there was too much sand, the pot became crumbly. Sand was the most common temper, but some women used crushed shell, crushed pieces of old pots, or plant fibers instead.

After mixing the clay with the temper, the potter added water until she could work the paste and form it into a roll or patty. She shaped the base of a pot using the bottom of an old pot as a mold, shaping the clay around it, or she might press out a disk of clay paste with her fingers. Once she was satisfied with the base, she made rolls of clay a foot or so long and about an inch in diameter. She built up the side of the pot by spiraling these rolls of clay around the base, higher and higher, thinning the sides as she built them up. As she added each new coil, she pressed it in place and smoothed it with a bit of shell or stone, or a piece of dried gourd.

When the shape and size were right, the potter put the pot aside to dry. After it was dry, she smoothed it once more and added a thin mixture of clay and water to the outer surface to create a finish called a *slip*. This gave a background for painting a design or for a polished surface. If there was to be a design, she painted it on freehand before she fired the pot; designs painted after firing were not permanent. Some potters cut designs into the paste with a sharp tool, pressed them on with a serrated shell, or stamped them with a carved paddle.

When the paint had dried, the potter put her pot, upside down, on stones over hot coals, with any other pottery that needed firing. She covered the pottery with old broken pots to keep the heat even. If flames or smoke touched it, they would leave black smudges. The temperature of the fire was about 1,200 degrees Fahrenheit, and the pottery remained on the fire for two or three hours. With tongs or sticks, the potter removed her pots after firing and let them cool.

Stone Working

For cutting and piercing implements, projectile points, axes, and knives, stone was the Indians' most important material. Stone that was easy to carve, like catlinite or soapstone, made excellent dishes and containers as well as pipe bowls. In fact, catlinite (named after the famous painter of Indian life, George Catlin) is often called *pipestone*. The Indians drilled colorful rocks like turquoise for beads to string into necklaces.

Making Stone Tools. Men worked stone by flaking, grinding, and polishing, matching the technique to the kind of stone. Flint is easy to chip or flake, but a granular stone like quartzite is less easy to control. Some stone, like slate, takes a very high polish. The earliest people to cross the Bering Strait undoubtedly knew simple stone-working techniques; later people developed their own in the New World.

Tools to work stone were other stones, bone, antler, wood, and copper. To make a projectile point, a man chose a suitable pebble or nodule of stone, and struck it to chip off some flakes and rough out a leaf-shaped blade. This usually was done with another stone called the *hammer stone.* Then with a more refined tool like a piece of bone or antler he put pressure first on one side, then on the other, detaching flakes to leave a sharp edge and the notches or stem required (see page 11). Taking time and care, an expert flint knapper could work very fine large or small points. Yurok stone workers made great ceremonial blades of *obsidian* (volcanic glass).

Drilling.   Stone was polished and ground with an abrasive, usually sand, moistened and held on leather or a wad of plant fiber, or with a block of sandstone, pumice, or other abrasive rock. Workers also drilled stone and shell, bone, ivory, and pottery with an abrasive. Drills were twirled by hand, with dry or wet sand at the point of contact to increase the friction. Drill heads were copper, stone, bone, and wood. Men also used slender, hollow cane filled with sand as drills. More complex drills rotated faster and cut more quickly. The strap drill was kept upright and in position by a wooden head that the driller held in his teeth. The driller wound a strap once around the shaft, then pulled it from side to side. The bow drill was similar except that the driller pulled the bow that held the strap from side to side with one hand, holding the shaft in the other. The more complex pump drill made the shaft revolve faster than the others did by a pumping motion which the driller gave to attachments slipped over the shaft. These drills could perforate even the hardest substances, like granite.

Leather Work

Women usually did all the skin dressing; only Pueblo men and a few in California processed hides. Except for some regional variations, the treatment for curing hides was the same in all areas. Nowhere did Indians apply the chemical most used for tanning hides today, tannic acid; instead they softened skins by physical manipulation.

First the woman skinned the carcass, and while the hide was still soft she staked it out, flesh side up, or stretched it in a frame. Then she scraped all fat and flesh from the skin. If she wanted fur, she left the hair on; if not, she scraped both sides with stone or bone implements. She then treated the hide with a skin-dressing mixture, usually a paste of mashed brains from the animal that supplied the hide, sometimes with a bit of the liver or marrow added. Human urine was another common skin-dressing material. After this treatment, she manipulated the hide to make it supple, sometimes by pulling it around the trunk of a rough tree, or over a stretched rope or a smooth rounded stake driven into the ground. Eskimo women often chewed skins to soften them. For a tan or buff color, the hide worker smoked her hides by suspending them over a low fire in a pit.

Indians also made rawhide, which is untanned or uncured leather, remarkable for its toughness and durability. Fresh hide was stretched on a frame or pegged to the ground just like hides being cured, but it was allowed to dry for several days without chemicals or manipulation. Plains Indians made their parfleche containers of rawhide, which, made into rawhide shields, also was excellent protection against arrows.

Metal Work

In pre-Columbian times, Indians north of Mexico did not know how to extract metal from ore by smelting. Around Lake Superior and the Copper River in Alaska, though, copper appeared naturally in pure form, and the Indians mined it. They shaped the nuggets of copper by hammering and grinding them, sometimes heating the copper early in the hammering, but not hot enough to melt the metal.

In the Midwest and Northeast where Indians traded Lake Superior copper, metalworkers hammered copper into breastplates, earrings, pendants, and other decorative and ritual items. They also made copper knives, projectile points, drills, and awls, but copper was too soft to replace stone for most utilitarian objects.

The Northwest Coast people got copper from the Alaskan source and hammered it into the ornamental shields known as coppers. With stones they pounded the metal flat, occasionally heating it to make it less brittle. To decorate the coppers, craftsmen hammered raised patterns into the copper from the back or incised designs on the front.

There is evidence that Indians used iron from meteorites when they were lucky enough to find it. They treated it too by hammering.

Basketry

Basketmaking is a very old craft in America. Archaeologists have found remains of baskets dating to around 8000 B.C. in the Basin. Natives of North America wove basketry everywhere, though it was rare in the Arctic. From it they made containers, mats, fish traps, hats, rainwear, and cradles. Women were the basketmakers, though men made fish traps and cradles in some areas.

Basket weavers used a variety of materials, depending on what grew nearby. Indians of the Northwest Coast made much of their work from spruce roots, and Southeastern people chose cane, reeds, and palmetto fronds. Other important materials were vines, grasses, and slender strips or twigs of wood. The two techniques in this craft were coiling and weaving. Woven baskets had a background of one set of parallel fibers, through which the craftsman wove other fibers crosswise. The coiled basket was built up in a spiral. (See pages 184 and 185).

Indians made some containers large enough to hold an adult and some so small that the weave was almost invisible. The latter probably were toys. Some basketmakers left their materials a natural color; others dyed theirs. To make a pattern, women wove in dyed or naturally colored fibers. Northwest Coast weavers painted some of their designs. Pomo basketmakers were famous for their work decorated with bird feathers and tiny shells or beads. Though experts give the Pomo credit for the most intricate and skillful work, other people of California, the Great Basin, and the Southwest produced very fine basket work.

A twined bag (height, 12 inches). The design depicts the human form in stick-figure technique. The upper figures are male; the lower two are female.

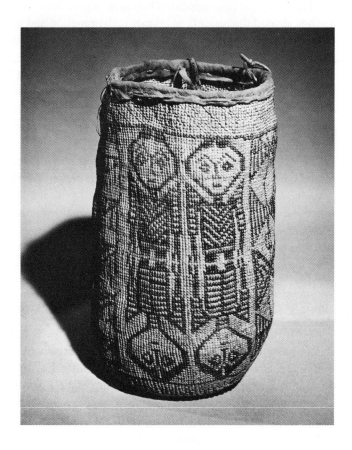

Western basketmakers often used their baskets for stone boiling, which required very tightly woven containers. Some of these could hold water even without further treatment, but for better waterproofing the women often coated their cooking baskets with pitch and asphaltum where they could get it.

Painting, Dyes, and Pigments

Indians applied color and designs to their persons, their clothes, their homes, and their tools. On their bodies, paint was both decorative and functional; it might indicate social connections, warlike intent, or great deeds. Men painted their shields with symbols of their guardian spirits and their tipis with designs telling of their success in hunting and warfare. In the Pacific Northwest, the painted and carved crest figures usually described family connections. Painting on pottery, katcina masks, and dolls in the Southwest often represented rain, clouds, and sun.

Indians applied paint with their hands or fingers, with sticks, and with crude brushes made of twigs or fibrous material chewed or pounded at one end until pliable. Sometimes they took paint in their mouths and sprayed it on. Plains people often used a piece of bone spongy enough to hold paint and sharpened to make a fine line. For paint containers, people often used shells, where they could find them, and the Pueblo made little clay pots.

Indians made their colors from plants and minerals. For paint pigments, they used inorganic materials. They got red, yellow, and browns from earth containing iron ore, black from soot or graphite, white from clay, limestone, and gypsum, and green and blue from copper ore. The artist ground the pigments on mortars and mixed them with grease or saliva. Dyes came from organic sources: brown and red from roots and barks, white and yellow from grasses and rushes, and others from berries and lichens. They used dyes to color quills, basket materials, yarns, and fabrics.

Textiles

In addition to hides and furs, people in some areas wore clothing made of woven fabrics. Indians made yarn for weaving from plant fibers like the inner bark of cedar and other trees, or, in the Southwest, cotton. They also used wool from buffalo, mountain goats, dogs, and other animals. Women did most of the weaving, though Pueblo men also wove. Only the Pueblo had a real loom; the other weavers merely suspended threads from a horizontal bar (perhaps stretched between two trees) and twined other yarns over and under. The foun-

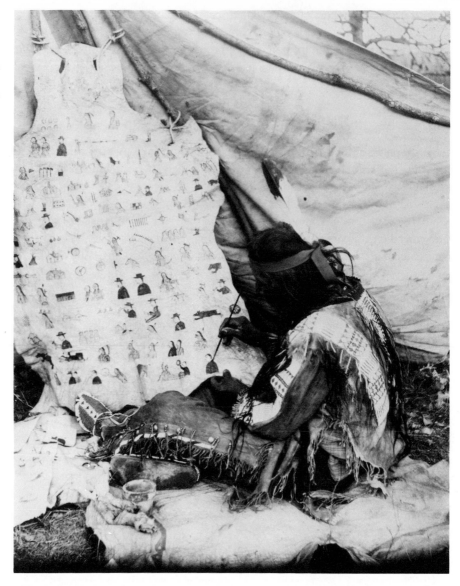

An Indian painting his tipi with designs most likely showing his prowess in hunting and warfare.

dation yarns (those hanging vertically from the bar) are called the *warp* yarns; the weaving yarns are called the *weft* yarns. Often the two were of the same material. Chilkat weavers on the Northwest Coast used warp yarns of cedar bark and weft yarns of mountain goat hair; the Great Basin people used warp of plant fiber and weft of strips of rabbit skin to make their rabbit blankets.

Weavers created patterns in their weaving by using dyed yarns rather than by changing the weave, which varied little in their woven products. In the Southeast, people sometimes used bird feathers to decorate their cloth of *bast* (inner bark). Chilkat blankets and skirts were woven work of great beauty, worn only by high-ranking individuals on special occasions. Pueblo Indians alone wore woven fabrics as their daily clothing. The Navajo learned weaving from the Pueblo. After they acquired sheep from the Spaniards, Navajo women began to spin sheep wool and weave their well-known blankets.

Toys

To amuse and quiet infants, parents made toys like rattles and objects hung from the cradle. Older children played with miniature copies of adult implements—bows, dolls, and sleds. Today these toys might be classified as educational, for the children learned some adult practices by playing. Even the toy katcina doll taught the children about the kinds of katcina spirits (see page 226). Of course, like all children, the young Indians also invented their own toys.

The Eskimo, with their long winter isolation, made more toys than any other native Americans. Their children played with toy boats, sleds, weapons, carved dolls and animals, and household utensils. Eskimo carved dolls and animals from wood, ivory, bone, and stone, often clothing dolls in furs and making beds, lamps, and other doll furniture. Children in all areas also played with toys like building blocks, balls, and tops, made from the native materials of their region.

Dramatic Arts

Every ceremonial presentation had its dramatic aspects. It is nearly impossible to separate what we would call the performing arts from the ritu-als in which they were imbedded. Regular patterns of movement, music, and recitation appeared in many ceremonies, but nonreligious drama, like plays, pantomimes, or operas, did not exist in pre-Columbian times, and neither did professional actors. Perhaps the closest any Indian groups came to our theater was the winter performances on the Northwest Coast, re-creations of clan and tribal legends in song and dance, with some spoken parts. These also included elaborate costumes greatly valued by their owners. Pueblo ceremonies in the open plaza also had expressive episodes, with dancers representing spirits, clowns, and heroes. Here too the dramatic effects were heightened by costumes, paint, and masks. Many Southwestern societies performed dances in public, including the very popular clowns or "delight makers."

Dance and Music

Like drama, dancing and music were an inseparable part of the military, religious, or social activities directed toward community welfare or personal glory. Unlike European dances, which are often a means of personal expression and social interaction, Indian dances were dictated by tradition and were mainly symbolic. Group dances, performed in a circle or oval, were the most common form in the Southwest, prairies, and woodlands, and straight-line dancing was popular in the Plains, Basin, and Plateau. The rhythmic gestures and movements of dancing varied from Pueblo dancing, which was slow, almost hypnotic, to the Plains kind, which sometimes approached frenzy. Some dances were only for one sex, and some were performed by just one dancer. Sometimes special clothing or costumes were required.

Dancing was usually accompanied by percussion instruments and chanting, the main form of Indian music. There were no purely instrumental performances, and no harmony singing or playing. Drums, rasps, rattles, and clappers were common, but the only Indian instrument that could play a melody was the flute or flageolet. This was used mostly for courting: a young man played love songs on it when he went wooing by blowing into one end and controlling the tones with finger holes.

Folklore

Indians had no written literature; their myths, legends, tales, and fables were passed down orally by each generation. Like the other arts, folklore played an important part in daily existence, reflecting the people's concerns and problems. In the absence of science as we know it, folklore explained the mysteries of life: why people die, why evil exists, and how nature works. It described the beginnings of the world and the creation of people and animals. It told about a tribe's origin and history, and the great deeds of their people. In addition, some tales had morals that showed what happened when someone did not observe the proper ways of his people. Such tales performed part of the function we call *socialization,* teaching children the traditional, proper behavior. And of course many stories were just entertainment, humorous tales to make people laugh, or adventure stories about some culture hero.

A rasp and a flute. To play the rasp a musician dug a small hole in the ground in front of him and placed the circular basket upside down over it. The pointed end of the rasp was placed top-center on the basket; the cylinder end was held in the musician's left hand. Sound was produced by running the scraper back and forth over the notched surface of the rasp. The basket and hole acted as an amplifier-resonator.

Characters in Folklore. While some folklore themes or characters stayed within one language group or culture area, many crossed cultural and linguistic boundaries, and some were almost universal. People everywhere told stories about animals, wise and powerful or weak and foolish. Most Indian societies also handed down fables about giants, little people, and witches. A common character was the trickster, who deflated the pompous and did many things forbidden to human beings. He provided not only comic relief from life's trials but a chance for vicarious enjoyment; listeners naturally sympathized with the way the trickster flouted social conventions. Often tricksters were animals: Coyote, Blue-jay, Raven, Hare, and Mink were among the most prominent. Bodies of legends about these beings are called "trickster tales." In the legends beginning the chapters of Part II, you have read of some tricksters: Coyote, Inktomi, and Manabozho (Chippewa) or Manabush (Menominee). In New England, the trickster was Gluskap or Kluskabe; and the Cree trickster was Wisagatcak, which Europeans mispronounced Whiskey Jack. Probably the popularity of trickster tales is the most characteristic feature of Indian oral tradition.

Another common figure was the Earth Diver, an animal (usually) who helped create the world. Earth Diver legends told about how the world began as a piece of earth or mud brought up from an endless sea that was all of existence. (See the legends on pages 164 and 165.) Usually Earth Diver gave his soil or mud to the culture hero, sometimes called Creator, sometimes Earth Maker. Occasionally Earth Diver himself created the world.

In many legends, Indians portrayed the culture hero not as an animal but as a human figure, a demigod or superman who put the world in its present state. Often Indian tales blended the hero with the trickster, showing him sometimes as human, sometimes as animal. Manabozho, Gluskap, and others appeared both wise and foolish, just as man does, at different times.

Folklore Themes. Parts of native American folklore were common to many areas, but culture areas did have their own typical themes and figures. Eskimo tales were less varied than those of most other peoples. The tale of the goddess Sedna, who created the sea mammals from her fingers, was told by most Eskimo groups, but there were few other Eskimo stories. Plateau people emphasized trickster pranks and mischief in their folklore—Coyote was trickster throughout the Plateau—and as you might guess, Northwest tales had much to say about social rank and proper behavior. The trickster theme also was popular there, and so were stories about sea mammals and salmon. Gluttony was a popular trickster motif along the Pacific Coast. The long winters and normally adequate food gave time for not only the clan dramas and winter ceremonials, but also much storytelling. California folklore was meager, like the Eskimo's, and focused on trickster and creation mythology, especially the Earth Diver theme.

All types of stories were told in the Plains, probably because of the peoples' varied backgrounds, and also in the Eastern woodlands, both north and south. Iroquois tales often dealt with cruel relatives, cannibalism, and monsters, as well as with creation. Twins, one good and one bad, were the Iroquois culture heroes. The Southeastern people emphasized animal tales of the Uncle Remus sort, with animals that behaved like people and plots with a moral (see pages 314 and 315). Southwestern people told many long and complicated stories of creation with many characters rising from lower worlds. The Subarctic Algonkians shared the legends of the other Algonkians, and the Subarctic Athabaskans tended to borrow their folklore from whatever cultures were nearest.

Among the agriculturalists, stories about how Indians got corn, beans, and squash were very common, and hunting peoples leaned toward story plots involving the dangers and problems of the hunt.

Religious Beliefs

Ideas about the supernatural were part of every aspect of Indian life. People looked for supernatural assistance in everyday doings as well as in life's crises. Hunters wanted spirit aid for success in hunting, agriculturalists for good crops, warriors for victory in battle. That much we know. But we have difficulty reconstructing pre-Columbian beliefs and practices, and the earliest written material comes to us from people who misconstrued what they saw and heard. For example, the idea of a sole god or "The Great Spirit" was simply incorrect interpretation on the part of observers. No groups in America north of the Rio Grande had such a monotheistic belief system. "The Happy Hunting Ground" was another popular fallacy Europeans ascribed to Indians.

Supernaturals of many sorts filled the Indian world. Some, like Sedna of the Eskimo, were gods and goddesses. Others were semidivines or demigods, culture heroes like Manabozho of the Algonkians. And then there were spirits of fields, trees, lakes, and other aspects of nature. Some Indians named these spirits, some did not. It is difficult for us to grasp how people felt in societies where every act and event had supernatural significance. To the Indians, the world of nature was alive with spirits, and generally superior to the human world. Spirits could withhold food and goods if people behaved badly, and could reward them for patience and perseverance.

Supernatural Power

Almost all Indian peoples believed in a general power beyond the spirits, a force in the universe that has been likened to electricity. It was impersonal; it ran throughout nature; and it could be tapped if one had the right knowledge and equipment. This was the force or power that the individual usually sought on the vision quest. But rarely is it clear exactly what difference Indians saw between this natural force and specific spirits. Perhaps they were never clear about it themselves, for they were quite practical and sought help from all sources. And they had no way of recording ideas of any tribal philosophers who may have thought about the nature of the supernatural. The Indian attitude toward supernatural aid seems to have been that if one type was good, more were better, and there were no hard and fast categories.

Though people throughout native America believed in a generalized world force, the words for it varied: Algonkians called it *manitu,* the Siouan, *wakonda,* and the Iroquoian, *orenda.* Other linguistic groups had their own terms, but the idea was the same: there was general power more potent than man. Some groups may have believed in power, spirit, and deity condensed into one being that early European observers recorded as the Great Manitu, but we really do not know how much of that was Indian and how much came from Europeans hoping to find Indian parallels to Christian beliefs.

Although we find no evidence of monotheism, some tribes seem to have had high gods or more important gods as well as lesser beings and the idea of a general world force. The Pawnee deity, Tirawa, lived in the upper sky above the Winds, the Sun, and the Stars, all of which were spirits. Tirawa had given everything necessary to mankind when he created the earth with the help of his fellow spirits, the four Air Powers: Wind, Cloud, Lightning, and Thunder. Stars looked after mankind and each was a patron of a Pawnee village. The Pawnee believed the offspring of the union between the warrior Morning Star and his mate, Evening Star, was a human girl, and the offspring of the Sun and the Moon was a human boy. They were the first human beings. The Pawnee thus believed in many supernatural beings besides Tirawa; they clearly were not monotheistic.

Another body of religious beliefs found throughout native American societies concerned physical and psychological conditions of human beings. Indians recognized that some kinds of disability, like broken bones and wounds, had natural causes, but they believed that many of the body's ills came from either the spirit world or witchcraft. Individuals could do little to prevent illness caused by witchcraft, but the right observances could keep them in good grace with the supernatural and prevent disease from that source. Therefore Indians carefully observed the tribal taboos, of which those associated with food and sex were most common; probably every tribe had some kind of food that was taboo.

Souls

Indians also believed in soul sickness, arising from loss or theft of the soul. If a victim did not recover his soul, he died. After death, according to some groups, the soul went to a western land or land of the ancestors. This afterworld was a dull place, a pallid copy of life, or a reverse image of life—by no means a "Happy Hunting Ground."

Algonkians conceived of the soul as a shadow; the Shasta thought it was invisible but could leave a trail and footprints. Omaha believed it glided through the air, and Bella Coola and Tsimshian thought of it as a bird or butterfly. Belief that the souls of the dead appeared as owls was fairly widespread. And many tribes believed in two souls, one that died when the body died, and one that might wander on, though it too might die. Some groups, like the Eskimo, believed in multiple souls. In some areas the soul of a dead person—the ghost—was greatly feared, for it tried to seek out the living, for whom it was lonely, and take them away. Even while they mourned for their dead, those people pleaded with the ghosts to go and stay away.

Religious Behavior

In almost all areas of America, Indian men and some women sought individual power. This was true regardless of what religious specialists their community might have, for personal power was essential for almost every endeavor. At the mercy of capricious nature, people knew that death from hunger, disease, or enemies was never far away; to survive, they felt a need for some powerful assistance. Calling the search for this help the vision quest may be misleading; in many culture areas, people could get power without having a vision. Most often, though, power did come through a vision.

Visions and Personal Power

Visions came usually in the form of animals, but occasionally as sun, stars, or other natural objects. The vision indicated that one had gained power through a personal protector, a guardian spirit that would protect the seeker and give him spiritual power. Usually one made contact with a spirit by acts of purification—bathing, sweating, fasting, vomiting—until the body and mind were clean and acceptable to the supernatural. Adolescent boys sometimes worked physically to make themselves receptive to a guardian spirit by dancing, self-flagellation, mutilation, or swallowing or inhaling drugs. At important times or crises in adulthood, people used the same ways of getting in touch with the spirit world. The power they received gave them special abilities in hunting, warfare, acquiring wealth, or reaching any goals they might desire.

The vision quest was by far the most popular way of getting power, but not the only one. The Blackfoot bought power in medicine bundles that contained powerful medicine (that is, sacred objects and charms), and sometimes charms and incantations were enough to bend the supernatural to one's will. Incantations acted upon the spirit world with compulsive force, if one adhered rigidly to the proper form. When incantations did not work, Indians blamed a lapse of memory or slip of the tongue. Beseeching the deities with prayer and pleas was another way of communicating. Prayers were more commonly addressed to animal, weather, and general spirits and deities than to the impersonal power, though one might approach it too in that way.

Religious Specialists

When one could not get results by personal contacts, it was time to call in religious specialists. Everywhere in native America there were shamans who could communicate with the supernatural easily and who usually had several personal spirits or "familiars." Along with shamans, the Pueblo and some other groups had priests. Whereas shamans got their power by direct contact with the supernatural, priests' powers came from formal training. Shamans might have some training as apprentices to old shamans, and priests might have visions, but the priests got their power from education rather than the personal religious experiences that were the essence of the shaman's power.

Shamans. The word *shaman* comes from Tungus, the language of the Tungus, a Siberian tribe well known for its shamanism. Both men and women were shamans, though in most societies women were not eligible until after menopause. The other names we use for shamans—medicine men, witch doctors, rainmakers, curers—indicate the wide range of shamanistic duties. The shaman's general ability to contact the spirit world meant that he was important and powerful almost everywhere, because people needed him and sought his advice. And since he could manipulate the supernatural, the shaman was often feared. The line between using the spirit world to benefit society and using it for selfish or antisocial purposes was narrow, and shamans often were suspected of witchcraft.

The shaman's greatest responsibility probably was curing. It was mainly the diseases thought to have supernatural causes that shamans treated, though most shamans had good knowledge of medicinal herbs and often treated problems like constipation and nausea as well. Supernatural disease had two causes: either it had been put into the body in the form of some object like a stone or stick by the supernatural or by a witch, or the soul had been lost or stolen. The shaman had to remove the object causing the illness or retrieve the soul. Sucking, through a straw or other implement or by placing the lips directly on the body, was the usual technique for removing the foreign object that brought sickness. The shaman usually concealed something in his mouth to spit out at the end of his performance, showing that the cure had been effective. Sometimes he bit his tongue and spit out a little blood too. To bring back a soul, people believed the shaman somehow sent his own soul or one of his spirits to recover it. Shamans performed these cures accompanied by chanting, drumming, dancing, tobacco smoking, and the like, usually with a number of people watching. The shaman often called for confessions from the patient, which would not cure germ-produced disease or organic disabilities but was very effective on psychosomatic disorders, because it reduced tension and relieved anxiety.

A Blackfoot medicine man. The painting on his face, necklace, and decorations on his fur hat all relate to his magical power.

Among all the curers, perhaps none was more aptly called a medicine man than the Navajo shaman. His cures took days and involved not only the usual activities but also preparing elaborate dry paintings. Navajo were more interested in bodily states than most other native peoples, and a curing ceremony always drew a large crowd of spectators.

In larger tribes, shamans tended to specialize: some treated with dreams, some sucked out disease, and some did little curing but emphasized weather control and predicting the future. In the small groups, one or two shamans took care of all needs including treatment with herbal remedies, setting broken bones, and cleaning wounds.

Payments for shamanistic services varied, and they were usually returned if the treatment did not work. Occasionally shamans were killed when a patient failed to recover.

Shamans often required the patient to appease the supernatural or make amends for his behavior, since much sickness was the patient's own fault for not observing taboos. Offenders atoned with both confession and punishment, appeasing the spirits with body mutilation and dietary restrictions. Confession of guilt, usually in public, was common among the Eskimo and Iroquois, and was often followed by mild punishments such as fasting or purging. On the Plains, making a vow to perform a ceremony was an accepted way of atoning for transgressions.

Shamanistic practices on the North American continent probably varied less than almost any other aspect of religion, but there were a few regional differences. In the Northwest, where rank was so important, some shamans inherited their power and combined religious functions with civil power by being house or town chiefs. The Hupa of California had a dancing shaman who located the cause of disease and a sucking shaman who cured it. Mojave shamans received their power by dreaming, as did many in California, and the Delaware also had dreamers who foretold the future. Eskimo shamans, besides curing, foretold weather conditions and located whales, seals, and other food animals. Shamans often went along on war parties even though war leaders were always expected to have their own power. Shamans were also very important politically in most tribes, partly because they were feared as well as respected. Shamans were least important among the Pueblo, where any undue individualism was suspect, and they were relatively unimportant in the Plains and the Plateau, where every man—and many women in the Plateau—sought spirit power and communicated often with the supernatural.

Priests.   Priests are specialists in group ritual, and priests in Indian societies organized and directed major tribal ceremonies. They acted not as individuals, like shamans, but as representatives of the tribe. Priests were most common in larger societies with elaborate religious systems. The Iroquois Keepers of the Faith, who were responsible for six major ceremonies each year, were typical priests. The most highly organized priesthoods developed among the Pueblo, but healing associations such as the Algonkian Midewiwin can be classified as priesthoods, and on the Northwest Coast the town or tribal chiefs performed priestly functions in the ceremonials. The Creek of the Southeast had town priests influential in civil and military affairs, and the Great Sun of the Natchez was considered a divinity, high priest of the tribe, and a descendant of the sun. The priesthoods actually controlled civil and military affairs among the Pueblo, whose government may be considered a theocracy.

It was their formal training in religious duties and ceremonial roles that separated priests from shamans. Also, priests often did not have personal contact with the supernatural. The length of training for ritual performances varied. The Midewiwin organization of the Western Great Lakes tribes was set up in degrees, and only a few ever attained the fourth degree in the Midewiwin hierarchy. Creek priests attended a school where they were trained in the necessary lore and sent out for direct contact with the spirit world. The Creek had three degrees of proficiency, and the war leaders and high priests for town ceremonies were chosen only from those who had reached the third degree.

All these ways of reaching the spirit world may seem ambiguous, and the many categories of spirit beings and types of religious behavior may look contradictory and overlapping, but Indians saw no inconsistency. They thought it only sensible to try every possible way of getting help.

Religious Ceremonies

The ceremonies in North America that we will consider are those that lasted for a day or more and had to do with the supernatural—not social ceremonies such as athletic events and puberty rituals or short medical ceremonies. Hunters and gatherers held ceremonies mostly for success in the hunt, plentiful wild-plant foods, and fertile game animals. Agriculturalists celebrated the crops, particularly corn, and controlled the weather. The famous rain dance was not one but many dances performed by Indians of dry lands to bring rain. In the Southeast, controlling weather meant more than bringing rain, for flood control was also important. Major ceremonies generally had something to do with the most important source of food. Most areas also had ceremonies for general well-being, world renewal, and thanksgiving, many of which were incorporated in the longer tribal ceremonials.

The whole tribe took part in some ceremonies; others belonged to an association or secret society. Some too were part public and part private. Many dances were performed for the entire community and were followed by private rites for members of the society sponsoring the affair, or for men of special rank or social status like chiefs and shamans. Almost always combinations of activities went on simultaneously—dancing, drumming, singing, prayer, recitation. Most ceremonies took place outdoors, but the Pueblo held many in the kiva, their ceremonial chamber. In other areas, special structures were raised for the occasion, like the lodge for the Sun Dance on the Plains. Many ceremonies called for long purification of those taking part before and after as well as during performances. Some ceremonies were held regularly at appointed times, like the solstice ceremonies of the Hopi, but others were held only when an individual vowed to give a performance—the Cheyenne Sun Dance, for instance. Others were held any time a contact with the supernatural seemed advisable.

Regional Rituals

The Arctic, Subarctic, Plateau, and Basin lacked the formal, lengthy ritual life that is truly ceremonial. There populations were sparse, and rites focused on individual rather than community occasions. Plains people had many ceremonies for tribal and personal well-being and to celebrate the life of the hunter, the most spectacular and widely performed being the Sun Dance. Some tribes gave an annual performance during the summer hunt when all the bands had assembled, while others held it only to fulfill a vow. The Sun Dance had common features everywhere: special preparation of the lodge or tipi, its ceremonial raising, dancing lasting one to four days. For almost all who observed it, the total period of the Sun Dance was eight days. Dancers blew whistles in many performances, and voluntary self-laceration was common in some groups. Other Plains ceremonies were held by the warrior or men's societies or, in a few tribes, women's societies.

In the Southwest, the Pueblo had almost endless ceremonial life—more than a hundred days out of each year, by one estimate. Part of almost every Pueblo ceremony took place in private in the kiva of the religious society officiating. Initiation into the societies was an important part of Pueblo ceremonial life. Pueblo ceremonials were rich in symbols of rain, clouds, and thunder.

The Navajo and Apache had extended curing ceremonies directed by shamans, and elaborate public girls' puberty ceremonies attended by masked dancers. These rituals were complicated and elaborate, with dry paintings, chanting, masks, and dancing, but they were not held with seasonal regularity like the great Plains or Pueblo ceremonials, and they were directed more toward individual health and well-being than the food quest or tribal life.

In California, extended ceremonies were tribal mourning observances or initiations into shamans' cults, first-fruit celebrations, world-renewal ceremonies, or performances for general well-being.

Northwest Coast peoples had many long, elaborate ceremonies, generally performed by cults or societies. One very important winter presentation, which

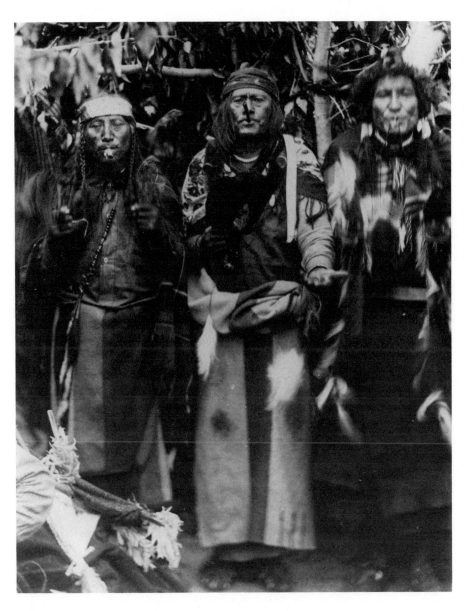

The three Indians shown here blow eagle-bone whistles as part of a Sun Dance ritual to ensure good weather during the ceremony. The Indian on the right wears a wreath of juniper or sage; the Indian in the center has a plume hanging from the little finger of each hand.

re-created myths in song and dance, was a chance for high-ranking individuals to prove their rights to social status. Almost all Northwest Coast performances had something to do with social rank. People there used more costumes than most others and carved very elaborate masks.

Major ceremonials in the East were for agriculture, good crops, good weather, and thankfulness for bounty from the spirit world. The Busk or Green Corn Dance was widely performed.

Sacrifice

Indians sacrificed to all kinds of supernaturals—spirits, deities, the sky, the sun, the four (or six) cardinal points, and the stars. They also sacrificed to the winds, thunder, mountains, various manitu, and personal medicine bundles and guardian spirits. Dead ancestors and relatives often were presented with gifts. In return for their sacrifice people expected to receive benefits and escape evils. Sacrifice pleased the supernatural, which responded by giving people food and good health, good weather, and success in war. Most sacrifices were individual: they might involve tossing bits of food into fires for the spirits, adding rocks to piles, or offering first fruits. War leaders made sacrifices before an expedition, throwing food in the fire or blowing tobacco smoke into the air. Shamans prescribed sacrifice to cure illness. However, there were some tribal sacrifices in which many people took part, such as the Iroquois communal White Dog Ceremony, in which a white dog was sacrificed.

Tobacco was by far the most common sacrificial offering. People smoked it in pipes or tubes and also offered it loose. The smoke was considered a gift to the supernatural. Food, clothing, and adornment were also sacrificed, and, less often, hunting and fishing equipment. Like the Iroquois, the Illinois, Cree, Ottawa, and others sacrificed dogs; in buffalo country, the skin of a white buffalo was an acceptable offering. Skins of bears, too, were offered, and sometimes game animals like deer, elk, and moose. In the Southwest, the Pueblo, Navajo, and Apache sprinkled corn meal on the ground.

A warrior's self-mutilation was a kind of sacrifice—giving a piece of himself such as a finger or a strip of skin—but the only regular human sacrifice was offered by the Pawnee to the Morning Star. They tied up a captive woman and slew her with arrows, sending the symbolic Evening Star (the victim) to seek her husband, the Morning Star. Perhaps the Iroquois' torture and killing of war captives was a kind of sacrifice, for those victims often were dedicated to the supernatural, but revenge really was a stronger motive there. Wives of the Great Sun and some of his servants were killed when he died, which might also be considered a kind of sacrifice.

To sacrifice a game animal, people killed it, then burned it on a fire, often removing it partially burned to eat the remains. People also made sacrifices by putting objects like foods and gifts on poles, in trees, or on rocks. A gift of that sort might calm any supernatural who was angry with human behavior.

Religious Paraphernalia

Tobacco. Though Indians smoked tobacco for enjoyment, it was primarily a ritual item. Besides smoking it, they often burned it like incense, or blew powdered tobacco into the air as an offering. Sometimes they blew puffs of smoke specifically toward the supernatural; sometimes they offered the stem of the pipe to the four cardinal points and up and down. Tobacco was in many ways a sacred plant, grown by hunters and gatherers who cultivated no other crops and grown only by men where women were farmers. In one form or another it was essential in many curing ceremonies; Indians believed it would cure disease and wounds, prevent hunger and thirst, and stimulate the weary. Sometimes they ate it as an anesthetic, as the Great Sun's wives and servants did before being sacrificed.

Sacred Objects. From wing bones men fashioned the whistles they blew during the Sun Dance, and they considered eagle and bear claws to be powerful charms. Eagles and bears symbolized nature's power, mystery, and majesty, and Indians worshiped them across the continent. Bones and claws were useful, but feathers and down were most important. They symbolized a warrior's deeds or coups; they were attached to masks, rattles, and prayer sticks for ceremonial occasions; and down was scattered in the air or sprinkled on costumes in ceremonies.

Many tribes had their own sacred objects in addition to the sacred items common to many. The Pueblo and some other groups used *prayer sticks* to honor or appeal to spirits. These were decked with feathers, plumes, or down to convey prayers to the supernatural, and with small packets of food or tobacco as offerings. The Kiowa of the southern Plains had a small stone image called *taime,* which vaguely resembled the head and shoulders of a man and was decorated with down, feathers, and images of the sun and moon. They kept it in a parfleche and exposed it only once a year at the Sun Dance. The four Medicine Arrows of the Cheyenne were sacred, and the Arapaho had a special flat pipe that was kept by a priest with an ear of corn and a stone turtle in a bundle opened only on special occasions. Warriors' own medicine bundles held supernatural power and symbols of their guardian spirits.

Charms or fetishes were objects that possessed power and brought luck and

success. Like rabbits' feet and four-leaf clovers, they were thought to enable the
owner to accomplish more than he would otherwise. Some peoples, like the
Zuni and Eskimo, manufactured them, carving animal forms of wood, rock, or
ivory. Other charms were natural objects such as bear claws and eagle feathers.
Charms found at the site of a vision were thought to have been given by the
guardian spirit. Some were gifts, others were taken from a slain enemy,
but in the owners' minds, fetishes had some connection with supernatural
power.

Masks. Masks were worn in many religious ceremonies, sometimes only by
priests and shamans, sometimes by all participants, because they were supposed
to intensify the presence of the supernatural. Some masks were merely prepared heads of buffalo, deer, or other animals, and some were very complex
with movable parts, of which the finest were made on the Northwest Coast. A
mask gave its wearer the qualities of the thing it represented, and it was usually
sacred in its own right. Masks were made only after the craftsman had attended
to purification and other rituals, and they were put away carefully after use. Hopi

and Apache were renowned for their masks in the Southwest, and the Iroquois for their false faces and cornhusk masks in the East.

In most areas, the wearer made his own mask, though Pueblo masks were clan property. Pueblo passed their masks and other ceremonial paraphernalia from generation to generation, making new ones only when the old wore out. But the Northwest Coast was an area of specialists, and there craftsmen made masks for others.

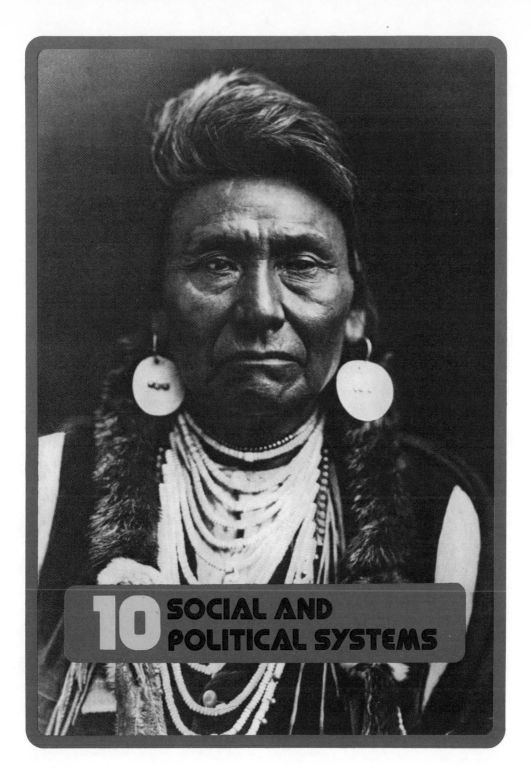

10 SOCIAL AND POLITICAL SYSTEMS

Everywhere human beings organize into groups, for human survival depends on cooperation with others. From the moment of birth, which places us in our first kinship group, we live our lives in social groups. In Indian societies, as in ours, social groups got the work done, devised and carried out ways to exploit the environment, supplied new members to society, taught those new members the traditional ways of doing things, and protected and fed all members. Kinship was the tie that formed the most important Indian groups, but these were supplemented by organizations based on common interests, occupation, social status, sex, age, and neighborhood or locality. Sometimes Indians ranked their social groups, like the Natchez classes and the Northwest Coast kin groups.

Marriage

Marriage was the beginning of a new family, and it also formed or cemented alliances between families because it bound kinfolk as much as it did the man and woman. Always some people were kept apart by the incest

Preceding page: Chief Joseph, leader of the Nez Perce in the 1877 conflict, was the son of a Nez Perce mother and a Cayuse father.

Ute couple. The man is wearing a hair-pipe breastplate, cartridge belt, breech-clout, and anklet. The woman is wearing a beautifully decorated pouch called a "bandolier bag" over her shoulder.

taboo: the society banned their sexual union because of their kinship. Parents, children, and siblings (that is, brothers and sisters) could not marry each other, nor could any cousins who called each other "brother" and "sister." In addition, wherever people had clans, they almost always observed clan exogamy—no one could marry anyone in his own clan. Tribes that were divided into two moieties usually practiced moiety exogamy. In a very few cases, residents observed village exogamy.

Most societies were very permissive about premarital sexual experiences, with a few exceptions. The Cheyenne prized female virginity and marital faithfulness, and the Northwest Coast people, especially those in the higher ranks, carefully guarded marriageable females to ensure their virginity at marriage. By far the greater number of peoples considered premarital sexual relations a normal and expectable experience.

Arranging a Marriage

Guided by the group's prohibitions, one chose a spouse, usually in consultation with parents and other kinfolk, who helped make a wise decision. If kin opposed the choice too vigorously, the couple could elope, but apparently that seldom happened.

Throughout pre-Columbian America, marriage was a civil matter, not a religious one. It rarely involved any ceremony, except for the upper ranks of the Northwest Coast and the chieftains of the Southeast. In most areas the couple, with family approval, decided to live together, and the rest of the people recognized them as married, though people did not always consider the marriage truly established until a child was born.

Bridewealth.   In the Plains and the Northwest, a marriage was not completed until the man presented a gift to the parents of the woman he wished to marry. That gift, called bridewealth or brideprice, was not a way of buying a wife but an acknowledgment that the parents were losing a daughter's services and should be compensated for that loss and for their time and effort in raising her. Bridewealth also established the rights of the man's kin line to the children of the marriage. Girls of high-ranking families brought the best bridewealth. As you would expect, horses were the bridewealth on the Plains, while cedar blankets, carved boxes, dentalia, and other goods were given on the Northwest Coast.

Elsewhere a man might make gifts to his wife's parents, but bridewealth was not so well defined or strictly required as in the Plains and Northwest. A Comanche woman expected her son-in-law to bring her a good portion of his game, and while there were no formal rules about it, people would have looked down upon any young man who did not fulfill this obligation.

Marriage was economically important for more than bridewealth and service; it joined the production efforts of man and woman. One person alone could not hunt, gather, cook, make clothing and tools, and protect himself, and without paid help, marriage was the best way of binding people for exchange of labor and mutual protection.

Residence. After marriage, the couple had to set up a home, sometimes moving into or near an existing household. The Iroquois man moved into his wife's longhouse; Hopi men and other Western Pueblo also moved in with their wives. Many times, women moved to join their husbands' households, or the couple might set up a new residence, though always in a community where one or the other had relatives. It was very unusual for a couple not to have some kinfolk nearby. Many families moved over the years, sometimes living with or near the man's kin, sometimes the woman's. No culture area had an unvarying residence pattern.

Affection and Divorce. Love had little to do with marriage, but husbands and wives expected that years of raising children and facing domestic problems together would make them fond of each other even if they felt little affection at the beginning. If a marriage proved unworkable, divorce was an acceptable way out, and in most areas one or the other spouse easily began the divorce simply by moving out of their common home. People separated for such reasons as sterility, laziness, lack of support, physical abuse, or incompatibility. Some groups, such as the Cheyenne, considered adultery immediate grounds for divorce, but others did not unless the adultery was frequent and flagrant. Bridewealth made divorce more complicated, because the girl's parents had to return the gifts unless the husband was obviously at fault. Among some matrilineal people, any woman who no longer wished to be married made a bundle of her husband's possessions and placed it outside the home. Seeing what she had done, he would take his things and return to his mother's home. Divorces usually required no more formality than marriage, and children of the marriage almost always stayed with their mother.

Polygamy

Most societies allowed *polygamy* (multiple marriage), though monogamy predominated everywhere. *Polygyny* (having more than one wife) occurred among all peoples except the Iroquois and the Western Pueblo, but few men could afford more than one wife even where custom allowed it. Even on the Plains after the horse came, where polygyny was most common, few men had more than four or five wives. *Polyandry* (having more than one husband) was very rare, occurring mostly among Eskimo and Basin people, where a woman might be married to two brothers. Some experts believe that even the Eskimo did not have true polyandry; they think that occasionally an older man would allow his younger brother sexual access to his wife, but only the older brother was married to her.

Sometimes polygyny followed the death of a spouse. Among all societies except those prohibiting polygyny, the practice of wife inheritance might lead to multiple marriage: a widow married her dead husband's brother, even if he already had a wife. In some places this practice was optional, in others it was mandatory. Another marriage custom in almost all tribes was somewhat similar, though it did not lead to multiple marriage: a widower often expected to receive a sister of his dead wife as a spouse. Both of these customs protected the single person, especially in environments where living alone meant almost certain death. When a dead spouse had no brothers or sisters, cousins took these roles. These practices emphasize how economically vital marriage was; the two sexes needed each other for much more than just sexual gratification.

It was not at all unusual among the Plains tribes for men to get wives by capturing them in warfare. Women captives were generally married by their captors, but most warriors married women of their own tribe first. Captives thus became secondary wives with low status, often no more than servants for the first or head wife.

The Family

Among the American Indians the family did most of the educating of the young and held the main responsibility for child rearing and welfare. In the very few societies that had formal schools, the schools provided training only for ritual positions. Within the family children learned to talk and to behave in approved ways; family life socialized children into adulthood. Parents, older siblings, and other relatives taught children etiquette, domestic duties, ceremonial behavior, craftsmanship, ways of getting food, and how to use weapons. Grandparents usually passed on folklore and tribal tradition.

The economic functions of marriage included the family as well; members pooled their labor and shared economic responsibility. Adults took care of the young, women by providing domestic care and men through hunting and defense. The extended family sheltered the aged, who in turn helped with child care and education.

The Indian family took several forms. The basic unit was the *nuclear family,* a

A Southwest family group beside a dwelling made of brush. The different designs painted on their cheeks denote different families.

man and woman and their children. Larger than the nuclear family was the *extended family,* which included another generation (that is, grandparents) or more wives. Another form was a group of sisters or brothers living together with their spouses and children, like the Iroquois longhouse family, with sisters and their husbands and children living in the same building. A true extended family was permanent; the people all lived together as a regular thing. All these types of family were found in aboriginal America, and almost all communities had some form of extended family.

Adoption

Children who had lost one or both parents and illegitimate children usually found a home with kinfolk who raised them as their own. War captives, particularly women and children, were often adopted too. Even adult male captives might be adopted to replace a dead family member, becoming faithful sons to their new parents though formerly they had been enemies.

Some tribes adopted members not only into families but into clans. A child or an adult adopted by an Iroquois family assumed not only the family connection but also the clan affiliation. On the other hand, among the Seminole, a child adopted into a family kept his biological mother's clan affiliation (Seminole were matrilineal).

Occasionally, whole groups were adopted. When the Tuscarora tribe moved north, the Oneida suggested to the League of the Iroquois that the whole tribe be adopted. The council agreed, creating the Six Nations where formerly there had been five.

Childhood

Children were universally desired, and were one reason a couple married. Infant mortality was high, and a child's death was considered a great tragedy. Few families had more than three children who lived to adulthood. Yet in spite of their love for children people sometimes practiced infanticide, deliberately killing a baby, usually because of famine and inability to feed the child. Infanticide—like killing or abandoning the aged—was practiced only in extreme circumstances. If a woman died in childbirth (and this was the most common cause of death among women of childbearing age), her baby might be buried with her even though it was alive. There was no way of caring for it unless another lactating woman could feed it, for Indians had no dairy animals in the days before Columbus. People also killed twins at birth in some areas where they were thought to be unlucky or evil, and many deformed children were not allowed to live. Infanticide was a decision to be made by the parents and was not criminal or illegal. It was a civic matter only if the child was older, when the clans or other kin groups might have some say in the matter.

The mother's kin group usually raised illegitimate babies, though illegitimacy was apparently not always accepted. A few reports from the various culture areas indicate some killing of illegitimate newborns, and a few abortions as well, though information is scant on that subject.

Children were taught to behave by various forms of reward and punishment. Very young babies were treated with great permissiveness in most societies; they were hardly ever severely punished, but were loved, praised, and cajoled into proper behavior. As the child grew and learned to walk, his parents, older siblings, and others ridiculed him for misbehavior. In some societies, ridicule was the strongest punishment, but spanking and other physical punishment were administered too. Muskogeans of the Southeast scratched a child's arms and back with the teeth of garfish as punishment. The scratches showed for several days and publicly shamed the offender. In matrilineal societies, the maternal uncle disciplined older children, but the younger ones were chastised by their parents. Grandparents were less agents of discipline than figures of affection and tenderness.

Parents set small tasks for their young children, initiating them into the work they would do as adults. Girls learned sewing, cooking, gathering, and other women's tasks, and boys patterned their ways after their father, uncles, and older brothers. Older adults taught tribal ethics, codes of conduct, and religious customs by oral instruction and by personal example.

Indian children shared with each other. There was little private property even in adult society, and children rarely quarreled over toys. Older children helped care for their younger brothers and sisters, and sibling rivalry too is not recorded as common. Because of high infant mortality, few Indian families had many children. Some, like the Cheyenne, spaced their children widely. Older children were taught that the arrival of a new baby was a joyous event that reflected well on the whole family.

Rites of Passage

Every known society recognizes periods of change or crisis when the individual leaves one social status and enters another. Often these periods are celebrated with rituals: the Hebrew bar mitzvah, for example, marks the transition from childhood to adulthood. Such a transition is called a *rite of passage*.

All Indian groups celebrated rites of passage, some observing more than others. Northwest Coast people of high rank observed a child's first teeth or first steps by giving a potlatch. In some Indian societies, initiation into an age-grade or warrior association was an important rite of passage.

These rites generally separate a person from his old status and incorporate him into a new one, and many of them take the form of symbolic death. The Central Atlantic Algonkian initiation rite witnessed by the English settlers was a ritual of this sort. The "death" destroyed the boy or girl as a child, to be reborn into the new status of adult. At transition times, especially at childbirth or when the child becomes an adult, Indians believed that individuals were in a state dangerous to themselves and to society. Society usually avoided the danger by segregating the individuals. Almost all Indian groups acknowledged four passages in one way or another: birth, naming, puberty, and death. Some tribes, especially on the Northwest Coast, celebrated many more changes of status, but these four are the most common.

Birth

Though Indians wanted babies, they attached less importance to the baby at birth than to its mother. In many societies she was believed to be in a state of supernatural danger, not to herself but to the males of the community and to their hunting equipment and spiritual well-being. The danger covered her entire pregnancy, so many Indian societies secluded pregnant women not only at delivery but also for the full nine months. During that time women observed food and activity taboos. Delivery usually took place in a special hut with one or more women in attendance. Usually the umbilical cord was put away until the child was older and the afterbirth was buried. In the Basin and in a few societies in California, fathers too observed taboos, staying in bed for a time after the birth and following a restricted diet. At the end of her seclusion, the new mother bathed, then she and the baby made a public appearance at a feast or some other celebration, where the baby was presented formally to the sun, the moon, or the supernaturals.

Mothers kept their babies in cradles of many styles, strapping the cradles to their backs for transportation, standing them upright, or hanging them from a tree. It is said that the lullaby "Rockabye Baby" was an Indian song and referred to the cradleboard hanging on a tree. Among the Seminole the baby stayed in a hammock, and in the Northwest the cradle was a wooden box.

Pregnant Indian woman. Many Indian societies separated women during their pregnancies from the men to protect the men from the state of supernatural danger they felt inhered in pregnant women.

Naming

Male and female names were often but not always different. Babies usually received a name when they were first presented to their father, clan, band, or community, but some groups called the infant "baby" or "boy" or "girl" until the child exhibited some characteristic suggesting a name. In clan systems, clan names often were used for new members, and in some groups, names came from mothers' or fathers' dreams. Sometimes names were given in memory of an ancestor, although among some people names of the dead were never reused or even mentioned. For a child of high rank on the Northwest Coast, the naming and presentation ceremony was a lavish potlatch at which the parents gave gifts to all guests.

Indian naming practices seem confusing because Indians often changed their names as they grew older. Though sometimes the childhood name was the only name for life, except for nicknames, children in many tribes got new names at puberty—at the first menstruation for girls, and at initiation for boys. In addition, a boy might take a new name after finding a guardian spirit or after his first war party. If a Natchez rose in rank from Stinkard to Honored Man by bravery in war, he took a new name. Boys might also take clan names after distinguishing themselves. On the Northwest Coast, the successor to a chief took the chief's titles and names, but he had to validate his rights to them by giving a potlatch.

Such naming practices bewildered the Europeans, who had no parallel custom. If an Indian dropped his childhood name when he received a new name at puberty, and many did, European record-keeping became very difficult—particularly when, over a valorous and long life, a man assumed ten or more names. Names were precious to their owners; assuming a name as a sign of honor or accomplishment was a very important occasion, marked with solemn rites.

In many societies it was considered bad manners to address someone directly by his personal name, which was thought of as private and sacred. Nicknames were used instead. In other societies, names could be purchased or loaned. All in all, names and the rites of naming were far more significant in Indian society than in Europe or in America today.

Puberty

Almost all North American people had special rites for a girl at menarche, her first menstruation, and many women went through similar but less rigorous observances during every menstrual period. Indians had two reasons for those rites: they believed that anything a girl did during her menarche influenced her whole life, and that menstrual blood was dangerous to hunters, game, and the supernatural. For these reasons girls were isolated and required to behave in certain ways. They were set tasks so that they would not be lazy, and they observed restricted diets so they would not be greedy. They used drinking straws and scratching sticks to keep from touching their heads, where supernatural influences were concentrated. While menstruating, they were careful not to pollute men's hunting equipment by touching it. On the Northwest Coast, where people coveted wealth, a pubescent girl did not work during her isolation, so that she might marry a chief and be waited on by slaves. Isolation and restriction usually ended with a feast at which it was announced publicly that the girl was ready to marry. Not all tribes had elaborate rituals, though; Hopi girls did not observe the taboos common elsewhere, but merely changed their style of hair dressing to show that they were marriageable.

Boys' puberty rites were not so directly connected with biological changes, but initiation ceremonies ending childhood were common, and some of them were true ordeals. Among the more severe trials were isolation and fasting, taking drugs, and body mutilation. Less severe practices included sweatbaths and taking part in a successful hunt. These exercises, like the girls' rites, were thought to influence the boy's future. On the Plains and elsewhere, some boys were initiated into associations at about the time of puberty, and the association's secrets were revealed to them by older members. Often several boys were initiated at the same time, especially in age-graded associations. The vision quest ordeal, on the other hand, was a solitary search for supernatural help. In southern California, visions were not left to chance. Boys were given a drink or infusion that induced hallucination. In some areas boys drank emetics and laxatives, symbolically wiping out the past and making a new, clean start.

Not all peoples held public ceremonies for girls and boys at puberty. Sometimes, as among the Hopi, girls were instructed by an older woman about the biological change and how to care for themselves. Boys sought a spirit helper, but without public recognition of their change from child to adult. There was some tendency for boys' puberty or initiation ceremonies to be dramatic where girls' rites were largely ignored, and vice versa, but this was by no means always true. In southern California, both girls and boys had elaborate public initiation ceremonies.

Death

The most common cause of death among women was childbirth; among men, it was warfare. The time of highest mortality for both sexes was infancy. Other causes of death were geronticide (killing or abandoning the aged) and suicide, which was not uncommon but about which we have very few data. Of course, many people died of disease and old age. After European germs spread

Tree burial, a practice among Indians of the western Great Lakes and the Plains. Often the bones were interred after the flesh had decayed.

through Indian communities, death rates leaped and disease became the major killer, far exceeding warfare.

Disposal of Bodies. Indians disposed of their dead in ways as simple as leaving the corpse on the ground or as elaborate as mortuary rites observed on and off for a year or more. Eskimo left their dead on the ground because they could not dig into permafrost, though they sometimes covered the bodies with stones. Disposal by burial was common, but Indians followed many other customs: cremating the corpse, embalming or mummifying it, disposing of bones in urns, and entombing bodies in trees or on scaffolds.

Most burials were in pits or graves in the ground, though some were in mounds or beneath houses. Many of the bodies were flexed, with knees drawn up, probably because that took less space—which was something to consider where people had only hoes and digging sticks. In the Southeast, secondary bone burial was common. Mourners buried the corpse, then exhumed it after most of the flesh had decayed. They called on a bone-picker, a ritual specialist unique to the Southeast, to remove all that was left of the tissues. Known as a Buzzard Man, he kept his fingernails very long to clean the bones efficiently, which he did in the presence of the mourners. Then the bones were either reburied or placed in a mortuary house. Sometimes bones were buried in communal pits called ossuaries, either individually or in urns.

In the Basin, human remains were often deposited in caves or fissures in rocks. Embalming and mummification apparently were used only in the central and south Atlantic coastal area. Tree or scaffold burials were widespread on the Plains: the bodies were wrapped in skins, then laid on a platform or scaffolding or in the crotch of a tree. On the Northwest Coast, the dead were placed in wooden mortuary cabins or in boxes or canoes raised on posts, which were decorated with the crests of the family line if the deceased was important. Cremation was a common means of disposal in California.

Mourning.   Mourning rites varied. Many people placed food and possessions of the dead person in or near the grave, which relatives might visit for a time with other offerings. On the Plains, a man's favorite horse was usually sacrificed at his death; slaves occasionally were killed in the Northwest, and often a wife among the Natchez. In some tribes, relatives mourned for a set time and many cut their hair, especially the widow. California tribelets mourned with much wailing and overt grief, with long ceremonies and an anniversary mourning ritual after one year, and sometimes again after another had passed. Among the Hopi, too, mourning meant wailing on the day of the death, and more crying a year later. Many people discarded personal ornaments or blackened their faces, and some gashed their arms and legs to shed blood as a sign of great sorrow.

Clans and Other Large Groupings

A clan is a unilineal descent group whose members consider themselves related, having descended from a common ancestor. Often the ancestor's name has long been forgotten, and clan members have come to believe that it was an animal or a spirit being. Clan names often refer to this supposed ancestor. The *unilineal* aspect of a clan means that membership passes through either the male or female line, but not both. To say a clan is *matrilineal* or *patrilineal* tells through which line descent is reckoned. In a matrilineal system, all children belong to their mother's clan. Because clans are almost always exogamous (meaning that marriage within the clan is forbidden), husbands and wives will never be of the same descent groups. In matrilineal systems, then, children will never belong to their father's clan; boys as well as girls belong to their mother's clan. Likewise, in a patrilineal system children belong to the fathers' clan, and patrilineal clan membership includes girls but is not passed on by girls.

Most Indian groups did not have clans. The Iroquois, Haida, Tlingit, Southeastern Indians, Western Pueblo, some Athabaskans, and Plains villagers of the upper Missouri were matrilineal. Some Plains villagers, the Upper Great Lakes people, and some California tribelets were patrilineal. All the rest of North America figured descent *bilaterally,* through both maternal and paternal sides.

Clan Rights and Duties

Being in a clan did not mean that children thought they were related to only one parent. Where they had clans, people still recognized relatives not in their own clan. The significance of clans was that they were responsible for property inheritance, rights to certain offices, and social control. In matrilineal societies, since the father was not a member of his children's clan, he had no authority over certain areas of their lives. The older male in his children's clan was their maternal uncle (mother's brother), who was responsible for some types of training that would have been left to the father in patrilineal or clanless systems.

Clan members often held their land in common. Iroquois clans held title to the longhouses and cultivated fields and also owned clan burial grounds. In the Northwest, clans controlled sections of the coast, fishing stations or strips of land along streams, and entire valleys for hunting. Pueblo clans too owned land, and also ceremonies and the masks, songs, medicine bundles, and dances that went with them.

Much tribal political and legal structure had to do with clan membership. Clans often had rights to chieftainships and council membership. The women of Iroquois clans selected members of the tribal council, who also formed the League council, and Omaha clans also nominated council members.

Clan members had individual duties and responsibilities as well. Clans regulated marriage, in that members had to observe clan exogamy. Each member also was obliged to support and defend other members and to observe clan taboos and rules.

Other Kin Groups

Some clan systems were further organized into *phratries* or associations of clans. Clans belonging to the same phratry usually observed phratry exogamy: one could marry neither a member of his own clan nor a member of the other clan or clans in the phratry. Phratries were most common in the Southeast, the Northwest, and the prairies.

Some tribes were divided into two segments called *moieties,* from the French word for "half." Indian moieties were usually, though not always, exogamous;

members of one moiety had to seek mates in the other. Membership in moieties was inherited matrilineally or patrilineally. Moiety functions usually were less important and less clearly defined than those of clans, except for exogamy, which was always clear wherever it existed. But moiety organization did have some common characteristics. It was customary for members of one moiety to perform the mortuary rites, conduct mourning observances, and offer comfort to those bereaved in the opposite moiety. In the Southeast, sports competitions usually pitted members of the two moieties against each other. And moieties often had important functions on ceremonial occasions. Each Creek moiety had specific parts to play in the Busk. Moiety divisions occurred among peoples with and without clan organization: a society could have a dual organization without being further divided into clans.

Pseudo-kinship

We saw in Chapter 3 how Eskimo trading partners and members of hunting parties entered into special relationships. Those men had no biological or marital connections but called each other by a kin name, putting each other into a special status anthropologists call *fictive kinship*. In many Indian societies, good friends might pledge themselves to lifelong blood-brotherhood or comradeship, a custom popular among Cree men. Two Cree boys would vow blood-brotherhood and thereafter call each other "brother" and each other's parents "mother" and "father." Hopi children had ceremonial parents (something like godparents), a "mother" for a girl and a "father" for a boy, who sponsored them for initiation into the Katcina Cult. Hopi ceremonial parents could not belong to the phratry of the children's real mothers or fathers.

In native American societies where all rights and status came only through kinship connections, people might extend fictive kinship to traders or other outsiders to give them rights in society. Fictive kinsmen had mutual duties and obligations like real kinsmen. If one died, the survivor might be held responsible for the other's family.

Associations

Associations are organizations built on some principle other than kinship. American Indian associations formed around mutual interest (military societies), religion (ceremonial societies), sex (men's and women's clubs), and age (age-graded associations). All provided mutual aid to members, and also education, recreation, and social control.

On the Plains, the military societies provided comradeship and mutual aid.

They also handled policing when large numbers of people assembled for hunts and tribal ceremonies, and they trained young men in the military arts. Usually they were not fighting units; members were or had been fighting men, but raiding parties assembled independently of the military associations.

Five Plains tribes had age-graded associations: Blackfoot, Hidatsa, Atsina, Mandan, and Arapaho. Members belonged to levels or grades according to their approximate ages, purchasing the rights and paraphernalia of each grade as they entered it. Though it was possible to skip grades, the membership of each group remained much the same as they advanced. Those age-graded groups functioned like the nongraded military societies of the Plains.

Associations, age-graded or not, were not exclusively for males. Women had societies too, age-graded among the Hidatsa and Mandan. These often formed as organizations of mutual interest or occupation—hide workers, beaders, or cultivators—but women sometimes joined curing or ceremonial societies with men.

The Hopi Katcina Cult (see pages 225–227) was a religious association that included all members of the tribe. It bound even non-kin Hopi together in ceremonial observances and common supernatural belief. Hopi men and women also entered other ceremonial societies limited to one sex. Most activities of Hopi cults or associations concerned the agricultural cycle and fertility. Other cult societies were the Kuksu Cult in California (pages 186–187), and the Iroquois False Face Society (pages 307–308). Associations on the Northwest Coast often have been called "secret societies," though membership was actually more exclusive than secret.

Among the Kwakiutl, nonmembers deeply feared the Cannibal Dancers, who were thought to be possessed by a cannibal spirit that could make them eat other Kwakiutl. During performances, Cannibal Dancers ate smoked carcasses of bears that looked enough like human cadavers to convince onlookers that the dancers really were eating human flesh. The Cannibal Society was powerful as well as feared; its members were high-ranking individuals who held significant political positions in Kwakiutl society.

The Midewiwin or Grand Medicine Society of the Great Lakes Algonkians was based on occupation. Entrance and advancement through its four grades were open to both men and women curers and required both payment and hard study. Members became wealthy and powerful as they passed through the levels because people respected them and feared their powers, and because many curers charged very high prices.

Though some associations included women, and a few were exclusively for women, associations were mostly male in pre-Columbian times. Domestic demands in primitive society left women little time to devote to club life, and the few women's associations usually were auxiliaries to men's groups or specialized in craft production.

Most associations in Indian societies were found in larger and richer groups. The Arctic, Subarctic, Basin, and Plateau had few non-kin organizations.

Games and Recreation

Moiety divisions generally meant ready-made athletic opponents, for one of the functions of moieties was to oppose each other in athletic events. In the Southeast, recreation between the two moieties was an important training exercise for warfare; the Indians there even called sports "little brother of war." Where people had no moiety divisions, competition was on a temporary basis, changing from game to game or from time to time. Except for this structuring of rivalry into the social system, games were surprisingly similar from coast to coast, regardless of culture area or linguistic affiliation.

Indian games were of two types: games of chance or gambling games, and games of skill or dexterity. Indians gambled with objects like dice or marked sticks, thrown at random to give a count or number, much like shooting craps. They also had guessing games, on which they bet a sum. An item, usually a special stick, was concealed in a team member's hand, and the opposing team tried

A group of California Indians gambling inside an earth-covered council house.

A vigorous game of lacrosse.

to guess who held it. Probably the best-known Indian game of chance, this is usually called "the hand game," and was accompanied by songs or chants.

Games of skill often required athletic prowess: archery, javelin throwing, racing, chunkey, and snow snake, for example. Chunkey, played in the Southeast, was an attempt to throw a pole at a moving stone ring or disk. Another version was called hoop and pole, which was played with a hoop covered with netting, rolled on the ground. Players shot at it with arrows or threw javelins at it. In snow snake, opponents slid a lance on snow or ice to see whose projectile would travel farthest. They also had team games: lacrosse, an Indian invention, was played by men, and women played shinny, something like field hockey, with a ball and stick. Children played games too, some of them much like their parents' games, and women as well as men took part in most games and sports. For men, though, these activities were more than just fun and recreation; these workouts hardened the players and made them more skillful warriors.

Women's Status

Women held a respected place in nearly all communities, with a very few exceptions like the Chipewyan and some other western Subarctic people. Europeans once believed that Indian women were menials, hardly more than slaves to Indian men, but they had misinterpreted the division of labor in native American society. When bands or communities moved, it was usually to search for food or to escape pressure from aggressive neighbors. Either way, men could not travel burdened with goods, utensils, or children, for they had to be free to use their weapons in hunting or warfare. Consequently, women seemed to Europeans like beasts of burden, since they carried all the family possessions on their backs. Early European arrivals were shocked to see women laboring in the fields, for European tradition said that farming was men's work. Measuring Indian customs by European standards caused many erroneous conclusions.

Indian women never were major political figures in any tribe (in fact, women have rarely been political officials anywhere in the world until recent times), but though they did not make community-binding decisions, their opinions and suggestions were highly regarded. Among the Iroquois particularly, women's right to nominate and depose the sachems gave them much political power. Men were very conscious of women's part in agriculture, too, for except among the Western Pueblo, women were the primary cultivators. In gathering wild-plant foods, women did nearly all the work. Even in the hunting societies like the Plains tribes, women's economic contributions were extremely important; no matter

Women washing the chaff and dirt from wheat winnowed by the wind; after washing, the wheat was placed in flat baskets to dry in the sun. Wheat became an important foodstuff after its introduction by the Europeans.

how many buffalo a man might kill, he could sell only as many hides as his wife or wives could cure. And, of course, everywhere women were responsible for nurturing new members of society.

Women were forbidden to take part in many male ceremonial activities, but in some areas they had associations and ritual observances of their own. In many matrilineal societies, women owned the family dwelling and the fields and they cared for the clan property. With men away from home hunting, fishing, or at war for days or even months, women had to be responsible for domestic economics, and they learned in childhood how to be self-reliant. Men made their own equipment and commonly supplied heavy materials for housing, but women had to do most of the craftwork like pottery, weaving, basketry, and skin dressing. Only in the Southwest and a few other areas where they were rarely away from home long did men take a hand in such manufactures. Labor in the home naturally fell to women because of the human reproductive cycle and the period of lactation, but just as women recognized men's importance in protection and subsistence, men were aware that women's contributions were indispensable.

Slavery

It is unfortunate that there are not more words in English for the varying degrees of servitude, because slavery in our society has implications that it rarely had among Indians. Except in a few cases, Indian slavery did not mean ownership of a human being as a chattel or possession. Only among the Northwest Coast people did it approach total bondage and power over life and death. The only hereditary slaves were in the Northwest, where children of slaves automatically became slaves, producing a permanent slave class. Even the Iroquois and Natchez, who rank after the Northwest Coast people as slaveholders and who tortured and sacrificed enslaved war captives, had no slave class, for children of slaves were freemen. Slaves almost always were treated as members of households, and not infrequently they married into the family.

Only on the Northwest Coast was commercial traffic in slaves common. Even there, slaves who had been captured in war might be ransomed by their kinfolk; in some tribes, they might purchase their own freedom if they could accumulate enough wealth. Women and children slaves in the Northwest were household drudges for high-ranking families, and male slaves helped with construction, canoe building, and the like. Most of their tasks were the same as those done by middle- and lower-class Northwest people. But slaves did live under definite restrictions in the Northwest. They were rigidly excluded from ceremonials, usually were prohibited from marrying free citizens, and occasionally were killed—Tlingit chiefs sacrificed slaves to be buried under the main posts of their houses at the time of construction. Of course, chiefs did not build houses often. Occasionally wealthy men sacrificed slaves at potlatches just to show how wealthy they were and gain prestige, but sometimes, for the same reason, wealthy men freed their slaves in a flamboyant gesture at a potlatch.

Outside the Northwest Coastal area, the words captive and slave were almost interchangeable, for most slaves were war captives. In some areas, like California, people were enslaved for debt. Life for most slaves probably was no harder or less pleasant than their captors' lives.

Political Organization

Among the functions of all human societies are maintaining internal order and making decisions that are binding on their members. In addition, most groups have some rules governing external relations or contacts with outsiders, like warfare and long-distance trade. We call the structures and relationships that perform these functions a society's political organization.

Unlike kinship structures, political structures are territorial—they occupy space. A group like a band, village, or tribe is defined at least partly by the fact that its members share (or divide) common territory. Even nomadic groups are not totally free-wandering, for their activities too occur within a certain region. Members of a political unit recognize the territory that is their common land, and they recognize land outside their boundaries as belonging to other political units. Anyone who wants to go through land not his own must either have some sort of safety pledge or risk being attacked.

Some native American societies had no specifically political structures. Among the Eskimo, political power and authority grew out of kinship or were vested in temporary leaders whom others followed out of respect for their competence. Other Indian groups, like the Natchez, had strongly centralized political organization. Most Indian societies lay somewhere between these two extremes. In many of them, groups such as clans made the important political decisions. A convenient and common way to classify the varying types and degrees of Indian political organization is as bands, tribes, and chiefdoms.

Bands

The simplest kind of political organization, the band, had between 50 and 150 people. It was made up of families who held territory in common for hunting, fishing, or gathering. A band was an egalitarian organization with no inherited power positions. Some sort of leader, often called a headman, acted for the

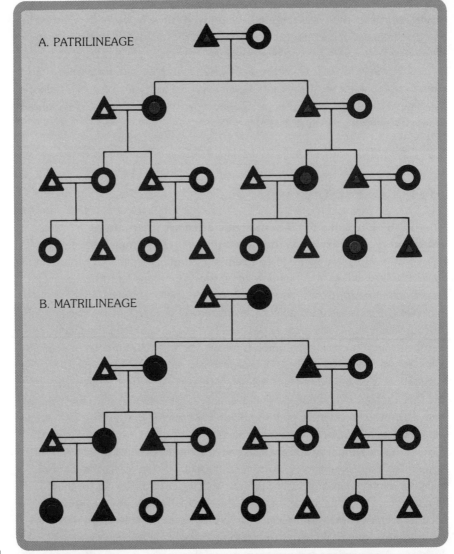

A. PATRILINEAGE

B. MATRILINEAGE

In patrilineal reck-
oning (A), descent
group membership
is passed from the
father to his chil-
dren, both male and
female, but only
males can pass on
membership. In
matrilineal reck-
oning (B), group
membership goes
from the mother to
her children, both
male and female,
and only women can
pass on membership.

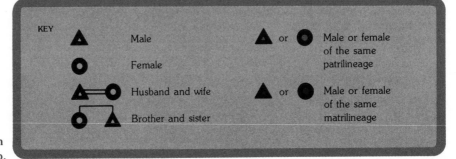

KEY

▲   Male

●   Female

▲═○   Husband and wife

○─▲   Brother and sister

▲ or ●   Male or female
of the same
patrilineage

▲ or ●   Male or female
of the same
matrilineage

group, but he had no power to enforce his decisions. People followed his suggestions because they respected his wisdom and had seen proof of his ability in the past.

Indian bands had little need for formal government, for social control was rarely a problem. Their population was small and homogeneous: everyone grew up with the same general experiences and about the same expectations. People held very little private property, and all shared food and supplies equally. The Paiute of the Basin were hunters and gatherers who recognized no political unit larger than the band, though several bands joined together each summer for rabbit or antelope hunts. Indian bands were commonly exogamous, and the Paiute arranged marriages too during this annual gathering.

Not all Indian bands were so nomadic as the Great Basin peoples. Where food resources were more plentiful and regular, people moved less often, following the seasons. Groups like the Klamath bands were really village groups, sedentary for the winter months and dispersed during the summer. The villages were close enough to do things together throughout the year, not just during an annual hunt. But since the Klamath units recognized no authority beyond their own community, we can consider them, too, as a band-level society.

Tribes

The tribe is difficult to define. Its members recognized that they belonged together; they spoke the same language, had the same customs, and married each other. They were often made up of bands, like the Plains tribes that gathered during the big buffalo hunts. Other tribes, like the agricultural Plainsmen and the Iroquois, were composed of villages rather than bands. Tribes in North America were much larger than bands, but even so they rarely exceeded 5,000 people.

The convenient and traditional way of referring to American Indian societies is to call them *tribes,* as we do throughout this book. Here, however, as we discuss political units, we need a more precise differentiation. In this section, the word *tribe* is meant as defined above. Elsewhere we will continue to use it in its more casual sense. *Nation* too can be confusing, especially the expression *Indian nation* as used in the popular press. *Nation* is not an appropriate term for societies north of Mexico; it implies a political complexity never found north of the Rio Grande in aboriginal times. None of these categories is absolute; they grade into each other, forcing us to be fairly arbitrary, for instance, when we distinguish a tribe from a chiefdom.

Tribes were usually much larger than bands, and had associations within them that took members from each of the component bands or villages. Warrior societies in the Plains had members from all the various bands, and medicine societies among the village tribes drew members from more than one village.

Clans also integrated tribes in that clan members were scattered through bands and villages. These pan-tribal associations and kin groups helped bond the units together and built tribal identity and unity. Without some such unifying device, tribes might have developed serious rifts between bands or villages.

Tribes, like bands, are egalitarian, in spite of the Europeans' habit of applying the word *chief* to leaders. Tribal leaders had little coercive power, for the chief's position rested entirely on the people's willingness to follow. Tribal chiefs governed with advice from a council, usually elders or headmen from the families, clans, or bands. Any policing was done by the associations and the tribal council, both of which had members representing all the bands or villages; their decisions helped avoid charges of favoritism or discrimination.

Chiefdoms

Chiefdoms have centralized authority, and they are not egalitarian. The political leader of a chiefdom has the socially recognized right to mobilize people and goods, and the society under him is stratified or ranked, with some social classes, individuals, or family lines considered higher, superior, or more prestigious than others, because of birth rather than achievement. The Natchez and the Powhatan were in this political category. The population of chiefdoms varied in North America, but most of them had fewer than 5,000 people.

The title *chief,* when it was used of someone like Powhatan, Pocahontas's father, meant a man of power who had force to carry out his orders. Plains chiefs usually were respected leaders, but they never had authority so absolute as Powhatan's. Plains chiefs were advisors. Both tribes and chiefdoms usually had different chiefs for different purposes—military, religious, and civil. Even the Great Sun of the Natchez had a war chief. Civil or peace chiefs were usually older men, once renowned warriors but now beyond youthful rashness, men who could be counted on to keep cool. The ceremonial or religious chief's position often was not clearly separated from shaman or priest, especially among the Pueblo. The war chief was of course a great warrior, a man others would follow. Some of these positions might be reserved for a family line or clan, but proven ability settled the choice even in chiefdoms. Rarely would one man act as two kinds of chief.

Other Political Classifications

Some Indian groups are hard to place in the categories we have been using. California peoples were organized in groups of autonomous villages called tribelets. Some of these lacked any tribal organization, having no overall leadership, and their only unifying force was their common language. Others had more definite political structure, with local units in villages led by headmen and chiefs who served as ceremonial and civil officials. These tribelets had strikingly large populations for hunters and gatherers with little political unity.

Because Pueblo religious societies ran the government, with religious officials also serving as political officials, their organization may be considered a theocracy. The Hopi lived in several villages on adjacent mesas, each village having its own religious or ceremonial associations. We would classify the Hopi as a tribe, even though the villages were mostly autonomous. Clan heads were leaders of the ceremonial societies and formed a council that considered village problems.

Some of the Southeastern people would be classified between tribe and chiefdom, showing characteristics of each. The Natchez may have been developing into a state, a politically organized body of people, when they were disrupted by Europeans; they certainly came closer to it than any other recorded group.

Councils

In all political groups larger than bands, the council was very important. Even the Great Sun of the Natchez had to listen to his council.

Sometimes Indian councils were groups of former warriors who had gained the community's respect for their bravery and military exploits. Other councils were clan elders representing all the tribal clans. The Pueblo councils included clan heads and leaders of ceremonial societies. Membership in the council could be based on kinship (leaders of clans), or territoriality (headmen of bands), and sometimes councilmen came only from specific families within clans. In some tribes councilmen held their position for life; others had limited terms of office.

Some councils, like the League of the Iroquois, had as many as fifty members; the Cheyenne tribal council had forty-four. Others had a dozen or fewer. In some tribes the council governed alone, while in others it acted as an advisory body for a ruler, like the Natchez Great Sun.

Councils acted as deliberative and legislative bodies. They discussed issues, and since the council members represented the bands, clans, and villages, they were a sounding board for the community's sentiments. In tribal organizations, council decisions were almost always unanimous. If the members could not reach unanimity, they kept deliberating. Most tribal government was democratic, but in a chiefdom the ruler could override his council. Only a very secure and personally powerful leader like Powhatan would have done so, however, and even he, we may be sure, listened to his council.

An Iroquois tribal council.

Social Control

As in all human societies, the most fundamental social control among American Indians was the socialization common to every member of the group. Adult Indians behaved properly most of the time because they had learned in childhood what the tribe considered right and wrong. Adults rewarded the child's proper behavior with praise, and punished improper or socially disruptive behavior with ridicule and shame. As children grew up, prestige and gifts were added to the rewards, while punishment became more severe, including locking up, restraint, or whipping. In the bands very little physical punishment was necessary.

Supernatural Control

Indians believed that the spirit world kept watch over human behavior, and that by withholding favors or protection the supernatural would punish those who neglected taboos. Some misbehavior, such as incest, was so dreadful that only the spirits could punish the wrongdoer by making him sick. In band societies, social control by these means was adequate; judges, courts, and policing officials were not needed.

Indians in some areas felt that wrongs would be avenged by witchcraft. If belief in it was strong, that could be a very effective way of dealing with social disorder. Pueblo Indians feared being accused of witchcraft as much as they did the results of witchcraft. Such fears were strong incentive to conform to social norms, for others might blame any abnormal behavior on the practice of witchcraft.

Control of Adults

Many of the ways of training children in proper behavior carried over as social controls for adults. Ridicule, gossip, and shame embarrassed violators of social convention enough to stop their socially disapproved behavior. Years of being socialized into culturally proper ways also made people feel guilty about misdeeds, and public comment and avoidance also kept people in line. And of course rewards such as prestige, gifts, and praise kept reinforcing good behavior all through life.

However, such informal controls were not always enough. Warrior societies could take coercive actions during tribal buffalo hunts on the Plains. They might take away a man's weapons, banish him from the hunt, or confine him to camp or even to his tipi. Occasionally the military societies could even impose capital punishment, for acts like premature hunting or stampeding the buffalo endangered the whole tribe's food supply. Such behavior was a crime against society itself.

Capital punishment, the ultimate social control, was rare among American Indians, and such extreme measures were used only for extreme provocation. Occasionally, though, it was the only way of preserving social order. Among the Eskimo, when a man had murdered several times, it was customary for the community to condemn him to death. With the community's sanction, one man executed the murderer. When social approval backed up this capital punishment, the kinfolk of the condemned man made no attempt to avenge him. Like the rest of the community, they recognized that this punishment was the only way of maintaining social order, and they accepted the verdict.

The one serious and largely uncontrollable disturbance was feuding, that is, aggression between two kin groups in the same society. It was dangerous because no one had a way of settling the feud, which perpetuated itself. For a murder within a tribe the victim's family sought revenge by murdering someone in the killer's kin group, who then sought revenge in their turn. On the Northwest Coast and in northern California, blood-money payments could resolve the feud, but in many places nothing could settle it once it got under way unless both groups accepted a peace chief or some other respected individual as a mediator. Otherwise the feuding could destroy the band or village. The Eskimo were the one group to settle private quarrels and disputes with a remarkable sort of word duel in the form of song (see page 89).

Economic Systems

The word "economics" covers all the ways in which people produce, distribute, and consume goods and services, including the items their technology produces and their ways of obtaining the raw materials they need to manufacture those items. We discussed the material bases of life in Chapter 9; here we will examine Indian ways of exchanging or distributing goods, and their ideas about property.

Property Rights and Land Tenure

Most Indian property was personal, like clothing, weapons, ceremonial apparatus, and subsistence and craft implements. The Plains giveaway and the Northwest potlatch customs tell us that some property was owned outright and could be disposed of according to the owner's wishes, even destroyed if he chose. Land, however, was almost never owned by individuals. Kin groups or communities had the rights to land, and Indians had no such concept as private ownership of real estate. This one difference of ideas caused great misunderstanding and hard feelings when Europeans arrived and tried to purchase Indian lands.

Agriculturalists by custom assigned garden areas to individuals or groups of kinfolk for cultivation. Where women were the gardeners (in all the agricultural societies except for the Pueblo), the produce was usually looked upon as theirs, but they always shared it. Families almost everywhere had the right to gather and fish at will within the tribe's or band's territory, and hunting land too was open to all in the local group. Along the Pacific coast and in the Subarctic, rights to fishing stations belonged to families, but only among the Yurok were fishing areas private property that could be sold. In the Western Great Lakes region, Indians recognized wild rice areas as belonging to families, who marked their territory by bending and tying off clumps of the grain. Still, all rights to land were rights to use it, not to destroy it, or let it lie unused. Any garden, fishing, or gathering areas that were not used for some time could be allotted to others if tribal or kin group authorities approved.

Communal housing too was kin group property, though in Plains tribes the skins and poles of a tipi belonged to the woman who cured the skins and raised and took down the tipi when the family moved.

Agricultural land was more uniformly controlled or owned by kin groups than hunting, fishing, or gathering territory, but every member of a band or tribe had rights to the produce of its land, whether those rights came from kinship connections or citizenship. And even in the few cases where property was clearly defined as belonging to an individual, he had to recognize claims coming from one group or another: the owner always let some groups of people, like his family, exploit his property.

Indians had intangible property too, like names, titles, songs, magical chants, and incantations. These almost always were privately owned and usually could be sold or given away, but on the Northwest Coast names and titles belonged to the kin group.

Inheritance

All peoples have ways of distributing property and rights from the dead to the living, a flow of belongings from generation to generation that is called inheritance. Communal or kin group property always remained with the group. No one person had the right to dispose of it or prevent another member of the group from using it.

A person could leave personal property to another, though. If he did not choose his own heir, a man's sons got his personal possessions and a woman's daughters got hers, where possessions did pass to the next generation. However, in some areas they were not passed on. In southern California, relatives burned the deceased's private belongings at the mourning ceremonies, and in the Plains, relatives often killed a dead warrior's favorite horse, though they might distribute others among the community. Distributing or destroying personal property was part of funeral ceremonies everywhere. One-family houses sometimes were inherited, but the Navajo and Apache burned or abandoned them after a death.

Trade and Commerce

Because natural resources are unequally distributed on this earth, some Indian societies had minerals, plants, and animals not available to others. Needing some kind of mutual exchange system, Indians built long-distance trading routes centuries before Columbus. Though actual routes are not known, we have plenty of evidence from burials and archaeological sites that mica and conch shells from the South, copper from Lake Superior, obsidian from the Rocky Mountains, and flint from Ohio circulated in some kind of regular trading network. Many other items probably were traded over shorter distances, but naturally we have no record of perishable items like foodstuffs. We know tobacco was traded after European arrival, but tracing it to prehistoric times is a problem because, though we have found pipes and other smoking devices, people must have used many of them to smoke kinnikinnik, not tobacco. Specialization in craft also brought trade in both raw materials and finished products. After contact, European guns, metal objects, glass beads, cloth, and horses entered the exchange systems.

Some tribes became famous as middlemen or traders. The Chinook controlled an important part of the Columbia River down which much trade passed (see pages 156–157). Huron territory was the heart of the early fur trade, and the Tobacco tribe even got its name from the part it played trading that plant.

Trade Routes. When most goods had to be carried on the human back, trade followed rivers wherever possible so that boats could be used. The Mississippi River and the Great Lakes were important tradeways. Overland trails that may have been made originally by seasonally migrating animals covered the continent.

Long trade routes were bound to lead through alien territory, and that called for ways of showing that the traveler's purpose was peaceful. Carrying the calumet or peace pipe was one of these. Even the trails heavily traveled by traders, migrating bands, and war parties were only a man's width, because Indians preferred to move in single file. Where they could, they chose routes to avoid hard, stony ground that wore out moccasins and dense undergrowth that slowed them down. In the North many trails crossed frozen rivers or lakes in the winter. The Sante Fe Trail and the Oregon Trail followed by frontiersmen were originally Indian routes, and maps drawn by the European colonists showed Indian trails like the one through the Cumberland Gap in Tennessee. Many trails later became paved roads and railroad tracks.

Media of Exchange. Indians had no general-purpose medium of exchange or commodity like money before European contact, but some items were used locally as standards of value and media of exchange. These things were not true money, though wampum has often been called that. It was valuable, but it was not currency. On the Atlantic coast, wampum became a medium of exchange after Europeans began using it; roanoke was another kind of shell the Indians used for both adornment and exchange. Both got their value from scarcity. The shells used for wampum, particularly the black or purple variety, were rare. One purple bead equalled two white ones in early times. The strung shell beads were convenient to carry as necklaces or belts. European glass beads later came in such quantity that the native shell lost its value. On the Pacific coast, dentalia were very valuable shells, and Indians used them for exchange. The value of each shell in this case depended on its length, not its color.

A wampum belt, used principally as a memory device by those tribes possessing no written language to record important historical events. These strings of polished beads, made from shell, also served as a currency between Indians and white settlers.

Away from the coasts, in the interior, pelts (especially beaver) were used for exchange and as a standard of value. Like wampum, they continued in use for a time after Europeans came. The Hupa of northern California used woodpecker scalps, and eagle feathers may have had a value for exchange among the Pueblo, who also used turquoise and shell beads. Many other items were used locally, but however prized they were, people still conducted most trade directly, by bartering goods, foods, and raw materials for each other.

Gift-giving

Most exchanges went on either within the tribe or with close neighbors, far more than occurred through long-distance trade. Within the group, gift-giving and sharing were the most common form of exchange. Indians gave presents at specified times such as weddings, when the two families exchanged gifts. Potlatches and giveaways were ways that wealthy men allocated food and goods on special occasions, described in previous chapters. These were actually leveling mechanisms, distributing wealth to many people instead of allowing it to accumulate in the hands of a few.

Most of these exchanges within the group or community were reciprocal, as most gift-giving is; even though no one says so, people generally expect a gift or action in return. Thus, gift-giving was more than a way of distributing goods and services, it was like social security. Reciprocity meant that one could always count on receiving in times of need if he shared in times of plenty.

Warfare

Indians settled their internal disputes according to regular patterns most of the time, but no group had any standard ways of solving intertribal conflict. The common solution was war. Wars for expansion of an imperialist sort did not occur in the areas covered in this book, and such wars were rare north of Mexico. However, wars did arise from economic causes. Hunters who pursued game into alien territory might be attacked, and offensive wars were fought to win control of food and perhaps mineral resources. After European contact, economic motives greatly increased tribal aggressions, as in the struggles to control territory for the fur trade. Defensive warfare too was necessary to protect homes, villages, women, and children.

In the East and on the Plains, raiding for captives, horses, and glory accounted for much aggression. But even there and on the Northwest Coast, where wars were fought mostly for captives, prestige, and revenge, there were no true military specialists. Even the warriors and the war chiefs were still hunters, not full-time warmakers.

Some areas, including the Arctic, Subarctic, and Great Basin, had no organized warfare. Other groups became much more warlike after they acquired horses, especially the Plains people and also those in the Plateau. Californians were not very aggressive except for some raiding. The Pueblo, on the other hand, though often described as very peaceful, had a fighting force of leaders and warriors to protect themselves against the nomadic Athabaskan raiders, and they had a priesthood in charge of war rites. However, they placed no high value on the warrior's way of life; anyone who killed had to go through long purification rituals. The very aggressive groups were in the East, the Plains, and the Northwest, and the Athabaskans in the Southwest.

Going to War

Preparation. Where warfare was frequent, physical training prepared young men to endure physical hardship. They learned to refrain from personal indulgence and to accept the decisions of their war leader. Prestige in warfare came from valorous achievement, and rights to insignia such as eagle feathers had to be publicly bestowed in religious ceremonies. Anyone who claimed war achievements he did not deserve was publicly humiliated, scorned not only by other warriors but also by the women and children of the tribe.

The war leader prepared by fasting and sexual abstinence and observed all the rites by which he could appeal to the supernatural. Followers joined him because they believed in his ability and his chances for success. During the conflict his leadership was autocratic; if a man in the war party was disobedient, the leader might order him whipped or send him home. Leaders usually appointed an alternate or two to take over if they were killed. Each man fought independently for most of the time, but tried to save any comrade in danger and to keep fallen tribesmen's bodies from being mutilated. Each was free to win as much prestige as he could. The leader had no rights over the glory gained by others, though he had the right to distribute the spoils of battle.

Many Indians thought of their battle horses as extensions of themselves; they dressed them accordingly, as these sketches show. Above, the horse bears the same trappings as his rider; below, both chief and horse wear elaborate headdresses.

Sioux war party. Most warriors carry coupsticks. The eagle feathers in their warbonnets signify their past coups.

The Battle.   The Plains Indians rode horses if they had to travel far to attack an enemy, but almost all their fighting, as in other areas, was hand-to-hand and on foot. In the Plains the leader would carry a war standard into battle, a ceremonial lance which he thrust into the ground and fought beside until victory or death. He was under honor not to leave unless a member of his own party pulled up the lance. To us, an act like that may seem the height of vainglory, but for the warrior it won praise and renown.

In a defensive fight, warriors tried to engage the enemy somewhere beyond the village limits to give women, children, and the elderly time to build breastworks or other physical shields and remove the young and incapacitated beyond the range of enemy fire. Women took part in defensive battle at close range, and in rare cases went into battle and fought as equals with the men. Most women who went with the war party were there to serve the men; often they were given a share of the loot.

Scalping

Mutilation of enemy dead was not universal, but scalping and beheading occurred in widely separated regions. Contrary to the common belief, scalping did not usually cause death, nor did it break or crush the skull. Probably the idea that it was always fatal resulted from the fact that the dead usually were scalped by their enemies. In fact, scalping was simply removing a piece of skin with hair attached, most often a patch about the size of a half dollar, from the crown of the head. If a living person was scalped, skin grew back over the wound but hair did not, leaving a small bald spot.

Warriors kept scalps they had taken as trophies and war insignia. Occasionally a warrior removed the whole top skin of the scalp, later dividing it into smaller pieces to decorate garments or horse trappings. If the fallen enemy was not dead, removing the entire scalp did kill him. Some Plains warriors stretched the scalp on a small hoop and carried it as a sort of banner at the end of a pole. Sometimes women carried the pole while they did a triumphal scalp dance when the war party returned. Some fighters wore a scalplock, a small lock or braid of hair, in defiance of any enemy.

Scalping was not unique to American Indians. Herodotus, Greek historian of the fifth century B.C., reported it among the Scythians in his time. And not all people of North America took scalps. As nearly as we can tell, it was mostly an Eastern war practice that spread into the Plains. Even there, however, counting coup—rather than scalping—was the usual measure of a warrior's prowess. Along the Northwest Coast, the trophy was the head itself; after beheading an enemy, the warrior might on the way home remove a scalplock from the head. In general, scalping increased after European arrival because colonists offered bounties for scalps of Indians fighting against them, but the practice itself appears to have been aboriginal.

U.S. cavalry officers examine the corpse of a hunter scalped by Indians.

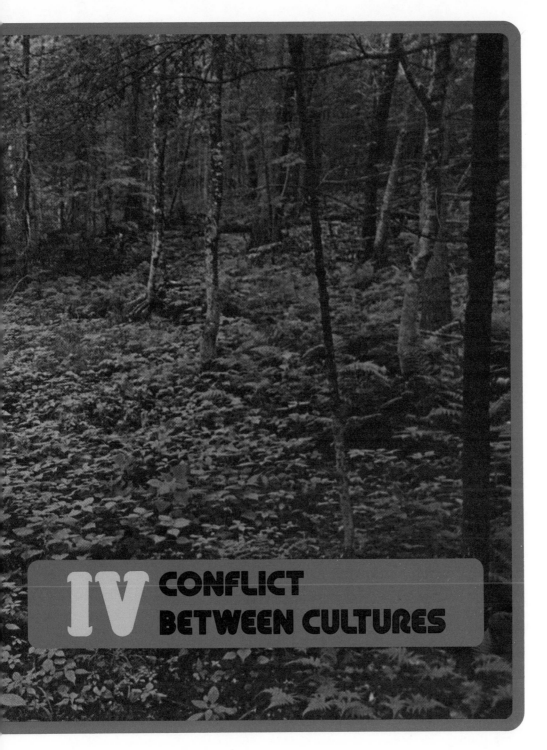

IV CONFLICT BETWEEN CULTURES

The glimpses we have had of Europeans as they came upon various Indian cultures have readied us for a historical look at the encounter and the results of their meeting. Overwhelming the native people, these invaders took control not only of the Indians' lands, but often of their very lives. While the European discovery of the New World brought change to Europe, it meant even greater change for the Indians. In spite of the many Europeans who tried to understand the Indians' ways of life and treat them fairly, there were many others who cheated the native peoples and took away their land.

Europeans also brought in diseases to which the Indians had no resistance, and thousands of Indians and Eskimo died in epidemics of smallpox, tuberculosis, and measles, among others. Many thousands more died in warfare with the Europeans, who met the Indians' bows and arrows and spears with guns. Sheer weight of numbers guaranteed that the advancing white population would

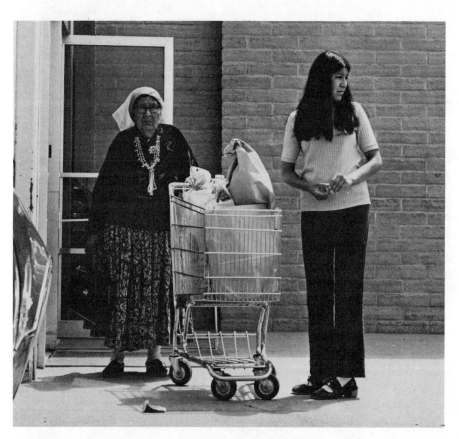

Preceding pages:
**The Eastern
woodlands.**

Two Indian women, whose dress reflects the difference in life styles between two generations, complete their shopping at a modern supermarket.

overcome the native people. People began to refer to Indians as the vanishing Americans.

Today, however, they are anything but vanishing; their birth rate is higher than that of non-Indians. In all that time many have not been assimilated, though absorption into the dominant culture has been the goal of most government policies. Earlier in their history, massive destruction nearly finished them as a people. More recently their story has been one of advances in education, employment, and self-determination. It is with the successes and problems of Indians and Eskimo today that we shall close Part IV.

Bibliography

Andrist, Ralph K.
1964   *The Long Death: The Last Days of the Plains Indians.*
        An account of the U.S. Army's final and decisive victory over the Plains Indians from a description of the Indian frontier of the 1840s to the Massacre at Wounded Knee in 1890.

Brandon, William
1961   *The American Heritage Book of Indians.*
        A very general and easy-to-read text of American Indian history.

Brophy, William A., and Sophie D. Aberle
1966   *The Indian, America's Unfinished Business.*
        The report of the Commission of Rights, Liberties and Responsibilities of the American Indian. Discussed are laws, values, political affairs, health, education, and economic development.

Brown, Dee
1970   *Bury My Heart at Wounded Knee.*
        A detailed account of the wars against the Indians from 1860 to 1890. An attempt to tell the Indian side of history.

Catlin, George
1841   *Letters and Notes on the Manners, Customs, and Conditions of the North American Indians.*
        Diaries and letters from a famous painter of Indian subjects. Fascinating accounts of culture change and the tragedy of disease.

DeLoria, Vine, Jr.
1969   *Custer Died for Your Sins.*
        The opinions of a Sioux Indian concerning the position and problems of Indians today.

Forbes, Jack D., ed.

1964   *The Indian in America's Past.*
        Includes speeches of Indian leaders, descriptions of U.S. policy toward Indians, and a section on contemporary Indians.

Greenway, John

1969   "Will the Indians Get Whitey?" *National Review,* March 11.
        A minority opinion about Indian history and contemporary Indians, one which many will disapprove, but students should be aware that such attitudes exist.

Kennedy, Michael, ed.

1965   *The Red Man's West.*
        Selected from *Montana, the Magazine of Western History,* articles on Indian history, religion, warfare, and culture change.

LaFlesche, Francis

1963   *The Middle Five.*
        Written by an Omaha Indian who became a professional anthropologist, this book tells of his life in a boarding school at the turn of the century. Gives an immediacy that accounts written by outsiders cannot attain.

Levine, Stuart, and Nancy O. Lurie, eds.

1970   *The American Indian Today.*
        Readings on culture change, Pan-Indianism, contemporary Indian tribalism, and legal problems of Indians.

Mooney, James

1965   *The Ghost Dance Religion.*
        An edited edition of Mooney's original work on the Ghost Dance and the Sioux uprising of 1890, eliminating the more technical parts and retaining a detailed account of the history of the Ghost Dance and a description of the ceremonies.

Spicer, Edward H., ed.

1961   *Perspectives in American Indian Culture Change.*
        Six studies of change in Indian ways of life from early contact to the present.

Steiner, Stan

1968   *The New Indians.*
        An energetic description of the beginnings of Indian power movements by a journalist.

Waddell, Jack O., and O. Michael Watson, eds.

1971   *The American Indian in Urban Society.*
        Studies of Indians undergoing the processes of adjusting to city life. Includes a chapter on government policies.

Walker, Deward E.
1972   *The Emergent Native Americans.*
       A collection of articles dealing primarily with contemporary Indians.

Washburn, Wilcomb E., ed.
1964   *The Indian and the White Man.*
       Collection of documents like treaties, letters, and statements by and about Indians.

Wax, Murray
1971   *Indian Americans, Unity and Diversity.*
       Contemporary situations and problems of Indians and some historical explanations of Indian treatment by government and individuals. Some very helpful statistics in the appendices.

Wilson, Edmund
1960   *Apologies to the Iroquois.*
       Fascinating study of contemporary Iroquois visited by the writer. The book includes Joseph Mitchell's article, "The Mohawks in High Steel," which relates the success some Mohawk have found in high-steel work.

Barnett, Homer G.
1957   *Indian Shakers.*

Other Pertinent Works

Cohen, Felix
1942   *Handbook of Federal Indian Law.*

Deardorff, Merle
1951   *The Religion of Handsome Lake.*

Leacock, Eleanor, and Nancy O. Lurie
1971   *North American Indians in Historical Perspective.*

Linton, Ralph
1940   *Acculturation in Seven American Indian Tribes.*

Prucha, Francis P.
1962   *American Indian Policy in the Formative Years.*
1971   *The Indian in American History.*

Spicer, Edward H.
1962   *Cycles of Conquest.*

Van Stone, James W.
1962   *Point Hope: An Eskimo Village in Transition.*
1967   *Eskimos of the Nushagak River.*

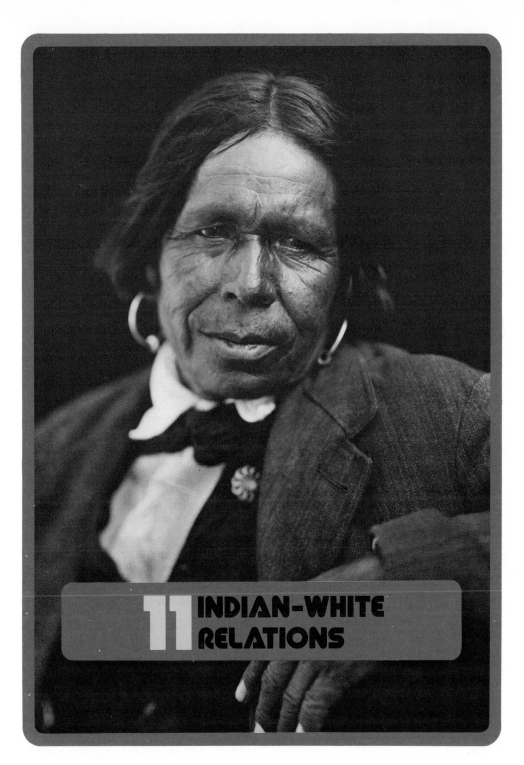

11 INDIAN-WHITE RELATIONS

Early in the eleventh century, Leif Ericson, a Norwegian, and Thorfinn Karlsefni, an Icelander, discovered a territory they called Vinland. We still do not know whether that was Labrador or the New England coast, but it was the first European landing in North America that we know of. The Norsemen called the people they met Skraellings, which was their word for "natives." Probably the Skraellings were northern Algonkians or possibly Eskimo, but their contact with the European explorers was so brief that no trace of it has come down in Indian or Eskimo legend.

Other European voyagers might have reached the shores of North America, blown there by storms or even venturing there deliberately, but if they did, they left no record. It took almost 500 years for another European to reach mainland North America. John Cabot landed in 1497 somewhere in what is now Canada, probably on the coast of Labrador or Newfoundland, and he claimed North America for King Henry VII of England.

Columbus, with his crews on the *Niña, Pinta,* and *Santa Maria,* is the European given credit for discovering the New World, and in terms of the far-reaching results of his landing in the West Indies, he deserves it. Floods of Europeans soon swept North and South America, coming face-to-face everywhere with the native Americans.

Preceding page:
A Pueblo dignitary.

Printed in 1651, this earliest known view of New Amsterdam shows Indians in canoes filled with furs, and ships of the Dutch East India Company.

European powers were fascinated by North America's commercial possibilities. Ponce de Leon sailed around a southeastern projection of the mainland, named it Florida, and claimed it for Spain in 1513. He found the natives hostile and did not venture inland. The middle part of North America's eastern seaboard was still largely unknown to European mariners in the early 1520s, but Newfoundland and Nova Scotia, called Codfish Land because fishing was so productive along their coasts, were familiar to crews of many European vessels who put into the bays for water, fresh food, and repairs. They must have had some contact with the natives, though they left no record of it. Between Codfish Land and Florida even the coast was unknown territory.

Early European Exploration

Between 1492 and 1763, no one European power was dominant in North America. France, England, and Spain were engaged in a physical and diplomatic power struggle for control, while colonists from a few other nations such as Holland hacked homes out of the forests.

Areas of Investigation

France, concerned for its fishing enterprises off the North American coast and hoping to find a northern waterway to the Orient, sent Jacques Cartier on exploratory voyages into the Gulf of St. Lawrence. There he made friendly contacts with the Algonquin (not to be confused with the Algonkian language) and Huron tribes. He went as far as 900 miles inland from the Atlantic by 1541, thus laying the basis for later French claims in North America. Some French settled far to the south in Florida, only to be destroyed by the Spanish in 1565. Religious wars in France kept its voyagers home for the next two generations.

Spanish troops, after destroying the French Florida settlement, built a frontier fort, St. Augustine, which grew into the first European town in North America. The Spanish set out for the interior from the Florida territory in 1539 under Hernando de Soto. At about the same time, Spanish explorers and troops under Francisco de Coronado entered the Southwest from Mexico. They were seeking Cibola, the legendary Seven Cities of Gold reported by survivors of an earlier expedition. The Spanish were in the New World mostly for wealth, especially gold, and legends sprang up throughout their territory about cities of gold. In 1539 a priest decided that the Zuni Pueblo must be Cibola. De Soto and his men marched westward from Florida across the South to the Mississippi River and then north. Coronado reached the Pueblo Indians, and his soldiers were the first Europeans to see the Grand Canyon of the Colorado. He then turned east to what is now Kansas, where he almost met de Soto. Both parties ran into many tribes of Indians along their way.

Following up late on Cabot's 1497 claim, the English, barred from the southern seas by Spanish sea power, turned north. In 1583, Humphrey Gilbert tried to start a colony in Newfoundland, and in 1587, Walter Raleigh did the same far to the south on Roanoke Island off the coast of today's North Carolina. But the first lasting English settlements in North America and the beginning of long-term contact with Indians were at Jamestown in Virginia and the Pilgrim colony in Massachusetts. These people were far more interested in Europe than in seeing the interior of the American continent, and generations passed before they went west of the Appalachians.

The French explored the Mississippi basin, their way made easy by the connecting waters of the St. Lawrence River, the Great Lakes, and the Mississippi. Jacques Marquette and Louis Joliet sailed down the Mississippi almost to the mouth of the Arkansas in 1673, charting the territory. Thus the general geography of the eastern third of the continent was mapped through the combined knowledge of Spanish, English, and French explorers.

Struggle in the East. Until the Revolutionary War, the English settled along the coast—east of the Alleghenies, all the way from Canada to Spanish Florida. Scattered among the British population were small groups of Dutch settlers, and blacks in the South, and a few French, Germans, and Swedes.

After the French and Indian War (1755 to 1763), in which England, France, and Spain fought each other for control of North America, England became the sole power east of the Mississippi, although France still held the Louisiana territory to the west. All three major European powers in colonial America needed and used Indian allies to supplement their forces in military campaigns. The Indians, long accustomed to hostilities between tribes, took sides against traditional enemies: some Iroquois tribes and some Algonkian speakers, for example, joined the Europeans to fight each other.

That conflict of Indian against Indian led Tecumseh, Pontiac, and some others to try to unite the Indians and drive out the Europeans. Perhaps there was a time early in the colonization when the combined efforts of the tribes could have expelled the invaders. But soon the Europeans came in such great numbers and their technology was so superior that Indian defeat was inevitable; and the Europeans turned on their Indian allies and drove them from their own territory.

Ten years before the American Revolution, Spain dominated the Southwest. France, forced out of the East by the Treaty of Paris, gave up to Britain all of Canada and Louisiana east of the Mississippi River, except New Orleans; thus the Eastern Indians suddenly became British subjects. Great Britain also acquired Florida from Spain, holding it for only two decades, from 1763 to 1783. Spain, meanwhile, took over Louisiana west of the Mississippi as well as New Orleans, only to agree in 1800 to transfer them back to France.

Exploration of the Northwest Coast.   With the Spanish established in Mexico, which then included much of California and the American Southwest, most of North America was known to Europeans. The last area to come under European scrutiny was the Northwest Coast. Gold and fur seekers from imperial Russia followed fishermen to the Aleutian Island chain. Then in 1741 Vitus Bering, a Dane sailing under the Russian flag, discovered the strait now named after him which separates Asia from the New World. From that moment, fur traders from Russia poured into Alaska seeking valuable pelts and advanced down the coast. Traders and explorers from other countries followed, among them James Cook and George Vancouver from England, and by 1793 all the coasts of North America were mapped.

European Goals

Indians thus met many different groups of Europeans, each with a different goal. In general, the English came to the New World to settle, build homes, own land, and raise families. The French came for commercial reasons, the fur trade primarily, and with the traders or immediately behind them came French priests to convert the natives. The Spanish came after gold, though their priests too came for converts. Like all generalizations, these statements tend to break down in the particular, but they are some help in understanding the different attitudes of people from the three most involved nations toward the American Indians. Because these goals and attitudes made the interactions and relationships among the many European and Indian groups very complicated, they are worth describing in greater detail.

The Spanish.   In the sixteenth and seventeenth centuries, the Spanish occupied strategic points along the Florida shoreline for military purposes. English privateers preyed on Spanish gold and silver bullion ships traveling with their cargoes from Mexico to Spain through the Straits of Florida between the mainland and Cuba. The Spanish used their forts as supply depots and ports of refuge for their ships. They were not interested in taking land from the Florida Indians or permanently settling there. Spanish priests came over, though, dedicated to saving souls, beginning a remarkably friendly and lasting contact between priests and natives.

In the Southwest the search for gold proved fruitless; Spanish commercial interest there waned, but again the secondary goal of conversion to Christianity remained strong. In fact, when the Rio Grande Pueblo resisted conversion and insisted on keeping their traditional religious practices, the clergy called upon the Spanish military to force Christianity upon the Indians. That destroyed peaceful relationships in that area. In California, the Spanish established missions backed by military might, but the California natives were less resistant to the clergy's appeals and did not fight for their traditional ways. Consequently Spanish rule there was gentler than in the Southwest, though they did punish Indians caught in their traditional religious practices, which the Spanish priests considered idolatrous, and forced them into an alien way of life. But the California fathers were generally kind in a paternalistic way and genuinely wanted to better Indian life, at least by Spanish Catholic standards.

The English.   English explorers and settlers landed all along the Atlantic coast, from Canada to the Carolinas. English and Indians were at peace and generally friendly at first, but the cordiality did not last. There were two basic reasons for the increasing conflict and distrust that soon separated them: religion and economics.

Puritan English settlers saw the Indians as heathens (non-Puritan and non-English) and devil worshipers, but more than that, many of them often believed the Indians to be less than human. While official Catholic doctrine proclaimed Indians to be human beings and therefore candidates for conversion, Protestantism, at least in its more rigidly Puritanical forms, denied their humanity.

Many English did not bother to understand or even learn about native values and beliefs. Most of them treated the Indians as heathens, inferiors, and undesirables, although there were a few notable exceptions like Roger Williams of Rhode Island Colony and William Penn and other English Quakers. Even when they managed to convert the natives, many English looked down on them and insulted Indian pride. Some theologians (Cotton Mather was the prize example) thought that Indians were too savage and too inferior even to profit from conversion. Naturally people with attitudes like those saw nothing but sin and horror in the idea of marriage between Europeans and Indians, so that intermarriage in the English-dominated area was rare.

One economic fact inevitably brought strife between Indians and English—and indeed between Indians and all Europeans: their difference in attitude toward land ownership. To the Indian, land was a free good, to be used but not owned. But for the English, owning their very own land was the goal that drew many, perhaps most, across the ocean. Most of the British immigrants were the poor, the dispossessed, and the younger sons of nobility who had no rights in land back home. They had dreamed of finding cheap real estate subject to complete private ownership, and that was what they came after. When an Indian gave up rights to land in exchange for goods, the English took it to mean sale of land into private ownership. They did pay for the land they took, but the Indians did not understand what the English meant by the transfer of property rights.

Such differences of opinion over land could lead only to conflict. Defending private ownership of land always brought political confrontation, and when that failed, warfare. Military activities were justified by religion. If Indians were heathen, inferior, perhaps not even human, it was perfectly all right to take their land, and if they resisted, it was all right to kill them. Thus religion was called on as an excuse for human destruction. In the Northeast, the English moved in and the Indians moved out.

Not all British were of this turn of mind, however. Many Scots who came to the New World were more sympathetic than Englishmen to Indian ideas and ideals. Scottish colonists, descendants of Scots who had lived for a century in Ulster, Northern Ireland, settled down in the Southeast. Unlike the English farther north, many of the Scots were single men, and they often married Indian women and set up homes and families. A fairly large population of mixed Scots-Indian descent grew in North Carolina, Tennessee, and Georgia. From that group came famed Indian leaders like Alexander McGillivray and Chilly and William MacIntosh of the Creek, and John Ross of the Cherokee. Scots who settled in Canada also became friendly with the Indians. Scottish fur trappers settled in the Athabaskan Subarctic, married Indian women, and produced a group of mixed-blood descendants.

The British established some schools to civilize and Christianize Indians. Dartmouth College was specifically set up in 1769 as an institution for Indian youths, and Harvard College and the College of William and Mary also were supposed to offer educational opportunities for Indians. Few Indians attended those schools, and before long their student bodies contained no one of Indian descent at all.

Trade goods were a far more powerful English influence than education. Guns and gunpowder, metal goods, and liquor were most important in commerce between English and Indians. The English also introduced domestic animals—horses, cattle, pigs, chickens—and appliances like the spinning wheel, loom, and plow. Indians of the East were using all these items in colonial times, before the Revolutionary War, and they also became accustomed to European household furniture, such as beds, and to English-style clothing. Pictures we have from colonial days show Indians not in buckskin but in calico, with cloth turbans on their heads.

The French.   French missionaries were at work from early times. In 1615, Champlain sent missionaries into the St. Lawrence area; first Franciscans, then Jesuits came. Some of the best information we have about Northeastern Indians

An eighteenth-century Mohawk sachem dressed in English-style clothing. He wears a cloth shirt, breeches, and hose.

comes from the Jesuits' careful study and recording of Indian customs. The Montagnais and Huron were particular targets for conversion. Working strenuously to halt the sale of liquor to Indians and to counteract its effects, the French clergy managed to get laws passed banning its sale, but when the Indians turned to the Dutch and English for supplies, the government reversed itself and again allowed alcohol to be sold in French territory. The missionaries kept trying to halt the traffic; they were out to help the people, not the government.

French contact with the northern Algonkian-speaking people was mostly sympathetic and friendly. French forces considered the Algonkians allies, and the French in general looked on Indians as human beings. Their Catholic doctrine was quite unlike Calvinist Protestantism: Indians were to be converted and then received as equals. European and Indian blood thus was mixed far more in French territory than anywhere else north of Mexico. The French respected most Indian institutions and even tried to learn Indian languages. Mixed-bloods spoke both French and Indian tongues, a political and economic advantage for the French.

French trade in guns gave their Indian allies an advantage over the other tribes and helped the French gain control over territory in the fur trade. The French also saw that Indian alliances would be bulwarks against the English threat. However opportunistic the French may have been, though, they usually treated the Indians as human and equal.

The French lost their hold on the New World largely because the Indians with whom they allied themselves were weaker than those allied with England. The League of the Iroquois was hostile to the French mostly because the League members were hereditary enemies of the French Indian allies, the Algonkian speakers and the Huron. Earlier, alliances with the Algonkians had helped France win a stronghold in the Northeast, but it was largely the Iroquois alliance with England that drove the French out. The Iroquois were better military strategists than the Algonkians, and the French had allied themselves with the weaker side.

Consequences of Contact

Religious Reaction

In spite of the determination of missionaries of many faiths, Indians did not change their religious beliefs and practices easily. Many Indians were perfectly willing to add Christian dogma to their religious system—the more gods and spirits the better. But few were willing to abandon the old ways for the new.

Like their ideas about land ownership, European and Indian approaches to the supernatural were irreconcilably different. Indians did not mix ethics with religion, and Christian morality was alien to Indian thought. Missionaries deplored dream and vision seeking, particularly when it involved drugs, and they tried to stop such practices. Whereas missionaries preached moral behavior as preparation for a future life, Indian philosophy was practical and immediate. Indians used religion to persuade the supernatural to help in the problems of living, not to attain future bliss. Indians pacified spirits with offerings and observed many taboos to compel the spirits to help them. Missionaries usually saw such practices as devil worship.

Indians believed too that the natural world had a dual existence: animals, plants, and places had spiritual as well as physical being, and proper ritual could compel them to help human beings. Missionaries, on the other hand, were horrified at the idea of many gods and of merely adding Christian practices to old beliefs. They wanted Indians to change completely, to abandon the traditional ways and the traditional gods—anything less was unacceptable.

The Spread of Diseases

Germs, which could cross all cultural boundaries, caused far worse devastation than any military action. Diseases to which Europeans had developed immunities spread among New World natives with immediate and disastrous results. Isolated for 20,000 years or more, Indians had no protection against the microbes of the Old World. Whole societies perished: within a hundred years of contact, disease had left no Indians in the West Indies, and it had cut down population in some other areas to one-tenth the numbers at contact. The Indians were helpless, and so were the agents of transmission, the newcomers, who could not halt the destruction they had unleashed on unresistant peoples. Scientific medicine had little to offer before the nineteenth century.

We do not know how many Indians died from disease. Mortality figures are no better documented than those on Indian population in general. Seven-eighths of California's population at the time of contact may have died of disease, while overall mortality has been estimated at 90 percent. But these are estimates based on estimates. We do know that far more Indians died of disease than by European aggression.

Some diseases, like smallpox, flared up in sporadic epidemics or outbreaks. George Catlin, the artist who painted many Indians in the nineteenth century, described a smallpox outbreak that virtually wiped out the Mandan on the upper Missouri River. Fur traders visiting a Mandan village in 1838 had accidentally introduced the disease. All the wives and children of a man Catlin had painted died of smallpox; the man lost all interest in life, refused to eat, and died of starvation. Only thirty or forty Mandan remained alive after the epidemic, and they were enslaved by their enemies, the Arikara.

About 1800, Edward Jenner invented a vaccination against smallpox, a disease as much dreaded in Europe as in America. Doctors tried to vaccinate Indian populations as the disease spread in the nineteenth century, but failed because there were few doctors in areas of high Indian concentration, and Indians who had not seen what smallpox could do resisted attempts to vaccinate them, believing their shamans' skill would protect them.

The Spread of New World Cultigens

Plants domesticated by New World people were botanically very different from Old World crops. Many of them became important in parts of the Old World where the traditional domesticates did not grow well. Old World cultigens like wheat, barley, and rice are not suitable crops in many areas where New World domesticates, especially maize and white and sweet potatoes, can flourish. Corn spread to Africa and southern Europe, the sweet potato to China, and the white potato to northern Europe, where it became known as the Irish potato because it became so important in the Irish diet.

Tobacco cultivation also spread around the world. Carib Indians in the West Indies smoked tobacco, as Columbus discovered when he landed there. They rolled the leaves to smoke them as cigars and also burned dried leaves, inhaling the smoke through hollow reeds. Spaniards introduced cigars into Spain in 1519, and Sir John Hawkins brought tobacco to England in 1573. Tobacco used as snuff and for chewing as well as smoking became popular in the Middle East before the end of the sixteenth century. Virginia Colony virtually pinned its life on its tobacco exports in the early seventeenth century. In the early years, colonists even used tobacco leaves as a medium of exchange.

Government Policies toward Indians
The Colonial Period

During the American colonial period, from about 1620 until 1756, England left relations between the colonies and the Indians to the local governments, for the most part. The only requirements were that settlers or colonies should pay for any Indian lands they acquired, and individuals could purchase Indian lands only with permission from the government. In 1756, the king centralized control of Indian affairs by appointing two superintendents, one for northern affairs and one for southern, to negotiate with Indians and regulate trade.

Contrary to popular belief, the official British policy was to compensate Indians for their lands. Though that compensation may seem to have been pitifully

inadequate, Indians had no other way of obtaining the European metal implements, mirrors, glass beads, and even firearms they wanted, and they were quite
willing to exchange rights in land for these treasures. Knowing no such thing as
private ownership of land, Indians probably did not realize that they were actually surrendering their property. And Englishmen did not realize that the Indians
did not share their idea of the exchange.

Treaties. Colonists considered Indians independent sovereign nations and
treated them as they would any nation, under international law. Accustomed to
centralized political power, the English assumed that each tribe had a chief who
had the right to sign for his tribe as the reigning official. In a few cases that was
so: the chief of the Powhatan and the Great Sun of the Natchez did have such
power. But most groups had no person with authority to sign away tribal lands,
though colonists rarely realized that.

As the colonists signed treaties which ceded tribal land to them, they were, in
effect, pushing the tribes out of their traditional regions. In some colonies, tax-
free land was set aside by treaty for the Indians within the colony's territory, and
the colonists further promised regular payments of goods and food to the Indians who moved onto that land. Thus in a small way the reservation system
began.

The Reservation System. The idea of reservations was not new. It had a respected place in English history. Under James I in 1603, English colonists trying
to take over a section of Celtic Scotland moved the native Celts onto reservations—those Celts whom they did not exterminate. The "removal" worked so
well that they used it again in Ireland a few years later, justifying the move on
the grounds that the Celts of both Scotland and Ireland were wild and primitive
folk, and civilized English would make better use of the land. Native languages
were suppressed and tribal customs were banned. Scottish and Irish children
were sent away to English schools to be "civilized." Change the names "Celts,
Scots, Irish" to "Indian" and you have described the reservation policy in North
America, a heritage from British colonialism to the United States.

After Independence

After the Revolutionary War, eastern pioneers continued to press westward, forcing still more Indians from their land. The new federal government, still treating
the tribes as independent sovereign states, worked out a program by which Indians exchanged their lands east of the Mississippi River for territory to the west.
Population in the West was light, and few whites sought western lands in early

Between 1776 and 1800 there was continuous strife between Indian and white. This engraving showing Indians attacking Daniel Boone appeared in 1812, and helped spread the fame of white America's first western hero.

federal days, though some eastern residents and government officials began to see a surge of white population to the Pacific Ocean as the nation's "manifest destiny." Those few recognized that sooner or later conflict with the western Indians had to come, and it did. Between the time of independence from Britain and the end of the nineteenth century, both Indians and whites did many cruel and treacherous things. The Indians, of course, were trying to save what was left of their lands and homes; the whites wanted more land rights.

The Bureau of Indian Affairs.   Indian removal from the East was accompanied by payments and promises from Washington of annual funds, goods, and food, plus guarantees that the new lands would not be taken from the Indians for "as long as the grasses shall grow and the waters run."

In 1824 the federal government established a Bureau of Indian Affairs in the War Department, a clear sign of the official attitude in Indian-federal relations: hostile. Although in 1849 the Bureau of Indian Affairs was transferred to the Department of the Interior, Indians had few contacts with white Americans that were not hostile. In 1862, the Homestead Act opened up Indian land in Kansas and Nebraska to white homesteaders. After the Civil War, ex-soldiers flooded the plains seeking homesteads. By the 1870s, the Indian tribes were no longer treated as independent sovereign states, but as domestic dependencies. Almost all Indians in Canada and the United States were by then living on reservations, though many tried to resist confinement. The reservations became prison camps, federal soldiers seeing to it that Indians stayed in their allotted areas. The government established reservation schools and boarding schools in an attempt to Anglicize Indian children. Agents were put in charge of the reservations, and though many of them were genuinely sympathetic toward the tribes, they could do little, for they did not set policy. Many agents were very poor administrators; worse yet, some were dishonest, keeping supplies and embezzling money intended for Indian welfare.

Allotment. In 1887, the Allotment Act permitted individual Indians to own parcels of reservation land outright, in hopes that the new owners would take to farming and ranching and turn into farmers on the European model. It did not work that way; individual Indians leased or sold their lands to whites. Also, the government sold to whites reservation lands that were not allotted to Indians, further decreasing Indian territory. By the turn of the century, the living conditions and psychological states of reservation dwellers were hopelessly low. Strict, supervised reservation life had not "civilized" the Indians, private ownership of land had not turned them into proud farmers and ranchers, nor had forced schooling "civilized" them.

No matter how hard lawmakers in Washington tried to enact legislation to relieve the Indians' most severe problems, no matter how interested they were in fairness, they could not control the frontier and reservation territory. Far from the nation's capital, men took law into their own hands or ignored it altogether. Supplies were sent to help the Indians adjust to reservation life, schools were set up, but more often than not the Indians never got the supplies or heard of the benefits they were entitled to. Crooked agents were legion. They became wealthy profiteering while Indians were inadequately housed, clothed, and fed. Substandard living conditions, coupled with disease, kept mortality high. Many who lived felt they had nothing to live for. Their lands were gone and the governmental authorities refused to let them follow traditional ways. A change so great in so short a time, loss of both land and freedom to wander, could only be destructive. It was forced on an unwilling people who had no part in the planning, and few of those who did plan had any real knowledge of conditions or desires among the people whose very lives were involved.

It seemed logical to planners who knew little about the diversity of Indian life that if they had land and an opportunity to farm, all Indians would settle down happily to an agricultural life. Many Indians, of course, had long histories as farmers, but many others did not. Besides, only the Pueblo men among all the Indians had done actual cultivation; the others considered farming women's work. Former warriors and hunters were emasculated psychologically when they were forced to turn to farming. With proper preparation a change like that probably could have been made over several decades or generations, but not all at once. And no one consulted with Indians or asked them to take part in decisions. Administrations changed in Washington; many social, religious, and government groups were sincerely interested; but too few really knew what they were doing.

Citizenship and the Vote. Although some individual Indians had been made citizens of the United States in the nineteenth century, Indians in general were not citizens, could not vote, and had little say in their own affairs. In 1924, Congress made all Indians who were twenty-one and older, on reservations or not, citizens of the country and enfranchised them for federal elections. Most states soon thereafter gave Indians the vote, though they still could not vote in New Mexico and Arizona until after World War II.

In 1934, Congress passed the Indian Reorganization Act, giving reservation Indians the right to establish tribal governments. The act also made funds available for loans to duly elected Indian councils to improve conditions on reservations and to undertake self-government. It had provisions for education and for agricultural and industrial credit. Allotment was discontinued, making it impossible for outsiders to buy any more reservation land.

Local Culture Contact and Change

Indian societies were not all alike, nor were all the Europeans who came to the New World the same. In general, European reactions to Indi-ans varied according to the newcomers' nationality, goals, and philosophies. Now let us see how European contact affected the native American people region by region.

The Northeast

Early in the sixteenth century, French and Basque fishermen and some from other nations fished for the rich schools of cod swarming off the Newfoundland banks. They set up small depots in natural harbors to dry their catch, and while ashore they traded European goods with Indians for fresh food. Along with the goods they passed on European diseases, which moved into the continental interior far more quickly than the explorers.

Fishermen soon saw how plentiful fur-bearing animals were in the North Atlantic area, and interest turned from fish to furs. Indians swiftly took advantage of the European desire for pelts and brought fox, mink, muskrat, and, above all, beaver to the coast to trade. French traders and fur trappers moved toward the interior along with Catholic clergy, who started small settlements. The priests and nuns were there for conversions, not furs, and they made close and friendly contact with Algonkian tribes on both sides of the St. Lawrence River. French traders built Quebec as a fur depot where Indians could bring pelts to exchange for firearms, kettles, cloth, and other European imports.

The Huron Indians, Iroquoian speakers, became the middlemen in the extensive fur trade of the north. They were friendly to France and to Indians west of them, but enemies of the other Iroquoian speakers, members of the League. The Huron, on the shores of the lake of that name, charged toll to other Indians bringing furs for trade. Making use of their friendship with the Huron, the French had the advantage in the first part of the seventeenth century. The English were struggling to stay alive in settlements farther south, so that the only problem the French faced was tribal warfare between friendly Indians and their enemies. In those fights, France was forced to take sides to keep the Huron loyal, making France the enemy of the League of the Iroquois.

As fur trade expanded, trappers moved farther west seeking new supplies of the fur-bearing animals, for unrestricted trapping was rapidly bringing some species in the East near extinction. The French penetration into the Algonkian Sub-arctic was swift, and with the accompanying disease it was deadly. Not only were animals being hunted to extinction; whole tribes, like the Beothuk, were dying out. Though French and Indians were friendly and each got desirable items from the other, Indian life as it had been before contact was destroyed, with disease killing vast numbers. Indian ways changed as their old hunting and gathering habits gave way to fur trapping, and they learned to depend on trade goods.

The Atlantic Seaboard

The land from southeastern Canada to the border of Spanish Florida was settled by the English. Dutch forces briefly held the Hudson River valley, but their impact was slight. English settlements sprang up rapidly on the coast and more slowly in the interior. The area was not good for furs; besides, the English had come to build homes, not trade. Indians helped the English settlers at first, teaching the colonists how to grow the New World plants and how to cook the new foods. A few interracial marriages took place; Pocahontas married John Rolfe and went to England. But soon the friendliness disintegrated, and acts of aggression, some quite frightful, came from both sides.

Before the Eastern Indians were driven out, killed, or destroyed by disease, they received European goods that changed many of their traditional ways. By the mid-1600s, Eastern Indians were wearing garments of European cloth, cooking with pots and pans, and hunting with guns. As the English learned about North American crops, the Indians began to raise chickens, horses, dairy cattle, and fruits such as peaches and apples. The Algonkian tribes took up European

Pocahontas, daughter of the chief of the Powhatan, who married an Englishman, John Rolfe.

styles of embroidery, in the Subarctic and Great Lakes region as well as on the coast, and with imported threads and beads combined those styles with their traditional curvilinear designs to produce attractive work on buckskin and cloth, on belts, moccasins, hats, and other clothing. People are often surprised to see how similar Algonkian design is to European peasant design. They are related through the combination of the needlework that the nuns taught the Indians in French territory and the traditional vine and leaf patterns of the Eastern Indians.

The Southeast

In the Southeast the Spanish held Florida, except for a brief period of British rule, until they ceded it to the United States in 1821. When Spanish priests arrived in Florida, they turned their attention to the Florida Indians, especially the Timucua in the northern half of the peninsula. Spanish military leaders looked on these northern Indians as buffers against English settlers and soldiers threatening from the Carolinas and Georgia. In the Southeast as in the North, the Indians fought each other as allies of warring European powers. And they suffered from fast-spreading European disease.

The Creek Indians sided with the English, the Timucua and Yamassee with the Spanish, and the French had allies in the Natchez and Choctaw along the lower Mississippi River. It was during the English-Spanish conflict in the early eighteenth century that the first groups of Creek separated from the main body and moved to Florida, where they became known as Seminole.

As in other Eastern areas, Indians rapidly acquired European material culture, and their traditional clothing, equipment, and furnishings disappeared. The Spanish introduced citrus crops as well as cattle in Florida, and the northern Florida Indians and the Seminole separatists put in orchards and raised herds of cattle. The Spanish word for cattle, *vaca*, remains in the Mikasuki (Seminole) vocabulary in the south Florida swampland as *waki*.

The Spanish made no effort to settle Florida with colonists or to take land from the Indians. Spanish soldiers were there only to protect Spanish trade routes; once the Florida Indians had been converted to Catholicism, no further interference came from Spanish sources. The Florida Indians lived in peace until the American Revolution, except for the disease that, as everywhere, decimated the population.

After the Revolution, military forces under Andrew Jackson invaded Florida and forced out the Spanish. In the brutal wars that followed—with federal losses higher than in any other Indian wars—Indians were all but eliminated from Florida and the rest of the Southeast. They were moved onto land west of the Mississippi, leaving only small and isolated settlements in the East, the Cherokee in North Carolina, the Choctaw in Mississippi, and the Seminole in south Florida. The rest were forcibly settled in the lands Congress called Indian Territory, now Oklahoma. The Indians took with them little but their knowledge and skills, and started a new life far from their homelands.

The Midwest

As trapping depleted the supply of animals in the East, Indian and European trappers pushed on to the Western Great Lakes, following the chain of lakes and streams to the Mississippi River. As in earlier colonial times, those most involved with the fur trade were the French. Until the middle of the seventeenth century, few Frenchmen did the actual trapping in the Western Lakes area because the Huron kept the sources of supply for themselves. However, the Huron were defeated by their traditional enemies, the League members, and after 1650 the French and other Indians moved into the rich Huron fur lands of the Upper Great Lakes.

This 1837 lithograph, one of a series published in Charleston, South Carolina, depicts a violent Seminole attack on a federal fort.

Contact between the Europeans and Indians of the Lakes and prairie went as it had in the East. Trade boomed and disease spread. Eastern tribes, pushed off their lands by settlers, moved into the Lakes territory and in turn pressed against the tribes there. The Midwest was the scene of jockeying for territory and favorable trade positions during the 150 years before the Revolutionary War.

Many French trappers settled down and married Indian women. Trade goods supplanted traditional Indian materials; steel and iron tools as well as firearms became common Indian possessions. Like the Scottish population of the Southeast, mixed-blood families often produced political leaders. Many of the Winnebago, Ojibwa, and Ottawa came to have French names. Catholic missionaries tried to convert Indians and also to keep the French traders from undoing the conversions, for the traders paid slight attention to religion.

Stimulated by new ideas from contact with Europeans, arts and crafts among the Lakes and prairie tribes literally blossomed. Women reproduced their traditional curved designs of flowers and vines with the imported beads and silk ribbons the French introduced. The Menominee, Potawatomi, and Winnebago developed an appliqué ribbon work to adorn the cloth clothing they now wore instead of buckskin.

English pressures began to change life for the Lakes Indians. The English dispossessed the tribes in the East, who began to move into the Midwest, creating pressures on the tribes there. English trade goods, often more plentiful and of better quality than the French could supply, filtered in from the East to tempt the Indians. French and English confronted each other all across the Northeast and Midwest, and the English won.

The prosperity the Indians had achieved under the French was lost as England became the sole European power. As in the East, English settlers eyed Indian land for home sites. Indians fought desperately under Pontiac, an Ottawa, to drive back the English in 1763. They failed, as they would under the Shawnee, Tecumseh, fifty years later.

England controlled the Great Lakes area only until 1776, when forced by the War for Independence to give it up to the new United States. After that, Indians had no chance to stay and rebuild. The new nation planned expansion into Indian territory; Indians lost their land and their traditional ways, and had to abandon the new life they had become accustomed to under the French. The disease that broke out again, and alcohol, the one item of trade they always managed to get, further disorganized their lives. Sadly, as wards of the government, they moved onto reservations.

Handsome Lake. Throughout history, in times of cultural stress, societies have turned to the types of religion often called *revitalization movements*. These have been especially common in situations of oppression and deprivation, and a number of them developed among Indians as they were defeated and driven off their lands by Europeans. The earliest and most enduring Indian religious response to economic and social threat was the Handsome Lake religion, which started in the very early 1800s.

Handsome Lake was a Seneca Indian, a tribal official (the name Handsome Lake is actually a sachem's or chief's title). He was not renowned as a warrior; before his religious awakening he had been something of an invalid, a heavy drinker, and subject to visions and trances. About 1800 his dreams and visions took a new direction. He believed that he was in communication with the spirit world and that the spirits gave him a message to preach to his people, the League of the Iroquois, who were sadly disunited by the Revolutionary War. Some had sided with the British, some with the colonists, and the League had disintegrated.

Handsome Lake had had some experience with different forms of Christianity. He had some Quaker friends, and he had probably been to some of the evangelical revival meetings that were popular among frontier folk of New York. Those camp meetings were held in tents where preachers roused congregations to religious frenzy. Handsome Lake's message combined Christianity and cultural revitalization. He preached that there was a god and a heaven, and that George Washington was there too. He combined traditional Iroquois beliefs with these new doctrines, not rejecting the old ways but emphasizing changed behavior and hard work. He taught that Indians should give up alcohol and turn to farming and animal husbandry. But he did not want them to be just like the whites. He urged his people to observe their kin obligations, to avoid divorce, and to take better care of Indian children. He thought Indians should remain neutral in all wars between the whites, but he wanted them to learn some white ways. Two boys from each tribe should attend white schools, he said, but all Indian children should not go to school.

Handsome Lake died in 1815, but his doctrine was taken up and memorized by followers. By mid-century it had been recorded in writing as the Code of Handsome Lake. It spread widely as a doctrine of reform while preserving Indian identity. The Code, originally quite revolutionary, came to stand for traditional ways, and today it still has many adherents, who are considered the conservatives among the Iroquois.

The Plains

Life on the Plains changed radically when the Indians acquired horses; in fact, the area's culture climax was the result of European contact. The Indians could cover two or three times as much ground as they had on foot, and as mounted nomads they could follow the buffalo herds. They also could accumulate more property now that they had horses to carry it. The horse totally changed their economy, and in so doing changed their social structure.

The period of cultural climax with the horse was as brief as it was dramatic: by 1850 the heyday was over. While it lasted it was so satisfying that the Indians forgot their old traditions and began to think they had always been horsemen. When the days of mounted freedom were over, nothing remained to take their place. The Plains people had no desire to return to old hunting and gathering ways or to turn to agriculture, even if they remembered such activities. Never had the men of the Plains tribes been farmers. Even in the groups with farming traditions women had been the cultivators. Farming was women's work, not fit for the hunter and warrior.

Because they had kept up cultivation in their new equestrian life, the Plains Village tribes did not lose quite as much as the mounted nomads. They went back to agriculture, though they too felt that farming was degrading work for a man. And it was a severe indignity to be confined to reservations.

The Fading of the Plains Tradition.   How did the flamboyant way of the Plains nomad end? It had begun while England and France were fighting in the East for control of North America, so that neither nation had time to interfere with the Plains development. After independence, the new United States was preoccupied with unity and federation; it too, for several decades at least, was too busy to consider expanding beyond the Mississippi. In fact, through the first part of the nineteenth century, the government saw the Plains Indians as a buffer protecting the United States from Spain and Mexico in the Southwest. The United States needed time to organize and develop a strong federal government, and for a while it had enough territory east of the Mississippi to contain its attentions. The horsemen of the Plains flourished in their dramatic new life without interference from Washington.

By 1850 the country was united and strong with nothing to fear from European powers. The fur trade, having wiped out much of the animal population of the East, was expanding into the Northwest. In 1849, gold was discovered in California. Settlers were beginning to agitate for homesteads in the West, and in 1862 the Homestead Act set up inexpensive 160-acre plots of land to meet this demand. All these events produced a new interest in the Plains and put pressure on the federal government to expand into that territory. Lewis and Clark had made their long journey through the Northwest, and people expressed interest in settling there, as far off as Oregon territory. The government began planning to confine the Plains tribes to specific areas.

The End of the Buffalo. As the horse had spread into the Plains from the Spaniards in the Southwest, so firearms came in from the French in the north. Mounted Indians with guns, especially after the repeating rifle was available, began to kill far more buffalo than bows and arrows ever had. White hunters, too, pursued the buffalo. In the old days Indians had used all parts of the buffalo—hooves, horns, sinew, even stomachs had been washed out and used as containers. But with their new killing power and the demand for buffalo hides,

White hunters shooting buffalo from a train.

Building the
Union Pacific
Railroad.

the hunters skinned the buffalo and took the hide, leaving the carcass to rot. Such waste had never been known before. Even when herds of buffalo had been stampeded over deadfalls—which was not frequent—the waste had not been that great. Buffalo began to disappear, hunted out as the fur-bearing animals had been a century before in the eastern Subarctic and Great Lakes regions.

Inevitably, the government responded to complaints and demands from its citizens by trying to confine the Plains Indians, preventing their free-wandering movements following the seasonal cycle of the buffalo. At first Washington or its agents tried to set boundaries for each tribe—not reservations, but borders within which the Indians were to be free to follow their accustomed way of life. But there was never enough territory within those boundaries. To pursue the buffalo, the tribes had to move over greater distances. The next federal move was to create reservations, none of which was large enough for the old hunting practices. By then the old wandering would have come to an end anyway, for the gun had done the trick; the buffalo were gone—almost overnight, it seemed. Those great herds of thundering animals, seemingly an inexhaustible source of food, clothing, shelter, and equipment, had vanished. Government agents reasoned that it was time for the Indians to settle down, to become farmers and livestock raisers. Of course, many of the lands appropriated for Indian occupa-

An 1886 photo of Geronimo, his son, and two followers wearing European-style garments. Geronimo and his followers terrorized ranchers on both the Mexican and U.S. borders for fourteen years.

Opposite page: During the intensity of the Indian-white conflict, recruiting posters, such as this, were issued. Note the promise of the right to plunder.

tion could not support agriculture; but the Plains warriors were not interested in farming anyhow.

Desperation on the Plains. Meanwhile, railway lawyers got Indians to sign over rights-of-way through Indian territory so that railways could be built. Many deeds were signed by Indians whom the whites considered chiefs but who had no right to sign away tribal lands or to make decisions for the tribes. The plains were crisscrossed with trails and railroads and invaded by Easterners who had no right to be there but who expected protection from the federal government.

Psychological blows fell one after another on the Plains people. Their source of food gone, little aggravations piling up broke the Indian spirit, leaving despair and a sense of futility. Under pressure from church groups, the government banned the Sun Dance as brutal and uncivilized. Missionaries tried to undermine the old religions and to prevent the vision quest, calling them barbaric, superstitious, and ignorant. Alcohol too was banned, but it was always available, and from it came solace, a way of forgetting and of achieving a new kind of vision. While Indians tried to forget by using intoxicants, whites used liquor to cheat Indians, to get them to sign away property or rights while drunk.

Desperate, a few men tried to do what no other Indians had been able to do: rally men of different bands and tribes to unite and fight back. But even at that late date, Indians had not learned to stand together. Unused to long-term mili-

ATTENTION!
INDIAN
FIGHTERS

Having been authorized by the Governor to raise a Company of 100 day

U. S. VOL CAVALRY!

For immediate service against hostile Indians. I call upon all who wish to engage in such service to call at my office and enroll their names immediately.

Pay and Rations the same as other U. S. Volunteer Cavalry.

Parties furnishing their own horses will receive 40c per day, and rations for the same, while in the service.

The Company will also be entitled to all horses and other plunder taken from the Indians.

Office first door East of Recorder's Office.

HAL. SAYR.

Central City, Aug. 13, '64.

General George Custer and his troops at the battle of Little Bighorn.

tary discipline, cooperation on a large scale, or integrated tactics, they made few successful forays, winning a few battles here and there but losing the war. After General George Custer was defeated at the battle of Little Bighorn in 1876, the Indian troops disbanded. The federal troops, though defeated in battle, replaced their losses and returned to destroy another day. Indians fought well in commando-like raids or ambushes on wagon trains of supplies, and finally in isolated attacks on travelers and homesteads. But the army always came back at them, organized, united, with supplies, personnel, and replacements the Indians could not muster. The end was bound to be in favor of the federal troops.

The Ghost Dance and Wounded Knee. Living a cramped and meaningless life on rations allotted by the federal government, the once free and proud Plains Indians turned to mystical comfort. Wovoka, a Paiute, claimed to have received a vision that directed him to journey from tribe to tribe and teach a new way of life, a new doctrine. His message was to give up European ways, to return to old customs that had been practiced before the Europeans arrived, to go back to the simple life, with no guns, no alcohol, no trade goods. Give all that up, and dance. Dance, and the Europeans would depart, leaving the land once more to the Indian peoples. Dance, and the great warriors of old—all the departed Indians—would return.

Some tribes took this as a message to return to the simple life; others saw it as aggressively antiwhite; but everywhere the people believed that the dancing would bring back the Indian dead. For that reason, this religious or revitalization movement came to be known as the Ghost Dance. Throughout the West, even into California, tribes laid down their arms. Wearily they turned away from conflict, and they danced. A slow, hypnotic dance it was, not anything wild and frenzied. Some groups wore shirts, called Ghost shirts, which were supposed to give magic protection against bullets.

Federal troops were everywhere, guarding against insurrection, and this strange behavior made them nervous. The troops were on edge, always expect-

**The Ghost Dance.
Women are chanting in a trancelike state.**

ing some attack, some ambush, remembering the battle of Little Bighorn and Custer's defeat; they could not believe that the Indians had given up. The Indian turn to the mystical, together with the soldiers' skepticism, led to perhaps the saddest confrontation ever between Indian and white. A band of Indians were camped under guard by the federal troops at Wounded Knee, South Dakota. On December 22, 1890, they assembled and began to dance. An army officer ordered them to stop. Someone, it is not known who, Indian or white, fired a shot, and the cavalry guard opened fire. Two hundred Indians and sixty soldiers soon lay dead. That was the battle of Wounded Knee, the last open confrontation between Plains Indians and the dominant society.

The Southwest

Spanish explorers under Coronado's leadership were the first Europeans to set eyes on the Pueblo Indians. Seeking the fabled Seven Cities of Gold, Coronado may have thought he had found them when he saw the Pueblo dwellings along the Rio Grande in 1540. But there was no gold, and the Spaniards claimed the land for Spain, stripped the Pueblo people of their food supplies, and moved on, leaving behind only the memory of pillage. Later, in 1598, Spaniards established a colony at Santa Fe as an administrative center for Spanish territory. The Pueblo people made no resistance and were easily dominated by the Spaniards. The Rio Grande settlements had never had any unity, and no one pueblo could stand alone against Spain's military might. The Spaniards did not strike out farther west into Hopi territory, but concentrated on the pueblos clustered along the river, where they easily imposed Spanish political and religious ways.

The traditional independence of each pueblo kept the Indians from uniting for nearly eighty years, but finally interference in their religious practices by Spanish priests goaded the Pueblo people into active resistance. They had borne Spanish military and political rule with little complaint, but the missionaries' determination to destroy "idolatrous practices" angered the people beyond endurance. The missionaries banned Pueblo dancers' masks, and when some Indians protested, the Spanish seized and hung them. By 1670, secret efforts were organized to unite the Pueblo.

Popé's Uprising. The resistance was led by a man named Popé, who had been a medicine man or shaman, imprisoned by the Spanish for sorcery. Released after being whipped—a great humiliation—he began to preach revolt, claiming that the spirits would side with the Pueblo to overthrow the Spanish. He promised too that if the Pueblo united and drove out the foreigners, not only would the Indians be able to practice their old religion, but they also could keep all the booty—the Spaniards' equipment and goods.

A picture drawn from a photo taken in 1890 after Wounded Knee. A large desperate group of Sioux, who fled the reservation to surrender, were slaughtered by cavalry, their tents destroyed, their bodies plundered.

The schedule for the uprising was kept very secret. Only Popé and a few trusted individuals who also had been flogged by the Spanish knew the details of the plot. Every pueblo had a leader in touch with Popé, who was to send a message to each leader to start the uprising in his town. The secret plans were leaked to the Spanish governor by a few Indians who refused to revolt. No one knew the date, however, and the Spanish mistakenly thought it was August 13. Tesuque pueblo started their revolt on August 11, 1680, and the others followed. The Spanish, taken by surprise, were driven out after much bloodshed and returned to Mexico.

Between 1680 and 1682, Spanish forces made some unsuccessful attempts to retake the Pueblo. For a while, Popé acted as a leader for all Rio Grande Pueblo, but the Indians faced unexpected problems. The food supply ran out, and marauding Apache attacked them. When Popé died around 1688, the Indians discovered that they were now dependent on Spanish trade. The Indians had equipment and firearms, but when something broke or wore out, they could not replace or repair it, nor could they make bullets. Famine, lack of central leadership, and the need for goods all created discontent among the Pueblo. In 1692, the Spanish made a stronger attempt to return and met little resistance. By 1696, all the Rio Grande pueblos were again under Spanish control. One group of the Rio Grande people fled to the Hopi, who had remained free of Spanish domination, and there built the town of Hano on the first mesa, where it still stands. The Pueblo never again revolted against European conquerors. In fact, in the nineteenth century, they joined with the Spanish in military forays against the Athabaskan raiders who plagued them.

Pueblo religion went underground after the Spanish reconquest. The Indians paid lip service to Catholic observance, but they continued their traditional religious practices privately in their kivas. The Spanish had less impact on other aspects of Pueblo culture, and life generally continued as in past ages, though the Pueblo accepted Spanish goods and learned to speak Spanish as well as their own tongues. The Spanish influence can be seen today in interior decoration and Spanish surnames as well as in Catholic ritual.

Athabaskan Reaction. Unlike the Pueblo, the other tribes of the Southwest were greatly changed by Spanish conquest. The Navajo acquired herds of sheep, and sheepherding became an important part of their economy. The Apache, some Navajo, and some tribes on the boundary of the Plains, like the Kiowa Apache, took to a life on horseback more typical of the Plains than of the Southwest. They concentrated on buffalo hunts and warfare, raiding not only the Pueblo but also Spanish settlements for metal tools, guns, and horses.

When the Spanish Southwest became United States territory in 1848, the Athabaskan tribes, with horses and equipment acquired from the Spanish, had lived as they pleased for many years. The Spanish or Mexicans had not tried to settle colonists on the land or tried to take land from the Indians. But the United States, especially after the Civil War, began to move troops into the area, and it suddenly became clear to the Navajo and Apache that the Americans were something new to contend with. The Americans offered the Athabaskans treaties, but the Indians were too divided to sign them. No one could be responsible for all the many autonomous bands. Americans set out on an organized conquest, rounding up Navajo and Apache, driving them starving from their lands and confining them in forts. Hostile Indian groups were thrown together far from their homelands. Imprisonment was cruel, but it did organize the Indians into cohesive units. It also impressed the Indians with the might of the federal government. Reservation lands were assigned to the Navajo, and the government gave them herds of sheep to reestablish sheep raising, which they had practiced for generations. The Navajo also raised horses and some cattle, and the women developed a new craft, blanket weaving, which they had learned from the Pueblo and Spanish.

Indian scouts, along with an interpreter and an officer, crouch for battle in Arizona's desert country.

The Apache were trained fighters who knew the rugged land far better than the American troops sent to control them. When placed on reservations, the Apache often refused to remain. It took many campaigns to subdue them, but the job was complete by the end of the nineteenth century. Agents encouraged the Apache to take up farming, but it appealed to them no more than to the Plains Indians. They too suffered despair and economic hardship, but eventually turned to ranching, and the western groups began to farm. The Ghost Dance found no converts among the Athabaskans because they feared the dead; the last thing they wanted was to have the dead return.

California

In 1542, hoping to find a waterway connecting the Pacific and Atlantic oceans, a cross-continent passage to the Orient, Juan Rodrigues Cabrillo sailed up the coast of California and into bays that looked as though they might lead inland. The first European to appear on the shores of California, he claimed the land for the Spanish crown. No other Spaniards followed him until the middle of the eighteenth century, when Spain began to fear encroachment by the Russians, who were then moving down the west coast from Alaska.

No one ever found a waterway between the oceans, for none existed, but the Spanish stayed to build missions and convert Indians. The first mission, San Diego, was established in 1769 where the city is today. Indians soon learned that they could get valuable trade goods at the missions, and they began to assemble and sometimes to live near the missions. Eventually Indians became virtual prisoners of the missionaries, who kept them at the missions by calling Spanish soldiers for help. Runaways were tracked down and whipped. Some offenders were even shot, and uprisings were quickly put down. The priests halted all the Indian ceremonies and refused to allow Indians access to shamans, or to cremate their dead. The Spanish fathers were determined to civilize the Indians, to teach them to work regular hours tilling the land and raising livestock.

The priests also taught the Indians to make adobe bricks for the mission buildings, which were almost like forts. The thick walls surrounding them had only one entrance, and the buildings themselves had thick walls with very small windows. Most missions had dormitories for unmarried Indians, one for men, one for women. Married couples and their children lived outside the mission walls, but they were not free to move away. After a generation or two, they no longer wanted to move away; having forgotten their old ways, they knew only how to live under the fathers' guidance.

Each mission aimed to be self-supporting. The Indians planted corn and European crops like wheat, fruit trees, and melons; wheat bread took the place of acorn bread. Women learned to weave cloth. Some Indians became sheepherders; they had freedom denied those working the mission fields because sheep had to move from pasture to pasture, and whole families went with them. While away from the mission herding sheep, the women gathered seeds and acorns and prepared food as in the past. But even the herders were kept under mission control. Soon all mission Indians dressed and ate like Spaniards.

The fathers taught blacksmithing to the Indians but never allowed them to own horses: they could escape too easily on horseback. Many Indians did escape, but most discovered that they no longer knew how to live in the wilderness and went back to the missions for food. They had become dependent upon European technology, agriculture, livestock, and tools such as metal axes and saws.

When the United States took over California from Mexico in 1846, the Indians ran into active persecution by whites. The newcomers who came from the East to live and farm had no knowledge of Indians and did not want them on the land. Justice for Indians was so rare that few mission Indians were left by the twentieth century.

California Indians north of the mission areas were not troubled by whites until the gold rush of 1849. After that, their story was one of continuous loss of territory and general destruction. Some reservations were set up by the federal and state governments, and some Indians began working for the new arrivals on the ranches and farms. But of California's dense aboriginal population only a few remain today.

The Plateau and the Basin

People of the Plateau felt the Europeans' presence in North America long before any came to their area. Trade goods had entered the Plateau in exchange for furs, and the tribes in the eastern part of the area had horses by the middle of the eighteenth century. The eastern Plateau and mountain slopes provided good grassland for pasturage, and some tribes of that area began to live a mounted life and became able horse raisers. The Nez Perce were noted for their fine horses, which Plainsmen often sought in trade. The Cayuse horse herds were so well know that the word *cayuse* entered the English language as slang for horse.

Life changed for the Plateau people who raised horses much as it did for the Plains people, though less drastically. War and war honors became important for the men, and war chiefs had high prestige. Of course, horse raising brought about many changes in clothing, equipment, and even housing. The movable tipi became the common shelter while men were hunting. Some of the Plateau warriors even began to wear feathered warbonnets.

Almost identical changes occurred in the Basin close to the Plains, though the dry lands in most of the region made horse raising impossible. The easternmost Basin people moved out into the grasslands and lived as nomadic hunters. The Shoshone, above all, became true mounted warriors, and the Comanche, once merely a band of Shoshone, became the terrors of the southern Plains. All these changes happened before Indians and whites actually met.

Contacts and Changes. The Lewis and Clark expedition was the first intimate contact between the Plateau and Basin Indians and whites. The interpreter for that journey was a Shoshone woman, Sacajawea, who was married to a French fur trapper. They were living among the Mandan Indians when Lewis and Clark came through. She said she would like to go with them when she heard that they were heading for the Pacific Ocean, explaining that she had wanted to see that great body of water ever since she first heard of it. So she went along, and gave birth to her first child while on the march. She made the journey easier by serving as an interpreter, and several times prevented aggression by suspicious tribes. Both leaders expressed their gratitude and spoke of their debt to her.

Traders and fur trappers followed through the Northwest, many with Indian wives. As in the East, trapping soon became big business, for the demand for fine furs in Europe and Asia never ceased. Traders and trappers never caused Indians much worry, except for the germs they carried, but the settlers from the East who eyed the Northwest for homesteads and farmlands were another story.

The Basin land was not desirable for agriculture, but both Basin and Plateau people felt the loss when the buffalo herds began to vanish; tribes like the Nez Perce and Shoshone suffered as keenly as the true Plains tribes. The Basin and Plateau folk were also targets for missionaries who considered Indian religious practices devil worship, worse than heathenism. The clerics, the settlers, the loss of the buffalo, and the high incidence of disease produced despair, disorganization, and finally apathy. The Nez Perce War of 1877, a final dramatic attempt to drive the enemy away, was the last resistance in the Plateau. It failed, and the Nez Perce were confined to a reservation that had been established for them two decades earlier.

The outcome of white encroachment was much the same for the Ute, Paiute, and other Basin tribes, though their lands were less desirable and the white pressures came later than elsewhere. The Basin people rarely saw whites until after the middle of the nineteenth century. Then the discovery of gold in California, and silver in Nevada, brought outsiders into the Basin. The men who came searching for precious metals were rough and cruel, few having families or social ethics to modify their behavior. In many ways they were the outcasts of white society, the most lawless sort of frontiersmen. The atrocities they inflicted on the peaceful small bands of Indians are almost unbelievable—it can even be said that the miners exterminated Indians deliberately. So it is not surprising that the man who originated the Ghost Dance was a Paiute. The dance itself was probably a traditional Basin dance with the new message added. But of course the Ghost Dance produced no more miracles for the Basin people than it did for the Plains. Miners and ranchers took over their land, and the few Indians who survived were placed on small reservations.

The Cult of Smohalla. In the Plateau a religious movement with some aspects of the traditional vision quest taught that Indians should ignore the intruders, give up new ways, and return to the old life. An Indian known as Smohalla (the name is really a title meaning preacher), born about 1815, visited a Catholic mission as a boy. He acquired some ideas about ritual from his experiences at the mission, and after distinguishing himself as a warrior, he turned to a life of preaching in about 1850. He traveled a great deal, once as far as Mexico, and visited many tribes. He claimed to have lived in the spirit world, where the Master Spirit told him that Indians should return to their primitive life. He held services on Sundays with ritual that combined Catholicism and the Ghost Dance. The cult had its own flag, and the congregation sang songs and did simple dancing to drumming. They also practiced confession. An important part of the doctrine was that dreams helped people to get religion; people reported their dreams at the services. Smohalla preached that the earth should not be plowed and that the land should not be sold. The Nez Perce in particular followed his doctrine.

The Northwest Coast

In the years after Bering's voyage to the Aleutian Islands and Alaska, Russian traders set up an outpost near Sitka and systematically hunted otters, seals, and other sea mammals almost to extinction. The Russian fur trade was a monopoly along the coast until 1867, when the United States bought Alaska. Though most of the Indians were not actually under Russian rule, they became dependent on Russians for the highly desired trade goods, especially metal implements. Some Spanish and British ships also touched the coast at a few points, and the Chinook traders on the Columbia River added European goods to their trade inventory.

With their new tools, especially metal woodworking tools, the Northwest Indians had a brief burst of creative activity similar to the artistic reaction in the East to ribbons and glass beads. Indian woodworking became larger and more elaborate, and the very large totem poles date from the period of metal tools. Among the items the Indians eagerly sought were metal pots and kettles and Hudson Bay blankets. Both Indians of the Northwest culture area and Athabaskans of the interior exchanged furs for these goods at traders' stores or traded them through the Chinook middlemen. Furs were so plentiful that Indians built up great wealth in trade goods.

Potlatching Explodes.   As in other areas, Europeans brought not only goods but disease, causing so many deaths that many positions of high rank were left vacant as legitimate heirs died out. The combination of new wealth and a high mortality rate directly affected potlatching. Wealthy people with no rights to high rank gave wildly extravagant potlatches to rouse support for their attempts to claim titles. In the late nineteenth century, potlatching became a chaos of consumption and waste, with commoners amassing goods to give away and even destroy as they rushed to outdo all rivals. The whole rank system began to crumble.

Eventually settlers moved into the area, and Indians began to feel pressure from white rule. Many Indians were kept off their old fishing, gathering, and hunting territory. Not long after 1850, Canada and the United States began moving Northwest and Western Subarctic Indians onto reservations. Economic and social disorganization asserted itself here as elsewhere. Alcoholism increasingly caused more and more of a problem. And as elsewhere, some of the people turned to a religious movement in an attempt to come to grips with the white intrusion and economic threats.

The Shakers.   Indians of the Northwest found solace in the Shaker Church, founded by a Puget Sound Indian named John Slocum. (This church is not to be confused with the German Shakers of the East.) Slocum believed that he had died and then returned to life, and that during his death he had been told by an angel that he was too wicked to enter heaven. The angel sent him back to set up a mission among Indians. His doctrine was not antiwhite. He was to build a church and preach against drinking, gambling, and betting on horse races. His message was that the dead would come alive and the ocean would disappear to make room for all the people. He preached curing by laying on of hands and believed that he was the medium of communication with God. Some time later, shaking was added to the curing practice when Slocum became sick and believed he had been cured by his wife's hysterics, which included shaking; thus the sect became known as the Shakers.

The Arctic

Eskimo-white contact was infrequent until the end of the nineteenth century, and very little culture change occurred until after World War II. In Canada, trading posts and missions appeared, stimulating the development of permanent Eskimo settlements like those that had been common in Alaska but traditionally lacking in the Canadian Arctic. These small settlements were clustered around the European outposts where new goods were available. The greater density of population (though the settlements rarely had more than a hundred people) spread disease as well as trade goods, and as in areas to the south, mortality from smallpox, measles, tuberculosis, and other diseases was high.

Imported rifles made hunting more efficient, and demands for furs, especially of the arctic fox, made trapping a new commercial pursuit. Many Eskimo hunters gave up seeking game and turned to fur trapping to get furs to trade for European equipment. Some took jobs for wages. With less time left to hunt, many Eskimo came to depend on imported foods. Besides, game resources, especially caribou, had been depleted by disease, scarcity of lichen forests (the caribou's main food source), and above all, overkill with guns.

Jobs for money as well as trade goods could be found at trading posts, missions, and, later, government and defense installations. Settling around these, Eskimo gave up not only traditional subsistence pursuits, but their housing and other material culture, for European types. Canadian Eskimo no longer lived so widely dispersed, and some groups, like the Caribou Eskimo, disappeared as a distinct group because of disease, famine, and movement away from the Barren Grounds.

In Alaska, even more people moved to towns and into wage labor than in Canada. Intensive commercial whaling by Europeans, Japanese, and Americans depleted that resource for the Alaskan Eskimo, and with the whalers came disease and alcohol. As in Canada, game became scarce as repeating rifles made killing more efficient. The Alaskans changed from hunting subsistence to a money economy, selling furs, ivory, and whalebone to traders. As towns, missions, and government posts increased, some people began to work for salaries or wages, completely abandoning hunting. Settlements in Alaska changed from native villages of one hundred or so people to concentrations in larger towns and even cities.

Canadian Government Policy

Canada's basic policy for dealing with Canadian Indians was spelled out in the Proclamation of 1763. That act provided that Indians would be removed from land only with their consent and the approval of the Crown.

The Canadian government did not make treaties with Indians until 1850. The treaties involved various things: setting aside land for Indian use exclusively, trusteeship by the government, control of liquor, and setting up schools. The treaties also ended all Indian titles to land; the use of land was theirs, but under government ownership. Lands that the French had set aside for Indians when Canada was under French control remained Indian land after the British took over. Reservations (called *reserves* in Canada) were established in lands already occupied by Indians or in very similar environments. Indians were never removed in large numbers from their original territories to other lands as they were in the United States.

The Indian Act of 1951 is the most recent definition of the Indians' legal position. Until that year, Canadian Indians did not vote and could not buy alcoholic beverages. By the Indian Act, a person is defined as an Indian who is registered as an Indian or is entitled to be registered as one. Names of Indians who are band members appear on Band Lists; anyone who is not a band member but is entitled to be registered is named on a General List. The Department of Indian Affairs keeps the lists. In Canada, being an Indian is a matter of legal definition.

Under the 1951 act, the government was charged with helping Indians take part in Canada's social and economic life. To do this, it has prepared programs in education, economic development, social welfare, sanitation, child and adult education, and business enterprise. It also oversees the administration of reserves and band funds and the descent of property.

Any Indian may decide to become enfranchised by giving up all rights as an Indian. When he becomes enfranchised, he receives a share of the trust fund of the band to which he belongs. Whole bands too may apply for enfranchisement and division of trust funds. The government approves enfranchisement only when the person is considered able to assume the duties and responsibilities of citizenship and to support himself and his dependents. Any woman marrying a non-Indian is automatically enfranchised. The government may declare the Indian wife and children of an Indian man applying for enfranchisement to be enfranchised. Any person who is enfranchised is defined by the government as non-Indian, his name is taken from the Band List or the General List, and Indian statutes no longer apply to him. He relinquishes his tax-free status and his claims to reserve land.

Today the liquor laws in Canada leave the sale of intoxicants to Indians to local option, to the provinces and the inhabitants of the reserves. Intoxication is, however, an offense everywhere in Canada.

Today Canada has about 250,000 Indians and 17,000 Eskimo. Indian affairs in Canada were under military jurisdiction in early years, but they are now under civilian control in the Indian Affairs Branch of the Department of Citizenship and Immigration, as are Canadian Eskimo. Parliament legislates for all Indians in all provinces; just as in the United States, Indian affairs are handled by the federal government, not the states. The Branch of Indian Affairs manages Indian lands and an Indian Trust Fund, and is responsible for Indian welfare, health, education, agriculture, and industry. Since 1951, Indians have been able to vote in national elections in Canada.

Canadian Indians today live in 561 communities known as *bands,* on reserve lands ranging from a few acres to more than five hundred square miles. These lands are set aside by the Canadian government for the use and benefit of Indians. About 25 percent of the Indian population lives off the reserves. Band governments consist of band councils and chiefs elected by band members. The councils work with representatives of the Department of Indian and Northern Affairs, making by-laws on local matters and conditions.

Most people who have compared Indian history and conditions in the United States and Canada think that Indians in Canada have generally been better treated by their government. White demand for Indian land has been less pressing, and the government has protected Indians against attempts to take their reserves.

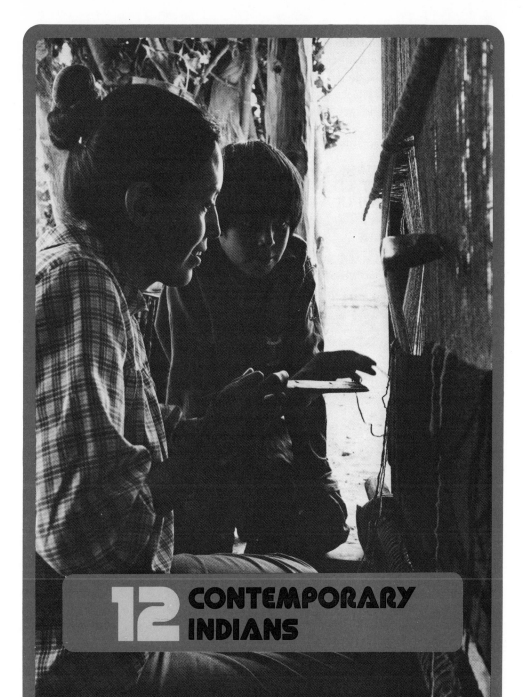

12 CONTEMPORARY INDIANS

More than 800,000 Indians and Eskimo live in the United States today, fewer than half of them on reservations. In the East scattered groups of Indians are mixed in the general population, speaking no language but English and living and working exactly like their non-Indian neighbors. Only on special occasions or holidays do they gather for ethnic activities, as Italian-Americans

INDIANS AND ALASKAN NATIVES IN THE UNITED STATES: 1960 AND 1970 POPULATIONS COMPARED.

State	1960	1970	State	1960	1970
Alabama	1,276	2,443	Missouri	1,723	5,405
Alaska	42,522[a]	50,654[b]	Montana	21,181	27,130
Arizona	83,387	95,812	Nebraska	5,545	6,624
Arkansas	580	2,014	Nevada	6,681	7,933
California	39,014	91,018	New Hampshire	135	361
Colorado	4,288	8,836	New Jersey	1,699	4,706
Connecticut	923	2,222	New Mexico	56,255	72,788
Delaware	597	656	New York	16,491	28,355
District			North Carolina	38,129	44,406
of Columbia	587	956	North Dakota	11,736	14,369
Florida	2,504	6,677	Ohio	1,910	6,654
Georgia	749	2,347	Oklahoma	64,689	98,468
Hawaii	472	1,126	Oregon	8,026	13,510
Idaho	5,231	6,687	Pennsylvania	2,122	5,533
Illinois	4,704	11,413	Rhode Island	932	1,390
Indiana	948	3,887	South Carolina	1,098	2,241
Iowa	1,708	2,992	South Dakota	25,794	32,365
Kansas	5,069	8,672	Tennessee	638	2,276
Kentucky	391	1,531	Texas	5,750	17,957
Louisiana	3,587	5,294	Utah	6,961	11,273
Maine	1,879	2,195	Vermont	57	229
Maryland	1,538	4,239	Virginia	2,155	4,853
Massachusetts	2,118	4,475	Washington	21,076	33,386
Michigan	9,701	16,854	West Virginia	181	751
Minnesota	15,496	23,128	Wisconsin	14,297	18,924
Mississippi	3,119	4,113	Wyoming	4,020	4,980
[a] Includes 5,755 Aleuts and 22,323 Eskimo.					
[b] Includes 6,581 Aleuts and 27,797 Eskimo.			United States	551,669	827,108

Preceding page: A Navajo mother and son weaving a rug.

Bureau of Indian Affairs Statistics Division, July 1972, from Census report PC(1)-B, Table 17.

may hold a parade to celebrate Columbus Day. In Rhode Island, for instance, people who consider themselves Narragansett Indians still hold "tribal" meetings. Biologically, these people have very little Indian in them—no one could distinguish them from the rest of Rhode Island's population. Yet they hold yearly festivals and support an "Indian" church. In most of their living habits, there is little to remind us of the former large tribes in the East.

California too has small groups who do not live on reservations. Most of those Indians are rural, and usually they work for wages in agriculture. They appear to be less assimilated into the general population than the Eastern nonreservation Indians, but their employment, schooling, and marketing often put them in contact with non-Indians. Their cultural distinctiveness seems to be decreasing.

Oklahoma has the largest Indian population; Arizona and California also have over 90,000 Indians. Congress designated Oklahoma "Indian Territory," where Eastern Indians were settled after being removed from their lands. Reservation lands once covered 30,000,000 acres. By about 1910, all except for the Osage reservation was allotted to individual Indians or sold to non-Indians. Today, descendants of people of many tribal affiliations live in Oklahoma, among them Creek, Cherokee, Seminole, and Osage, but the only reservation there is Osage. Many Oklahoma Indians live in rural areas where they often control or actively participate in county government; others have settled in Tulsa and Oklahoma City.

All these people think of themselves to some degree as Indians, though their amount of Indian genetic inheritance may be as little as a sixteenth or less. Yet most are not federally recognized as Indians: they are not covered by federal Indian law or eligible for the services offered by the Bureau of Indian Affairs. Hundreds of thousands of others who are part Indian, an eighth or more, do not think of themselves as Indian or count themselves Indian in the United States Census. Being Indian, then, is a matter of culture and, to some extent, choice—not just blood or biology.

Since World War II, more and more Indians have moved from rural areas and towns and from reservations into cities. Los Angeles has more than 25,000 Indian residents, almost all from out of state, and other western and midwestern cities also have thousands of Indian residents. Of the Indians age sixteen and over who are employed, 50 percent work in urban areas.

Reservations

Reservations are the more than two hundred tracts of land set aside by the United States government in treaty, statute, or executive order for the use and benefit of Indian tribes. Some reservations are solid blocks of tribal land; others are interspersed with sections of land belonging to non-Indians. Some reservations are restricted to one tribe, though many are home to several tribes. Membership in a tribe or rights to a place on a reservation are determined by requirements set by the tribe or its governing body. How much Indian blood one must have to claim tribal membership varies from tribe to tribe.

Reservations fall under two different jurisdictions. Most are federal trusts controlled by the federal government, but others are state reservations, especially in New York, Pennsylvania, and Maine—and in California, where they are often called rancherias. The only federal reservations east of the Mississippi are in the Western Great Lakes area and in New York state, and those of the Cherokee in North Carolina, the Seminole in Florida, and the Choctaw in Mississippi. Largest of all is the Navajo reservation; with more than 14,000,000 acres, mostly in Arizona, it completely encloses the Hopi reservation. Navajo population is also largest—nearly 100,000, according to the 1970 census.

Indian Rights on Reservations

Indians who live on reservations are free to come and go or to live anywhere else they choose and can afford. The government is the trustee of Indian land, not the master of individual Indians any more than it is of other citizens. At one time, some Indians were considered "wards" of the government, but no longer. The reservations are not prison camps; they are not even enclosed. Many major highways run through reservation land, and outsiders frequently travel them, often without realizing that they are on a reservation.

Reservation Indians have rights in their land and can live on it without paying land taxes. They share in sales of mineral wealth, land rentals, and agricultural produce from the land. Each individual's share may be a cash payment, or it may be a share in investments or improvements made for all the tribe, such as housing, recreation facilities, or college scholarships. Indians do pay the other taxes that are levied on the general citizen—income tax, sales tax, and even real estate tax if they buy land outside the reservation. No Indian can sell his share of reservation land, though he can usually bequeath it to his heirs if they are tribal members.

Indians have the same voting rights as all other citizens. For federal, state, and county elections they vote in their districts, wards, or precincts, and all are enfranchised at the age of eighteen. Eligibility to vote in tribal elections is determined by the tribe. Non-Indians living on reservations usually are not allowed to vote in tribal elections, though of course they can vote in the other elections. Indians also can run for office in general as well as tribal elections. Many have held state and federal office in the western states where Indian populations are large.

SOME FEDERAL INDIAN RESERVATIONS

ARIZONA
  Ak-Chin
  Camp Verde
  Cocopah
  Colorado River
  Fort Apache
  Fort McDowell
  Gila Bend Papago
  Gila River
  Havasupai
  Hopi
  Hualapai
  Kaibab
  Maricopa
  Navajo
  Papago
  Salt River
  San Carlos
  San Xavier Papago
  Yavapai

CALIFORNIA*
  Agua Caliente
  Alpine Washoe
  Big Pine
  Bishop
  Cabazon
  Cahuilla
  Campo
  Capitan Grande
  Chemeheuvi
  Colorado River
  Fort Independence
  Fort Mojave
  Fort Yuma
  Hoopa Valley
  Hoopa Valley Extension
  Inaja Cosmit
  La Jolla
  La Posta

Lone Pine
Los Coyotes
Manzanita
Mesa Grande
Morongo
Pala
Pauma
Pechanga
Ramona
Rincon
Round Valley
San Manuel
San Pasqual
Santa Rosa
Santa Ynez
Santa Ysabel
Soboba
Sycuan
Torres Martinez
Tule River
Twenty-Nine Palms
X L Ranch

COLORADO
  Southern Ute
  Ute Mountain

FLORIDA
  Big Cypress
  Brighton
  Hollywood

IDAHO
  Coeur D'Alene
  Duck Valley
  Fort Hall
  Nez Perce

IOWA
  Sac and Fox

KANSAS
  Kickapoo
  Potawatomi

LOUISIANA
  Chitimacha

MICHIGAN
  Bay Mills
  Hannahville
  Isabella
  Keweenaw Bay
  L'Anse
  Ontonagon

MINNESOTA
  Deer Creek
  Fond du Lac
  Grand Portage
  Greater Leech Lake
  Lower Sioux
  Nett Lake
  Prairie Island
  Prior Lake
  Red Lake
  Upper Sioux
  White Earth

MISSISSIPPI
  Choctaw

MONTANA
  Blackfeet
  Crow
  Flathead
  Fort Belknap
  Fort Peck
  Kootenai
  Northern Cheyenne
  Rocky Boys

*Only major reservations listed. California also has many rancherias—very small land trust areas.

Continued

SOME FEDERAL INDIAN RESERVATIONS (Continued)

NEBRASKA
- Omaha
- Santee
- Winnebago

NEVADA
- Battle Mountain
- Carson
- Duck Valley
- Duckwater
- Elko
- Ely
- Goshute
- Las Vegas
- Lovelock
- Moapa River
- Odgers Ranch
- Pyramid Lake
- Reno-Sparks
- Ruby Valley
- South Fork
- Stewart School
- Summit Lake
- Walker River
- Washoe
- Winnemucca
- Yerington

NEW MEXICO
- Acoma
- Alamo Navajo
- Canoncito Navajo
- Cochiti
- Isleta
- Jacarilla
- Jemez
- Laguna
- Mescalero
- Nambe
- Navajo
- Picuris
- Pojoaque
- Sandia

- San Felipe
- San Ildefonso
- San Juan
- Santa Ana
- Santa Clara
- Santo Dominto
- Tesuque
- Taos
- Ute Mountain
- Zia
- Zuni

NEW YORK
- Allegany
- Cattaraugus
- St. Regis
- Tonawanda

NORTH CAROLINA
- Cherokee

NORTH DAKOTA
- Devil's Lake
- Fort Berthold
- Sisseton
- Standing Rock
- Turtle Mountain

OKLAHOMA
- Osage

OREGON
- Fort McDermitt
- Umatilla
- Warm Springs

SOUTH DAKOTA
- Cheyenne River
- Crow Creek
- Flandreau
- Lower Brule
- Pine Ridge
- Rosebud

- Sisseton
- Standing Rock
- Yankton

UTAH
- Goshute
- Navajo
- Skull Valley
- Unitah and Ouray

WASHINGTON
- Chehalis
- Coleville
- Hoh
- Lower Elwha
- Lummi
- Makah
- Muckleshoot
- Nisqually
- Ozette
- Port Gamble
- Port Madison
- Puyallup
- Quileute
- Quinault
- Skokomish
- Spokane
- Squaxon Island
- Swinomish
- Tulalip
- Yakima

WISCONSIN
- Bad River
- Lac Corte Oreille
- Lac du Flambeau
- Menominee
- Oneida
- St. Croix
- Stockbridge Munsee

WYOMING
- Wind River

Reservation Facilities

Reservations are not totally rural; they usually have towns or villages, and a few include small cities. In recent years industry has developed on a few reservations, but most Indian territory is far from major transportation centers and skilled work forces, so that industrial development has been slow. The lack of industry and other job opportunities has been a major reason for the movement to cities. Most reservations do, however, have small shopping centers or a few stores.

On the Navajo reservation there are still over two hundred trading posts, even though towns have grown up there too. The relationship between Navajo and traders benefits both. Set up in remote areas, the posts are stocked with up to several thousand items of food and merchandise, many of which the people would have to travel far to get otherwise. Traders often provide services as well, like burying the dead, a task the Navajo are most reluctant to undertake. Navajo also can pawn jewelry with traders or get credit from them when they are in financial straits. The trader, of course, makes a profit. At one time many traders were unfair because they had a monopoly on trade, but today laws regulate trading practices, and the Navajo are better educated and too sophisticated to be cheated easily.

A Navajo trading post. There are more than 200 well-stocked trading posts on the Navajo reservation.

BUREAU OF INDIAN AFFAIRS ORGANIZATION*

SECRETARY DEPARTMENT OF THE INTERIOR

COMMISSIONER OF INDIAN AFFAIRS

DEPUTY COMMISSIONER

CONGRESSIONAL & LEGISLATIVE AFFAIRS STAFF

INTERGOVERNMENTAL RELATIONS STAFF

PUBLIC INFORMATION STAFF

POLICY PLANNING STAFF

OFFICE OF INDIAN SERVICES
- DIVISION OF HOUSING SERVICES
- DIVISION OF LAW ENFORCEMENT SERVICES
- DIVISION OF SOCIAL SERVICES
- DIVISION OF TRIBAL GOVERNMENT SERVICES
- DIVISION OF TRIBAL PLANNING SERVICES

OFFICE OF TRUST RESPONSIBILITIES
- DIVISION OF TRUST FACILITATION
- DIVISION OF TRUST SERVICES

JOINT USE ADMINISTRATIVE OFFICE

OFFICE OF ADMINISTRATION
- EEO STAFF
- CONTRACTING STAFF
- AUDIT STAFF
- ADP PLANNING AND POLICY STAFF

SUPPORT SERVICES
- DIVISION OF ADMINISTRATIVE SERVICES
- DIVISION OF SAFETY MANAGEMENT
- DIVISION OF PROPERTY MANAGEMENT
- DIVISION OF ADP SERVICES
- DIVISION OF PERSONNEL MANAGEMENT

MANAGEMENT SERVICES
- DIVISION OF PROGRAM DEVELOPMENT AND IMPLEMENTATION
- DIVISION OF MGMT. RESEARCH & EVALUATION
- FINANCIAL MANAGEMENT
- DIVISION OF ACCOUNTING MANAGEMENT
- DIVISION OF FACILITIES ENGINEERING

OFFICE OF INDIAN EDUCATION PROGRAMS
- DIVISION OF PROFESSIONAL RELATIONS
- DIVISION OF INTERNAL SERVICES
- INDIAN EDUCATION RESOURCES CENTER

OFFICE OF TRIBAL RESOURCES DEVELOPMENT
- DIVISION OF INDIAN BUSINESS ENTERPRISE
- DIVISION OF FINANCIAL ASSISTANCE
- DIVISION OF JOB PLACEMENT AND TRAINING
- DIVISION OF TRANSPORTATION

AREA OFFICES

* As of March 1975, about 40 percent of the main division of the BIA organization were headed by Indians. This percentage, of course, only reflects the status at that time.

At one time both state and federal laws prohibited sale of alcoholic beverages to Indians. In 1953, Congress gave Indians the right to buy liquor off reservations under the same conditions and regulations as non-Indians. However, the ban against selling liquor on reservations remained in effect unless the tribal government voted for legalization. Now some tribes allow sales on their reservations and some do not.

The Bureau of Indian Affairs

The reservation's administration is supervised by the Bureau of Indian Affairs, with a central office in Washington, D.C., and area offices throughout the country. Chief executive of the BIA is the commissioner of Indian affairs; helping him are assistant commissioners in charge of such fields as administration, community services, and economic development. Area directors are in charge of regional offices that supervise the agencies for the reservations. Superintendents (sometimes referred to as agents) are in charge of the agencies. Three agencies, Cherokee, Seminole, and Miccosukee, do not fall under any area office but are directly under the Office of the Commissioner.

If a tribe has organized and formed a government under the provisions of the Act of 1934, that government takes a large part in planning and making deci-

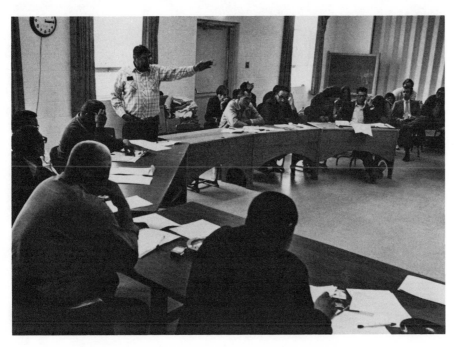

A Sioux tribal council in session.

sions for the tribe. That act, the so-called Indian Reorganization Act, aimed at reviving or restoring Indian uniqueness and identity. It set up the mechanism for tribal government on reservations and encouraged Indian art and customs. Each reservation also has a superintendent from the Bureau of Indian Affairs personnel (more than half of whom are of Indian descent). Superintendents are the head officials of the local agencies, and may live on reservations, though most do not. Sometimes one agency administers one large reservation, but not always, especially if the reservations are small. For example, three Florida Seminole reservations are under one agency and thus one superintendent.

Where reservation residents are well-educated, the tribal government has more say in making decisions. When there are fewer educated people, the superintendent has to handle more decisions because the Indians feel inadequately prepared to make judgments. The superintendent and his aides are supposed to be advisory; still, friction often builds between the superintendent and the Indian government, even though Indians may like individual superintendents very much. The superintendent usually has a small bureaucracy working with him on land development, education, and other affairs, and other residents feel as though they are being controlled by the bureaucracy.

Both Indian reservation residents and the federal government are trying to realize the full productive potential of reservation lands. Here a Navajo sheepherder drives his sheep out to graze.

Indian coal miner. Mineral resources are now being tapped on many reservations.

Reservation Land

Although it might seem as though Indians have much reservation land—altogether some 50,000,000 acres, or a little less than the state of Minnesota—much of it is unproductive. Many parts are useless for agriculture or stock raising, and too far from centers of population and transportation to be useful for industrial development. Nevertheless, some is good agricultural land, some is good for grazing, some is well timbered, and a few places are rich with mineral resources. The Osage reservation, for example, has rich oil fields. A major aim of both federal government and Indian residents is to develop the land for economic return, raising the standard of living while preserving the territory's beauty and productive potential. Thus Indian timberland is reforested under contract with lumber companies or by Indians themselves so that lumber resources will not be depleted. Land management is an important job of the Bureau of Indian Affairs and its local representatives. Still, so much Indian land is not productive that lack of opportunity has drained population to other areas where employment is better.

Reservation Housing

Very few Indians still live in traditional structures. Tipis appear only for summer celebrations of a few tribes on the Plains. Although some Navajo continue to live in hogans, and many others have built hogans for ceremonial purposes or storage, more and more Navajo have moved into cabins or ranch houses. Even the hogans that remain have changed. The ancient pointed wooden structure covered with earth is rarely seen on the reservation today. The common hogan form now is six- or eight-sided, made of horizontally laid logs, plastered with mud or even entirely covered with earth for insulation.

On Fort Peck Reservation in Montana, a few Assiniboin and Sioux live in sod houses or cabins very much like those that housed nineteenth-century pioneers. No one lives in tipis, and most of the population have ranch-style homes or western farmhouses. In the towns on Fort Peck, Indians may live in flats above stores, and the towns also have housing developments as well as individually built homes just like those of western towns off the reservation.

Perhaps more traditional housing is still used by the Florida Seminole than any other Indian community, but even there new styles are catching on. The traditional open-sided, palmetto-thatched *chickee* still stands on Big Cypress Reservation. It is good shelter for the tropics, letting air flow freely. But the Seminole also have two other types of buildings, concrete-block ranch houses and wooden housing built on a poured cement slab. The block houses, despite their unattractive name, are typical of Florida construction. Florida state law specifies that type of structure, even for the most elegant housing, because it is hurricane-proof. The wooden buildings were started in the late 1960s as part of a mutual-help home building program on many reservations. The wooden buildings are open-walled like the *chickees,* but they are screened and have complete plumbing and electrical wiring.

Although Indians have abandoned most traditional house forms for ranch and farmhouse types and wooden cabins, some of this reservation housing is sadly substandard. Many homes are still little more than tarpaper shacks, without hot and cold running water, electricity, screening, and reasonable sanitation. Recognizing these inadequacies, federal and tribal governments have tried to improve Indian housing with mortgage loans and mutual-help building programs. These programs include professional plumbing and electrical work, but much of the carpentry and other labor is done by men of the community, helping each other.

Though much remains to be done to improve reservation housing, it is not all inadequate. Homes on reservations range as widely in appearance, sanitation, and maintenance as they do anywhere else. A lot of reservation housing is attractive, with modern facilities, and clean. The worst is very bad indeed, but many homes compare very favorably to housing in the rural white communities near the reservations. Almost all reservation dwellings are electrified, even the few traditional structures still in use.

Reservation Life

Just as there is no typical Indian tribe, there is no typical Indian reservation. Reservation lands vary from sawgrass and cypress swamplands in south Florida to plains in northern Montana and deserts in Arizona. Some reservations are large—the Navajo is nearly 25,000 square miles; some are small—rancherias in California may be only a few acres. Some reservations have towns and others are totally rural.

Work and Recreation. Daily life on a reservation involves the same kind of activities other rural Americans engage in. The children go to school, walking if it is nearby or taking buses if it is at some distance. Women do housework and wage work. Many Indian women work for their agency or tribe as clerks and secretaries, nurses and nursing aides, or teachers and teacher aides in the schools. Where there is industry, both men and women may do wage work. Men also do many kinds of work for the agency or tribe, from administration to work on road crews and general maintenance, and often cattle ranching and farm work. Men and women may continue traditional crafts, though usually to sell their products

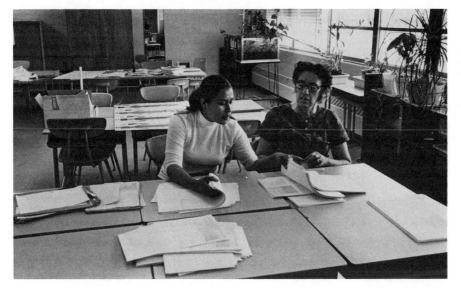

A teacher's aide with her student. Many Indian women are now working in this capacity.

rather than to use them. Adults and children go to town for shopping and entertainment, watch television, and take part in sports like baseball, basketball, swimming, or, especially in the West, horseback riding competitions or rodeo performances. Reservation life in general is much like that of neigboring non-Indian areas.

Many reservations, particularly the larger ones, have their own police force, in which the men find work. Other reservation people have voted to accept the county or state police. On Sundays, the people may go to one of the churches on the reservation or in neighboring towns. Missionaries from many denominations or Indian ministers may lead the churches, which may include Indian religious groups like the Native American Church or the Longhouse People.

Indians and Whites.   Relations between reservation Indians and whites vary a good deal. In many places white people living close to reservations dislike and discriminate against Indians, often fearing competition for jobs. The only contact between Indians and whites of the area may be of the most unfortunate sort. Whites may know only the Indians who have gotten into trouble for drunkenness, theft, or other undesirable behavior while in town. The whites rarely meet Indians socially as equals. Prejudice among small-town whites toward neighboring Indians prevents meetings that might create real understanding and friendship. Whites who live some distance from reservations, on the other hand, often are more tolerant and interested in Indian life and problems. Yet their image of Indian life may be romantic and equally erroneous: they see the Indian as a noble but vanishing savage, someone it may be fashionable to know.

Tourists visiting Indian reservations are often insultingly naive. Many expect Indians to be primitive, unable to read, write, or even speak English. Tourists are often incredibly rude without realizing it when they take photographs without permission and make derogatory or unpleasant remarks in front of Indians as though the Indians were unable to understand. Without knowing it, such visitors increase reservation people's suspicion and animosity toward non-Indians.

Reservation Culture

Little of the great variety of cultures that Indians had when Europeans first landed on this continent remains on reservations today. A veneer still distinguishes Hopi from Seminole from Chippewa, but on all reservations patterns of life are very similar. Visitors going from reservation to reservation get the feeling that they have seen it all before. The life-styles all seem very much alike, regardless of the people's cultural traditions. And those life-styles seem much like those of the rural white communities of America, especially the poorer ones. All over the continent Indian people have adapted to reservations in similar ways, to the point that some anthropologists have begun to talk of a *reservation culture.*

Reservation culture, the various tribes' common response to outside pressure and stress, has been described as sterile, depressing, and above all, boring. It is the primary reason that the ambitious and educated leave the reservations and return only to visit. Cultural vitality and variety seem to have been washed out by the overriding similarity all reservation people have experienced in isolation and overdependence on the BIA. Reservations look to many like an intellectual, cultural, and economic backwater, housing the inept and unambitious.

Changes after World War II

Two significant programs for Indians were launched by Congress in the 1950s. Behind each was the idea that Indians should no longer live in a special relationship to the government, that opportunities should be created to put Indians still on reservation lands back into general American society. One plan became known as *relocation,* and the other as *termination.* Before we discuss these two plans, let us look at the ideas behind them.

The Development of Indian Policies

Early in its history, the United States gathered in immigrants from many nations, making the idea of national integration or the "melting pot" theory popular, as it has been ever since. Although ethnic, racial, and religious enclaves did form in the United States, and majority populations throughout history have discriminated in one way or another against the minorities, the general melting-pot philosophy has always been strong. Most people, whether government workers or scholars, assumed that Indians would be absorbed into American society if they were given a chance. And many were—perhaps more than were not. But some continued to think of themselves as Indian and refused to integrate with the dominant community. Except for legislation designed to remove Indians to western territory, most governments acts aimed at assimilation. The Allotment Act was passed with the idea that private ownership of land would stimulate assimilation.

One major piece of legislation stopped the trend toward assimilation—the Indian Reorganization Act of 1934. However, after World War II, the mood of Congress and of influential people connected with Indian affairs reverted to the feeling that Indians really should be assimilated.

Many thought that Indians were kept from assimilation by poor education, poverty, and especially isolation from the American mainstream. It seemed that Indians had simply become so dependent upon the BIA that they no longer could make their own decisions or lead their own lives. It was a vicious circle. The BIA controlled the Indians both directly and subtly, because government officials thought Indians could not manage their own affairs, and the more the bureau made decisions, the less the Indians could do so, for they never got any practical experience.

Termination

In the 1950s, the idea spread that in spite of such deadening dependence on the government, some Indians had the economic understanding, stability, and education to break away. Several members of Congress thought that the Klamath and Menominee reservations, with their wealth of marketable lumber and people who were trained and competent in logging and milling, were ready to stand without government support. Seconding that position were others who questioned whether some citizens should have a relationship to the federal government denied to other citizens. After the war the feeling grew in the dominant population that ethnic and racial minorities should have the same rights as the majority, and that special treatment for one group was really discrimination against others. Indians, on the other hand, saw attempts at assimilation as just another move by whites to take away Indian land. The problem of assimilation and its solution were hotly debated and very difficult to handle because they touched off so much emotion on both sides.

In 1953, Congress passed a resolution that came to be known as termination. It severed the special relationship between the government and the Menominee, Klamath, and some smaller groups; those reservations were declared terminated. A cash settlement was paid for the land, which in some cases was distributed to individuals and in others was invested for tribal members. Perhaps the large amount of money persuaded many Indians to vote for termination.

Although the majority vote on the reservations affected by this resolution was for termination, some voted against it, and some did not vote at all; and after termination, many of those who voted for it regretted their act. For the Menominee, the settlement was tied to a possibility that government funds due the tribe would be withheld if they refused to vote for termination. Wisconsin created a county out of the Menominee reservation, and the new county residents had to pay real estate taxes. Many could not pay taxes nor could they pay for the county services that formerly were supplied free by the federal government. The Klamath managed somewhat better, but they too suffered financially. It was soon apparent that many Menominee and Klamath were not as ready for independence from the bureau as had been thought. Once again, the years of government control had encouraged dependence; no one was properly prepared for freedom from supervision.

In December 1973, under much pressure from Menominee and some others, Congress voted to reverse Menominee termination. It is too soon to assess this legislation. Wisconsin favored restoring federal supervision so that the state would not have to try to cover services formerly paid for by the federal government. The other terminated areas have remained terminated, and they are now under the jurisdiction of their states. Termination is still the official government policy, though none has occurred since 1961.

Relocation

Reservation populations began to rise after World War II, and there were few job opportunities on most reservations. Some Indians had moved to cities before and during the war because of the boom in war-related jobs. Many of those people stayed in cities, returning to reservations or the rural areas of their childhood only for visits.

In 1951, the BIA launched an employment assistance program popularly known as relocation; because areas with high employment were all urban, the employment program necessarily moved people to cities. Relocation started in a small way, operating in only a few cities. By the 1960s, however, relocation placement centers had been established in many others. The cities most prominently involved early in the program were Chicago, Denver, Los Angeles, and Oakland, California.

Under this program, the move to the city started on the reservation. Interested Indians, both men and women, applied there for training or jobs. Counseling was provided to prepare the relocated people for their city experience, and through it the local BIA personnel tried to eliminate anyone they believed obviously unable to cope with city living. Many of the young Indians just after the war already knew quite a bit about city life from their education, television, time in military service, or visits to family and friends living in a city. Adjustment was harder for older people. Certainly in the first years of the program both Indians and government officials had hopes that were not always realistic.

In the city, the BIA city office helped find housing and periodically talked with the new arrivals to help them adjust. A relocated individual might go into an education program leading to a degree or diploma, or into on-the-job training. After the period of training and adjustment, specialized government services ceased, and the new city Indian was on his or her own.

Relocatees almost always changed living quarters and often jobs after they came to know their new surroundings. In some cities Indians concentrated in one section; in others, they dispersed. After his personal government contacts

Many Indians have assimilated into city life and pursued successful careers. One such example is this Indian art director of a prestigious New York advertising agency.

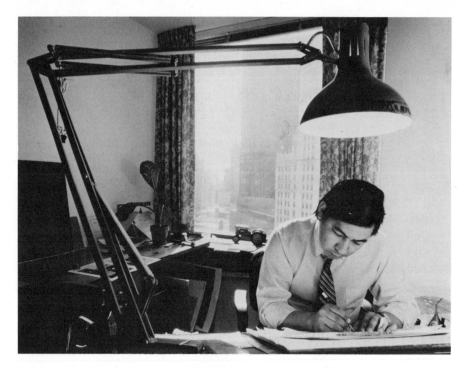

were severed, any Indian who needed help from public agencies had to go to those serving all residents of the city, not just Indians.

Success of Relocation. Even though many of the people settled in cities by the program later returned to reservation living, it must be judged successful in terms of numbers resettled. Well over 100,000 Indians have entered cities as relocatees, and many others have come on their own without BIA assistance. Most Indians think it has been a good program—at least the goals are good. Usually any dissatisfaction arises from breakdowns in help, information, or counseling either in the city or on the reservation before the move.

How well any individual Indian reacts to city life has depended too on the sophistication on his home reservation. People from the Great Lakes and northern Plains reservations usually have been to public schools with non-Indians. Most of them speak only English, and they are quite familiar with such things as public transportation. Indians from more isolated reservations, especially where English, if it is spoken at all, is a second language and where many traditional customs are still common, find it much harder to adjust to city life. More sophisticated Indians may not like the city, but their reasons are the same as those of the general population: noise, dirt, traffic, and crowding. The more traditional relocatees feel alienated, lonely, and perhaps frightened. For them adjustment is very much more difficult, sometimes impossible. They probably will not stay long in the city regardless of job opportunities.

One of the relocation program's goals was to train people who planned to go back to reservations to use their new knowledge. Unfortunately, many of the educated have not gone back because they can find few ways of using their new skills there. This and other programs such as college training thus have caused a "brain drain" from the reservations. Young, educated Indians are on reservations as visitors, not residents.

Adjustment to Urban Life. Happiness in city life seems to depend most on adequate preparation and realistic expectations. Membership in a stable group, usually one's family, also makes adjustment easier. If the family group is not stable, divorce, drunkenness, or abandonment will affect the whole family and may make city life worse than reservation life. Back on the reservation, people with family problems still can find other relatives and long-time friends to turn to. Personal characteristics also contribute to adjustment to city life. The ability to be flexible and take misfortune and new situations in stride make life less stressful in the city or anywhere else.

Having a place for meetings and recreation also eases newcomers into the unfamiliar and busy rounds of urban living. As city Indian populations have grown, Indian centers have been established to meet this need. The first, started in 1952, was the Chicago American Indian Center. These centers generally try to support an Indian way of life in the city and to help solve problems of urban life by providing a social outlet. Originally they specialized in recreation because many city entertainments were beyond the means of Indians. Since the relocation program began operating, some centers have grown to provide social welfare, psychological and legal counseling, and education programs ranging from Headstart preschool to high school classes or adult education classes leading to the GED (a general education certificate of high school equivalence).

With more Indians living in cities, some perhaps inevitable conflicts have come up between reservation and nonreservation Indians. Because so many Indians live off the reservations, some reservation governments have changed voting regulations. Some tribes have refused to allow off-reservation voting because those left on the reservation believed the others were opposed to their interests. Off-reservation members of the Colville tribe in Washington tried to have tribal status terminated and the reservation assets sold and distributed to tribal members. Those living on the reservation were able to vote down the attempt at termination, but such differences are bound to continue as the move to cities continues.

Education

Very early in the history of European-Indian contact, Europeans de-cided that one way to transform Indians into "civilized" people was through education on the European model. Although some early colonists did think the difference between Europeans and Indians was biological and un-changeable, many others believed that the distinction arose from experience and tradition. They reasoned that proper schooling would erase the differences if enough young Indians could be persuaded to go to school.

In the East in colonial times, some private organizations, usually religious, set up schools either specifically for Indians or with programs for Indians. The United States government entered the field of Indian education in the early nine-teenth century. However, it had neither the personnel, facilities, nor skills to get directly into education, so Congress appropriated money, called the Civilization Fund, to be used by churches and other private institutions to educate Indians. Many treaties required that the federal government arrange for the education of Indian children; in those early days, many tribes were eager to learn to read and write so that they could compete with whites for jobs. The Cherokee refused to let missionaries work in Cherokee territory unless the sponsoring church set up schools. Federal funds also supported occupational training programs or man-ual labor schools.

Sequoyah

One man did not wait for Europeans to educate him. The son of a Cherokee mother and British father, Sequoyah took part in both Indian and European tra-ditions. He was a silversmith and blacksmith as well as a fairly prosperous farmer. During his lifetime (about 1770 to about 1843), the Cherokee were los-ing territory to white settlers year by year. Though he could neither read nor write and knew no language but Cherokee, he was convinced that literacy was the secret of white power. He was sure that his language could be written, and when he was about thirty, he set out to invent a system of writing for Cherokee.

He first tried to create a symbol for each word—a method too elaborate to work, for even he could not remember what all his symbols meant. Eventually he realized that he could represent each Cherokee *syllable* by a symbol, calculating that the language had eighty-six syllables. He then invented a syllabary of Chero-kee characters, composed of capital and lower-case letters of the English alpha-bet, some turned upside down, and some original symbols of his own.

He taught his daughter his system, showing all doubters that she could read anything he wrote. Cherokee back in the East as well as Sequoyah's neighbors in Arkansas accepted his system. In 1828, the Cherokee published a newspaper, *The Cherokee Phoenix,* running news in English and in Cherokee. Sequoyah is the first known person who, though illiterate, created a whole system of writing. The sequoia tree and Sequoia National Park memorialize his name.

Early Indian Schools

The privately operated schools of the early years were set up on reservations or in Indian territory. The first one off the reservation, Carlisle Indian School, was established in Carlisle, Pennsylvania, in 1879 and continued there until 1918. It was more famous for football teams than for academic excellence. Jim Thorpe, the famous Sauk-Fox Indian football and track star, got his start at Carlisle. During World War I, Carlisle was turned over to the army and permanently closed as a school because it was too far away from the centers of Indian population.

During the last quarter of the nineteenth century, the government began to build federally administered Indian schools close to Indian populations. In the late 1800s, most Indian schools were boarding schools where the children lived, returning to their kinfolk only during holidays. Behind the boarding schools were two theories of Indian education. One was that the only way to educate young Indians for assimilation into white society was to remove them completely from tribal influences. The other was that setting up as many separate day schools as it would take to cover all reservation groups would weaken academic quality and overstretch the educational budget.

Probably few of the children taken from their families—sometimes by force—thought of Indian boarding schools as an opportunity. But being children, they were flexible enough to live through separation from their families, and many went on to graduate from those schools with a sense of accomplishment. Nevertheless, many people, non-Indians and Indians, saw the cruelty in a program that took children, some hardly more than infants, from their homes and forced on them an alien and generally authoritarian way of life. Eventually the outcry against such practices resulted in the establishment of more day schools on Indian lands. Still, where populations were sparse and settlements widely scattered, children could not go to day schools, so some boarding schools still operate. They are run by the Bureau of Indian Affairs not only for children far from public schools and Indian day schools, but also for those who need home care as well as education because of sickness, death, or broken families. In addition, schools operated by churches or other private institutions care for about 10 percent of Indian children in school today.

An Indian classroom. The federal government has substantially upgraded the quality of Indian schools.

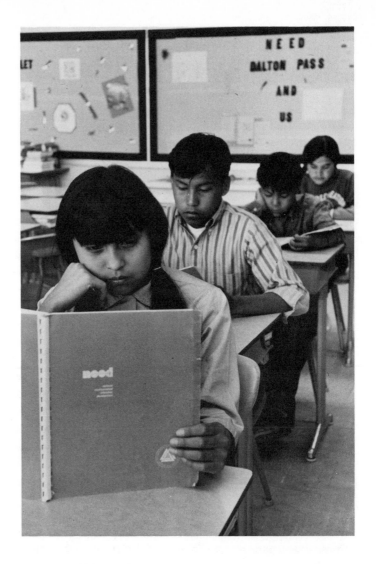

Government Schools Today

Federal day schools and boarding schools cover kindergarten through twelfth grade. The government also offers vocational or technical training beyond the high school level in three schools operated by the BIA: Haskell Institute in Kansas, which grants a two-year associate's degree, Chilocco Indian School in Oklahoma, and, for training in arts and crafts, the Institute of American Indian Arts in Santa Fe. None of these schools offers the equivalent of a four-year college education. For that academic level, Indians must enter schools that are also open to the general public. Two more federal schools offer medical training under the Department of Health, Education, and Welfare: the Indian School of Practical Nursing and the Intermountain School Health Center. For those interested and academically competent, the BIA provides some loans for college education, and many tribes have college scholarship funds.

On the Navajo reservation in Arizona, the Navajo Community College was chartered by the tribe in 1968. First housed temporarily in a BIA high school, it now has its own campus at Tsaile. To emphasize that it is a Navajo institution, ten dormitories are shaped like hogans. The college offers a two-year program of study leading to an associate of arts degree in academic studies or a certificate of proficiency in vocational fields. The curriculum also has courses on Navajo language and culture.

The college is operated under a ten-member board of regents appointed by the Navajo Tribal Council. About 70 percent of the administration is Navajo. Indians other than Navajo also attend, as well as a few non-Indians. The Navajo tribe appropriated a million dollars for the first phase of construction, and the federal government provides the operating funds and pays tuition, room and board, and book fees for all Indian students at the college.

Indian dropout rates at all levels are higher than those of the general population. Educators believe there are three reasons for this. First, where English is not the primary language, as in most Navajo settlements, the language handicap is great. Indian children who must learn English are much older than their classmates from the general population, a position which can embarrass or discourage them. Most Indians with major language handicaps fail to catch up to their age level. Second, many Indian children and their parents do not value scholastic achievement as much as members of other ethnic groups do, and thus they are not so highly motivated. Third, many Indians can see no benefit in the kind of education that is represented by the schools. School subjects used to seem very remote from Indian life. Today this view seems to be changing as most Indian parents realize that their children need certain basic skills to get desirable jobs and goods. More and more, parents are encouraging children to stay in school.

Most Indians of school age are not in government schools but in state public schools. When reservation Indian children attend these, the federal government pays the school district to compensate for the fact that Indians pay no state land tax to support the schools. Indian children in federal schools must meet the same educational requirements and standards as other public school students because BIA schools must meet the standards of the state in which they are located. Indian children also are subject to the state's compulsory attendance laws whether they are in state or federal schools. No children can grow up without attending some schools, so the literacy rates of Indian children today are almost as high as for children from the general society. However, Indian children more often drop out as soon as they have reached the age at which their state lets them leave school. In 1970, a third of Indians twenty-five years and older were high school graduates.

Health

Since 1955, health services for reservation Indians have been handled by the United States Public Health Service, Division of Indian Health, of the Department of Health, Education, and Welfare. Before that, the Bureau of Indian Affairs supplied health services. Off-reservation Indians use the same services as other citizens, public or private depending upon their means. Reservation health services are provided by the federal government because state services or private physicians are hard to reach from reservation areas far from population centers. Because Indians do not pay state property taxes on reservations, they do not have state coverage for many services, including health. The Public Health Service has contractual arrangements with hospitals for surgical, gynecological, and in-patient care, and the bureau operates some hospitals itself. The federal government also helps with other health services, such as constructing sanitary facilities and sewage systems, and testing water.

American Indians have some special health problems, including high rates of trachoma (an eye disease), tuberculosis, and diabetes. Others are common infectious diseases and forms of dysentery and gastroenteritis that come from poor sanitation and diet. On the other hand, some disorders are only about half as common among Indians as in the general population, including cancer, heart disease, and strokes. The Indian birth rate is almost twice that of whites; the average life expectancy is about six years less than for members of the general population.

Indians who speak English as a second language or not at all often have trouble communicating with doctors and other health officers. Trained bilingual medical aides have bridged this gap in many cases. Relationships between patient and doctor are better when the doctor is an Indian, but many Indians who get a medical degree do not go back to reservations to practice. In fact, the doctor shortage is acute on some reservations. Of course, most of the problems Indians face in finding adequate health care are not unique, but are shared by all people in isolated areas or in lower socioeconomic classes where information is inadequate, misinformation is widespread, and shortages in medical personnel are constant.

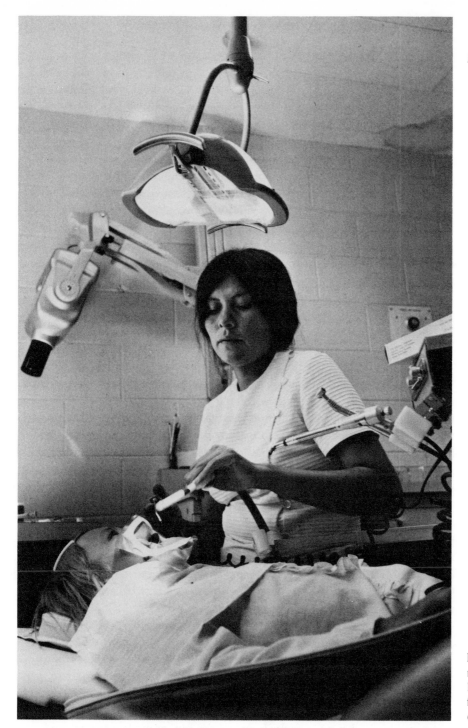

Indian dental technician. Reservation health services are funded by the federal government.

Religious Change

In spite of unflagging efforts by Catholic and Protestant missionaries, Christianity did not make great strides among Indian peoples. It was too exclusive, requiring that they abandon old ways. Left to themselves, Indians preferred to combine elements of old and new.

Many Christian denominations claim Indian members today, and some traditional Indian practices and beliefs are still strong in areas with dense Indian populations. Religious organizations that Indians have found appealing combine old beliefs and Christianity. The religion of Handsome Lake, described earlier, still has followers among the Iroquois. The meeting place is a longhouse, and today the movement is usually called the Longhouse Religion. Shakerism too has continued as a local religion in the Northwest, also combining Christian and traditional Indian beliefs.

The Native American Church

The newest and most important religious movement among Indians today is the Native American Church, often called the Peyote Cult. (*Peyote* is a nonaddictive hallucinogenic drug.) This cult spread after the Ghost Dance declined in the Plains just before 1900, replacing the Ghost Dance in many tribes. After 1900, the Peyote Cult became popular in other areas, especially the Southwest and Midwest. It has never had much following in California, which some anthropologists say is explained by the common use there of another hallucinogen, *Jimson weed* (see Chapter 5). The use of the two drugs seems to be mutually exclusive.

The Native American Church has about a quarter of a million members. It combines something of the vision quest and belief in general supernatural power with the Christian Trinity; its doctrine teaches that God is a great spirit and Jesus a guardian spirit. Christian morality is woven into its precepts: brotherly love, honor, trust, the golden rule, and some ethics derived from the Ten Commandments, such as no adultery or divorce. Members believe especially in total abstinence from alcoholic beverages.

Though the doctrine or belief derives much from the Bible, peyote ceremonialism bears little resemblance to Christianity. The Peyote Cult uses many trappings from traditional Indian ritual: feathers and rattles, bone whistles, drumming, and eating peyote to achieve a vision. The ritual varies from group to group, but meetings usually begin at sundown with one man, the peyote chief, in charge. He is assisted by other officials in the church. Peyote, the bud of a cactus species, is chewed in its dry form and spit out, or made into a tea and drunk. The ritual chief administers the peyote to the congregation accompanied by drumming and singing. The songs, called peyote music, often deal with subjects from the Bible, but they can also be nonsense verses taken from a drug-induced hallucination. Sometimes peyote acts as an emetic, causing many novices to vomit. Peyote is used with careful control; it is regarded as a sacrament. At dawn a woman brings in drinking water because peyote makes one very thirsty; then the participants eat breakfast together.

Indians in Today's World

Indians hold about as many different jobs and enter as many professions as the general American population, but Indian unemployment is very much higher. Only a small percentage of employed Indians are in occupations requiring college degrees. One reason is, of course, that the percentage of Indians holding degrees is much smaller than in the general population. Also, many Indians entering the professions no longer identify themselves as Indians.

Indians on reservations generally have a higher rate of unemployment than nonreservation Indians because jobs on reservations still are scarce and usually call only for unskilled workers. Until recently these jobs depended mainly on farming, stock raising, and similar enterprises. Though efforts have been made to bring industry to reservations, wage work from such sources is still rare. In addition, reservations are overpopulated, reservation land is not productive, and competition is tremendous for whatever jobs do exist.

Poor education has been another great cause of Indian unemployment. As we have mentioned, the dropout rate of Indians at all educational levels is high. Reservation schools are employing teachers specially trained to handle Indian problems like language and motivation, and many school systems in cities with large Indian populations have special curricula to stimulate Indians to work for scholastic achievement and to correct deficiencies. Of course, one reason many Indians lack motivation to finish school is that even those who have diplomas find it hard to find work on reservations. Students educated elsewhere who had hoped to return to their home reservations to use their education to benefit the tribe often have found no suitable jobs.

Economic Success

It may seem that Indians either abandon Indian ways or live in poverty and ignorance, but that is not the case. Though no one can deny the economic and educational problems they face, many Indians have reached economic self-sufficiency without losing their Indian identity. Indians on some reservations have been outstandingly successful in developing resources. The Western Apache are an example that other Indians can point to with pride, for they have developed a cattle-ranching industry fully competitive in the general market. In fact, stock raising has turned into an important economic opportunity in unlikely places, such as Big Cypress Seminole Reservation in Florida. Big Cypress is in a south Florida swamp area that seems completely unsuitable for cattle land. But the Seminole, with BIA and state aid, have drained large areas and turned them into pasture for herds of Angus cattle. For Seminole interested in raising cattle, this has been a great economic opportunity.

Mohawk Indians have received a great deal of publicity for their work in high steel construction for skyscrapers and bridges. Long ago in colonial times, English surveyors noticed how little fear of heights Mohawk displayed, and in 1886, when a railway bridge was built across the St. Lawrence River near a Mohawk village, some Mohawk men were employed. Engineers and company officials were impressed by the men's agility and confidence, and since that time, Mohawk have worked in high steel all over this continent. They have been involved in building most of the major bridges and skyscrapers, among them the Empire State Building and the George Washington Bridge. These Mohawk steel workers live today in several apartment buildings within one neighborhood in Brooklyn, New York, not on the Canadian or New York State Iroquois reservations, though they often visit there.

Cattle ranching. On many reservations Indians have developed a lucrative cattle-ranching industry that is competitive with the general market.

Mohawk Indians constructing a bridge in Vancouver, British Columbia. They have long been known for their lack of fear of heights and for their great agility.

The Northwest Coast Indians have been quite successful in commercial salmon fishing, and also working in the fish canneries. Some of their success may come from the competitive personality their ancestors showed in the potlatch, but they have profited too because of the Alaska Native Brotherhood. During the second decade of this century, a group of Tlingit Indians organized the Alaska Native Brotherhood to oppose discrimination in employment, education, and citizenship rights. It has grown to include many Alaskan Eskimo and Indians as well as the Tlingit. The brotherhood became active in labor relations in the fishing industry and fought for nonsegregated schools in Alaska; a Canadian Indian organization with similar aims was formed in British Columbia. The primary goal of the brotherhood has been acculturation—the adoption by Indians of non-Indian ways—and it has always had strong Christian leanings though it is not connected with any denomination. In recent years the organization has been trying to encourage Indians to be more active in politics.

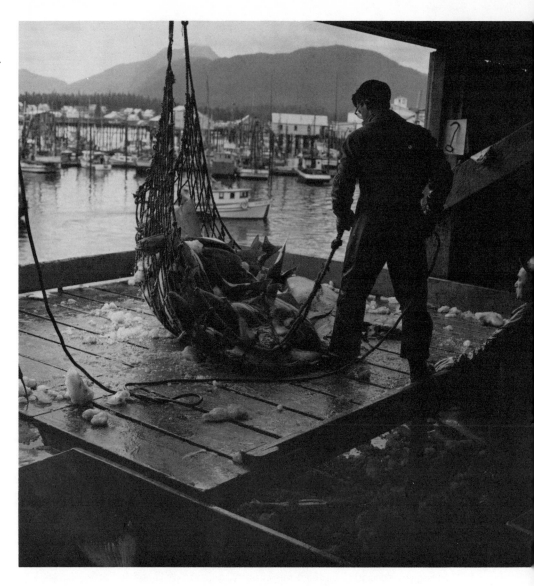

Alaskan Indians un-
loading halibut.

Economic Hope

Both Indians and BIA officials see recreational development on reservations as
an important way to create jobs and income in the future. Some tribes have already built motels, camp grounds, restaurants, and the like on reservation territory. Also, because most tourists and visitors show interest in Indian traditions,
the performance of dances, celebrations, and ceremonials would allow Indians
to practice traditional ritual display and make money at the same time.

Selling arts and crafts to tourists already brings in supplementary income in many areas. Since the Indian Reorganization Act of 1934, federal officials as well as Indians themselves have promoted commercial sale of traditional Indian works. Public recognition of these productions has helped build pride in the Indian cultural heritage. Some artists and craftsmen have won national recognition for their skill and talent. One of the most famous is Maria Martinez, a potter of San Ildefonso Pueblo. Her pottery, known as black-on-black, is in some of our great art museums. The School of Indian Art in New Mexico has developed its own special style and has turned out many Indian artists, most of them from Southwestern tribes. Other Indian artists hold positions in art departments of universities or paint and teach privately. Basketry is going through a renaissance, especially in California and the Southwest, as is woodcarving in the Northwest. Also in the Northwest, argillite (often erroneously called slate) carved into bowls or statuary has become a new medium for expressing traditional motifs and styles.

After the Spanish introduced silver work to the Pueblo people, the Zuni became master silversmiths, and the Navajo too began to produce strikingly beautiful silver products using Spanish designs. The squash blossom necklace with the pendant called the *naja,* a Spanish gypsy symbol to ward off the evil eye, is treasured not only by Navajo and Pueblo, but by anyone fortunate enough to own one.

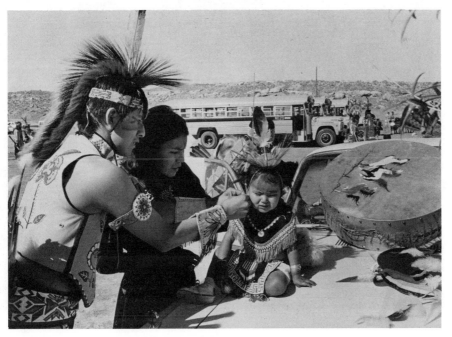

A ceremonial Indian festival in Gallup, New Mexico.

Navajo blankets, of wool homespun from Navajo sheep, are an important source of income to those who weave. Most colors used in these blankets today are modern aniline dyes, but some weavers still take the time to make and use the old natural dyes. Prices may seem high—a good blanket about 4 by 6 feet costs several hundred dollars—but for the time that goes into making the blanket, the pay is low.

Ceremonial costumes of all tribes are much brighter now than traditionally, for they too are colored with aniline dyes. Most modern costumes combine items from many culture areas: Indians of the Great Lakes now perform dances wearing the feathered bustles and headdresses of Plains Indians. Beaded designs include patterns from widely separated tribes as well as from European peasant styles. Art styles today are truly pan-Indian, with the emphasis on being *Indian,* rather than of a particular tribe.

The Eskimo, traditionally skilled carvers in bone, ivory, and antler, have turned to soapstone, the material used long ago for oil lamps, to produce a sculptural art that has great appeal. The Canadian government helps retail these figurines, and some museums now have fine collections. The subjects are the people and animals of the Arctic: fat walruses and plump seals dozing on their flippers, gamboling polar bear cubs, chunky Eskimo mothers with babies on their backs. The animal figures are in the tradition of Eskimo good-luck charms or amulets, carved during times of famine as magical devices to bring the game or to appease the spirits.

Economic Development in Canada

In the Canadian Subarctic, besides some wage work in towns, many Indian men continue to trap, hunt, and fish for a livelihood. They have increased the production of fur-bearing animals with new techniques and management developed in cooperation with the provincial governments. Canadian Indians also are going into the commercial fishing industry. And some Indians today make their living as guides to sportsmen.

The Canadian government has especially encouraged Indians to produce traditional arts and crafts. Items that sell well are moccasins, gloves, jackets, and *mukluks* (the sealskin boots worn by Indians and Eskimo of the Northwest Territories). In the Northwest Coast area, woodcarvings of totem poles and masks bring important supplementary income.

Recognizing the need for long-term economic objectives, the Canadian federal and provincial governments and private organizations have helped to develop mineral resources on Indian reserves and to create business opportunities such as stores and gas stations.

Political Movements

Indian organizations that have been active in national political and economic affairs are the National Congress of American Indians (NCAI), the National Indian Youth Council (NIYC), and the American Indian Movement (AIM). NCAI is the oldest of the three. It was founded in 1944 "to protect, conserve and develop Indian land, mineral, timber and human resources; serve legislative interests of Indian tribes; improve health, education and economic conditions." It is composed of both tribes and individuals, and more than a hundred tribes are affiliated with it. NCAI conducts research on Indian problems as a service to Indian tribes, has a legal aid program for Indians, and runs a lobby in Washington to present Indian needs and wishes. In general, it appeals to industry and commerce for greater employment of Indians, and tries to promote legislation to improve Indian conditions and to secure Indian rights.

The National Indian Youth Council

The National Indian Youth Council was founded in 1961 by a group of young Indians during a conference of American Indians at the University of Chicago. It received some national recognition when members conducted a "fish-in" in the state of Washington in 1964: NIYC members and some others fished in the Nisqually and Puyallup rivers in Washington, defying state law. This effort through civil disobedience to preserve Indian rights to traditional fishing sites, and the resulting publicity, brought national attention to Indian economic problems.

The issue behind the fish-in was whether or not Indians were subject to state regulations on hunting and fishing. The Indians claimed that under the Medicine Creek Treaty of 1854 they were guaranteed fishing rights. The state of Washington contended that net fishing (the kind of fishing the Indians did) was against conservation laws. The State Fisheries personnel tried to remove Indians' nets from the Puyallup River, and Indians shot at them. Police came in, subdued the Indians with tear gas, and arrested sixty. The case was eventually settled in favor of the tribes, however, allowing limited net fishing by Indians only.

The American Indian Movement

The American Indian Movement, founded in Cleveland in 1968, is generally thought to have radical leanings, and many Indians want no part of it. It was the moving force behind the confrontation between Indians and federal forces at

Wounded Knee, South Dakota, in 1973. On February 28 of that year, Indians under the direction of AIM took at least ten Indian hostages at Wounded Knee and demanded concessions from the federal government: that the Senate Foreign Relations Committee hold hearings on treaties made with Indians; that the Senate begin full-scale investigation of government treatment of Indians; and that another inquiry be started into all Sioux reservations in South Dakota.

Members of AIM occupied a trading post and church at Wounded Knee, and federal police surrounded the town. Inhabitants of Pine Ridge Reservation,

In 1973 a few hundred Indian militants seized a trading post at Wounded Knee, South Dakota, in order to focus national attention on Indian problems. The seizure, however, turned into guerrilla warfare with loss of life and also loss of public sympathy.

where Wounded Knee is, claimed that AIM was interfering in internal tribal affairs and did not represent the reservation. The chairman and council of Pine Ridge said the occupation was tied to the struggle for political control of the reservation. Through the next few months, the conflict grew, with AIM demanding that the tribal chairman step down, and the chairman insisting that the nonresidents (AIM people) be expelled. Gunfire exchanges became frequent, finally killing two people. The seventy-day occupation ended on May 8, with nothing really changed. Most reservation Indians were very upset and angry at the shooting and occupation and destruction by fire of their homes and other buildings. While most Indians disavowed tactics AIM used, others—most of whom are not on the reservation—believe that such measures are the only way to win justice. Support, membership, and leadership for AIM have come mostly from younger, nonreservation Indians.

Alcatraz

Late in 1969, in another political action, eighty-nine Indians occupied the island of Alcatraz. That occupation by Indians was not sponsored by any particular organization. The occupiers found justification for their move in an old Sioux treaty which they claimed gave Indians the right to occupy any unused federal land. They said they wanted a center for Indian studies set up on the island.

The island had no supply of fresh water, so the Army Corps of Engineers provided a water barge and permitted food to be delivered to the island. Later, when the Indians proved to be more determined to stay than the government had expected, the authorities shut off electricity and water supplies. In April 1970, the Department of the Interior submitted a plan to turn the island into a national park with "an Indian flavor." The Indians rejected the proposal.

Finally, in June 1971, the government forcibly removed the remaining fifteen Indians from the island for interfering with the Coast Guard's attempt to repair navigation aids there and for stealing copper wire, which the Indians had claimed along with the island.

Occupation of the BIA Building

In late October 1972, a group of activist Indians organized a protest which they called the Trail of Broken Treaties. They meant to dramatize Indian grievances, for they thought that Indians had too long been silent on Indian health, housing, education, and neglected treaties. Joined by some members of AIM, they went to Washington, D. C., to discuss Indian problems with BIA personnel. They

Alcatraz Island was occupied by a group of Indians claiming rights by treaty to all abandoned federal land. The occupiers wanted Alcatraz to be turned into an institute of native American studies. Lack of food and water eventually led to the Indians' departure.

planned a peaceful demonstration to gain social and economic benefits, but the Indian leaders of the protest came to feel that their talks with the BIA officials were without result and that the government was generally disinclined to discuss any serious matters with them.

On November 2, about five hundred Indians, AIM members and participants in the Trail of Broken Treaties, took over the BIA offices in protest. They scuffled with police inside and outside, but no arrests were made, and word came from high officials to let the Indians remain in the building. They held the offices until November 8, when they left after reaching an agreement with White House negotiators to hear Indian proposals for aid and solutions to their many problems.

During the occupation, the Indians did over a million dollars' worth of damage to furniture and equipment in the building, and when they left they took documents and records as well as Indian paintings and artifacts. Most of the militants were urban Indians; the government charged that they did not represent the Indian peoples. However, the government agreed not to prosecute those who seized the building, and allotted $60,000 in government funds to help them get home. Then some Indian members of the National Tribal Chairmen's Association inspected the damage and called for investigation and prosecution of the militants; their president blamed the government for letting militants occupy the building. Many Indians who had not been involved were particularly disturbed over the destruction and theft of treaty and land documents recording vital negotiations on Indian rights. They said that the acts of destruction were self-defeating, harmful only to Indians, not to government personnel.

Taken alone, this kind of action may be seen by many as either futile or merely an attempt at publicity for individuals. Yet it does prove that young Indians are politically aware and active. Many people, while deploring acts of destruction and violence, are encouraged that some Indians are beginning to take steps on their own rather than leaving planning and action to the BIA.

Predictions

Everywhere traditional native American ways are changing. Today's Indians are not like their ancestors of Columbus's time, and those people were not like the first who came across Beringia many thousands of years ago. Yet some traditions remain, and some tribes, especially the Pueblo, have kept many of their ancestors' customs. Other groups have revived old ways for festivals and ceremonies, both for commercial profit and from pride in their past.

Some of the old variety of Indian culture is still there, but socioeconomic and educational differences are far more important among Indians today. Indians have entered general North American society at every level including the learned professions, and they are as much affected by social and economic conditions in their country and in the world as any other member of society.

Since World War II, Indians have awakened to the idea that they can control their future. With their own political organizations, they have learned how to pressure the government to let them make their own decisions, and to persuade business and industry to employ more qualified Indian people. They have encouraged their young to seek more education. Indians are increasingly taking over Indian affairs, assuming the obligations and duties of citizenship as well as demanding the rights due them. They are making their own suggestions about what can be done to help their people and are insisting on the right to take part in pertinent decisions at all levels.

Predicting the future is a hazardous undertaking; but it seems likely that old traditions of art, mythology, and kinship responsibility will last or will be revived, but only as a veneer over industrial life. No Indian wants to live his life in a tipi or expects to subsist by hunting and gathering any more than whites want to live in log cabins. Indians recognize that the idea of holding onto a way of life that passed more than a hundred years ago is as unrealistic as it is insulting. It implies that Indians somehow cannot change—or can change only in degrading ways. Instead, Indians want to be able to make their own decisions and to keep up a private life as traditional as they may wish, while entering fully into public, industrial life. In this they are no different from any other ethnic group. Perhaps the real problem Indians must face in the future is not their loss of traditions, but their inadequate preparation for making their own choices in life. They have lived too long under the repressive influences of a paternalistic bureaucracy. Indians will continue to rebel against the indignity of being told how to behave and what to do, and will demonstrate not only their regained self-respect but a well-developed sense of social responsibility.

BIBLIOGRAPHY

This bibliography contains fuller citations for the works listed in the bibliographies appearing in the text, along with other suggested references.

Abbreviations used:

APAMNH   Anthropological Papers of the American Museum of Natural History. New York.

ARBAE   Annual Reports of the Bureau of American Ethnology. Washington, D.C.

BBAE   Bulletin of the Bureau of American Ethnology. Washington, D.C.

MAAA   Memoir of the American Anthropological Association.

MAES   Monograph of the American Ethnological Society. Seattle: University of Washington Press.

UCPAA   University of California Publications in American Archaeology and Ethnology. Berkeley and Los Angeles.

UPMAP   University of Pennsylvania Museum Anthropological Publications. Philadelphia.

YUPA   Yale University Publications in Anthropology. New Haven.

Aberle, David F.
1966   *The Peyote Religion among the Navaho.* Chicago: Aldine.

Andrist, Ralph K.
1964   *The Long Death: The Last Days of the Plains Indians.* New York: Collier Books.

Astrov, Margot, ed.
1946   *American Indian Prose and Poetry.* New York: Capricorn Books. Also
       published as *The Winged Serpent.* New York: John Day, 1946.

Balikci, Asen
1970   *The Netsilik Eskimo.* Garden City, N.Y.: Natural History Press.

Bandelier, Adolf
1890   *The Delight Makers.* New York: Dodd, Mead & Co.

Barnett, H. G.
1957   *Indian Shakers.* Carbondale: University of Southern Illinois Press.

Basso, Keith
1970   *The Cibecue Apache.* New York: Holt, Rinehart and Winston.

Beaglehole, Ernest
1935   *Hopi of the Second Mesa.* MAAA 44.

Benedict, Ruth
1923   *The Concept of the Guardian Spirit in North America.* MAAA 29.

Birket-Smith, Kai
1958   *The Eskimos.* 2nd ed. New York: Humanities Press.

Boas, Franz
1888   *The Central Eskimo.* ARBAE 6:390–669.
1966   *Kwakiutl Ethnography.* Helen Codere, ed. Chicago: University of Chicago Press.

Brandon, William
1961   *The American Heritage Book of Indians.* New York: Dell Publishing Co.

Brinton, Daniel G.
1876   *The Myths of the New World.* 2nd ed. New York: Henry Holt & Co.

Brophy, William, and Sophie D. Aberle
1966   *The Indian, America's Unfinished Business.* Norman: University of
       Oklahoma Press.

Brown, Dee
1970   *Bury My Heart at Wounded Knee.* New York: Holt, Rinehart and Winston.

Bunzel, Ruth
1932   *Introduction to Zuni Ceremonialism.* ARBAE 47:467–544.

Caldwell, Joseph
1958   *Trend and Tradition in the Prehistory of the Eastern United States.* MAAA 88.

Catlin, George
1841   *Letters and Notes on the Manners, Customs, and Conditions of the North American Indians.* Reprint. New York: Dover Publications, 1973.

Codere, Helen
1966   *Fighting with Property.* MAES 18.

Cohen, Felix
1942   *Handbook of Federal Indian Law.* Washington, D.C.: U.S. Government Printing Office.

Deardorff, Merle
1951   *The Religion of Handsome Lake.* BBAE 149.

de Laguna, Frederica
1960   *The Story of a Tlingit Community.* BBAE 172.

Deloria, Vine, Jr.
1969   *Custer Died for Your Sins.* New York: Macmillan.

Densmore, Frances
1926   *The American Indians and Their Music.* New York: The Women's Press.

Dobyns, Henry F.
1966   "Estimating Aboriginal American Population." *Current Anthropology* 7:395–449.

Douglas, Frederick H., and René D'Harnoncourt
1941   *Indian Art of the United States.* New York: Museum of Modern Art.

Downs, James
1966   *Two Worlds of the Washo.* New York: Holt, Rinehart and Winston.
1972   *The Navajo.* New York: Holt, Rinehart and Winston.

Dozier, Edward
1966   *Hano, a Tewa Indian Community in Arizona.* New York: Holt, Rinehart and Winston.
1970   *The Pueblo Indians of North America.* New York: Holt, Rinehart and Winston.

Driver, Harold E.
1969   *Indians of North America.* 2nd ed. Chicago: University of Chicago Press.

Drucker, Philip
1951 *The Northern and Central Nootkan Tribes.* BBAE 144.
1955 *Indians of the Northwest Coast.* New York: McGraw-Hill.
1958 *The Native Brotherhoods.* BBAE 168.
1966 *Cultures of the North Pacific Coast.* San Francisco: Chandler Press.

Dunn, Dorothy
1968 *American Indian Painting.* Albuquerque: University of New Mexico Press.

Eggan, Fred
1937 *Social Anthropology of North American Tribes.* Chicago: University of Chicago Press.
1950 *Social Organization of the Western Pueblos.* Chicago: University of Chicago Press.
1966 *The American Indian.* Chicago: Aldine.

Ewers, John
1955 *The Horse in Blackfoot Indian Culture.* BBAE 159.
1958 *The Blackfeet.* Norman: University of Oklahoma Press.

Farb, Peter
1968 *Man's Rise to Civilization as Shown by the Indians of North America from Primeval Times to the Coming of the Industrial State.* New York: Dutton.

Feder, Norman
1965 *American Indian Art.* New York: Harry N. Abrams.

Fletcher, Alice, and Francis LaFlesche
1906 *The Omaha Tribe.* ARBAE 27.

Forbes, Jack D., ed.
1964 *The Indian in America's Past.* Englewood Cliffs, N.J.: Prentice-Hall.

Ford, C. S.
1941 *Smoke from Their Fires.* New Haven: Yale University Press.

Fowler, Melvin L.
1969 *Explorations into Cahokia Archaeology.* Illinois Archaeological Survey.

Garbarino, Merwyn S.
1972 *Big Cypress, A Changing Seminole Community.* New York: Holt, Rinehart and Winston.

Gearing, Fred
1962   *Priests and Warriors: Social Structure of Cherokee Politics in the 18th Century.*
       MAAA 93.
1970   *The Face of the Fox.* Chicago: Aldine.

Gifford, Edward W.
1928   *Pottery-Making in the Southwest.* UCPAA 23:353–73.

Greenway, John
1969   "Will the Indians Get Whitey?" *National Review* 21 (March 11).

Griffin, James B., ed.
1952   *Archaeology of the Eastern United States.* Chicago: University of Chicago Press.

Grinnell, George B.
1923   *The Cheyenne Indians.* 2 vols. New Haven: Yale University Press.
1961   *Pawnee Hero Stories and Folk Tales.* Lincoln: University of Nebraska Press.
1962   *Blackfoot Lodge Tales.* Lincoln: University of Nebraska Press.
1962   *By Cheyenne Campfires.* New Haven: Yale University Press.

Heizer, Robert F., and Alan Almquist
1971   *The Other Californians.* Berkeley: University of California Press.

Heizer, Robert F., and M. A. Whipple
1951   *The California Indians.* Berkeley: University of California Press.

Hickerson, Harold
1970   *The Chippewa and Their Neighbors.* New York: Holt, Rinehart and Winston.

Hodge, Frederick W.
1906–10   *Handbook of American Indians North of Mexico* (2 parts). BBAE 30.

Hoffman, Walter J.
1891   *The Midewiwin or "Grand Medicine Society" of the Ojibwa.* ARBAE 7:143–300.
1893   *The Menomini Indians.* ARBAE 15:11–328.

Honigman, John J.
1954   *The Kaska Indians.* YUPA 51.

Inverarity, Robert B.
1950   *Art of the Northwest Coast Indians.* Berkeley: University of California Press.

Jenness, Diamond
1928   *The People of the Twilight.* Chicago: University of Chicago Press.
1955   *The Indians of Canada.* Bulletin 65. 3rd ed. Ottawa: Canadian National Museum.

Jennings, Jesse D.
1968   *Prehistory of North America.* New York: McGraw-Hill.

Jennings, Jesse D., and Edward Norbeck, eds.
1964   *Prehistoric Man in the New World.* Chicago: University of Chicago Press.

Jones, David E.
1972   *Sanapia, Comanche Medicine Woman.* New York: Holt, Rinehart and Winston.

Joseph, Alice, R. B. Spicer, and Jane Chesky
1949   *The Desert People: A Study of the Papago Indians.* Chicago: University of Chicago Press.

Josephy, Alvin M.
1965   *The Nez Perce Indians and the Opening of the Northwest.* New Haven: Yale University Press.
1968   *The Indian Heritage of America.* New York: Alfred A. Knopf.

Kennedy, Michael, ed.
1965   *The Red Man's West.* New York: Hastings House Publishing Co.

Kluckhohn, Clyde
1944   *Navaho Witchcraft.* Boston: Beacon Press.

Kluckhohn, Clyde, and Dorothea Leighton
1962   *The Navaho.* Rev. ed. New York: Doubleday.

Krause, Aurel
1956   *The Tlingit Indians.* MAES 26.

Kroeber, Alfred L.
1925   *Handbook of the Indians of California.* BBAE 78.
1939   *Cultural and Natural Areas of Native North America.* UCPAA 38.

Kroeber, Theodora
1961   *Ishi in Two Worlds.* Berkeley: University of California Press.

LaFarge, Oliver
1956   *A Pictorial History of the American Indian.* New York: Crown Publishers.

LaFlesche, Francis
1963   *The Middle Five.* Madison: University of Wisconsin Press.

Landes, Ruth
1968 *Ojibwa Religion.* Madison: University of Wisconsin Press.
1970 *The Prairie Potawatomi.* Madison: University of Wisconsin Press.

Lange, Charles H.
1958 *Cochiti, a New Mexico Pueblo.* Austin: University of Texas Press.

Lantis, Margaret
1947 *Alaskan Eskimo Ceremonialism.* MAES 11.
1960 *Eskimo Childhood and Interpersonal Relationships.* MAES 33.

Leacock, Eleanor
1954 *The Montagnais Hunting Territory and the Fur Trade.* MAAA 78.

Leacock, Eleanor, and Nancy O. Lurie
1971 *North American Indians in Historical Perspective.* New York: Random House.

Levine, Stuart, and Nancy O. Lurie, eds.
1970 *The American Indian Today.* Baltimore: Penguin Books.

Lewis, Theodore, and Madeline Kneberg
1958 *Tribes that Slumber: Indian Tribes in the Tennessee Region.*
      Knoxville: University of Tennessee Press.

Linton, Ralph
1940 *Acculturation in Seven American Indian Tribes.* New York: Appleton-Century.

Lowie, Robert
1910 *The Assiniboine.* APAMNH 4:1–270.
1916 *Plains Indian Age Societies.* APAMNH 11:877–992.
1935 *The Crow Indians.* New York: Holt, Rinehart and Winston.
1954 *Indians of the Plains.* New York: McGraw-Hill.

Lurie, Nancy O.
1966 *Mountain Wolf Woman.* Ann Arbor: University of Michigan Press.

McFee, Malcolm
1972 *Modern Blackfeet.* New York: Holt, Rinehart and Winston.

McGregor, John C.
1965 *Southwestern Archaeology.* 2nd ed. Urbana: University of Illinois Press.

Marriott, Alice
1945 *The Ten Grandmothers.* Norman: University of Oklahoma Press.
1948 *Maria, the Potter of San Ildefonso.* Norman: University of Oklahoma Press.

Martin, Paul S., George Quimby, and Donald Collier
1947   *Indians before Columbus.* Chicago: University of Chicago Press.

Meggers, Betty J.
1972   *Prehistoric America.* Chicago: Aldine-Atherton.

Meggers, Betty, Clifford Evans, and Emilio Estrada
1965   *Early Formative Period of Coastal Ecuador.* Smithsonian Contributions to
       Anthropology I. Washington, D.C.: U.S. Government Printing Office.

Mishkin, Bernard
1940   *Rank and Warfare among Plains Indians.* MAES 3.

Mooney, James
1965   *The Ghost Dance Religion.* Chicago: University of Chicago Press.

Morgan, Lewis H.
1851   *League of the Ho-De-No-Sau-Nee or Iroquois.* (Several editions.)
1965   *Houses and House-Life of the American Aborigines.* Chicago: University of
       Chicago Press.

Mowat, Farley
1954   *People of the Deer.* London: Pyramid.

Murdock, George P.
1972   *Ethnographic Bibliography of North America.* New Haven: Human Relations
       Area Files.

Nabokov, Peter
1967   *Two Leggings: The Making of a Crow Warrior.* New York: Crowell.

Neihardt, John G.
1951   *When the Tree Flowered.* Lincoln: University of Nebraska Press.
1961   *Black Elk Speaks.* Lincoln: University of Nebraska Press.

Oberg, Kalvero
1973   *The Social Economy of the Tlingit Indians.* MAES 55.

Opler, Morris E.
1941   *An Apache Life-way.* Chicago: University of Chicago Press.

Ortiz, Alfonso
1969   *The World of the Tewa Indians.* Chicago: University of Chicago
       Press.

Osgood, Cornelius
1936   *Contributions to the Ethnography of the Kutchin.* YUPA 14.
1937   *The Ethnography of the Tanaina.* YUPA 16.

Oswalt, Wendell H.
1973   *This Land Was Theirs.* 2nd ed. New York: Wiley.

Owen, Roger C., James Deetz, and Anthony Fisher
1967   *The North American Indians, A Sourcebook.* New York: Macmillan.

Parsons, Elsie C.
1939   *Pueblo Indian Religion.* 2 vols. Chicago: University of Chicago Press.

Prucha, Francis P.
1962   *American Indian Policy in the Formative Years.* Cambridge: Harvard University Press.
1971   *The Indian in American History.* New York: Holt, Rinehart and Winston.

Quimby, George
1960   *Indian Life in the Upper Great Lakes.* Chicago: University of Chicago Press.

Radin, Paul
1926   *Crashing Thunder, the Autobiography of a Winnebago Indian.* New York: Appleton-Century.
1956   *The Trickster: A Study in American Indian Mythology.* New York: Philosophical Library.
1971   *The Winnebago Tribe.* Madison: University of Wisconsin Press.

Ray, Verne F.
1963   *Primitive Pragmatists: The Modoc Indians of Northern California.* MAES 38.

Reichard, Gladys A.
1950   *Navaho Indian Religion.* New York: Pantheon Press.

Ritzenthaler, Robert E., and Pat Ritzenthaler
1970   *The Woodland Indians of the Western Great Lakes.* Garden City, N.Y.: Natural History Press.

Rohner, Ronald, and E. C. Rohner
1970   *The Kwakiutl Indians of British Columbia.* New York: Holt, Rinehart and Winston.

Sanders, William, and Joseph Marino
1970   *New World Prehistory.* Englewood Cliffs, N.J.: Prentice-Hall.

Secoy, Frank R.
1953   *Changing Military Patterns of the Great Plains.* MAES 21.

Simmons, Leo W.
1963   *Sun Chief: The Autobiography of a Hopi Indian.* New Haven: Yale University Press.

Slobodin, Richard
1966   *Metis of the Mackenzie District.* Ottawa: Saint Paul University.

Speck, Frank G.
1907   *Ethnology of the Yuchi Indians.* UPMAP 1.
1919   *Functions of Wampum among the Eastern Algonkian.* MAAA 6.
1935   *Naskapi.* Norman: University of Oklahoma Press.
1940   *Penobscot Man.* Philadelphia: University of Pennsylvania Press.

Spencer, Robert
1959   *The North Alaskan Eskimo.* BBAE 171.

Spencer, Robert, and Jesse D. Jennings, eds.
1965   *The Native Americans.* New York: Harper and Row.

Spicer, Edward H.
1961   *Perspectives in American Indian Culture Change.* Chicago: University of Chicago Press.
1962   *Cycles of Conquest.* Tucson: University of Arizona Press.

Spier, Leslie
1921   *The Sun Dance of the Plains Indians.* APAMNH 16:451–527.
1928   "Havasupai Ethnography." APAMNH 29: 81–391.
1930   *Klamath Ethnography.* UCPAA 30.

Spinden, Herbert J.
1908   *The Nez Perce Indians.* MAAA 2:165–274.

Spindler, George, and Louise Spindler
1971   *Dreamers without Power: The Menomini Indians.* New York: Holt, Rinehart and Winston.

Spindler, Louise
1962   *Menomini Women and Culture Change.* MAAA 91.

Steiner, Stan
1968   *The New Indians.* Evanston, Ill.: Harper and Row.

Stern, Theodore
1966   *The Klamath Tribe.* MAES 41.

Stevenson, Matilde C.
1904   *The Zuni Indians.* ARBAE 23.

Steward, Julian H.
1933   *Ethnography of the Owens Valley Paiute.* UCPAA 33:233–350.
1938   *Basin-Plateau Aboriginal Socio-political Groups.* BBAE 120.

Stewart, Omer C.
1941   *Northern Paiute.* Anthropological Records of the University of California (Berkeley) 4:361–446.

Strong, William D.
1929   *Aboriginal Society in Southern California.* UCPAA 26.

Swanton, John R.
1911   *Indian Tribes of the Lower Mississippi Valley.* BBAE 43.
1946   *The Indians of the Southeastern United States.* BBAE 137.
1952   *The Indian Tribes of North America.* BBAE 145.

Tanner, Clara Lee
1957   *Southwest Indian Painting.* Tucson: University of Arizona Press.

Teicher, Morton I.
1960   Windigo Psychosis. *In Proceedings of the 1960 Annual Spring Meeting of the American Ethnological Society,* Verne F. Ray, ed. Seattle: University of Washington Press.

Thompson, Laura, and Alice Joseph
1944   *The Hopi Way.* Chicago: University of Chicago Press.

Thompson, Stith
1971   *Tales of the North American Indians.* Bloomington: Indiana University Press.

Thwaites, Reuben G., ed.
1896–1901   *The Jesuit Relations and Allied Documents.* Cleveland: Burrows Bros.

Trigger, Bruce B.
1969   *The Huron.* New York: Holt, Rinehart and Winston.

Underhill, Ruth
1953   *Red Man's America.* Chicago: University of Chicago Press.
1956   *The Navahos.* Norman: University of Oklahoma Press.
1965   *Red Man's Religion.* Chicago: University of Chicago Press.

Van Stone, James W.
1962   *Point Hope: An Eskimo Village in Transition.* MAES 36.
1967   *Eskimos of the Nushagak River.* Seattle: University of Washington Press.

Voegelin, Carl, and F. M. Voegelin
1966   *Map of North American Indian Languages.* American Ethnological Society. Seattle: University of Washington Press.

Waddell, Jack O., and O. Michael Watson, eds.
1971   *The American Indian in Urban Society.* Boston: Little, Brown.

Walker, Deward E.
1972   *The Emergent Native Americans.* Boston: Little, Brown.

Wallace, Ernest, and E. A. Hoebel
1952   *The Comanches, Lords of the South Plains.* Norman: University of Oklahoma Press.

Washburn, Wilcomb E.
1964   *The Indian and the White Man.* Garden City, N.Y.: Doubleday.
1971   *Red Man's Land—White Man's Law.* New York: Charles Scribner's Sons.

Wax, Murray
1971   *Indian Americans, Unity and Diversity.* Englewood Cliffs, N.J.: Prentice-Hall.

Wedel, Waldo R.
1961   *Prehistoric Man on the Great Plains.* Norman: University of Oklahoma Press.

Willey, Gordon
1966   *An Introduction to American Archaeology.* Vol. 1, *North and Middle America.* Englewood Cliffs, N.J.: Prentice-Hall.

Wilson, Edmund
1960   *Apologies to the Iroquois.* Includes Joseph Mitchell, "The Mohawks in High Steel." New York: Random House.

Wilson, Gilbert L.
1924   *The Horse and the Dog in Hidatsa Culture.* APAMNH 15:125–311.

Wissler, Clark
1916 *Costumes of the Plains Indians.* APAMNH 17:39–91.
1938 *The American Indian.* New York: Oxford University Press.

Wormington, Hilda Marie
1957 *Ancient Man in North America.* Denver: Denver Museum of Natural History.

FILMS

All the following films are 16 mm and with sound except Nanook of the North, *which is a silent film. I have used all these films and recommend them.*

The fifteen films in the American Indian Film Series, produced by the University of California, Extension Media Center, Berkeley, California, 94720, are all in color:

Acorns: Staple Food of California Indians. 28 min.

Basketry of the Pomo: Introductory. 30 min.

Basketry of the Pomo: Ornamentation. 21 min.

Basketry of the Pomo: Techniques. 33 min.

Beautiful Tree—Chishkale (about California Indians and acorns). 20 min.

Buckeyes: Food of California Indians. 13 min.

Calumet, Pipe of Peace (Great Plains). 23 min.

Dream Dances of the Kashia Pomo. 30 min.

Game of Staves (California games). 21 min.

Kashia Men's Dances (California Pomo). 40 min.

Obsidian Point Making. 13 min.

Pine Nuts (Great Basin). 13 min.

Sinew-backed Bow and Its Arrows. 24 min.

Totem Pole (Northwest Coast). 27 min.

Wooden Box (Northwest Coast). 33 min.

Films by other producers:

Circle of the Sun (Indians of Alberta). 30 min. Color. Contemporary Films/McGraw-Hill, 1221 Avenue of the Americas, New York, N.Y., 10020.

Corn and the Origins of Settled Life in Meso-America. 40 min. Color. Educational Services, Inc., 1730 Eye St., N.W., Washington, D.C., 20006.

Fishing at the Stone Weir (Netsilik Eskimo). 2 parts. 60 min. Color. Educational Services, Inc., 1730 Eye St., N.W., Washington, D.C., 20006.

The Longhouse People (Iroquois who still practice the Longhouse Religion). 25 min. Color. Encyclopedia Britannica Educational Corp., 425 No. Michigan Ave., Chicago, Ill., 60611.

Loon's Necklace (Northwest Coast legend filmed with masks; excellent). 5 min. Color. Encyclopedia Britannica Educational Corp., 425 No. Michigan Ave., Chicago, Ill., 60611.

Nanook of the North (documentary of Eskimo life in 1922). 54 min. Black and white. Athena Films, 165 W. 46 St., New York, N.Y., 10019.

Navajo Night Dances. 11 min. Color. Coronet Instructional Media, Division of Esquire, 65 E. So. Water St., Chicago, Ill., 60601.

Vision Quest (traditional quest of Plains Indians re-enacted). 30 min. Color. Montana State University, Bozeman, Mont., 59715.

Washoe (contemporary Washo Indians). 56 min. Black and white. McGraw-Hill Films, 1220 Avenue of the Americas, New York, N.Y., 10020.

The National Film Board of Canada, located at 1251 Avenue of the Americas, New York, N.Y., 10020, produces superior films; among them are the following:

Caribou Hunters (Cree and Chippewa). 18 min. Color.

People of the Potlatch. 21 min. Color.

The Lake Man (mixed blood Indian in western Canada; contemporary). 27 min. Black and white.

GLOSSARY

aboriginal   the population native to an area from the time of its earliest occupation.

adaptation   a change in structure, function, or form that leaves an animal or plant better adjusted to its environment.

adobe   a kind of clay used in building, either applied like plaster or made into sun-dried bricks. Adobe became a major building material in the Southwest after Spanish contact.

age grade   a subdivision of a society in which membership is based on age. Members of an age grade form a social group and engage in various activities together.

association   an organization built on some principle other than kinship. American Indian associates formed around mutual interest, religion, age, and sex, and provided aid, education, recreation, and social control.

atlatl   a board or stick, 20 to 24 inches long, fitted with a handle on one end and a groove or peg at the other, used in throwing a dart or spear.

babiche   rawhide strips for snowshoes, netting, thongs, and other uses.

band   a simple level of social organization with groups of fifty to a hundred people in families or other kin groups, living and finding food together. A band might be composed of brothers with their wives and younger children.

bast   the inner bark of a tree.

berdache   a man who chose not to follow the ideal masculine ways of the Plains warrior, and instead led a woman's life. He was not necessarily a homosexual, and his way of life was considered socially acceptable.

bilateral descent tracing descent equally through the maternal and paternal sides of the family.

blood money material retribution paid for injury, loss of life, or loss of property.

bow drill a drill consisting of a straight stick that is rotated by a string looped around the stick and pulled rapidly back and forth.

bridewealth gifts given by the groom's family to the bride's family as compensation for the loss of her services.

buffalo chips buffalo dung, used as fuel by the Plains Indians and later by the European settlers.

bull boat a cup-shaped boat used only to cross rivers. It had a framework of saplings covered with skins.

burial mound a grave for one or several people covered with a hill of earth.

cacique the Spanish name for the head of a medicine society, who was also the head of the town.

calumet a pipe with a long stem, also known as a peace pipe. It was smoked before going to war, on trading expeditions, and at peace councils; in it tobacco was also burned as an offering to the spirits.

carnivore a meat-eating animal.

catlinite a soft, easy to carve stone, ideal for pipe bowls, dishes, and other containers; also called pipestone.

chickee the traditional Seminole house, an open-sided palmetto-thatched structure.

chiefdom a stratified society, having centralized authority and a leader who was set apart from or considered superior to his followers.

clan a kinship group descended either through men or through women from a common ancestor.

Clovis point a spearhead specialized for mammoth hunting, lance-shaped, with a mildly concave base, larger than a Folsom point, and with fluting extending one-quarter to one-half the length of the base. Clovis points, found from coast to coast, are always associated with the Big Game Hunting tradition.

copper   a one- to four-foot shield-shaped plaque made of copper, used as a symbol of prestige on the Northwest Coast.

coup stick   a small stick carried into battle by Plains Indians to touch the enemy. Touching a live enemy in battle brought great glory; the act was recounted back home by striking a pole with a coup stick.

cultigen   a cultivated plant.

culture   the collected ways of life led by a group of people, including all their knowledge, customs, institutions, and material goods.

culture area   a geographically distinct region within which various groups developed similar ways of life.

deadfall   a trap that lets a weight such as a heavy log fall on an animal thereby killing or disabling it.

dentalia   long, pointed shellfish that became an important medium of exchange on the Northwest Coast.

diffusion   the exchange of material objects, information, and techniques among various cultural groups.

earth oven   a shallow pit dug in the ground, used for cooking food. The food is wrapped and placed in the pit on top of hot stones or coals, and covered over with earth until cooked.

effigy mound   an enormous earthwork shaped to represent an animal.

epicanthic eye fold   a small fold of skin covering the inner corner of the eye. It is the characteristic that creates the so-called slant eyes common to people of the Mongoloid race.

ethnographic analogy   a comparison between the facts we have about pre-historic peoples and what we know about similar groups who live today or who lived in the recent past. Used carefully, information about living groups can be helpful in reconstructing a picture of ancient societies.

exogamy   the practice of selecting your spouse from a group other than your own.

extended family   a domestic group consisting of a nuclear family plus another generation (grandparents), or more wives. It could also be a group of brothers or sisters living together with their spouses and children.

family (linguistic) a major category for classifying languages. Two or more related linguistic families comprise a linguistic phylum.

fictive kinship a special relationship in which people accord each other the status of kinsman, such as blood brothers or ceremonial parents. Fictive kinsmen have mutual duties and obligations like real kinsmen.

first fruit ceremony a public activity celebrating the first catch of game fish or animals or the first plants of the season.

flute a long rounded groove, such as those on the surface of Folsom and Clovis points.

Folsom point a spearhead specialized for bison hunting, with parallel edges, a concave base, and flutes or grooves extending the entire length of the point. Folsom points are always associated with the Big Game Hunting tradition, and are found only in the North American High Plains.

geronticide the abandonment of aged persons who could no longer make an economic contribution to their group. It was practiced only under extreme conditions, and for the benefit of the whole group.

gorge a double-pointed piece of bone with a line attached in the middle, used much like a fish hook. Swallowed by the fish, it lodged in the throat, and the catch could easily be hauled in.

guardian spirit a spirit, usually in the form of an animal, which acted as a personal helper for its possessor, helping him win success in life. Guardian spirits usually appeared to those who sought them in a vision quest.

hair pipe a long tubular bone strung into a breastplate by Plains warriors.

hammer stone a hard stone used to strike another, chipping off pieces to be fashioned into tools, such as projectile points or flint blades.

headman a leader, somewhat like a chief, whose authority rests on consent of the group he leads.

hogan the traditional Navajo house, a circular log-framed, earth-covered structure, its doorway always on the east.

Homo sapiens the scientific name for the genus and species to which all human beings belong.

horticulture plant cultivation with hand tools like hoes and digging sticks.

impound   the confined area into which animals are driven so that they can be killed easily.

infanticide   the abandonment or killing of a newborn infant, who could not be fed because food was scarce or its mother ill or dead. Infanticide was practiced only under extreme conditions, and for the benefit of the whole group.

jerky   a strip of dried meat.

katcina   a good spirit, believed by the Hopi to bring rain. Katcinas were said to have come from the Underworld with the people; men were allowed to impersonate them and dance to make it rain.

katcina doll   an image of a katcina, given to children to teach them about the many katcinas.

kayak   an Arctic canoe made of skins stretched over a frame of wood, covering it completely except for the open space where the paddler sits.

kinnikinnik   a substance consisting of sumac, dogwood, willow bark, and sometimes tobacco, smoked by men of the Great Lakes region. *Kinnikinnik* is an Algonkian word meaning "mixture."

kiva   a chamber, often subterranean, used by some Southwestern tribes for ceremonial purposes.

labret   an ornamental lip plug, inserted through a hole pierced in the lip.

lean-to   an open dwelling consisting of a single wall, supported at an angle.

longhouse   an Iroquoian dwelling, 50 to 100 feet long and about 20 feet wide, which housed several related families. It had a door at each end and was gabled or vaulted, like a long, narrow barn.

maize   corn.

manitu   an Algonkian belief similar to the Iroquoian orenda and the Siouan wakonda, a great supernatural force flowing through the universe.

mano   the upper stone used on a metate to grind corn and other grains. It is held in the hand and moved back and forth over the metate.

matrilineage   a descent group in which membership is inherited through mothers.

medicine bundle   the sacred container in which a Plains warrior carried his "medicine," items that had a kind of supernatural power similar to good-luck pieces, sacred talismans, or religious relics. Strangely shaped stones, bones, or feathers symbolized the warrior's visions or the animals that sent him power; these were his "medicine."

metate   the trough-shaped lower part of a grinding stone, used for milling corn and other grains.

microblade   a small, narrow flake of stone with sharp edges. A microblade could be used for making toothed saws, or as the point of a spear or harpoon.

moiety   a kin group consisting of half a tribe. The two moieties of a tribe might compete in sports or perform important rites for each other.

mother-in-law avoidance   a behavior pattern, designed to reduce the usual tension between a man and his wife's mother, by eliminating almost all face-to-face interaction between the two.

mukluk   a sealskin boot worn by Indians and Eskimo of the Northwest territories.

naja   a Spanish gypsy symbol believed to ward off the evil eye. The naja design appears in Navajo squash-blossom necklaces.

nuclear family   a domestic group consisting of a married couple and their offspring.

obsidian   volcanic glass.

orenda   for the Iroquois, the source of supernatural power. It was a great invisible force that flowed through all the world, and could be tapped through dreams. It is similar to the Algonkian manitu and the Siouan wakonda.

ossuary   a communal pit where the bones of exhumed corpses were buried.

oulachon   an oily fish known as the candlefish because it burns like a candle when a wick is run through its body.

outfit   a Navajo group composed of matrilineally related extended families living fairly close together. Members of an outfit farmed together, held common land rights, and had a headman who represented the group in dealings with outsiders.

palisade   a tall fence of sharp, pointed poles.

parfleche a container used by Plains Indians, which was actually a giant rawhide envelope. When packed, it expanded to the size and shape of a small chest.

patrilineage a descent group in which membership is inherited through fathers.

patrilocal the residence pattern in which a married couple and their children live in or near the husband's father's home.

pectoral a large chestplate of bone worn by Plains warriors.

pemmican an Indian dish made of dried, pulverized meat and berries, mixed with suet or other fat. Pemmican remains edible after a year of storage.

permafrost permanently frozen subsoil.

phratry an association of clans. This social grouping was most common in the Southeast, the Northwest, and the prairies.

phylum (linguistic) a major category for classifying languages. A linguistic phylum contains divisions called families.

physical anthropology the study of man's animal origins and his genetically determined nature. Its main study is human evolution, using both the fossil remains of man and his ancestors, and the distribution of hereditary variations in living peoples.

pipestone a soft, easy to carve stone, ideal for making pipes, dishes, and other containers.

pit house a semisubterranean dwelling constructed over a pit, made of a frame covered with dirt removed from the pit.

Pleistocene the last major geologic epoch, beginning more than two million years ago and ending about 10,000 years ago. In this period the great glaciers spread over much of North America.

polyandry the form of marriage in which a woman has more than one husband.

polygamy a form of marriage in which there is more than one husband or wife.

polygyny the form of marriage in which a man has more than one wife.

potlatch a large feast given by some Northwest Coast peoples, usually to validate a social title in public. The potlach included singing, dancing, and giving away large amounts of valuables.

prayerstick   a stick covered with feathers, plumes, or down, used by the Pueblo and some other groups to convey prayers to the supernatural. Also attached to it might be small packets of food or tobacco as offerings to the spirits.

pueblo   an apartmentlike dwelling of clay, mud, or stone. *Pueblo* is a Spanish word meaning "town."

reservation   a tract of land set aside by the United States government in treaty, statute, or executive order for the use and benefit of Indian tribes.

reserve   the Canadian term for an Indian reservation.

revitalization movement   a special kind of religion, usually occurring where people are oppressed and deprived. A main element in movements is an attempt to recreate the happier times of the past.

rite of passage   a ceremony marking an important event in the life cycle, such as puberty rites, marriage, or death rites.

roach   a stiff ridge of hair two or three inches high, running from the forehead to the back of the neck, and sometimes padded out with red-dyed deer hair. The roach was a common male hair style in the East.

sachem   an English version of an Algonkian word for "chief," synonymous with sagamore.

sagamore   a sachem.

sand painting   a picture made by dribbling colored sands, minerals, pollen, or other fine material into designs 3 to 12 feet in diameter. The paintings had elements that stood for serpents, stars, mountains, and other natural features. Sand paintings were used in rituals by Pueblo, Navajo, and some Mission Indians. Also called dry paintings.

scalp lock   a lock of long hair grown on an otherwise bare head by men in the East as a challenge to enemies.

scraper   a stone implement used to scrape leather, smooth wood, or remove fat from the underside of a skin.

shade   a four-posted, brush-roofed shelter without walls that allowed air to circulate freely while protecting against the sun's searing rays.

shaman   a religious specialist, such as a medicine man or a ritualist.

shovel tooth   a physical trait occurring in Asian and North American Indian populations. The inner side of the upper central incisor teeth is hollowed out, giving them a scoop or shovel shape.

sibling   a brother or a sister.

slash-and-burn agriculture   a method of preparing fields for farming by cutting and then burning the trees on the field to be planted.

socialization   teaching children the traditional, proper behavior expected in their culture.

subsistence pattern   the way in which a group of people obtains its food, as by hunting and gathering, herding, or agriculture.

sweathouse   a small building in which people gather to sweat, as in a steam bath, often for ritual purification or to socialize.

temper   fine bits of stone, shell, or fiber mixed with clay in making pottery, to keep the clay paste from splitting and cracking as it is heated.

totem pole   an elaborately carved cedar log, usually depicting animals and supernatural beings. This Northwest Coast art form honored dead chiefs, marked the graves of important people, served as portals to houses, and in general was a sort of coat of arms indicating owner's rank and title.

travois   an A-shaped sled consisting of a platform or net and two supporting poles. The narrow end was placed over a horse's or dog's shoulders, an the broader end dragged behind.

tumpline   a strap placed across the brow and connected to a bundle carried on the back, easing the burden.

tundra   the level, treeless plains of the Arctic region.

umiak   an open boat used in the Arctic, made of hide stretched over a framework of lashed wood.

unilineal descent   kinship traced solely through males or females. If descent is traced through males, it is patrilineal; if traced through females, it is matrilineal. A clan is a unilineal descent group.

wakonda a Siouan belief similar to the Iroquoian orenda and the Algonkian manitu, a great supernatural force flowing through the universe.

wampum strings of white and purple shell beads woven into belts by the Algonkians and the Iroquois. They could be used for adornment, but more important, wampum designs represented treaties, agreements, and records of events. After European contact, wampum became a medium of exchange.

weir a fish trap that allows water to pass through but obstructs the way for fish; the fish are confined and easily caught.

wickiup a conical or domed hut of poles covered with brush, matting, or bark strips, with a center fire pit and a smoke hole in the roof.

wigwam a domed dwelling made of bent poles or saplings, tied together and covered with sheets of bark, hide, or woven matting.

INDEX

ARCTIC

SUBARCTIC

NORTHWEST-COAST

PLATEAU

CALIFORNIA

GREAT BASIN

PLAINS

EAST

SOUTHWEST

CULTURE AREAS